SCHNELLBOOTE

SCHNELLBOOTE

A COMPLETE OPERATIONAL HISTORY

LAWRENCE PATERSON

Seaforth
PUBLISHING

First published in Great Britain in 2015 by
Seaforth Publishing,
Pen & Sword Books Ltd,
47 Church Street,
Barnsley S70 2AS

www.seaforthpublishing.com

British Library Cataloguing in Publication Data
A catalogue record for this book is available from the British Library

ISBN 978 1 84832 083 3

All photographs from the author's collection.

Typeset and designed by M.A.T.S., Leigh-on-Sea, Essex
Printed and bound in Great Britain by CPI Group (UK) Ltd, Croydon, CR0 4YY

Contents

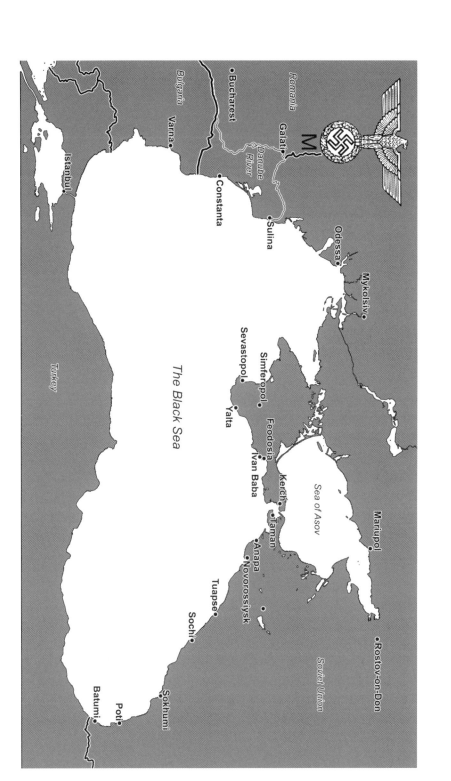

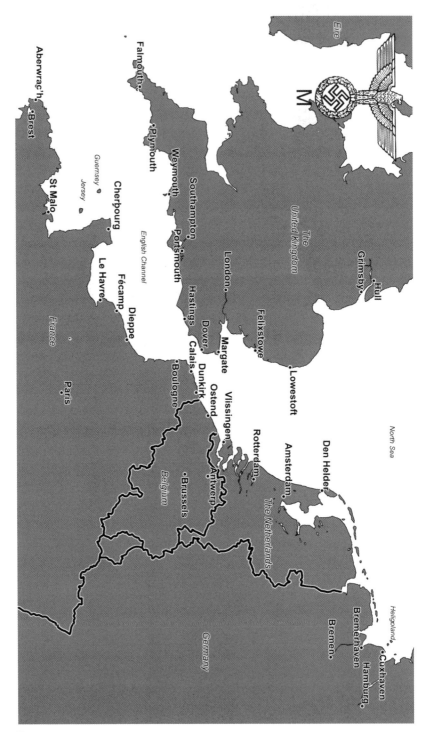

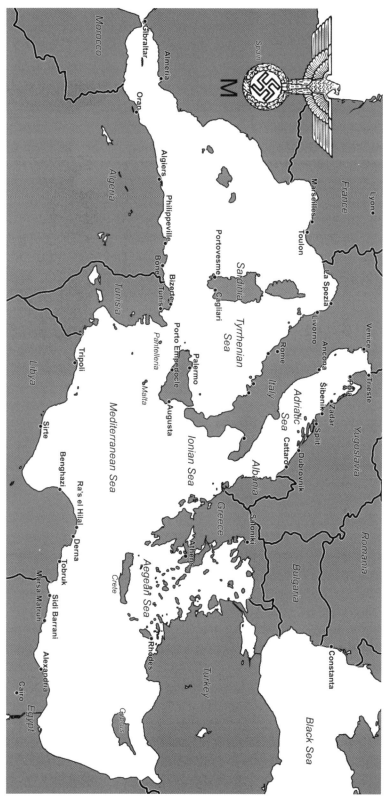

Foreword

THE history of the Kriegsmarine S-boat service mirrors that of most naval components of Germany's Third Reich. Involved in an unexpected war at a time when their service was barely beginning to recover from the previous conflict, it is a story of often startling military achievement against superior enemy forces, before the long, inexorable decline toward defeat six years later. Within these pages I have pre-dominantly focused upon S-boat operations within the chronology of the Second World War. Where applicable there are, of course, the develop-mental aspects of Germany's S-boats, but to fully explore that subject would require its own book.

The S-boat, or *Schnellboot* in German, was the Kriegsmarine's equivalent of the Allied motor torpedo boat: small, highly-manoeuvrable and heavily armed motor launches that provided a coastal cutting-edge to naval forces. With a main armament of two torpedo tubes (with a single reload available for each), the S-boats were primarily designed for the interdiction of coastal merchant traffic traversing waters unsuitable for U-boats. As we will see, they were frequently used in roles not entirely suited to their purpose by a Kriegsmarine that was under-strength from the outset of the war. To the Allies the S-boat became the 'E-boat' for reasons that have never fully been confirmed, the most likely explanation being that the nomenclature stands for 'enemy boat'.

Interestingly, although U-boat flotillas were loose organisational structures which largely dealt with logistical concerns at home ports, playing no role in combat planning, S-boat flotillas were closely knit fighting units, designed for the boats to operate in concert with one another. U-boats were lone-wolf hunters controlled from a central location in France or Germany (BdU Headquarters), whereas S-boats were subordinate to local Kriegsmarine commands; flotilla commanders were frequently involved in missions, either as a boat commander or in the role of mentor to young skippers making their first war patrols.

The S-boat war had many facets. Not just a war against merchant shipping tonnage, it was also frequently used as the only viable means that the Kriegsmarine possessed of countering enemy naval power, particularly on the eastern front. However, while it is easy to relate the ebbs and flows of such battles in terms of boat numbers and shipping tonnage, the humanity of the war at sea can never be forgotten. It remains a story of people caught up in the maelstrom of war, ships sinking in flames into a frequently unforgiving sea.

Told from the German point of view, the names of various ports and cities (particularly in the east) are those that were used by the Kriegsmarine, as are times unless quoted otherwise. Some words have retained their original German form, the notable exception being 'Heer'. Although it is inconsistent, I have retained the term 'Army' throughout the book, while Luftwaffe and Kriegsmarine are used for the two other major services. Somewhat inexplicably, many readers become confused over what the Heer actually is: hence the inconsistency.

Glossary

B-Dienst – German naval radio listening service (*Funkbeobachtungdienst*)

FdS – S-boat Command (*Führer der Schnellboote*)

FdT – Torpedo-boat Command (*Führer der Torpedoboote*)

FdZ – Destroyer Command (*Führer der Zerstörer*)

Heer – German Army

Kriegsmarine – German Navy from 1935 to 1945

Luftwaffe – German Air Force

LCT – Landing Craft Tank

LST – Landing Ship Tank

ML – Motor Launch, small British vessel designed for anti-submarine and harbour work

MGB – Motor Gun Boat, larger, more heavily armed development from ML

MTB – Motor Torpedo Boat, similar to MGB but torpedo carriers with fewer guns. S-boat equivalent

OKH – Supreme Army Command (*Oberkommando des Heeres*)

OKL – Supreme Air Force Command (*Oberkommando der Luftwaffe*)

OKM – Supreme Naval Command (*Oberkommando der Kriegsmarine*)

OKW – Supreme Military Command – all three services (*Oberkommando der Wehrmacht*)

PT boat – Patrol Torpedo boat. American equivalent to MTB

R-boat – German motor minesweeper comparable in size to S-boat (*Räumboot*)

SKL – Naval warfare command, responsible for planning, execution and direction of naval warfare (*Seekriegsleitung*)

Kriegsmarine ranks

Seamen

Matrose	Ordinary Seaman
Matrosen-Gefreiter	Able Seaman
Matrosen-Obergefreiter	Leading Seaman
Matrosen-Hauptgefreiter	Leading Seaman (4.5 years service)
Matrosen-Stabsgefreiter	Senior Leading Seaman
Matrosen-Stabsobergefreiter	Senior Leading Seaman

Junior NCOs

–maat	Petty Officer
Ober-maat	Chief Petty Officer

Senior NCOs

Bootsmann	Boatswain
Stabsbootsmann	Senior Boatswain
Oberbootsmann	Chief Boatswain
Stabsoberbootsmann	Senior Chief Boatswain
Obersteuermann (ObStrm)	Quartermaster
Stabsobersteuermann (StObStrm)	Senior Quartermaster

Officers

Fähnrich zur See (FzS)	Midshipman
Oberfähnrich zur See	Sub Lieutenant
Leutnant zur See (LzS)	Lieutenant (Junior)
Oberleutnant zur See (ObltzS)	Lieutenant (Senior)
Kapitänleutnant (Kptlt)	Lieutenant Commander
Korvettenkapitän (KK)	Commander
Fregattenkapitän (FK)	Captain (Junior)
Kapitän zur See (KzS)	Captain
Kommodore	Commodore
Konteradmiral (KA)	Rear Admiral
Vizeadmiral (VA)	Vice Admiral
Admiral	Admiral
Generaladmiral	no equivalent
Grossadmiral	Admiral of the Fleet

1
Introduction

THE development of the torpedo during the nineteenth century opened fresh vistas for naval architects to explore. As well as the submarine, new surface craft evolved into the torpedo boat, destroyer (essentially an enlarged torpedo boat) and, finally, the motor torpedo boat. Small and agile motor torpedo boats (MTBs) found particular favour with the Italian and British navies. During the First World War, three Royal Navy junior officers suggested that such shallow-draught vessels operating at speed would be able to pass over defensive minefields in order to attack the German fleet at anchor. Although committed to action, their successes were few, not least of all because the craft's design required the torpedo to be launched over the stern tail-first. Italian naval planners were also fielding such craft, sinking two Austro-Hungarian capital ships in the last two years of war. For their part, the German Navy also introduced such craft, though more defensive in nature.

At first they had developed pilotless wire-guided craft, armed with a remotely detonated explosive charge in the bow. These *Fernlenkbooten* (FL or remote-control boats) were used in action against British monitors shelling the German U-boat bases in Belgium, but with no real success. The Kaiserliche Marine then turned to the development of crewed boats, initially small, fast motor launches tasked with clearing anti-submarine nets laid by the Royal Navy outside Zeebrugge and Ostend. Three boat-yards were approached to provide these craft, the most prominent being the Lürssen boatyard at Bremen, established by innovative boatbuilder Friedrich Lürssen in 1875 and run since 1916 by his son Otto. The following year *LM1* was launched for the navy. The designation LM (*Luftschiffmotorboote*) reflected the fact that they were each powered by three powerful and lightweight Maybach Zeppelin engines.

1

An FL boat manhandled into its shelter for protection from enemy bombs in Flanders.

Lürssen was not the only boatyard engaged in producing the first six boats ordered in January 1917. Both the Naglo and Oertz shipyards had been contracted, though both yards had diversified – unsuccessfully it transpired – into aircraft design during the pre-war years.

LM1 and *LM2* were built by Lürssen, *LM3* and *LM4* by Naglo, none of them possessing armament other than a 3.7cm cannon. Their primary use was dictated by bow-mounted net cutters. However, from Oertz's *LM5* onward the armament included a 45cm bow torpedo and a single machine

LM boat undergoing sea tests outside Zeebrugge.

gun. Averaging a maximum speed of approximately 30 knots, fourteen LM boats were incorporated into the German Naval Corps Flanders, seven into the Baltic (*LM7–13*), and several skirmishes with Allied units are recorded, though without much success. In fact, only a single sinking has been attributed to these first small motor torpedo boats: the British transport steamer ss *Penelope*, torpedoed and sunk on 24 August 1917 by ObltzS Peytsch less than six hundred metres from Swalfer Ort Lighthouse in the Gulf of Riga.

The firm Rolandwerft at Hemelingen also produced several LM boats; *L18* and *L20* commissioned in 1917, *LM17* the following year and *LM19* in 1919 after hostilities had ceased. Results had been relatively meagre for Germany's first foray into small motor torpedo boats, but with the harsh terms of the Versailles treaty severely curtailing the size of any German fleet, interest remained high in continuing to develop such coastal defence vessels.

The post-war Weimar Republic was not allowed any U-boats on strength, their total surface strength, excluding minesweepers, limited to 'six battleships of the "Deutschland" or "Lothringen" type, six light cruisers, 12 destroyers and 12 torpedo boats'. This final class, limited to not exceed 200-tons displacement, elicited further MTB development – a

An LM boat on anti-submarine patrol off Flanders. The tiny size is all too apparent.

3

type of craft not explicitly covered by the treaty terms. The Reichsmarine immediately began experimenting with speedboat concepts once more, taking strong cues from the British and Italian navies. Several LM boats that had been built at the war's end were transferred back into the navy and re-designated *Unterseeboote Zerstörer*, UZ for short. It was these that were first used to develop what would become future S-boat combat tactics, exercising against target hulks in small groups of two and three, using speed, low silhouettes and light grey camouflage that merged with the horizon.

Like much German military development, S-boats were hidden behind dummy civilian corporate fronts. The head of the Reichsmarine had entrusted Kapitän zur See Walter Lohmann, chief of the Reichsmarine's transportation division, to administer an accumulated 'black fund' of unofficial money that enabled armament development to take place under the noses of the Allied Armistice Control Commission. In this he was assisted by the officer who would go on to head Germany's minesweeping service, ObltzS Friedrich Ruge. Together they established, amongst other things, TRAYAG (Travemünder Yachthafen AG) in 1924 as a base and shipyard for the development and trial activities for fast MTBs. The following year they inaugurated the High Sea Sports Association (HANSA) for training of personnel in basic seamanship, small motor and sailing boat usage as well as radio communication. The Neustädter Slip GmbH was created as a repair and training plant for sport boats (and S-boats) in 1925 and the following year 60,000 Reichsmarks (RM) was given to the Motor Yacht Club of Germany for the testing of TRAYAG motorboats. The subterfuge proved successful – not only for MTB development, but also U-boat and aircraft projects.

During 1926 the Bremen firm Abeking & Rasmussen (designers of minesweepers, torpedo boats and submarine chasers in the last war, future designers of R-boats in the next) built the Experimental Boat K with a stepped planing hull; Travemünde's Caspar Werft built the *Narwhal*, a large planing hull, and Lürssen built the *Lür*, a displacement-hulled boat. At first, attention was clearly placed on the planing hull concept that was successfully used for speedboats. In flat calm waters this hull shape enabled a boat to effortlessly skim across the water surface – 'planing', where the weight of the craft is supported by hydrodynamic lift rather than simple hydrostatic lift (displacement buoyancy). However, the future German MTBs were most likely to operate within the North Sea, which was frequently beset by heavy swells. Therefore it was Lürssen's displacement hull that was chosen by the Reichsmarine as the starting point for MTB planning. Their attention was then drawn to a design Lürssen had created for a private customer – the *Oheka II*.

The customer, Otto Hermann Kahn, was an extremely wealthy investment banker, philanthropist and patron of the arts who had moved from Germany to the United States in 1893. During 1926 he placed an order with the Lürssen boatyard for a high-speed motor launch capable of both river cruising and use in the North Sea. One year after his order had been placed, Kahn's speedboat was delivered, sporting radical new features that would see it become the fastest boat in its class worldwide. It carried the best features of a displacement hull – extreme seaworthiness even in heavy weather – and a planing hull towards the stern that would provide the requisite hydrodynamic lift when travelling at speed. Constructed of wooden planking over alloy frames, the boat was lightweight, increasing its overall speed and performance

The combination exactly suited the Reichsmarine's needs. The craft's sizeable displacement would also bear the weight of two forward-firing torpedo tubes mounted toward the bow. Lürssen was asked to build another of the same basic design in November 1929, with the addition of two detachable torpedo tubes and on 7 August 1930 this boat, named *UZ(S)16* was commissioned into the Reichsmarine. The 'S' stood for '*schnell*' and was added in order to differentiate this vessel from the former LM First World War boats. She was renamed twice more: to

S1 and *S2* at sea shortly after commissioning.

Wachboot W1 (guard boat) in March 1931, and finally to *Schnellboot S1* on 16 March 1932. The term 'Schnellboot' had actually been used as a cover name for the development of MTBs; now it was a brand new class of warship.

S1 was constructed of mahogany and light metal composite, powered by three 900hp Daimler-Benz petrol engines as no marine diesels were available at that time. The Reichsmarine had commissioned both MAN and Daimler-Benz to develop lightweight high-speed diesels specifically for the S-boat, though *S1* was ready well before the new diesels were. She was 26.5m (87ft) long with a beam of 4.2m (14ft) and a draught of 1.1m (3ft 6in) making *S1* the largest high-speed coastal motorboat of the time, but still capable of 39.8 knots. As well as the two First World War vintage 50cm torpedo tubes there was a single 2cm flak weapon on the stern deck. Crewed by twelve men, the boat was capable of operating in a sea state up to 5 on the Beaufort Scale (equating to a wind speed of between 17 and 21 knots and waves up to six feet high).

Although *S1* was the smallest of the designs that would follow, the interior layout remained similar throughout the war. Internally, seven bulkheads separated eight watertight compartments. From bow to stern, the first compartment contained a trimming cell, the anchor chain storage locker, the forward 'head' and then Feldwebel and Unteroffizier (NCO and junior officers) quarters, holding six bunks in total and having natural light provided by portholes in the hull. Next came the captain's cabin (again with hull portholes) on the starboard side opposite the radio room to port, which also doubled as the radioman's quarters. Fuel tanks (6,000 litres/1,300 gallons) lay directly under the bridge, followed by the first engine room, where the port and starboard engines were housed with a central walkway. The following compartment was engine room 1, holding the central engine, flanked by walkways either side, and two more fuel tanks (8,000 litres/1,750 gallons). Both engine rooms were provided with numerous skylights to provide as much natural light as possible into the relatively spacious working space. A built-in Ardex fire-extinguishing system helped reduce the risk of fire. Immediately astern of this lay the small galley, stern 'head' and the crew room, ultimately capable of housing up to fifteen men, atop the roof of which was the location of the 2cm Rheinmetall MG C/30 flak weapon. Here the cabin roof protruded above deck level, allowing portholes on either side. Finally, rudder gear and two more fuel tanks (4,000 litres/880 gallons) occupied the sternmost part of the boat.

Each bulkhead was designed to withstand flooding and light damage from shell splinters, and constructed of wood stiffened with aluminium. The engine beds were steel and each engine compartment ceiling was removable plating to enable the replacement of worn-out machinery. The boat had a double layer of hull planking, the inner hull nailed to the boat's longitudinal frames, the outer layer riveted directly over the top. The deck itself was more planking, covered with canvas and then painted with a durable, waterproof, non-slip synthetic resin paint.

Although possessing excellent qualities and built to a high design specification, work began on an improved class almost as soon as testing began on *S1*. During 1931 construction of the *S2* class (four boats numbered *S2* to *S5*) started; these were commissioned into service between April and July 1932. The boat's length had been increased to 27.9m (90ft) and the displacement also increased to 49 tons. This allowed an improved layout and added machinery, including a 100hp auxiliary Maybach engine which could operate the central propeller. Designed for use when the boat was embarked on silent running, it was ultimately found to be surplus to requirements and phased out of future classes. All three main engines received superchargers, and two extra rudders were added outboard on each side of the main rudder. These two smaller independent rudders were directly behind the screws and when operated at high speed they could be inclined up to 30°, keeping them horizontal in the water, creating additional

S1, *S2* and *S3* photographed as part of the 1st Schnellbootshalbflottille.

water flow around the screws and diminishing the stern wake – a distinct advantage for combat craft attempting to minimise the chance of detection. Ingenious, this became known as the 'Lürssen effect'. In addition, the scooped end to each torpedo tube which had featured on *S1* was replaced with a vertical aperture sealed with a hinged door.

Like *S1*, the torpedo tubes were detachable. This precaution had been taken lest the S-boats be seen for what they were by Allied observers monitoring adherence to the Versailles treaty. Indeed, the head of the Reichsmarine, Admiral Erich Raeder, issued an order on 10 February 1932 outlining the secrecy required.

> In view of our treaty obligations and the Disarmament Conference, steps must be taken to prevent the 1st S-Boat-Half-Flotilla ... from appearing openly as a formation of torpedo-carrying boats as it is not intended to count these S-Boats against the number of torpedo-carrying boats allowed us.

> I therefore order:

> 1. *S2-S5* will be commissioned in the shipyard Lürssen, Vegesack without armament, and will be fitted with easily removable cover-sheet-metal on the spaces necessary for torpedo-tubes. The same will be arranged by TMI [Inspectorate of Torpedoes and Mining] in agreement with the naval arsenal, for the boat *S1* which will dismantle its torpedo-tubes, on completion of the practice shooting, for fitting on another boat.
> 2. The torpedo-tubes of all S-boats will be stored in the naval arsenal ready for immediate fitting. During the trial runs the torpedo-tubes will be taken on board one after the other for a short time to be fitted and for practice shooting so that only one boat at a time carries torpedo armament. For public consumption its boat will be in service for the purpose of temporary trials by the TVA [Technical Research Establishment]. It should not anchor together with the other, unarmed boats of the Half-Flotilla because of the obvious similarity of type. The duration of firing, and consequently the length of time the torpedo-tubes are aboard, is to be as short as possible.
> 3. Fitting the torpedo-tubes on all S-boats is intended as soon as the situation of the political control allows it.[1]

With five S-boats in commission, the 1st Schnellbootshalbflottille was formed under the command of Kptlt Erich Bey and intensive training of crews began.[2] As of July 1932 the strength of the unit stood at five boats, *S1* to *S5*. On 26 August 1932 orders for *S6* to *S9* were placed, the first to feature new marine diesels. These boats were again lengthened, this time to 32.4m (106ft) overall, the beam increased to 4.9m (16ft). Displacing 59 tons now, *S6* was powered by three lightweight MAN L7 Zn 19/30 two-stroke diesels, which proved inadequate, reaching only 32 knots, although they still had the advantage over petrol engines of reduced risk of fuel explosion and fire during operations. An inline, double-acting, non-reversing engine, the *L7* produced a maximum of 1320HP but its weight exceeded the specifications originally laid down, reducing overall speed. From *S7* onwards a 'knuckle' was introduced into the bow to increase seaworthiness and prevent the bow from 'burying' into heavy waves. *S7* to *S9* also hosted MAN diesels, *S10* to *S13* Daimler-Benz, the latter a more compact power plant. Daimler-Benz's MB502 was a 16-cylinder V, four-stroke that produced 1320HP although its lighter weight, lower fuel consumption and added superchargers resulted in the boat having 25 per cent more power than those carrying the MANs. Furthermore, these engines proved more reliable and also contributed to the S-boat's stealth, exhaust gases being nearly invisible, as opposed to the dark exhaust produced by its contemporary.

The complement aboard the new boats had increased to twenty-one men (though this was variable) and the armament had changed beginning with *S6*: the 50cm torpedo tubes were replaced with what became the German naval standard 53.3cm tubes as well as the addition of a forward mounted machine gun at the bow for both anti-aircraft and surface firing purposes. Generally, the crew consisted of commander (commonly an *Oberleutnant zur See*), first mate (*Ober-* or *Bootsmanmaat*), one helmsman (*Matrosengefreiter*), semaphore and lookout men (*Matrosengefreiten*), engine telegraph man (*Matrose*), two seamen (*Matrosen*), chief engineering NCO (generally an *Obermaschinsten*), three engineering NCOs (*Ober-* or *Maschinenmaaten*), six engine room ratings (*Heizergefreiten* or *Heizern*), two radio men (*Funkgefreiten* or *Funkgaast* for radio work and decoding) and a torpedo mechanic who doubled as cook (*Torpedomechanikergefreiten*).

Originally, the early S-boats were provided with the First World War Bergman MG15 water-cooled machine gun, though these were later superseded by the standard Wehrmacht MG34. The torpedo tubes remained exposed, passing through a steel bulkhead behind the machine gun mounting. It was also here between the two tubes that the boat's inflatable dinghies were stored, thought to be protected from enemy fire by the tubes themselves. To the rear of the bulkhead was the cabin that contained the bridge/wheelhouse, to its rear an externally mounted mast

An S-boat is commissioned into the Reichsmarine.

from which spread the complicated array of radio antennae. The boat could carry four torpedoes: two within the tubes and a further two on deck racks for reloads. Those torpedoes within the tubes had been open to the elements on *S1*, but now rested behind hinged flaps. Up to eight depth charges could be carried on the stern deck immediately behind two large smoke dischargers for use in evading the enemy. Three additional boats to *S7*'s specifications were built for export to China, five for Bulgaria and eight for Yugoslavia.

The officers and men of the 1st Schnellbootshalbflottille were initially accommodated aboard a depot ship, the converted steamer *Nordsee*, captained by ObltzS Eberhard Godt (later to move over to U-boat operations). However, this ship was not ideal for use with the mobile S-boats, being both too slow and too old. New fleet tenders were commissioned to assist operational S-boats in their operations. In principle it was decided to allocate each S-flotilla its own tender, which was used to refuel and rearm the boats and also to function as a floating barrack for six crews. On 24 September 1934, Blohm & Voss's *Tsingtau* was commissioned into the Reichsmarine as the first purpose-built S-boat tender (*Schnellbootbegleitschiff*), similar in design and purpose to the Deutsche Werke-constructed U-boat tender *Saar*, built at the same time. In overall

A pre-war photograph of destroyer *Friedrich Ihn* with an S-boat alongside, showing the relative scale of the two ship types.

command of S-boat activities was the post of Führer der Torpedoboote, established in September 1933 and responsible for all destroyer, torpedo boat and S-boat operations.[3]

On 12 June 1935 *S9* was commissioned into a new flotilla within a new navy. The Kriegsmarine had supplanted the Reichsmarine and had been publicly announced by Adolf Hitler on 16 March, a little under two years after he had taken full dictatorial control of Nazi Germany. At the same time the 1st Schnellbootshalbflottille was renamed 1st Schnell-bootsflottille. Full-scale rearmament was now openly underway, almost helped by the signing of the Anglo-German Naval Agreement which allowed a Kriegsmarine one-third the size of the Royal Navy – a move that Great Britain mistakenly believed would allow some form of arms limitation to be placed upon Germany. By the year's end *S10* to *S13* were in service, all powered by the more reliable 16-cylinder Daimler-Benz MB502. As if to confirm the choice, in May 1937 all operational S-boats made a journey around Denmark from Heligoland to Kiel, those equipped with the Daimler-Benz engines experiencing a trouble-free passage, all those with MAN suffering multiple mechanical failures.

The original S-boats that had been powered by petrol engines (*S1* to *S5*) were decommissioned and sold to Spain in December 1936, as was *S6*, powered by its unreliable MANs. It was there that the combat capabilities of the S-boats would be tested for the first time.

2
Spain and the Gathering Clouds of War

July 1936 – October 1939

IN July 1936, following years of political and religious turbulence, Spain erupted into civil war. A right-wing uprising led by General José Sanjurjo y Sacanell at the head of the so-called Nationalists attempted to wrest control of the country from President Manuel Azaña's democratically elected, though divisive, Republican government. Sacanell was killed in a plane crash only days after the uprising began, as was his primary strategist who co-ordinated the attempted coup – Don Emilio Mola y Vidal – leaving Nationalist forces in the hands of General Francisco Franco. The ensuing civil war swiftly captured the attention of most of western Europe.

Politics in the interwar years throughout Europe had largely polarised into two opposing viewpoints – those for or against Communism on the one hand, Fascism on the other. Although the roots from which the Spanish Civil War grew were far more tangled and complex, this simplistic view of Left versus Right gripped the continent, a fact understood and encouraged by the Nationalists who declared their fight as one against Communism and 'ungodliness'. For their part, the Republicans trumpeted their standpoint as anti-fascist. While the Western democracies adopted a primarily non-interventionist standpoint, the Fascist countries Italy and Germany were soon providing aid to Franco, while Communist Russia (and to a lesser degree the French Popular Front government) did likewise to the Republicans.

Of all three German armed services, the Kriegsmarine probably benefited the least from their experience during the Spanish Civil War. Participation was initiated in August 1936 when three officers and specialists arrived in Spain to advise the Nationalist command about mine warfare, signals and coastal artillery. This small group was expanded upon the creation of the Condor Legion, the naval portion named Gruppe Nordsee, and largely consisting of communications personnel.

The First World War vintage Bergman MG15 water-cooled machine gun, used as bow weapon aboard early S-boats.

At sea, the Nationalist cause could muster very little by way of fighting craft, as the majority of Spain's navy had rallied to the Republicans, overthrowing and executing their Nationalist officers. Thus it was that Italy and Spain provided assistance in both men and materiel, initial German efforts including the deployment of warships to evacuate German nationals.

The Kriegsmarine quickly formed a small operational control staff – Sonderstab W – to co-ordinate covert military supply transports by German freighter to Spain. In total they would go on to organise 170 voyages during the civil war. There would be two threads running in German commitment to Spain: covert and overt. Overtly, the Kriegsmarine eventually contributed three pocket battleships, six cruisers, twelve torpedo boats and fourteen U-boats to coastal patrols as part of the international military presence in Spanish waters, all overseen by Vizeadmiral Rolf Hans Wilhelm Karl Carls. The Kriegsmarine's initial purpose was part of a humanitarian relief mission, rescuing 9,300 refugees from the fighting, including 4,550 German nationals.

On 3 August, at the behest of the French government, an international 'non-intervention agreement' was proposed, designed to stop the potential spread of war beyond the Iberian Peninsula. Somewhat cynically, Germany declared to the United Kingdom that 'no war materials had been sent from Germany and none will', signing the agreement towards the end of the month. A naval patrol was established using French, British, German and Italian ships to enforce an international arms embargo on both warring sides. The Kriegsmarine was allotted the patrol area between Cabo de Gata (Almeria) and Oropesa. Ironically, most of Spain's Mediterranean coast was policed by the very nations bringing weapons to Franco.

Covertly, however, two U-boats passed through the Straits of Gibraltar as part of Operation Ursula, and equipment and men were ferried to Spain for use by the Nationalists.[4] Part of that would involve the first six S-boats that had been commissioned into the Reichsmarine.

In Kiel, the officers and men of 1st S-flotilla were gathered in the wardroom of the *Tsingtau* where they were addressed by their flotilla commander KK Heinz Dietrich von Conrady. He was enlisting volunteers to travel to Spain to train Nationalist naval crews to operate the seven S-boats sold by Germany to Franco's forces. After some deliberation, von Conrady selected thirteen men to form the small S-boat contingent commanded by the erstwhile skipper of *S3*, Fregattenkapitän Manfred Fuhrke.

The volunteer contingent embarked aboard the steamer *Capri* in Hamburg, bound for La Coruña, carrying supplies for the Nationalist forces which included S-boat torpedoes. The boats themselves would follow aboard the freighter *Uhenfels*, arriving early in 1937.

Training for the Spanish crews began as soon as their German instructors arrived and the boats had been refitted for sea. Trials were conducted in the Bay of Biscay and almost immediately the S-boats were found to be incompatible with the frequently heavy seas in what was a notoriously turbulent part of the Atlantic. Operating between Santander, Gijon and Bilbao, the boats were subject to long approaches to and from their testing grounds, and floundered in heavy swells. The decision was made to relocate south and once again they were loaded by floating crane on to the deck of a German freighter – *Drachenfels* – and transported to Hielva near Cadiz. Unfortunately, during unloading by floating crane an accident damaged *S3*; the strong wooden beams supporting the boat snapped and *S3* plunged 12m (40ft) to hang suspended in *Drachenfels'* railing. Two merchant seamen riding the S-boat hull were hurled to the deck, one killed, the other severely injured. It was an inauspicious start to the S-boats' redeployment. *S3* was eventually freed and the remaining boats unloaded using the ship's smaller crane. The battered hulk of *S3* was deemed beyond repair and she remained on land, acting as a source of spare parts for the remaining vessels that were officially commissioned into the Nationalist Navy as 'LT' boats (*Lancha Torpedera*) under their new Spanish names: *S1* became *Badajoz* (*LT15*); *S2, Falange* (*LT13*); *S4, Requete* (*LT11*); *S5, Oviedo* (*LT12*); and *S6* was renamed *Toledo* (*LT14*).

Ultimately, although there was action elsewhere at sea during the civil war, the S-boats remained largely ineffectual. The German training contingent found their Spanish counterparts relatively lacklustre in their desire to patrol on a war footing, going so far as to suspect mechanical sabotage on behalf of some in order to keep their boats in port. While other German servicemen – particularly on land and in the air – garnered considerable experience from the war, the S-boat men returned to Germany in April 1937 having gained little, losing their commanding officer Manfred Fuhrke on 30 April when his Ju52 transport plane, also carrying six Condor Legion fighter pilots, was shot down by Republican fighters while travelling from Seville to Rome.

The Spanish S-boats had little success, although mines laid by *Falange* and *Requete* south of Almeria crippled the British destroyer HMS *Hunter* patrolling on 13 May 1937 as part of the non-intervention force. In turn, on 18 June *Falange* was set afire and sunk off Malaga after the S-boats had moved to the northeast, near the centre of the land battle.

The new generation of S-boats had been blooded in combat, albeit under a different flag and using already obsolete designs. Meanwhile, the S-boat

Pre-war postcard photograph of *S8* at sea. The white bow numbers were painted out during the last days of peace.

service was slowly expanding, though not without opposition from within the Kriegsmarine itself. Admiral Carls, Kriegsmarine Fleet Commander, demanded a halt to S-boat production as he judged them too dependent on weather conditions to be reliably used in combat. Nonetheless, meetings at SKL, including former commanders of 1st S-flotilla KK von Conrady and KK Schubert, were productive for the fledgling S-boat service and expansion was agreed.

During 1935 four more S-boats were ordered from Lürssen, acting as testing platforms for new engine configurations. Based on the *S7* design, the size had once again increased to accommodate new machinery. Each boat measured 34.6m (113ft 6in) long, 5.1m (16ft 8in) wide with a draught of 1.5m (4ft 11in). Whereas *S1* had displaced 39.8 tons, now *S14* displaced 97 tons. The armament remained unchanged, but 11-cylinder MAN L11/Zu engines now pushed the boat to a maximum speed of 37 knots. These MAN engines were certainly upgrades of the company's previous efforts, but were larger and heavier, with the resultant need for an increase in S-boat size.

Unfortunately, although improved, these four-stroke, 11-cylinder engines were rife with disadvantages when weighed against Daimler-Benz. Their physical size and weight was considerably greater and mechanical problems continued to plague them. The long crankshaft was prone to torsion-induced damage and the engine's high centre of gravity frequently placed undue stress on engine mounts, particularly during high-speed manoeuvring, potentially causing them to crack. Despite attempts to solve these issues, the faultless performance of the Daimler-Benz engines in the four boats numbered *S10* to *S13* decided the issue and the Kriegsmarine henceforth used only the latter for future S-boats. However, this would ultimately cause its own problems. Daimler-Benz was heavily involved in providing engines for the Luftwaffe and would remain so throughout World War Two. This, in turn, would cause severe delays in the production of S-boat engines and the Kriegsmarine's ability to launch new boats.

Between June 1936 and March 1938, *S14* to *S17* were commissioned, forming the basis of a new flotilla to be based in Wilhelmshaven and coming into existence in August 1938. Pre-war experiments at minelaying using *S14*, *S15* and *S16* were considered a success; removable mine rails were fixed to port and starboard for rolling ground mines off the stern. Minelaying was to become a mainstay activity of S-boats.

Although the Daimler-Benz MB502 had proved highly dependable, an improved model, the MB501 was soon available for production. A 20-

Another pre-war postcard showing *S19* at sea. The eagles gracing both sides of the bridge were removed at the beginning of hostilities. The original photo shows the boat number painted white on the hull, removed by the censor.

cylinder V engine that generated 2050HP, it was first used in trials aboard the boats *S18* to *S25* and exceeded expectations. Due to the versatility of the engine and its proven reliability, this would become the basic S-boat engine that continued to serve through the war. Later, from *S139* onwards, a motor-driven supercharger became a standard fitting, raising the power output to 2500hp. This supercharged version was redesignated the MB511.[5]

On 1 August 1938 the 2nd S-flotilla was formed in Wilhelmshaven, with depot ship *Tanga*, commissioned on 21 January 1939, later joining the boats. Flotilla commander was Kptlt Rudolf Petersen who had already served as skipper of *S9* and been recently promoted. Petersen had joined the Reichsmarine as a cadet in 1925, commissioned on 1 October 1929 and initially served aboard torpedo boats and light cruisers. He spent two years in the naval oceanographic service, before returning to torpedo boats. On 1 September 1935 he was promoted to Kapitänleutnant and one month later joined the S-boat service. Whilst skippering *S9*, Petersen was also given command of a training company for officer cadets and in August 1938 he completed his Admiralty staff training at Mürwik's Naval Academy and was promoted to command the newly established 2nd S-flotilla. Petersen's new unit allowed for a reshuffling of available S-boats as training intensified — and not without risk. On 14 June 1939 *S13* collided with the Kriegsmarine oceanic research ship *Meteor* while exercising in the Baltic Sea. The Schnellboot's starboard bow was completely smashed in, though she remained afloat and was towed to Kiel for repairs that would last until 1940.

As war clouds gathered on Germany's horizon, Adolf Hitler ratified a naval construction plan for a balanced fleet in the same vein as the Royal Navy or Germany's previous Kaiserliche Marine: the so-called Z-Plan. This included an S-boat strength of seventy-five boats by 1946 and by March 1939 orders had been placed for boats numbered up to *S37*; *S23* was the last of these boats to be commissioned before the outbreak of hostilities.

Diplomatically, Hitler's government was internationally belligerent. Relations with Poland had soured over Hitler's territorial demands on Danzig and the 'Polish corridor' that connected Germany to East Prussia. On 31 March 1939 Great Britain 'guaranteed' Polish sovereignty in the face of potential German invasion, angering Hitler enough to threaten the

The 20mm flak weapon which was mounted on early S-boat stern gun platforms.

official abandonment of the Anglo-German Naval Treaty of 1935 during a speech in Wilhelmshaven at the launch of the battleship *Tirpitz*, a threat he carried out on 28 April 1939.

By August 1939 the two S-flotillas were positioned in strategically important areas in the event of potential war, identification hull numbers painted over to ensure military secrecy. The 1st S-flotilla remained in Kiel with the *Tsingtau*, while the 2nd S-flotilla had relocated to the small island of Heligoland with the *Tanga*. The eight newer boats were mainly allocated to Kptlt Sturm's flotilla in Kiel, Kptlt Petersen's unit strength being only six. On the evening of 24 August, Sturm's flotilla accompanied the Führer der Torpedoboote, KA Günther Lutjens, aboard the destroyer *Leberecht Maass*, from Swinemünde to Pillau. There, the following day Sturm met with Lutjens and his staff and received instructions to patrol the Baltic five miles east of Gdynia, the plan being to blockade Polish naval forces therein. Hitler set an initial attack date for 26 August, but cancelled at the last moment in a case of uncharacteristic diplomatic nervousness. In Pillau the S-boats remained at readiness, three Polish destroyers reported by German B-Dienst operatives as having put to sea on alert. Finally, at 0445hrs on 1 September, Kriegsmarine units received notification that they were at war, Sturm's S-boats taking up position on calm seas in naval grid square AO1935. Two minutes later the old battleship *Schleswig-Holstein* opened World War Two by bombarding the Polish military transit depot at Westerplatte, Danzig.

As fighting raged on an almost unexpected level ashore, the S-boats' first wartime day was uneventful, two used primarily as despatch boats shuttling orders between German destroyers. On 2 September Sturm was ordered to position his flotilla to intercept any vessels attempting to pass through suspected gaps in Polish minefields east of the Hel Peninsula. It was here the following day that ObltzS Georg Christiansen found Polish steamer *Lloyd Bydgoski II*, recently commandeered by the Polish Navy for use as a picket ship. Christiansen fired a warning shot across the Pole's bow, allowing the small crew to take to their lifeboat before sinking her with a prolonged 20mm artillery attack: the first sinking by the Kriegsmarine S-boat service – and the last for 1939. As the *Lloyd Bydgoski II* disappeared beneath the waves, Great Britain and France were declaring war on Germany and the stage was set for the Kriegsmarine to clash with two of the world's most powerful navies.

With limited scope for action after the threat from Polish destroyers was eliminated by Stuka dive-bombing attacks, the 1st S-flotilla was sent back to Kiel with the *Tsingtau*, ordered to continue onward to the North Sea and pass into the control of Commanding Admiral West. En route Christiansen's *S23* stopped another freighter, which was identified as German steamer *Phoebus* and allowed to continue its journey to Königsberg. Over the days that followed, the flotilla transited the Kaiser Wilhelm Canal to Wilhelmshaven and then on to Heligoland, where the boats of the 2nd S-flotilla had been stationed since the outbreak of war. On 5 September Petersen's flotilla had suffered its first wartime damage after *S17* encountered unexpectedly stormy conditions in the North Sea during a routine patrol. The boat's keel was broken, although ObltzS Hans Schultze-Jena and his crew were able to limp back to Heligoland. Chief Engineer ObMasch Werner Eigenbrod was later singled out for his calm handling of the emergency and keeping the crippled vessel afloat. Ultimately, the boat was so badly damaged that after transfer to the Kriegsmarine Werft in Wilhelmshaven it was decommissioned; the troublesome MAN engines were removed and kept for spare parts.

Shortly thereafter, Petersen's flotilla transferred to the Baltic, embarking on further training exercises, before joining patrol lines in the western Baltic near Øresund in an unsuccessful attempt to prevent Polish submarine *Orzel* from escaping to England. Fears had also arisen that Royal Navy submarines prowled the region. The unit had undergone a reshuffle

S-boats travelling in line and communicating by semaphore early in the war; later on, intercepted radio communications were frequently the undoing of S-boats on patrol.

and by mid October fielded seven boats: *S10*, *S11*, *S12*, a repaired *S13*, *S14*, *S15* and *S16*. The elderly *S9* had been placed into reserve undergoing repairs in Kiel after suffering a piston seizure, *S12* transferring from 1st S-flotilla to take its place. *S15*'s captain, LzS Bernd Rebensburg, was replaced after he and a watch officer from the depot ship *Tanga* were badly injured in a car accident, ObltzS Wilhelm Zimmermann taking command of his boat. A little over two months later, Zimmermann in turn departed, replaced by ObltzS Carl Eberhard Koscky, whose *S14* was in reserve undergoing extensive overhaul. Zimmermann was beginning the so-called *Baubelehrung* of the first of a new series of S-boats, *S30*, launched on 10 September and undergoing final fitting-out. The concept of the *Baubelehrung* had come about during the days of Germany's Imperial Navy. Rather than bring together a new vessel's crew from whatever available personnel there were, often taking an extended period for the crew to meld with both the vessel and each other, the prospective crew were brought to the shipyard as the vessel neared completion. There they gained an insight into the construction of their ship and began to familiarise themselves with their future stations under the eyes of the skipper and chief engineer.

The appearance of *S30* displayed some of the most fundamental changes to S-boat design as a result of operational experience garnered thus far. Two new design models had been in construction since 1938: four boats of the *S26* class numbered *S26* to *S29*, ordered in August 1938, and the first eight of what would eventually be sixteen *S30*-class boats. The latter design had originally been built for export to the Chinese Navy, but with the outbreak of hostilities they were appropriated by a Kriegsmarine desperately under-strength for a war against the British and French navies. These keels had been laid first and so the *S30* boats would be commissioned out of numerical sequence as the first *S26*-class boat was not commissioned until 25 May 1940.

While internally the *S30* class was similar to the *S10*, using the 2000HP Daimler-Benz MB502 engines, externally it incorporated some important advances, the most obvious being a heightened forecastle that enclosed the torpedo tubes. This would remain a feature on all subsequent designs, increasing seaworthiness and the reserve buoyancy of the boat. The covered torpedo tube also vastly eased their maintenance demands, as they were no longer as exposed to the corrosive effect of seawater and weather-related problems. However, there was little to obstruct the flow of water over the bow and into the boat's open bridge in front of the wheelhouse and so two distinctively curved upward flanges were added to shelter the torpedo crews.

The bridge of all S-boats up to the *S18* class was actually in front of the wheelhouse: raising it to the wheelhouse roof in subsequent models increased all-round visibility, as well as the observable horizon.

The bridge atop the wheelhouse of an *S26*-class boat.

The *S30* boats were 2.2m (7ft 2in) shorter than *S26* and 20cm (8in) narrower. This in itself seemed relatively unremarkable, but would eventually pay dividends when it was found that the *S30* class could just manage to navigate the Rhine–Rhône canal system, eventually allowing them to transit from the North Sea to the Mediterranean.

The *S26* class improved on the command and control by setting an open cockpit into the wheelhouse roof, increasing the visible horizon, providing greater shelter and allowing the captain to occupy a centralised position from which to direct his boat. The boat was still helmed from inside the wheelhouse, with which the captain could communicate via speaking tubes and glass windows. The final, most obvious, difference was that the hull portholes were eliminated, increasing structural integrity.

The S-boats continued to patrol the German portion of the North Sea and within the Baltic, providing security for larger surface units or operating as submarine hunters, neither of which suited this type of vessel. The low bridge of an S-boat yielded a near horizon; the spotting of enemy periscopes or torpedo tracks at a distance that allowed evasive manoeuvring was almost impossible. Despite carrying depth charges, ASW work was wholly unsuitable. In fact, in months to come, depth charges were frequently fitted with floats to delay their descent and used as a means of deterring surface pursuit. Escorting larger, slower ships meant that the S-boats were operating well below their planned operational speeds, generally using only the central engine, resulting in increased strain upon it, in turn requiring more frequent overhauls and repairs on only one of three power-plants. OKM were demonstrating that they had little concept of how to actually utilise their S-boats to full advantage. This, coupled with planned operations curtailed through worsening winter conditions, resulted in a seemingly ineffective service, MGK West (Marinegruppenkommando West) going so far as to claim in November 1939 that S-boat groups had 'fallen short of expectations in every respect', a sentiment that would soon lead once again to plans to limit the construction of new boats.[6] It was an inauspicious start to the S-boats' combat service.

On 4 October MGK West formally requested the permanent return of 2nd S-flotilla to its ranks, complaining that the few destroyers available were unsuited to the task of intercepting British merchant shipping. The request was declined and Petersen's unit continued to plough through increasingly wintery Baltic seas, acting as both escort and submarine hunter, while MGK West made plans to send 1st S-flotilla on its first mining mission in the Thames Estuary.

3

Norway

April 1940

THE planned siege of Great Britain involved the disruption of maritime traffic. U-boats, destroyers and S-boats were all assigned minelaying duties that ranged from the Humber to the Thames Estuary, although S-boats had at least twice been forced to cancel planned missions due to foul weather.

In Swinemünde KzS Hans Bütow became FdT on 30 November; the following day Kptlt Heinz Birnbacher was named chief of the 1st S-flotilla, replacing Kurt Sturm. Sturm for his part transferred to the staff of Admiral der Nordsee. The flotilla had grown with the commissioning of ObltzS Kurt Fimmen's *S24* on 18 September. The 1st S-flotilla now stood at six operational vessels: *S18*, *S19*, *S20*, *S21*, *S23* and *S24*, which continued to patrol the North Sea around Heligoland until ordered into the shipyard for extensive overhaul. Winter weather was proving ever more prohibitive for S-boat operations, harbours frequently experiencing severe ice that trapped the boats, and the opportunity was taken to rest and refit.

Petersen's 2nd S-flotilla briefly engaged on anti-submarine operations in the western reaches of the Baltic during December alongside ships of the 11th U-Bootjäger Flotilla, although no contact with the enemy was actually made. The crews at least received experience in the handling of depth charges as the S-boats blew columns of empty water into the sky. By the year's end there were five more boats launched, three commissioned. *S30*, *S25* and *S31* were all in active service by the New Year, followed in March by *S32* and *S33*. Each flotilla would comprise six to eight active duty boats, with two in reserve as training vessels.

During the first half of January, the 2nd S-flotilla continued torpedo training in the Baltic, severe icing of Kiel harbour and the Kaiser Wilhelm Canal preventing a scheduled refit in Wilhelmshaven until February.

24

The S-boat's life raft, here stowed forward of the hatch leading to the compartment housing the main fuel tanks.

Following their shipyard time the 2nd S-flotilla resumed active patrolling in the North Sea with *S14*, *S15*, *S16*, *S30*, *S31*, *S32* and *S33*, an unsuccessful submarine hunt northwest of Heligoland undertaken on 29 March. As part of the search, the three older boats were loaded with six RMA/RMB hemispherical magnetic ground mines for trial purposes. While the newer boats remained almost dry on deck even in rough weather, the three older ones suffered, ObltzS Obermaier signalling from *S15* that they were forced to return to harbour, struggling to keep station. Unfortunately, as they turned for Heligoland, *S15* rammed *S32* to starboard – the entire bow section smashed in. *S32*'s damage was relatively

25

light, but Obermaier's boat limped back to harbour and was consigned to the shipyard for twelve weeks of repairs. The young captain was transferred to new boat *S34*, commissioned on 30 April.

Meanwhile, a military storm was brewing around Norway. German naval planners had debated the necessity for bases on Norway intermittently since 1906. There were those who reasoned during the interwar years that had the Kaiserliche Marine been able to operate from Norwegian ports, rather than the constricted Baltic Sea, their wartime experience would have been remarkably different. Furthermore, German rearmament depended on iron ore exports from Sweden's Kiruna mines, French occupation of the iron-rich Alsace-Lorraine region under Versailles treaty terms having denied Germany this vital military resource. The Swedish iron was transported from the port of Luleå when the harbour was ice free, or alternately by rail to the Norwegian port of Narvik and transported by ship to Germany. Germany's military command rightly feared that this crucial transport system could be severely disrupted by British mining of Norwegian coastal waters. This would force German shipping away from the coast and into the North Sea, dominated by the Royal Navy. The Altmark incident in February served to hasten German invasion plans, fuelling speculation that Britain was not overly concerned with maintaining Norway's neutral status.

In fact, Winston Churchill, as First Lord of the Admiralty, had long advocated the mining of Norwegian waters for this express purpose. Denied permission, his Operation Wilfred remained stalled until 3 April 1940 when the Admiralty received reports of a German naval build-up within the Baltic. A second British operation, Plan R4, for the occupation of key Norwegian and Swedish ports and mines had also long been in development and was activated as an apparent by-product of assistance rendered to Finland following Russia's invasion attempt of November 1939. However, on 2 March 1940 British requests to send troops through Norway and Sweden to aid Finnish forces – whilst occupying the target areas, thus presenting the two Scandinavian nations with a fait accompli – were denied. A Russo-Finnish armistice signed nine days later prevented any such attempt being made under the guise of military assistance.

Both Germany and Britain were vaguely aware of the other's intentions and finally, on 28 March, Churchill was given permission to begin laying Wilfred's minefields. On 8 April a Royal Navy Task Force led by HMS *Renown* laid mines near Bodø; however, they were already too late. The combined forces of Operation *Weserübung* were already at sea and began landing the following day.

Weserübung was the first genuinely 'combined arms' operation that Germany had mounted, with OKW overseeing co-ordination between the three Wehrmacht services. Of paramount importance was the naval contingent, not only for the subjugation of enemy naval forces but for the transporting and logistical support of the Army's ground invasion. Air support by the Luftwaffe would provide an umbrella of security and also allow for the deployment of airborne troops in both Denmark and Norway.

Denmark would be pacified first by a swift assault, paratroops making their combat debut by landing and seizing the Storstrøm Bridge, connecting the island of Falster with Sjælland, and the coastal fortress on Masnedø Island. Further drops were made to secure the airfield at Aalborg, a major stepping stone for future Luftwaffe operations in Norway.

S-boats escorting troop transports during Operation *Weserübung*.

The Kriegsmarine would field eleven groups of surface ships and nine U-boat groups to screen the landing forces from potential attack by the Royal Navy (a disastrous failure, as it transpired). While the two battleships *Gneisenau* and *Scharnhorst* would prowl offshore in support, Warship Gruppe 1, comprising ten troop-carrying destroyers and two freighters, would strike at Narvik. Gruppe 2 was led by the cruiser *Admiral Hipper*, accompanied by four destroyers targeting Trondheim. Gruppe 3 attacked Bergen, led by the light cruisers *Köln* and *Königsberg*, with the artillery training ship *Bremse*, two torpedo boats and Heinz Birnbacher's 1st S-flotilla. For this operation the flotilla fielded *S19*, *S20*, *S21*, *S22* and *S24*, supported by the tender *Carl Peters*.[7] Further south at Kristiansand, Rudolf Petersen's 2nd S-flotilla was part of Gruppe 4, led by the light cruiser *Karlsruhe* alongside three torpedo boats. Petersen's flotilla included *S7*, *S8*, *S17*, *S30*, *S31*, *S32* and *S33*, as well as the tender *Tsingtau*. Gruppe 5 attacking Oslo and Oslofjord centred on the heavy cruisers *Blücher* and *Lützow*, accompanied by torpedo boats and minesweepers. Gruppe 6 attacked the telegraph station at Egersund with four minesweepers. The remaining warship groups sailed for Danish targets. Gruppe 7's objectives were the towns of Nyborg and Korsör which flanked the Great Belt. This attack was headed by the obsolete battleship *Schleswig-Holstein* with auxiliary units and minesweepers. Gruppe 8 sailed for Copenhagen with the minelayer *Hansestadt Danzig* leading a small group of patrol vessels, while Gruppe 9 occupied the small Danish town of Middelfart and the bridge over the Little Belt with cargo ships and patrol vessels. The last two groups passed through the Kaiser Wilhelm Canal and landed on objectives on Denmark's North Sea coastline; Gruppe 10 sailed to Esbjerg and the island of Nordby, with the escort ship *Königin Luise* leading minesweepers; Gruppe 11, comprising minesweepers, sailed for Thyborön, the western entrance to Limfjorden. Follow-up invasion troops would be transported in a virtual shuttle of escorted merchantmen.

On 6 April the FdT KzS Hans Bütow briefed the commanders of both Schnellboot flotillas on the operation that was already underway. Covert German supply vessels had been despatched to Norwegian ports on 3 April and in the days that followed there were Allied sightings of German naval units along the Norwegian coast, fuelling speculation that they were attempting a breakout into the Atlantic. An advance echelon of eight merchant ships acting as disguised tankers had quietly sailed to strategically position themselves along the routes of the impending invasion, followed by seven disguised supply ships which would attempt to put into the target ports carrying heavy weapons.

Bad weather began to develop in the area, leading to rough seas and patches of thick fog. In these difficult conditions the opposing sides began to blunder into one another. Polish submarine *Orzel* sank German troopship SS *Rio de Janeiro* on 8 April (carrying 313 Luftwaffe troops and flak weapons bound for Bergen) and reported sighting uniformed infantry men among the wreckage. Norwegian fishing boats and a destroyer came to the Germans' aid and also reported a startling number of troops.

However, the British Admiralty were distracted by the sinking of HMS *Glowworm*, which had blundered into the *Admiral Hipper*, ramming and disabling her before being sunk herself. Skirmishes around Oslo began on the night of 8 April when Gruppe 6 brushed with a Norwegian patrol vessel, but the ambitious German invasion began in earnest the following morning. At 0500hrs the German ambassador in Oslo informed the Norwegian government both verbally and in writing that they were 'requested' to place themselves under German military protection. A similar note had been delivered to the Danish government. The latter acquiesced under protest, with Denmark subdued within six hours despite some localised fighting that left over two hundred German troops dead. Norway refused.

Landings began as planned on all Norwegian objectives. Birnbacher's 1st S-flotilla was engaged in the assault on Bergen and already one boat down before fighting began. In the early hours of 8 April the spearhead of Gruppe 3, cruisers *Köln* and *Königsberg*, had sailed from Wilhelmshaven, accompanied by *Bremse*, *Leopard* and *Wolf* of the 6th T-Flotilla and the S-boat tender *Carl Peters*. Between them they transported the staff and two battalions of the 69th Infantry Division, as well as Pioneers and Luftwaffe and Kriegsmarine artillery units. The torpedo boats and tender rendezvoused with 1st S-flotilla in Cuxhaven in thick fog. After an hour at sea, *S19* and *S21* collided, ObltzS Kurt 'Bobby' Fimmen's *S19* running into *S21*'s stern. Rendered barely seaworthy, *S19* was towed by *Wolf* to landfall in Bommel Fjord where the crew began repairs.

In Bergen defensive forts opened fire on the approaching German ships. Despite being hampered by fog the 210cm cannon of Kvarvan battery scored two hits on the *Königsberg*; *Bremse* and *Carl Peters* were also damaged by smaller calibre guns. Aboard *Königsberg* the engines, firefighting mains and auxiliary power were all damaged and two of her 3.7cm anti-aircraft gun positions put out of action. The main batteries continued to fire, however, and Birnbacher's S-boats began ferrying troops ashore to directly assault the battery, three soldiers aboard *S22* being wounded during the attack. With Luftwaffe assistance, the Norwegian defenders were eventually silenced, whereupon the S-boats continued ferrying men and equipment ashore. The crew of *S24* also seized control of the 250-ton Norwegian minelayer *Uller* which had begun mining the harbour approaches.

A British reconnaissance flight revealed the presence of the two cruisers and later, between 1830hrs and 2000hrs, Wellingtons and Hampdens from three different squadrons attempted to bomb them, but failed to register a single hit, three men being killed by machine-gun fire from a Wellington. With *Königsberg* unfit to sail and troops well and truly ashore, *Köln* and the torpedo boats began their return to Germany lest they become trapped

S-boat tenders played a vital role in the invasion of Norway. Here a torpedo reload is lowered aboard a waiting S-boat.

by Royal Navy forces. Tied at the Skoltegrund Mole in the most effective defensive posture available, *Königsberg* was attacked once more, this time by Skuas of the Fleet Air Arm. Set on fire and abandoned, she capsized the following day, her crew incorporated into coastal defence units.

On 14 April Birnbacher's 1st S-flotilla was bolstered by the arrival of *S23* and *S25* from Wilhelmshaven. Conquered Bergen needed defending. Vizeadmiral Otto von Schrader had been designated Admiral of the Norwegian West Coast and had little reliable intelligence of what Allied intentions were. With *Königsberg* sunk and *Köln* and the torpedo boats in Germany, he was left with captured inoperable Norwegian coastal forts, the damaged *Bremse* and *Carl Peters*, the six boats of the 1st S-flotilla, a minesweeper, two aircraft tenders and three auxiliary ships. The S-boats were repeatedly grounding ashore, rudders and propellers taking sustained damage as the inexperience of S-boat crews in constricted waters began to tell; *S22* was disabled for nearly two weeks with propeller damage. Coupled with the strain of constant harassment by Fleet Air Arm Skuas that killed at least one man and wounded others, Birnbacher's men were becoming increasingly fatigued.

The depot ships in Norway provided accommodation as well as supplies for the *Weserübung* S-boats.

South of Bergen a small group of Norwegian warships and auxiliaries had gathered at Uskedal, and on 18 April Birnbacher's flotilla was despatched to make reconnaissance sweeps of Hardangerfjorden and ascertain the location of any enemy ships. With reports of German 'destroyers' approaching, the Norwegian torpedo boat *Sæl* moved to intercept, encountering *S23* and *S21*. Using their speed advantage, the S-boats launched an attack with 20mm flak weapons. Torpedoes were fired from both S-boats but they passed under the keel of the shallow-draught Norwegian, hit and holed instead by gunfire, taking on water, but managing to use her superior fire power of twin 37mm cannon to immobilise *S21*. *S23* closed on *Sæl* to draw fire and soon both Norwegian 37mm guns were out of action, a single machine gun left firing. As *S21*'s crew managed to restart their engines, the Norwegian's machine gun seized, and her captain Fenrik Gulbrandsen ordered the sinking ship thrown into full reverse and beached to allow the crew to escape. A third German torpedo also missed, but hit nearby rocks, the concussion tearing *Sæl*'s bow off. Seven Norwegian sailors were wounded before the S-boats, now joined by *S19*, retreated at the approach of a second Norwegian warship.

With the Norwegian presence confirmed and a planned breakout of the Bergen beachhead imminent, von Schrader ordered a direct attack on Uskedal led by the 1st S-flotilla as well as *Bremse* and two auxiliaries (*Schiff 18* and *Schiff 221*) carrying infantrymen. Birnbacher's flotilla numbered five operational boats, *S22*, *S23*, *S24* and *S25*, together with *S19*, which was first into action as she laid a smokescreen under which the auxiliaries landed their troops. Norwegian artillery had opened fire and the minelayer *Tyr* joined the battle, damaging one S-boat before shellfire from *Bremse* disabled the ship. Before the minelayer could be scuttled, two S-boats roared alongside and captured her. This marked the end of organised Norwegian resistance and the town fell to the Germans. *Bremse* and three of the undamaged S-boats next headed to Stavanger to continue ferrying troops to Bergen.

Birnbacher and his overworked S-boats were again required for the escort of an amphibious landing force on 25 April, escorting *Schiff 18* and captured passenger ship *Kong Olav* to Granvin. With the troops successfully ashore, Birnbacher's boats cruised toward Ulvik in a reconnaissance sweep, finding several merchant ships at anchor. Intending to capture the vessels, the S-boats radioed minesweeper *M1* for support from her heavier weapons. *S21* pulled alongside the 2,380-ton motor freighter *San Miguel*, *S23* approaching *Afrika*, a 6,503-ton German steamer that had been captured by the Norwegian Navy, and men from

S19 began boarding the small 162-ton *Eidfjord* as the two remaining S-boats stood guard to seaward. Unbeknownst to the Germans, they had been detected by nearby Norwegian infantrymen, who had hurriedly established ambush positions with machine guns in the village. They opened fire on *S19*, the effect devastating on the immobile and exposed German crew; the boat was repeatedly hit as men jumped off *Eidfjord* and attempted to find shelter. *S19* itself reversed away from the coastline as Kptlt Birnbacher brought *S25* racing in to pull escaping men from the sea and return fire. *M1* then arrived, her captain Kptlt Hans Bartels enraged to see men being targeted while struggling in the water, and ordered his guns to immediately open fire; the village of Ulvik was set ablaze and soon in ruins. By 0845hrs the firing ceased. The Norwegian defenders had retreated and two of the merchant ships were settling on the seabed, their seacocks opened before the arrival of the Germans. *Eidfjord* was boarded again and sailed with the S-boats and *M1* back to German-held territory. Birnbacher had been wounded in the left arm during the brief but sharp battle and his flotilla had taken several other casualties: ObltzS Hermann Büchting (commander of *S25*), ObltzS Bernd Klug (commander of *S21*) and nine other sailors had all been wounded; Oberfähnrich zur See Herbert Spickenbom, aboard as part of his officer training, was killed and later buried in St Mary's Churchyard, Bergen. *S25* was temporarily taken over after repair by the

Kapitänleutnant Heinz Birnbacher, wounded in fighting near Ulvik on 25 April, shakes hands with Admiral Hermann Boehm.

flotilla adjutant, LzS Karl-Friedrich Künzel, while LzS Siegfried Wuppermann took over *S21*.[8]

A less spectacular attack took place on 27 April when boats of the 1st S-flotilla operating alongside *M1* engaged what they took to be an enemy cruiser or destroyer in Sognefjord, only to discover that it was the obsolete destroyer HNoMS *Garm* that had already been attacked and sunk by Luftwaffe bombers during the previous day.

On 2 May Birnbacher's S-boats hunted the submarine HMS *Trident* which had attacked 5,295-ton German freighter SS *Claire Hugo Stinnes* in Bjørnejorden. Torpedoes had missed the freighter as she was travelling in ballast and high in the water, but several hits from the submarine's deck gun had run her aground.[9] The S-boats searched in vain, although unbeknownst to them they narrowly missed *Trident* with one depth charge

Admiral Hermann Boehm, named commander of Kriegsmarine forces in Norway after *Weserübung*, on inspection tour aboard an S-boat at sea in Norwegian waters.

which caused the submarine's bow to rise nearly enough for bilge water to flood the main motors. However, *Trident* remained concealed and made good her escape.

Meanwhile, Rudolf Petersen's 2nd S-flotilla had taken part in the assault on Kristiansand. Gruppe 2's major surface vessels had sailed from Wesermünde at 0500hrs on 8 April, the cruiser *Karlsruhe* escorted by torpedo boats *Luchs*, *Seeadler* and *Greif*, with S-boat depot ship *Tsingtau* accompanying them. Between them they carried infantry, bicycle infantry and naval artillery units. As the group approached Kristiansand in the early hours of 9 April, *Greif* was detached to land elements of the 163rd Infantry Division on Arendal to capture the telegraph station and sever one of two telegraph cables joining Norway and Britain. The remainder continued to Kristiansand, though thick fog forced *Karlsruhe* to lie outside the narrow entrance fjord. Instead, he ordered the three most modern S-boats (*S30*, *S31* and *S32*) with *Luchs* and *Seeadler* to ferry infantrymen from the cruiser ashore. As the transfer of troops began, Odderöy's coastal battery opened fire on *Karlsruhe*. Unable to bring all guns to bear, the cruiser backed off to present a full broadside as *S30* and *S31* raced to land troops that could deal with the forty-man Norwegian battery. Under direct attack with Luftwaffe support and *Karlsruhe* shellfire, the battery surrendered before midday and *Karlsruhe* entered Kristiansand to unload all remaining troops.[10]

Inside the military harbour, the crews of the 2nd S-flotilla helped take control of an impressive haul of captured enemy equipment, including two small obsolete submarines, a destroyer, two torpedo boats and various patrol craft. They also retrieved *U21*, which had been interned by Norwegian forces on 27 March after running aground off Oldknuppen Island due to faulty navigation.

The subjugation of Norway would take a further two months, with Norwegian forces capitulating on 10 June 1940. However, although the German operation had been a success, the Kriegsmarine had been severely mauled, losing two heavy cruisers, two light cruisers, ten destroyers and six U-boats. Others had suffered severe damage, leaving just three cruisers and four destroyers as the only major surface units in service. S-boats were ordered to remain in the Norwegian ports, safeguarding the German coastal traffic. The 1st S-flotilla remained under the command of Admiral von Schrader in his role as Admiral der Norwegen Westküste, while the 2nd S-flotilla was placed under the control of Der Befehlshaber der Sicherund der Ostsee, Vizeadmiral Hermann Moontz. FdT initially exercised immediate control of S-boat deployment as Moontz's subordinate, but with few combat units, FdT returned to Germany to oversee the formation of new S-boat units and the return to active duty of

S-boats in harbour at the end of hostilities in Norway, photographed for *Die Kriegsmarine* magazine.

damaged boats. *S9*, *S14* and *S16* were judged to be obsolete, only of limited use after the strain on their MAN engines resulted in problems unworthy of repair.

Petersen's 2nd S-flotilla acted in co-operation with minesweepers and the few serviceable torpedo boats to escort transports of men and equipment between Germany, occupied Denmark and Norway. However, once again, this proved an unsuitable deployment for the fast attack boats. The wear and tear of running on a single engine severely tested the power-plants' endurance and necessitated premature replacement. Alternately, if the boats ran on two engines the steering was difficult to control; three engines and the lowest speed was too fast for the slow transports of the Kriegsmarine convoys. Nonetheless, their commitment was necessary, with a lack of surface ships available. After the depredation of *Weserübung*, the Kriegsmarine was severely under-strength at a time when Hitler embarked on his most ambitious gamble yet: the invasion of France.

4
Invasion in the West

April 1940 – May 1940

THE 2nd S-flotilla was transferred to the North Sea on 24 April alongside all functioning torpedo boats. SKL had decided that shipping in the German Bight was at greater risk of Allied interception, and so Petersen's flotilla came under the control of von Schrader's Admiral der Norwegen Westküste command, despite strong objections from Moontz's Baltic command. As if to prove the wisdom of the transfer, the 2nd S-flotilla boats sighted French destroyers that had broken into the Skagerrak in the early morning. Converted trawlers of the 7th Vorpostenboot came under ineffectual French fire before the S-boats arrived to chase the destroyers away. *S30*, *S32* and *S33* were then transferred to Wilhelmshaven, while *S31*, *S34* and *S36* continued to operate from Norway, using Stavanger as their base, while *Tsingtau* remained in Kristiansand. The laying of defensive German minefields in the North Sea and Skagerrak continued, the S-boats used as protective escort for minelayers. On 8 May the 2nd S-flotilla was thus engaged when it encountered a Royal Navy Task Force centred on the cruiser HMS *Birmingham*, which had been despatched into the North Sea to disrupt the German minelaying.[11]

S31, *S34* and *S13* were all en route from Stavanger to Wilhelmshaven during that afternoon, the latter due for repairs to engine damage caused by grounding. To the south, *S30*, *S32* and *S33* were at sea, *S32* briefly detouring to the Danish harbour of Esbjerg with engine problems. All bar the damaged *S13* were re-routed to intercept the British surface group converging on the German minelaying mission west of the Fisher bank.

On the British side of the hill, three of the destroyers had become detached from the main group of fourteen ships, HMS *Kelly* and *Kandahar* engaged on hunting unsuccessfully for *U32* with depth charges, HMS

Bulldog veering away to destroy a floating mine with gunfire. The three ships formed a loose group as they raced to rejoin *Birmingham*, briefly opening fire on a Dornier 18 flying boat sighted at 2052hrs. By this time HMS *Bulldog* was trailing behind the two faster K-class ships and, with fog beginning to close in and concerns over the destroyer's fuel situation, HMS *Kelly*'s captain Lord Louis Mountbatten ordered speed reduced to 28 knots to allow *Bulldog* to catch up. At 2244hrs lookouts aboard *Kelly* sighted a dim shadow approximately six hundred yards off the port bow. It was ObltzS Hermann Opdenhoff's *S31* lying in wait with *S34*.

Luftwaffe–Kriegsmarine co-operation – particularly with the S-boat service – was relatively ineffective during the Second World War, never fulfilling a fraction of the potential soon to be discovered by the British. However, in this case, a sighting report from the Dornier Do18 that had spotted the three destroyers allowed the S-boats to lie in wait across the expected enemy track. *S31* fired both torpedoes, one hitting HMS *Kelly* in the forward boiler room and ripping a 50ft hole from keel to waterline. The

S-boats fanning out from their line-astern travel into attacking formation.

ship immediately stopped, swiftly developing a 13-degree list to starboard. The boiler had been thrown off its mountings to starboard and scalding steam added to the confusion and casualties. Dead in the water, HMS *Kelly* appeared doomed.

Aboard the stricken ship, Mountbatten was unsure of whether the attacker had been U-boat or S-boat and ordered HMS *Bulldog* to drop depth charges, Opdenhoff having retreated in the certain belief that his target was fatally holed. The men aboard *Kandahar* too believed *Kelly* had sunk, but those aboard HMS *Bulldog* could still see her lying with decks awash, enveloped in smoke and steam, and prepared to take the stricken ship in tow. In ever-thickening fog, Lieutenant Commander J P Wisden's ship began towing HMS *Kelly* toward shore, the latter ditching all depth charges and any removable weight in an effort to keep afloat. After half an hour, at approximately 0010hrs on 9 May, British lookouts heard high-speed marine diesels to starboard. Minutes later *S33* appeared out of the fog, ramming into HMS *Bulldog*'s starboard quarter. The impact angle was slight, deflecting *S33* forward into HMS *Kelly*. Aboard *S33* the crew began firing both the forward machine gun and stern-mounted flak weapon before ramming *Kelly* at the break of the forecastle, driving at high speed down the awash starboard deck, tearing loose the ship's whaler and motor cutter as well as smashing davits and guardrails. Aboard *S33* there was pandemonium as the steel guardrail stanchions tore through the wooden hull, smashing the bow to pieces. In moments *S33* broke away, disappearing into the fog, the engines stuttering and dying. The S-boat's helmsman had fallen across the drive lever when the collision happened, cutting the throttle completely. Neither side were visible to each other now, HMS *Bulldog* and *Kelly* continuing their slow limp to shipyards on the River Tyne.[12]

Aboard *S33* the crew assessed their situation. Nine metres of the starboard bow had been smashed in and compartments VIII and IX were completely flooded, although bulkhead number VII held fast and kept the rest of the boat dry. The young captain, ObltzS Hans Schultze-Jena, had received minor injuries from flying splinters, which had slashed the entire length of the boat. The forward part of the torpedo tube was wrecked by the impact and sporadic British small-arms fire had riddled the S-boat's dinghy. Although hidden by fog, *S33* lay only 60m (200ft) astern of the two destroyers and blind British fire was continuing. Schultze-Jena ordered scuttling charges rigged while the chief engineer, Obermaschinist Werner Eigenbrod, assessed the damage. Once the engines were restarted, *S33*

Although not entirely suitable as an ASW vessel, S-boats were often charged with finding enemy submarines. Here a crewman loads depth charges aboard in preparation for patrol.

made way at reduced speed to leave the area and attempt a return to Germany, two hundred miles distant. The engines were largely undamaged and *S33* was capable of a respectable 20 knots. The remaining three S-boats reached Wilhelmshaven without further incident, Schultze-Jena's damaged boat entering harbour nearly six hours after its flotilla-mates with only dregs of fuel left in the bunkers, to be immediately consigned to the shipyard.

It was commonplace for S-boats to travel independently back to port after an operation, frequently having lost contact in fast-moving battles. During an attack the captain and senior petty officer, as well as any officer under instruction who was aboard to 'learn the trade', were on the bridge, one seaman at the steering-wheel, another ready to fetch any required charts. Two signallers with binoculars were behind the bridge, torpedo rating at the starboard torpedo tube and senior seaman at the port torpedo tube. Engine-room personnel remained on duty and were not allowed on deck during a mission. Seldom working alone, S-boats usually attacked in pairs (a *Rotte*) or larger numbers, remaining in visual touch after leaving harbour for as long as possible and then continuing to pass any necessary signals via VHF radio (*Ultrakurzwellen*).

Despite heavy damage to *S33*, the mission was rated successful; the offensive nature of the S-boats had been proven in direct action against enemy warships. S-boat tactics practised in the Baltic had yielded the first major S-boat victory: attack and then retreat at speed under cover of a smokescreen to enhance natural elements of fog or darkness. On 16 May 1940 ObltzS Hermann Opdenhoff became the first S-boat man to receive the Knight's Cross.[13]

The day after the S-boats' triumphant return, the border between Germany and its Western neighbours erupted with the beginning of *Fall Gelb* and the invasion of France and the Low Countries. German troops poured into the Netherlands, Belgium and France in another combined arms offensive, though with little naval participation. At sea, small coastal U-boats were laying mines and harassing British traffic in the North Sea and English Channel, but Dönitz's U-boat strength was woefully inadequate. MGK West made urgent appeals to SKL for the immediate transfer to the English Channel of S-boats, though SKL vacillated for two days before complying. Commanding Admiral Norway had deemed it essential that he retain various surface units – including one S-flotilla – for the protection of coastal convoys, particularly those supplying hard-pressed Wehrmacht units in Narvik, where the battle continued to rage.

However, although SKL agreed in principle, there were too few resources available to keep the S-boats committed in two theatres. German forces still swept through the Netherlands, which capitulated within five days and was fully occupied within seven. Belgium surrendered on 28 May, eighteen days after the German attack had commenced and in France, though the battle would draw out until June, Prime Minister Paul Reynaud contacted Winston Churchill on 15 May and told him: 'We have been defeated ... we are beaten; we have lost the battle'.

Standing by to deploy a depth charge at sea; each charge was manually released from its individual wire restraint.

Now that the Dutch coast is in German hands, Naval Staff considers the operational facilities for S-boats on the Belgian and French coasts and in the Channel to be particularly good in view of the nature of this area and the experiences of World War I. Further developments in the situation on land indicate that we shall soon be mopping up Northern France and Western Belgium and that there will be large-scale evacuations of troops by the enemy from the harbours of Northern France and Belgium.

At this time it is imperative that we have a sufficient number of S-boats for operations in this area. Every effort must be made to use Den Helder and, as soon as possible the Hook of Holland also, as bases for S-boats.

In view of these urgent operational requirements, the S-boat operations from the south Norwegian coast, although important, must take second place. Hence the 1st S-flotilla is being withdrawn from southern Norway and placed at the disposal of Marinegruppenkommando West for use on operations in the southern North Sea.[14]

The port at Den Helder was investigated as a permanent S-boat base, requiring the building of bombproof shelters and ammunition stockpiling. Mines strewn about the harbour by the retreating enemy were to be cleared using captured steamers as makeshift Sperrbrecher. S-boats were earmarked as naval cover for Group Stein – Heer units launching an amphibious assault from Walcheren and South Beveland Islands across the Scheldt river – as well as the interception of Allied troopships at Ostend. Stein was ultimately abandoned, but the commitment to operations along the Belgian coast remained absolute as Allied merchant and naval traffic intensified west of Ostend. The S-boats were the only surface force felt capable of taking the battle to the enemy.

On 19 May the nine S-boats of both the 1st and 2nd S-flotillas (*S22*, *S23*, *S24* and *S25* of the 1st S-flotilla and *S13*, *S30*, *S31*, *S32* and *S34* of the 2nd S-flotilla) made their way to the German island of Borkum with the tender *Carl Peters*. *S24* had passed through the Kaiser Wilhelm Canal after transfer from Norway, having doubled as convoy escort to Germany. While in the canal near Rendsburg, British aircraft laid mines along the waterway, flying directly above *S24*. The crew later lamented that they had not been given the required permission to fire on the aircraft which, they claimed, 'they could have riddled'.[15] All nine boats went into action during the following night, 20 May.

The S-boats embarked upon a reconnaissance of Ostend, Nieuport and Dunkirk, although their operation was somewhat hampered by a full moon.

At 2005hrs three British Avro Anson aircraft of 48 Squadron engaged on a 'Dutch patrol' unsuccessfully attacked the outbound boats southwest of Ijmuiden with bombs, the nearest explosion 20m (65ft) abeam of *S30*. Flak from the weaving S-boats hit the lead aircraft in the starboard wing and Flight Lieutenant Stephen Dodds was forced to ditch, with all four crew killed. In the early hours of 21 May *S32* fired two torpedoes at one of two darkened steamers sighted near Nieuport. Estimated at 2,000 tons, one torpedo was a 'surface runner' and missed, while the other struck amidships. The resulting explosion and pillar of flame prompted the captain to report the vessel as 'probably carrying fuel or munitions', no longer visible once the flames had subsided and presumed sunk.[16] *S25* fired two torpedoes at what was identified as a 'French torpedo cruiser and destroyer' west of Dunkirk, missing the destroyer *Sirocco*. All boats returned to Borkum by noon on 21 May. SKL recorded that 'the fact that the boats managed to fire on destroyers in the immediate vicinity of the enemy ports justifies the expectation that continual operations from the Dutch coast will attain further successes.'[17]

There then began a stream of S-boat sorties against targets gathered near Dunkirk and the eastern end of the English Channel. During the night of 22 May, eight boats of the 1st and 2nd S-flotillas sortied to attack patrolling destroyers between the Thames and Ostend. It was an exceptionally still night, the noise of S-boat diesels drifting across the sea, their enemy apparently mistaking them for aircraft and throwing searchlights into the sky. However, not all of the enemy were so easily fooled and the 2nd S-flotilla boats were halted off the Scheldt Estuary by parachute flares, breaking off an attempt to enter the Thames Estuary. However, ObltzS von Mirbach's *S21* and ObltzS Christiansen's *S23* of 1st Flotilla were able to find one of the three destroyers from the 2ème Division de Contre-Torpilleurs (*Chacal*, *Léopard* and *Jaguar*) which had sailed from Brest on 21 May. Having briefly put in to Cherbourg, they were instructed to carry explosives and demolition crews to the three ports of Boulogne, Calais and Dunkirk to prepare them for destruction before the Germans arrived. *Jaguar* was assigned Dunkirk, suffering two dead as a result of aircraft attack in transit, arriving on station off Dunkirk Harbour a little after midnight. Nearby, the wreck of the 5,482-ton tanker *Niger* still burned fiercely forty-eight hours after it had been hit by Luftwaffe attack. Alerted by accurate radio intelligence, *S21* and *S23* lay in wait and at approximately 0045hrs they fired all torpedoes, one from Christiansen's *S23* hitting *Jaguar* on the port side immediately below the bridge. *Jaguar* was doomed; the burning ship was towed toward shore and abandoned near the beach of Malo-les-Bains, thirteen men killed in the attack and twenty-three injured.[18] The two S-boats immediately came under fire but managed to escape the area unscathed.

A rather flowery account of the attack was later printed in Germany's main newspaper, the *Volkischer Beobachter* on 1 January 1941, signed by ObltzS von Mirbach:

AN S-BOAT TRIP OFF DUNKIRK

When darkness had blotted out the whole sky, we became aware of two fiery arcs just above the horizon to the south. 'That can only be Dunkirk and Calais,' I tell my men who ask me about this. According to a reconnaissance report of our aircraft the British are preparing further evacuations for which the required destroyers are said to be lying ready.

As the possibility of sinking something there seems to be favourable, the Commanding Officer of the Flotilla tells two boats, one of which is mine, to proceed as far as possible towards the harbour entrance and to attack the transport fleet. We therefore separate from the other boats and make for the entrance of Dunkirk harbour.

Slowly we approach the French coast. Gradually a bright fire rises above the horizon; at first we cannot ascertain the cause of this fire, but we soon realise that the burning object is on the sea. As we had feared at the outset of the undertaking, the moon slowly comes out, almost round, from a bank of clouds and throws a wide silvery track on the water.

I cannot put on paper the oaths we used at the sight of the moon, we felt as though we were being offered up on a plate to the enemy destroyers and guard ships. Soon we saw in the direction of the moon several guard ships which, in my opinion, must be lying off the approaches to Dunkirk. As they are too small and not worth a torpedo, we keep out of their sight. In a curve we gradually creep near to them and now recognise the bright fire as a burning tanker which, probably, our dive-bombers hit and which now pierces the darkness like a brilliantly flaming torch.

As most of the night still lies before us, we decide to lie in wait as near to the guard ships as possible. Our main attention is focused on the dark horizon to the west. For our only danger threatens from that side, as a destroyer approaching from the dark sector can only be made out very late, whereas the small S-boat on the moonlit stretch of water can be seen from a considerable distance.

We had not been lying in wait for long, when our companion, who was slightly more to the west, reported a shadow in a northwesterly direction. I quickly turn my binoculars and in a few moments I can locate the shadow. The news goes through the boat in a flash.

My feverish impatience gives way to complete calm, as action is now required. As on innumerable occasions in peacetime I give the requisite orders and keep my eyes glued to the slowly enlarging shadow. Now I have to judge its speed and course as accurately as possible, in order to make the correct calculations for my torpedo.

Without the need of arranging matters with the other S-boat, everything works as on manoeuvres at home; for it is obvious that we are both after the shadow which turns out to be a large French destroyer of the type they call 'torpedo-cruiser' and we intend to make it impossible for the ship to avoid the torpedoes.

Now the destroyer passes the burning wreck and shows us a wonderfully sharp silhouette. At this moment it is a question of keeping a firm hold on one's nerves, in order to let the enemy come so close that the torpedoes cannot miss, because slight alterations of course, for which there is always time, quickly negative the calculations made before firing the torpedo.

I notice slowly that the hunting fever is gripping me. Another quick glance sideways at the guard ships, which fortunately have not become suspicious, although they are really near enough to have been able to discover us, but they have apparently dozed off in the slight swell.

Sharply the order is given: 'Both tubes ready! Tube one – fire! Tube two – fire!'

Twice the boat shivers in all her timbers by the vibration caused by the discharge of the torpedoes which vanish into the water with a gurgling sound. A glance towards the other boat shows that my companion has fired as well.

Hurrah! A sky-high sheet of flame shoots out of the destroyer. Then – another one. Two hits! We all shake hands with cries of triumph and from the engine-room there is a positive yell of joy. Through my binoculars I see clearly how the destroyer is listing and a few moments later only the curve of the ship's side can still be seen above the surface, half hidden in smoke and steam issuing from the burst boilers. Over the grave of the destroyer there is a great mushroom of smoke which the wind slowly bends sideways. Our thoughts turn for a moment to the brave seamen who have fallen by our hand, but – such is war.

Part of the popular *War Stories for German Youth* series: 'S-boats for Dover'.

We have not much time, because over there the detonations have put everything on the alert. The guard ships emit black smoke, a sign that they are getting underway in order to drive us off. Ashore lively Morse transmission of the signal stations is seen. The long fingers of the searchlights excitedly probe over the water. As we can still be cut off from Ostend, we make off at high speed, for it will soon be dawn. With a vibrating din the engine revolutions increase, the bow rises out of the water and we are off; not for nothing are we called 'Schnellboote'.

After the two remaining 2nd Division destroyers delivered their demolition crews, they proceeded to patrol the coastline between Boulogne and Dunkirk, radio communication from one of the French captains intercepted by B-Dienst reporting that the British destroyer HMS *Vanoc* was in Boulogne to evacuate British troops. All indications pointed to a large-scale withdrawal of Allied forces pinned against the coast.

The S-boats were moved closer to the front line as soon as possible. German naval surveyors found that the British had cleared all Dutch and German aerial mines from the Hook of Holland, and deemed this harbour of more immediate use than Den Helder. Nevertheless, all available S-boats put into Den Helder on 23 May, apart from *S22*, *S24* and *S25* which transferred to Wilhelmshaven for weeks of repairs to engines and exhaust systems.

The following night four 2nd Flotilla S-boats – *S13*, *S30*, *S32* and *S35* – mounted an unsuccessful patrol near Dunkirk, missing a sighted destroyer with torpedoes. On the night of 25 May another pair of boats from the flotilla were attacked both outbound and inbound by British aircraft, one claimed as shot down by flak from *S34*.

On 26 May four S-boats slipped from Den Helder, *S24* and *S25* sailing for the waters north of Ostend, while *S13* and *S30* planned to prowl the seas off Dunkirk. ObltzS Wolfdietrich Babbel's *S13* was forced to abort due to damage to the boat's rudder and main driveshaft. While returning west of Ijmuiden, lookouts sighted the wake of an enemy submarine running shallow. Depth charges were dropped that resulted in an oil slick and the sighting of 'hammocks and interior wooden panelling'. The appearance of a lifeboat with the designation *O21* led Babbel to claim the Dutch submarine destroyed.[19] *S13* successfully docked in Den Helder before transferring to the shipyards in Emden for repairs.

The 1st S-flotilla's *S24* and *S25* also claimed success. They sighted a British destroyer escorting a steamer near Zeebrugge and closed to the attack. It was HMS *Vega* operating as part of Operation Lyster, the British Admiralty plan to sink blockships at Ostend and Zeebrugge to prevent their future use as U-boat bases. The largest vessel allocated to the operation that included MTBs, patrol boats and minesweepers, HMS *Vega* was escorting blockship *Atlantic Guide* into position when ObltzS Detlefsen's *S24* launched torpedoes, claiming the destroyer hit and sunk. In reality the premature detonation of a torpedo had barely caused any damage aboard *Vega* at all and the two S-boats were forced away by machine-gun fire which peppered their superstructures.

Both at sea and ashore the situation had become increasingly chaotic for the Allies. On 27 May Operation Dynamo began; the following day Belgium formally surrendered to the Germans. The British Expeditionary Force and whatever Allies could be accommodated aboard available shipping were to be lifted from the beaches at Dunkirk and evacuated to Britain. For their part, the German High Command would make a serious blunder when the Army and Waffen SS forces that had the Allies pinned inside the Dunkirk pocket were ordered to halt before a final attack. Göring's Luftwaffe was to be used to pound the British into submission, a task they were ultimately unable to complete. The forces on land were the only ones strong enough to crush all enemy resistance and Hitler had effectively held them in check. At sea, the Kriegsmarine had few resources available for the task, as notes on an SKL meeting reflect:

> On 26 May Chief, Armed Forces High Command [OKW] asked Chief of Staff, Naval Staff by telephone what operational possibilities Naval Staff foresaw for naval forces against the evacuation of enemy troops from the Belgian and northern French area. Naval Staff's opinion is seen from the letter to OKW/Führer Headquarters in which it is pointed out first that the Hoofden/Channel area is not suitable as an operational area for large vessels. Destroyer and torpedo boat operations must be delayed for the present, since the losses incurred in Norway, the important transport escort assignments and the newly planned operations urgently require retention of these forces. On the other hand, operational conditions for S-boats are especially favourable in the Hoofden and should be fully exploited; U-boat operations are rendered difficult by navigational conditions and enemy defence measures.[20]

So it was that the S-boats would be called upon to intensify their pressure on the myriad ships involved in Operation Dynamo. On the night of 27 May *S21*, *S32*, *S33* and *S34* sailed from Den Helder. They almost immediately came under air attack which they successfully evaded. The RAF had recognised the threat posed by the small, agile German craft and assigned squadrons to operate 'anti-E-boat sweeps' as the British

The crew relaxing in harbour; the nearest man is leaning out of the hatch for engine room 1, which housed the engine that operated the central screw.

evacuation got underway. It has never been completely confirmed why the British designation for the *Schnellboote* became 'E-boat', the most popular and logical explanation being that they were 'Enemy boats'.

In the early hours of the morning Obermaier's *S34* sank a loaded transport estimated at 2,550 tons from a 'strongly escorted convoy' off North Foreland. Obermaier had in fact hit the 694-ton steamer *Abukir* crowded with more than two hundred British troops – including a military mission that had been sent to liaise with the Belgian High Command – alongside fifteen German prisoners of war, six priests, and fifty women including a party of nuns from Bruges and a small group of British schoolgirls. *Abukir* had already avoided Luftwaffe attack before *S34* fired the first two torpedoes. Both missed as the steamer zigzagged from what it took to be U-boat attack. Obermaier retreated to reload before returning and hitting her amidships with one of a second salvo as *Abukir* tried to ram *S34*, still in the mistaken belief that she was a surfaced U-boat. The crippled steamer sank within one minute. Obermaier departed and British destroyers later rescued survivors numbering only five crew and twenty-five passengers. It was alleged by the ship's master, Captain Rowland Morris-Woolfenden, that Obermaier lingered long enough to shine a searchlight on the survivors in the water and open fire with machine guns at them, an account that was reported in the British press. Aside from any ethical considerations, this would be extremely hazardous for an S-boat which relied on speed to leave the scene of any attack as swiftly as possible. Indeed, *S34*'s KTB tells that the S-boat behaved exactly as normal and retreated at high speed, some debris from the exploding *Abukir* having even landed on the S-boat's deck. Elsewhere it is related that men still aboard ship opened fire with a Lewis gun at what they thought could be a U-boat conning tower, instead hitting lifeboats.[21] It was an especially tragic – and highly emotive – postscript to the first S-boat sinking of a British merchant ship.

At sunset the following evening *S25*, *S34* and ObltzS Wilhelm Zimmermann's *S30* sailed from Den Helder to operate near the well-lit Kwinte buoy. Despite once again coming under air attack while outbound, all three S-boats arrived on station without loss. Using the *Lauertaktik* principle – in which S-boats were spaced one nautical mile apart, approaching the presumed target convoy in line before dividing on a broad front and attacking – Kptlt Siegfried Wuppermann deployed his three boats and waited for an hour before moving west with *S25* and *S34*, leaving Zimmermann on station. A little past midnight *S25* and *S34* attacked the sloop HMS *Shearwater* south of Fairy Bank but missed with all torpedoes. Meanwhile, Zimmermann observed the approach of a destroyer leading a straggling column of ships. HMS *Wakeful* had taken 640 troops off the Dunkirk beach, all housed below decks to lessen topweight on the destroyer. The captain, Commander Ralph L Fisher, had been warned by Admiral Ramsey that there were likely to be German destroyers, S-boats and U-boats headed to Dunkirk and the watch was doubled as *Wakeful* steamed along Route Y used for Dynamo traffic. Ninety minutes into their voyage Kwinte buoy's white light showed on the horizon. Fisher ordered his zigzagging destroyer's speed increased to 20 knots, reasoning that with the glare of the buoy almost anything could hide in the darkness beyond, sighting two torpedo tracks only 150m (165yds) on the starboard bow as the order was made.

'Thunderstruck,' Fisher whispered, 'You don't mean to say those bloody things are going to go off when they get here?' His First Lieutenant, Walter

Scott, was admirably impassive. 'You know, I'm rather afraid they are.'

'Good God!' [Leading Seaman James] Ockenden heard Fisher yell then. 'Hard a-port!'[22]

It was too late. Zimmermann's first torpedo fired from 600m (650yds) distant narrowly missed the bow, but his second hit amidships on the starboard beam. *Wakeful* was split clean in two by the explosion and sank in seconds. Three officers, one petty officer, the ship's surgeon, one NAAFI worker, ninety-two naval ratings and all but one of the embarked soldiers were killed in either the explosion or rapid sinking, trapped below decks before they had any chance to escape. Zimmermann retreated to reload as British ships arrived to rescue whatever survivors they could find. Unfortunately for them, the numerous signal lights and flares used in the rescue attracted the small Type II U-boat *U62* which torpedoed the destroyer HMS *Grafton*. In the pandemonium that followed, both *S30* and *U62* faded away into the darkness while British ships collided and nervously opened fire at one another.

The three S-boats came under air attack once again before reaching Den Helder, escaping damage with a barrage of accurate flak and swift manoeuvring by the young skippers. The success of S-boats in fast-moving hit-and-run operations proved the exceptional abilities of the boats and their highly motivated crews. On 30 May SKL ordered all operational S-boats immediately placed under the direct control of Generaladmiral Alfred Saalwächter's MGK West in order to maximise their effectiveness. Effective intelligence gave a very clear view of the Allied situation: transit routes used in the evacuation and even orders given to Allied shipping not to fire on any sighted ships until they could be absolutely positive they were hostile. The advantage was squarely in the hands of the Kriegsmarine, though they lacked the numbers to fully capitalise on it. The previous night *S21*, *S32*, *S34* and *S35* had sailed, but in the mist and rain sighted nothing except numerous Allied patrol vessels and one small steamer, unable to press home any attacks. *S32* reported bearing damage and returned to Wilhelmshaven for the central engine to be changed. However, on 30 May the 1st S-flotilla successfully went into action with *S23*, *S24*, *S26* and *S30*. At 0210hrs ObltzS Detlefsen's *S24* torpedoed the French destroyer *Cyclone* near Kwinte Bank. *Cyclone*, the flagship of France's 2nd Destroyer Flotilla was en route to Dunkirk, engine trouble limiting speed to 16 knots, when Detlefsen's first torpedo was seen streaking ahead of the ship, passing from port to starboard at only 10m (30ft) distance. The second did not miss, despite being sighted approaching and Capitaine de Vaisseau Yves Urvoy de Portzamparc throwing his ship into evasive manoeuvres. Hitting the bow, the ship appeared critically damaged to Detlefsen and he claimed her as sunk, retreating into the darkness to reload. In fact, despite the bow section having been completely blasted away, *Cyclone* was afloat and capable of maintaining a speed of 5 knots. De Portzamparc requested escort by nearby Polish destroyer *Blyskawica* and together they made their way slowly for Dover.

Nearby, and less than ten minutes later, another French destroyer, *Sirocco*, passed in front of the stationary *S23* and *S26* and was hit by two torpedoes, one from each S-boat. The first double salvo had grazed the destroyer's bow without exploding, the second pair hitting the stern. *Sirocco* was laden with 770 troops plucked from Dunkirk's beaches, nearby destroyer HMS *Vega* reporting a column of flame nearly 200ft high illuminating the end of the French ship. Immobilised and listing badly to starboard, she went down in two minutes with fifty-nine crew and over six hundred troops aboard, as well as the colours of the 92nd French Infantry Regiment, which its colonel had risked his life to smuggle out of Lille after encirclement by German troops. It has been asserted that the destroyer was finished off by Luftwaffe bombing, but all Luftwaffe units had been grounded on 30 and 31 May, only resuming their attacks on 1 June.[23]

Shadowed by Royal Navy MTBs and destroyers, the S-boats returned triumphantly to Den Helder. SKL reflected on the success achieved thus far within their War Diary:

> The S-boats have thus sunk [*sic*] five enemy destroyers to date in the Hoofden (six in all) without loss to themselves. Excellent proof of the usefulness of the S-boat and the training of their commanders. Fresh evidence has been given of the special suitability of S-boats for use in the Hoofden/Channel area, which had already been shown in the Great War by the first successful operations by these boats. Exploitation of the flanking position of the coasts of Flanders and northern France with regard to the lines of communication between Great Britain and France, as well as with regard to the shipping route from the Channel to the Thames Estuary, opens up great prospects of success for the S-boats at these focal points in constant naval operations. We must expect, as happened in the Great War, that the enemy will very soon set up a systematic defence organisation by disposing permanent lines of patrol vessels and S-boats and having constant air patrol. It is possible that particularly this activity by enemy planes (dive-bombers), which experience

has proved must be regarded as especially dangerous for S-boats in consequence of their speed and manoeuvrability, will make sorties considerably more difficult and make it necessary for our boats to have constant air cover during their sorties. Further developments must be awaited. If enemy patrol becomes stronger it remains to be investigated whether S-boat sorties will have to be supported later by single destroyers or torpedo boats.[24]

Within the margins of this entry, Admiral Otto Schniewind – SKL's chief of staff – correctly surmised the fact that any such ideas about tying S-boats to destroyer escort would limit their 'freedom of attack', nullifying the very advantages of using such fast and agile craft. However, the call for fighter protection inbound and outbound was constant from the headquarters of both S-flotillas. Indeed Kptlt Petersen wrote within the 2nd S-flotilla KTB:

Despite constant requests to Marinegruppenkommando West for fighter protection, there has been no fighter escort for the previous thirteen S-flotilla operations within the Channel. The fact that, so far, no losses have been suffered through bombing attacks must not lead to the conclusion that fighter escort was superfluous. The successes of the S-boat missions, which are to be regarded as only brief forays due to the short nights, are greatly reduced by any delays on the outward journey.

In fact the Luftwaffe was for the first time showing its deficiencies in combat, albeit in no way due to the skill or determination of its pilots. Co-operation with the Kriegsmarine was generally sketchy at best, and opposition from the RAF had proven stiffer than anticipated.

During the last night of the month the 2nd S-flotilla boats *S21*, *S22*, *S34* and *S35* attacked the evacuation route off Ruytingen, encountering a heavy Allied patrol boat. The boats encountered numerous patrol vessels, although ObltzS Obermaier in *S34* hit what he believed to be a 4,000-ton munitions ship, the huge explosion pointing to its suspected cargo. In fact, he had destroyed the 416-ton Royal Navy ASW trawler HTM *Stella Dorado*, which had ironically been involved in the rescue of *Sirocco* survivors the previous night. Believing themselves under U-boat attack, three other converted trawlers began searching for the assailant, HTM *Argyllshire* subsequently being hit by a torpedo from OlbtzS Kecke's *S35*.

The S-boats' return to their new harbour base at the Hook of Holland was again harassed by enemy aircraft, Hudson bombers of RAF 206 and 220 Squadrons specifically tasked with keeping S-boats away from Allied transports. The Fleet Air Arm's 826 Squadron had also begun operations against S-boats off the Belgian coast with Albacore biplanes. On 2 June a planned S-boat operation near North Goodwin was called off following severe air attack northwest of Dunkirk delaying the outbound boats. Petersen's call for fighter escort was echoed again, MGK West agreeing that planned operations were becoming impractical without Luftwaffe cover. However, SKL declined to liaise directly with Luftwaffe Command, stating that fighter cover during daylight or bright nights may be 'desirable', but was by no means essential to operations. MGK West was instructed to arrange fighter cover locally with the offices of General-feldmarschall Albert Kesselring's Luftflotte 2. This they duly did, but the despatch of junior officer ObltzS Bernd Rebensburg (former commander of *S15* and now ashore as a staff officer) to deal with Kesselring probably did nothing to emphasise the importance placed on their discussions. The desired Luftwaffe commitment was of covering fighters and heavy fighters for S-boats during daylight, also capable of attacking such targets deemed too small to be engaged by torpedo.

Owing to the fact that Kesselring's forces were already heavily taxed by bombing missions in support of the land battle, there was clearly no guarantee that aircraft would be available to protect the S-boats. The ultimate objective was for direct tactical co-operation via radio between the S-boats and aircraft, similar to the manner in which armoured troops harnessed the power of the Luftwaffe for their blitzkrieg. However, due in large part to the lack of maritime training provided to pilots and the Luftwaffe's resistance to the establishment of a maritime strike force, this never transpired. The close inter-service co-operation that the British would begin to establish was something never matched by Germany's armed forces.

Marinegruppenkommando West ambitiously planned to move 1st S-flotilla to a forward base at Boulogne. There it was felt that, in conjunction with torpedo boats and heavy shore batteries at Calais, the S-boats could contribute to the complete blocking of the English Channel to enemy shipping, with the subsequent advantage of allowing U-boats to pass through the narrow waterways into the Atlantic. However, at sea S-boats were encountering greater obstacles than ever. On the night of 3 June numerous air attacks harassed two groups of S-boats, thick fog then

Travelling at speed in line astern.

hampering their hunting near North Goodwin. Enemy escort ships and patrol vessels fired flares into the night sky preventing any approach to Dunkirk. As Operation Dynamo reached its climax, it was apparent that the Allies had successfully neutralised the S-boat threat.

In the Hook of Holland the first boats of the brand new 3rd S-flotilla arrived to join the fray on 4 June. Kptlt Friedrich Kemnade had captained *S11* and *S15* during the years 1936 and 1937 before training and service as torpedo officer aboard the cruiser *Emden*. On 23 May 1940 he transferred to the Baltic to oversee the formation of a new S-flotilla, taking over from ObltzS Werner Töniges who had begun the task eight days previously and who stayed on as the flotilla's senior skipper. The 3rd S-flotilla was originally formed from reserve boats of the two operational flotillas and the newly commissioned S-boat depot ship *Adolf Lüderitz*, replaced by *Tsingtau* once training had begun. The working-up period for a new flotilla had at least twenty days' training at sea: mastering individual boat exercises, operating in the standard attack formation of pairs (*Rotte*), with up to three pairs at a time, practising torpedo firing and attack procedures, reconnaissance practice, gunnery practice and flotilla formation exercises.

Kemnade arrived at the front with only one of his flotilla's boats, *S11*, followed soon after by *S12*, which had been forced into Wilhelmshaven for repairs on one engine. The 3rd S-flotilla would come to consist of *S1*, *S10*, *S11*, *S12*, *S13* and *S54* (commissioned in August), once again showing the urgency that the Kriegsmarine attached to committing every combat-worthy vessel to the battle. On 3 June *S11* accompanied two 1st Flotilla boats on patrol from Rotterdam against Dunkirk convoy traffic. Leutnant zur See Paul Poppe's *S33* encountered a single steamer, but missed with a surface-running torpedo, instead strafing the target with his quick-firing 20mm flak weapon before breaking off the attack amid enemy machine-gun fire.

Aircraft from Luftflotte 2 had begun to provide cover for the Schnellboote. On 4 June *S21*, *S22*, *S34* and *S35* of the 2nd Flotilla sailed to the waters off North Foreland, escorted both in and out by four Messerschmitt Bf109s, although the mission during the light and clear night yielded no results, as strong British patrol presence prevented approach to the coastal convoy route.

Inspired by the mistaken belief that the worst effects of enemy air power were thus countered, MGK West requested that Boulogne be speedily expanded as an S-boat base. FdT Hans Bütow believed that due to the state of the harbour installations, many of which had been destroyed by retreating troops, the earliest that S-boats could begin operating from the port would be two weeks distant. Naval Command, however, disagreed. They reasoned that shallow-draught S-boats were impervious to whatever ground mines may have been laid and, as long as suitable camouflage netting and anti-aircraft posts could be established, the boats could begin operations from Boulogne immediately. Both torpedo and minelaying missions against the English coast were being planned, as the focus of the battle switched from Dunkirk to the battle of England itself. Operation Dynamo officially ended on 4 June 1940, the final French rearguard in Dunkirk surrendering to victorious German troops. Operation Cycle would see the evacuation of 3,321 British and French troops from Le Havre between 10 and 13 June, while Operation Aerial would continue until 25 June from ports predominantly on France's Atlantic coast and beyond the reach of S-boats.

5

The Battle for England

June 1940 – August 1940

FOLLOWING the end of Dynamo, the war continued to rage in France and Norway. *Fall Rot* – the invasion of France – began on 5 June as German forces pushed past the Somme river and outflanked the monolithic defences of the Maginot Line to the southeast. In Norway, German and Allied troops continued their seesaw battle in Narvik, although the debacle in Belgium and France forced Allied evacuation; the final Norwegian forces on their own mainland surrendered on 10 June as the country went into what would become years of uneasy occupation.

Coffee atop the open bridge of an S-boat underway.

On 6 June boats from all three S-flotillas sailed from their new base at the Hook of Holland into patrol areas along the Downs. Their primary target was the busy coastal convoy route that stretched between the Thames and Firth of Forth.[25] Great Britain possessed a proportionately high coastline to land mass and the resources of the nation – coal being of the highest importance – were predominantly found in the less populated north, but required in the densely populated, high-consumption areas in the south, particularly London. The precious commodity was also required to fuel industry and power stations of the south.

The 1st S-flotilla fielded *S22*, *S23*, *S25* and *S26*, the 2nd S-flotilla *S21*, *S34* and *S35*, and 3rd S-flotilla *S11* and *S13* in their first attempts at hindering this crucial trade route. These latter two boats proceeded to North Goodwin to draw enemy patrol vessels, before swinging eastwards. The 1st Flotilla passed through British patrol lines north of South Goodwin and searched the Downs between South Foreland and Deal, although a smattering of attacks against empty steamers and small ships met with no success. Torpedo failures were rife at this stage of the war, something that also plagued the U-boat service. The three boats of the 2nd Flotilla stopped at the southern point of Goodwin Sands and searched the eastern portion of the Downs without result. They reported constant and intense searchlight activity, although frequently the searchlights were drawn skyward as they mistook prowling Allied aircraft as potential Luftwaffe intruders, ironically allowing the S-boats to remain unseen. However, the S-boats were harassed by Allied aircraft, bombs missing *S13* by only 50m (55yds).

Again on the night of 8 June six boats of the 1st and 3rd S-flotillas were thwarted in the Downs and the Thames Estuary, a strong British patrol line including MTBs and aircraft preventing any breakthrough, while providing no worthwhile targets. This depressing pattern was repeated on the two following nights, with attacks against destroyers and merchant ships all unsuccessful, *S30* even watching a torpedo pass beneath the keel of an enemy destroyer without detonating. During the brief clear nights the S-boats were frequently fired upon, and used smokescreens and high speed to escape. The Kriegsmarine were well aware of the evacuations taking place as part of Operation Cycle from the Seine Bay and pressed yet again for the S-boats to base further west, following the advance of the Wehrmacht's land forces. While MGK West stubbornly resisted the movement of flotillas to Boulogne until mines could be thoroughly swept and anti-aircraft weapons emplaced, SKL remained insistent.

Naval Staff is of opinion that neither the enemy situation nor the mine situation off Boulogne has a decisive influence on S-boat operations. The great advantage of using S-boats is just that they are independent to a great extent of the mine situation. In critical cases a favourable tide can be utilised. If necessary operations can be carried out with an intermediate stop in Boulogne, the Hook of Holland can then still be the main base until it is possible to transfer a depot ship. Naval Staff fears that if clarification of the mine situation is awaited, prospects of success will decline through another enemy deviation owing to the rapid developments in the situation on land. At present there is heavy transport traffic from Cherbourg to Le Havre.[26]

For his part, FdT also pressed for increased flak protection for any S-boats deployed to Boulogne, somewhat mollified by promises of a nearby fighter group placed on standby to intercept any British move against the harbour.

On 11 June Petersen's 2nd S-flotilla began the transit from Rotterdam to Boulogne, *S1*, *S20*, *S31*, *S34* and *S35* arriving at 0400hrs, mistakenly fired on by German coastal artillery who had not been informed of their presence. Fortunately, their enthusiasm outstripped their accuracy and no shells hit. However, the transfer had been detected by British radio monitoring and four Blackburn Roc aircraft of Coastal Command's 801 Squadron dive-bombed the S-boats. The unwieldy British aircraft had taken off at 1201hrs from Detling airfield and reached Boulogne thirty-four minutes later, identifying their stationary targets as 'painted light grey in position south side of the harbour'. The British aircraft hit the crane jetty alongside the moored boats in the Loubet Basin, one successfully diving to strafe all five boats. The Rocs encountered no opposition at all, detecting no flak, although the S-boats' 20mm cannon managed at least some defensive firing. After their return to England, the squadron commanding officer recommended a second strike using small bombs. The same four aircraft took off again at 1525hrs, each carrying three 250lb (113kg) and forty 20lb (9kg) bombs. Upon arriving over Boulogne they found that the S-boats had moved to the Promenade Quay by the Southern Railway terminal building. This time they claimed a direct hit on one S-boat and damage to two others. Once again they reported no resistance, machine-gunning a coastal battery and parked trucks as they flew back over the French coast, bound for Detling.

Behind them, Boulogne's port was in chaos, although no S-boats were sunk and only minor damage inflicted, the most serious being a life raft destroyed by bomb splinters. However, as well as fourteen dead French civilians, the 2nd S-flotilla suffered seven dead, including the skipper of *S35*, ObltzS Hans Kecke. Twenty-two others were wounded, including ObltzS Zimmermann, the commander of *S30*, ObMasch Werner Eigenbrod (chief engineer aboard *S1*) and LzS Gernot Goehle, commander in training. The following day, six Albacores of 826 Squadron returned to Boulogne to repeat the attack, but by then the S-boats were gone. Obviously vulnerable – as feared by MGK West – they had transferred rapidly back to Rotterdam, awaiting the arrival of a mixed flak battalion despatched by Luftflotte 2 to Boulogne before they would return. With no trained S-boat officers available, owing to the total commitment of every available crew in the Channel, on 15 June ObltzS Wilhelm Meentzen was transferred from his post as watch officer aboard torpedo boats to the S-boat arm and assumed command of *S35*. Replacing the severely wounded Zimmermann, the first officer aboard *S30*, LzS Ullrich Roeder, took his boat to Wilhelmshaven for engine overhaul.

At sea the S-boats continued to sail into combat without success. Bright nights and high phosphorescence levels within the sea allowed many target vessels to detect and avoid torpedo attacks, others being foiled by defective 'surface runners'. S-boats were using the steam-powered G7a torpedo. Capable of 40 knots, it outstripped the G7e electric (and thus 'wakeless') torpedo by 10 knots. The G7a's turbine engine was powered by steam created by the burning of decahydronaphthalene (Decalin) fuel mixed with compressed air and could be used at an 'ultra-fast' speed of 44 knots, although this often overloaded the turbine before the components were reinforced in 1942. The speed was essential for a torpedo that was not only noisy but visible, U-boats using them only at night and the silent G7e electric torpedo by day. The G7a could be fitted with either an impact fuse (*Aufschlagzündung*, or AZ) or magnetic fuse (*Magnetzündung*, or MZ). The latter relied on the ship's magnetic field detonating the torpedo as it ran beneath – theoretically more destructive as the explosive shock wave was amplified through water. However, the G7a was inadequately tested before being put into full production, causing a crisis within both the S-boat and U-boat service.

After mass torpedo failure experienced by U-boats, particularly off Norway in April, tests were undertaken that showed the magnetic fuse to be faulty, particularly in northern latitudes. During 1936 the Torpedo Test Institute (TVA) had conducted firing tests against suspended nets, showing that both G7a and G7e torpedoes had a tendency to run deep, therefore passing under the target and failing to explode if using contact fuses. This was deemed acceptable as it would be solved by the magnetic fuse, the same magnetic fuse that now proved faulty. The final insult was a new four-fingered contact fuse which had replaced the reliable two-fingered version used during the First World War. Test-fired only twice in 1937, it was so delicate that if the torpedo struck the target at an oblique angle the main fuse rod would bend and not fire the warhead. It was something of a debacle for the U-boats, perhaps less so for S-boats, and by July most of the depth-keeping and contact fuse problems had been remedied enough to make the G7a a more reliable weapon.

Despite Allied evacuation shipping now completely out of S-boat range after the end of Operation Clyde, the Kriegsmarine were still determined to bring the S-boats forward from the Netherlands; 2nd S-flotilla returned to Boulogne on 17 June with three boats, *S19*, *S31* and *S35*. A fourth boat, *S1*, had been forced to turn back due to engine damage in transit, attacked by three Lockheed Hudson bombers during her return to Rotterdam, though the zigzagging boat put up a fierce barrage of flak and escaped damage. Crews were quartered north of Boulogne in a hotel in the small coastal town of Wimereux, while flotilla personnel readied the boats for operations.[27] Two boats sailed that night against a convoy southwest of Dungeness. Both *S19* and *S31* were committed to the action after *S35* suffered engine failure in her starboard diesel. The attacking S-boats suffered torpedo failures against enemy destroyers, who pursued the Germans at high speed and with heavy gunfire. Under a full moon the S-boats were clearly visible, deploying smokescreens as they made off at high speed for Boulogne. Meanwhile, four further boats had arrived in Boulogne during the early hours of the morning: *S26* (on 'loan' from 1st S-flotilla) and *S32* from Rotterdam.

Grossadmiral Raeder visited Boulogne, which now also held the 2nd R-boat flotilla, but continued to deny permission for the construction of concrete S-boat shelters, camouflage to be used as defence from air attack (a decision reversed in 1942). Le Havre had also been put forward as an ideal base for S-boat operations, only slightly damaged during the Allied retreat and home to extensive French naval facilities, including the Schneider gunnery workshop. Führer der Torpedoboote began sketching plans to transfer S-boats from Boulogne once torpedo and fuel storage and supplies could be provided in Le Havre. Like Boulogne, anti-aircraft defence would be required, the small harbour at Fécamp also revealing its suitability as an emergency port for S-boats and small coastal U-boats.

The 2nd S-flotilla now bore the brunt of the Schnellboote fight against England. Kemnade's 3rd S-flotilla had returned to Germany after ten

Grossadmiral Erich Raeder congratulates ObltzS Götz Frhr von Mirbach on his recently awarded Knight's Cross during a visit to Boulogne in June 1940.

days in the combat zone to train new crews, docking first in Kiel before travelling on with *Tsingtau* to Saßnitz on Rügen Island where training would begin. Birnbacher's 1st S-flotilla was in Wilhelmshaven undergoing much needed engine overhauls. On 17 June Heinz Birnbacher became the second S-boat man to be awarded the Knight's Cross, for bravery in the field and exemplary leadership. Elsewhere the war in France neared its climax. Though it was far from an easy victory, with French resistance stiffening as they fell back on their own supply lines, the German advance appeared inexorable. Paris fell on 14 June, the Maginot Line cut off and eventually beaten into submission until an armistice was signed on 22 June, coming into effect three days later. On 10 June Italy had somewhat cynically entered the war against the Allies, attacking in the French Alps and along the Mediterranean coast, though stopped almost immediately by French defenders.

On 19 June the S-boats finally drew blood once more when *S19* and *S26* sailed into the waters off Dungeness, finding the Canadian steamer ss *Roseburn* in bright moonlight. ObltzS Töniges fired two torpedoes, both of which missed and, rather than retreat for the five minutes it would take to reload, he opted instead to close on what he estimated as a '4,000-ton steamer' and open fire with his boat's 20mm flak gun. This allowed ObltzS Fimmen to bring *S26* into firing position, hitting *Roseburn* with torpedoes. Ashore, Ben Tart of the Observer Corps was on duty and later recalled the attack:

We saw this ship – we now know it was the SS *Roseburn* – coming up. She was not in the convoy and it was light as day, a full moon. She was a mile or two off the Point (Dungeness) and almost immediately we could hear, before we saw, the torpedo boat [*sic*]. He came right up behind the *Roseburn* right under the rays of the moon; you could see the silhouette of the *Roseburn*. At first he fired many tracers, but she kept going, and the next thing she went up with a huge bang, and Jerry turned round and went off as fast as he could go.[28]

The 3,103-ton Canadian was sailing independently from New Brunswick, Canada, to the Tyne with a cargo of pit props and began sinking slowly by the bow. A lifeboat launched from the nearby RNLI station approached and took off the crew and their luggage, the lifeboat's skipper Coxswain Doug Oiller then going aboard and advising the captain to beach his doomed ship at Dengemarsh.[29]

The pair of jubilant S-boats returned to Boulogne, where they were singled out for praise regarding the close co-operation that had resulted in their victory. The following day dawned with strong winds and high seas keeping the boats harbour-bound and it wasn't until the night of 21 June that five boats took to the sea again, bound for Dungeness. The successful *Rotte* of *S19* and S26 departed first, the remaining three following soon after. The trio sped in line abreast, *S35* the central boat, *S32* to starboard and *S31* to port. A little past midnight they were over-flown by a British aircraft and less than half an hour later *S32* exploded in sheets of flame as it ran onto a floating mine, possibly laid by the same aircraft. The entire forepart of the boat was destroyed and what was left reared stern-first into the air before rapidly sinking. Seven men went to the bottom with her, including her commander ObltzS Carl-Eberhard Koscky. Three men were wounded, one, Chief Engineer StObMasch Wilhelm Bartels, later died of his injuries on 24 June. Koscky's two companion boats returned to Boulogne with the survivors.

During the morning of 23 June, the repaired *S1* and ObltzS Wolf Dietrich Babbel's newly commissioned *S36* arrived to bolster Petersen's flotilla. A mission was planned that night for all six boats, once again focused on the coastal shipping lane off Dungeness. However, the now virtually obsolete *S1* once again experienced engine problems and was forced to remain in port. The remaining five boats slipped from harbour in two *Rotten*: *S31*, *S35* and S26 in *Rotte* 1, *S19* and S26 in *Rotte* 2. ObltzS Babbel's new *S36* attacked a '5–6,000-ton' steamer with torpedoes during the early morning – the 3,477-ton British tanker ss *Albuera*, sunk two miles southwest of Lydd Light with seven crewmen killed and twenty-nine men rescued by Dutch ship *Merope*. *S19* also torpedoed a steamer estimated at 5,000 tons, although this time the estimate was wide of the mark, as torpedoes sank the 276-ton motor vessel *Kingfisher*, southeast of Beachy Head. The coaster had been travelling from Milford Haven to London when she went down with one crew member killed.

German intelligence reported an increase in the number of Royal Navy MTBs being brought into the area between Dover and Ramsgate, indicating that the S-boat threat was beginning to tell in British Admiralty thinking. There was clearly traffic running along the south coast of England, detected by radio interceptions from B-Dienst, and sightings by naval units, aircraft and land stations at the Channel's narrows. The Germans reasoned correctly that if their enemy accepted the increased risk of this sea route closest to German forces, then the Thames was clearly a main supply hub. German military strategists had already surmised that British west coast ports were unable to handle the intake of convoyed supplies and subsequent distribution alone, while the route that trailed around the north of Great Britain and down the east coast constituted a significant detour that would not only consume valuable fuel but extend already long voyages even further. With this in mind, Cherbourg was now planned for use as the second major French S-boat harbour. This would open up the seas west of the Isle of Wight to attack, widening the potential hunting ground for targets. Now that France was subjugated – the British Channel Islands soon occupied by German forces – the entire British south coast was vulnerable to attack.

Marinegruppenkommando West requested immediate transfer of anti-aircraft defences to Cherbourg (and Brest, due to open as a U-boat base), whilst maintaining those already in place at Boulogne. The FdT secured accommodation for Cherbourg S-boat crews in the small nearby town of Urville-Nacqueville, quartered in the Hôtel de la Plage, while fuel supplies, torpedo storage and crew transport were all put in place. Once mine-sweepers confirmed the harbour as safe, elements of the 1st S-flotilla, fresh from engine refits, transferred to their new base during the night of 27 June. *S19*, *S24* and *S26* made the voyage from Rotterdam to Cherbourg via a sweep of the sea off Beachy Head, although no targets were sighted. The 2nd S-flotilla sighted only enemy MTBs and the destroyer HMS *Greyhound* once the weather had cleared enough for a resumption of operations, *Greyhound* reporting a brush with *S1*, and forced to break off its patrol in heavy seas. The following night they fared little better, attacking the small British trawler *Wellard* and missing with a clutch of surface runners. During the night of 29 June the three boats of the 1st S-flotilla made their first thrust from Cherbourg into the area west of the Isle of Wight. Strong searchlights probed from the British coast and no targets were hit. A 979-ton steamer SS *Helder* was sighted and attacked during the return voyage to Cherbourg, but missed.

Photograph taken by *Propaganda Kompanie* war correspondent Hoffmann on 14 July 1940.

Two nights of unsuccessful patrolling by both flotillas marked the beginning of July, boats of the 2nd S-flotilla chased by three British destroyers during their return. Unable to reach advantageous firing positions, *S36* dropped two depth charges on deep settings, hoping they would explode beneath their pursuers. Although it failed, it may have helped discourage the British pursuit.

ObltzS Mirbach's *S20* arrived in Cherbourg on 3 July to bolster the 1st S-flotilla to four boats that took to the seas during the night of 4 July. What would become known as the Battle of Britain was looming, and the first phase of the Luftwaffe's assault against the enemy was shipping strikes in the Channel. During 4 July Ju87B Stukas of Sturzkampfgechwader 2 based at Beaulieu made a successful attack on convoy OA178 in the English Channel, sinking one freighter and damaging five more. The convoy of fourteen ships had only a single escort, the corvette HMS *Clarkia*, and no air cover since departing from Southend-on-Sea during the previous day. The convoy was to pass through the Channel into the Western Approaches and there disperse to various Atlantic destinations. Several of the convoy's ships elected to take shelter in Portland Harbour where thirty-three Ju87s soon returned to bomb and sink the 5,500-ton anti-aircraft ship HMS *Foylebank* and the tug *Silverdial*, damaging three more freighters.[30]

The Stukas had taken a high toll from OA178 and that night the four boats of the 1st S-flotilla put to sea from Cherbourg to attack the remaining ships east of Portland. A little past midnight the S-boats sighted three ships and closed in for action in the standard *Rotte* formation. During the confused high-speed battle that followed, Mirbach's *S20* hit and sank the zigzagging 4,343-ton steamer SS *Elmcrest* with torpedoes, the first impacting to port in her coal bunker. As the crew were ordered to abandon ship, Mirbach fired his second torpedo from starboard, which passed under a lifeboat and into the engine room. The ship capsized, sixteen crewmen going down with her. Mirbach also claimed a second freighter of '5-6,000 tons' attacked and sunk. Fimmen's *S26* hit the 6,972-ton tanker SS *British Corporal* in the stern, a huge column of water flying into the dark sky as the rudder was blown away and a jagged hole torn in the side, exposing steam pipes and carnage. A second torpedo hit in the boiler caused a catastrophic explosion and Fimmen claimed a '12,000-ton tanker sunk'. The crew abandoned ship, but after rescue were able to return and inspect the damage. Although severe it was not mortal, and the ship was towed to harbour, where the bodies of two missing crew were later recovered. Fimmen also claimed a steamer of '8,000-tons' hit and sunk. The latter was 5,500-ton freighter SS *Hartlepool*, hit in the propeller, which caused a sympathetic detonation of stored ammunition for the stern gun. Captain Rogerson ordered his ship abandoned – under protest following Royal Navy orders – after Fimmen opened fire with machine guns, the sole injury inflicted being the chief officer's nose cut by a bullet graze. Like *British Corporal*, however, the ship was later towed in to Weymouth. *S19* reported missing two targets, but is actually probably responsible for the sinking of 3,514-ton Estonian freighter SS *Kolga*. German radio intelligence confirmed the destruction of *British Corporal* and also picked up mention of Dutch steamer SS *Britsum* sinking, although she had been hit and set ablaze by the earlier air attack.

The result of this combined aircraft and S-boat action had been the severe depletion of OA178, so much so that Winston Churchill penned one of his famous 'Action This Day' memos on 5 July to the Admiral Sir Thomas Spencer Vaughan Phillips (Vice Chief of Naval Staff) and Admiral Sir Henry Ruthven Moore (Assistant Chief of Naval Staff):

> Could you let me know on one sheet of paper what arrangements you are making about the Channel convoys now that the Germans are all along the French coast? The attacks on the convoy yesterday, both from the air and by E-boats, were very serious, and I should like to be assured this morning that the situation is in hand and that the Air is contributing effectively.[31]

Their response was to stop convoys of large 'OA' Atlantic-bound ships from passing through the English Channel. Henceforth they would traverse Scotland, starting from Methil, Fife, and heading north before swinging down the west coast of the British Isles. The sole convoy traffic to use the English Channel was to be the CW (Southend-on-Sea to Yarmouth, Falmouth and St Helens) and CE (St Helens to Southend-on-Sea) convoys of coastal steamers that began on 6 July. Churchill demanded that each convoy receive fighter cover from at least six aircraft, something that the RAF were incapable of guaranteeing as they began to face the full attention of the Luftwaffe.

Somewhat flushed with success, four boats of Birnbacher's flotilla put out from Cherbourg during the night of 5 July into the area of Portland and the Isle of Wight. The *Rotte* consisting of *S20* and *S26* fired three torpedoes at a freighter estimated at 3,000 tons, but missed. However, *S19* from the second *Rotte* hit a steamer estimated at 6,000 tons, which split in two and sank thirty miles south of the Isle of Wight. No sinking records match Töniges' attack. The flotilla's next sortie on the night of 7 July produced nothing except enemy retribution. Under a clear sky and due to the brightness of the night, the S-boats were chased to within five miles of Cherbourg by Royal Navy destroyers and MTBs, German artillery fire from newly installed coastal batteries covering the S-boats once in range.

However, that same night the 2nd S-flotilla sailed from Boulogne into the area south of Beachy Head and Dover. Petersen's flotilla had been bolstered by the arrival of *S34* from Wilhelmshaven, as well as *S22* and *S23*, both belonging to the 1st S-flotilla. With this temporarily enhanced strength, Petersen sent his boats to sea, ObltzS Babbel's *S36* torpedoing and sinking the converted trawler HMT *Cayton Wyke* of the 9th Anti-submarine Group south of Dover, killing seventeen crewmen.

Lookouts at night aboard one of the earlier model S-boats, before the addition of an open bridge atop the wheelhouse.

Bad weather kept the boats in harbour until 9 July when *S21* and *S24* made an ASW sweep from Cherbourg south of Portland, although they were thwarted once again by bad weather and forced to break off the outward voyage. In the same heavy seas *S19* and *S26* searched unsuccessfully for the crew of a Ju87 which had crashed in the Channel. It was a task that was to become familiar to the S-boat crews.

The emphasis was now placed on minelaying and the closing of the Thames to merchant traffic. While aircraft were capable of sowing minefields over larger areas, S-boats could be more exact in where the lethal barrages were laid, advantageous should the same waterways be traversed by an invasion fleet in the near future. FdT was against the use of the fast attack craft in this role, considering it contrary to every principle of S-boat operations. The boats could only carry a small number of mines each, the extreme weight making the boats stern-heavy. He went so far as to record in his own war diary that, 'The use of S-boats as minelayers had been forbidden in a fundamental OKM order.'[32] However, his objections were overruled and on the night of 10 July Petersen's 2nd S-flotilla used newly assembled cranes at Boulogne for loading four EMC anchored mines each aboard *S22*, *S23* and *S25*. Both *S34* and *S36* were loaded with twelve explosive buoys, used as an anti-minesweeping measure. The flotilla now numbered seven, with the arrival earlier that day of LzS Ullrich Roeder's *S30*, and he and *S35* would act as guard boats for the others laying the deadly field.

Meanwhile, the 1st S-flotilla continued with torpedo patrols. The same night that mines were laid off the Thames, four of the Cherbourg boats raced to intercept a convoy with destroyer escort reported by Luftwaffe aircraft twenty miles southeast of the Isle of Wight. The target was not found, although *S26* attacked 352-ton coaster MV *Mallard* with machine-gun fire and torpedoes, sinking the ship and killing six of her nine crewmen. The accompanying *S24* rescued the three survivors who were returned to France as prisoners of war.

The following afternoon *S19*, *S20*, *S24* and *S26* all put to sea from Cherbourg looking for downed Luftwaffe fliers following a Stuka attack on coastal shipping. The Luftwaffe's *Kanal Kampf* had begun in earnest, with dive-bombers attacking shipping while fighters patrolled above, hoping to lure RAF fighters over the Channel and into combat. The S-boats fired on a prowling British aircraft, but failed to find the Luftwaffe men. One of the Stuka crews eventually made landfall in France after thirty-eight hours adrift and had actually seen the S-boats searching in the distance, but mistaken them for British and waited silently for them to pass by.

Released from minelaying, Petersen's 2nd S-flotilla left port to attack a convoy reported between Kentish Knock and Shipwash in the Thames Estuary during the night of 11 July. East of North Foreland the S-boats passed a double-masted wreck in the shallow waters and eighteen minutes later *S23* struck a mine. Eight metres (26ft) of the stern was demolished and the engines wrecked, although miraculously there were no serious casualties. While the remainder of the crew transferred aboard *S30*, ObltzS Christiansen and the Chief Engineer StObMasch Burmeister remained aboard as a towline was attached and the crippled boat dragged slowly south to Calais. Apprised of the situation, Kptlt Petersen requested immediate fighter cover, but meanwhile the damaged boat sank deeper into the sea until eventually the towing attempt was abandoned. As soon as the two men were retrieved, *S23* was sunk with scuttling charges.

The following day both flotillas were laid off duty, their return to offensive operations on 13 July beginning an unsatisfying run of fruitless missions, encountering mainly enemy MTBs and other patrol vessels of which none were successfully attacked. Convoys were sighted by aircraft and shore observers, but the S-boats seemed unable to penetrate an increasingly thick enemy defence. Despite the S-boat attempts and more successful daily Luftwaffe raids, Allied merchant traffic of the CW and CE convoys was continuing to pass through the English Channel. Heavy shore batteries were not yet ready to engage the enemy shipping, the Kriegs-marine appealing for Army help to supply heavy motorised or railway artillery as a temporary anti-shipping offensive measure.

As S-boat torpedo patrols continued to be frustrated by British destroyers and MTBs, Petersen's 2nd S-flotilla stepped up its minelaying missions, sowing fresh fields on at least seven nights between 16 and 25 July. Occasionally the boats would encounter strong enemy forces and alter the target area, but accurate navigation allowed for precise mapping of where the mines were laid. As well as the EMC mines, captured Polish naval mines were deposited off Harwich in the North Sea. On the night of 25 July when this latter field was complete, the 2nd S-flotilla boats put into Ostend instead of Boulogne, allowing greater range to be covered along the convoy routes of England's east coast. Crews were quartered in a comfortable hotel in the small nearby town of De Haan.

Weather occasionally foiled attempts to put to sea during the latter half of July and flotilla war diaries tell of skirmishes with MTBs and pursuit by enemy destroyers until within sight of the French coast. However, on the night of 24 July two *Rotten* of the 1st S-flotilla sailed from Cherbourg: *Rotte* 1, *S19* and *S27*, bound for the waters southwest of Portland and *Rotte* 2, *S26* and *S20*, headed for the eastern coast of the Isle of Wight. At 2310hrs *Rotte* 1 sighted a white light to starboard and turned to investigate. At first they believed they had found the crew of a Dornier Do18 flying boat shot down during the day, but instead they came upon a large 'two-funnelled, 18,000-ton steamer'. Both S-boats fired one torpedo each, missing wide of the mark. The steamer stopped and two more torpedoes sped toward the drifting target that was displaying white lanterns fore and aft. Again the torpedoes flew wide of the mark, *S19* opening fire with its flak weapon.

Nearly fifteen minutes had passed before ObltzS Klug's torpedo crew were ready to fire once more, the single torpedo arcing toward the target as a surface runner, but still exploding against the ship's stern. The large ship began to sink and both S-boats retreated into the darkness. Tragically, she was the French steamer ss *Meknes*, an elderly 6,127-ton ship being used to repatriate 1,300 French officers and men from Britain back to Vichy France under Armistice terms.

Although the ship was lit, both Klug and Töniges, aboard *S19*, denied that French national colours were displayed, as asserted by the British Admiralty. While the British protested strongly that the Red Cross had been made fully aware of the passage of the neutral ship and its passengers, neither the German government nor the Armistice Commission had been informed, FdT going as far as to say within his KTB that the torpedoing, while regrettable, was perfectly legal and may have even been a British attempt to place a French ship occupied by French personnel in harm's way in order to sway public opinion against Germany. Regardless of the reality of the sinking, 416 men perished, the remaining survivors pulled from the sea by Royal Navy ships and lifeboats.

The sinking of the *Meknes* made headlines around the world and was touted as an example of German callousness. Statements were made in the British House of Commons condemning the attack on a humanitarian mission and propaganda leaflets were dropped in France and circulated amongst French troops still in Britain, attempting to dissuade further repatriation to Vichy. The French survivors were sent to the Royal Navy training establishments at Fareham, Trevol and Skegness, where they were given rest and fresh clothes. The leader of the newly established Free French Navy, Admiral Émile Muselier, visited the officers and men in the company of a British naval liaison officer attempting to enlist new recruits. Despite strong British propaganda concerning the sinking of the *Meknes*, Muselier was received coolly at best and gained no extra men for his service. The French survivors remained determined to return home and be with their families. Perhaps the situation was not helped by the enlisted men's view of their own officers, most of whom had been first away in lifeboats as the *Meknes* went down.

As Petersen's 2nd S-flotilla continued minelaying from Ostend, Birnbacher's 1st Flotilla boats continued torpedo patrols. On the night of 25 July a particularly successful attack was launched south of Brighton by three boats, *S19*, *S20* and *S27* (*S26* having transferred back to Kiel for engine overhaul). During the day westbound convoy CW8 of twenty-five merchant ships with destroyers escorting were pounded by Stukas and five steamers destroyed.[33] As the S-boats neared the battered convoy, two escorting destroyers turned to engage them, chasing them back towards France before the ships were hit by aircraft and artillery fire from the French mainland, seriously damaged and forced to withdraw. Meanwhile, the Luftwaffe reported the exact whereabouts of the enemy merchant ships for the S-boats. That night, in between squalls of rain, each of the flotilla boats successfully sank one British freighter each. *S19* torpedoed the small 646-ton steamer SS *London Trader* (claimed as a 10,000-ton steamer); *S20* torpedoed 1,013-ton SS *Broadhurst* (claimed as a 6–7,000-ton tanker) after the ship had turned to face an attack by a different S-boat, thus presenting a broadside target and being hit in the starboard bow. The ship's forecastle collapsed and *Broadhurst* went under in five minutes with only twelve survivors. Von Mirbach also claimed a second ship aflame. *S27* torpedoed 821-ton SS *Lulonga* (claimed as a 10–12,000-ton steamer) and aboard *S19* Töniges reported seeing another steamer capsize as it abruptly turned to avoid a torpedo, also raking a 2,000-ton ship with gunfire. Although the estimation of the enemy vessels' sizes was wildly inaccurate, it was a successful night for the flotilla which retreated unscathed into the darkness, mooring in Cherbourg after dawn on 26 July.

Three nights later four of the flotilla's boats were despatched to search for a British 'cruiser' hit and damaged by Luftwaffe bombers. The British ship had sailed from Portland during daylight, directly contravening standing Royal Navy orders. Detected by newly installed Freya radar at Cap de la Hague near Cherbourg, the ship was attacked and badly damaged, the S-boats *S19*, *S20*, *S21* and *S27* being despatched to finish her off. At 2223hrs a cloud of smoke was sighted and the boats sped toward their target, pre-empted fifteen minutes later when a huge detonation was seen from the burning ship which immediately sank. The destroyer HMS *Delight* was gone, six of her crew killed in the earlier bombing, the remainder taken ashore by rescue ships.

The operations undertaken by the 1st and 2nd S-flotillas followed the same routine throughout the weeks that followed. Petersen's boats sailed from Ostend whenever weather permitted, to continue laying mines in an attempt to close the English Channel and blockade the Thames. However, it continued to be an unpopular assignment for the fast attack craft, not purely because of the additional peril of skirmishes with enemy forces while weighed down with a cargo of extremely heavy weapons, but because the results of the patient and dangerous task could never be readily ascertained.

On 13 August Grossadmiral Raeder visited Cherbourg, where he addressed S-boat commanders from both flotillas. Petersen and his men expressed their 'regret' that so far there appeared to have been no definite successes as a result of their various minelaying operations, apart from some possible trawler sinkings. Whilst Raeder and his staff found the attitude understandable, they were at great pains to point out that intelligence reports showed that, indirectly, the minelaying was causing considerable problems for the British, both in psychological and material terms. There was evidence of direct hits, although captured French military communiqués revealed that even before the fall of France the Allies were making every effort to conceal mine casualties. The importance of the task was stressed to FdT and both S-flotillas, OKM drafting a letter acknowledging their 'patient efforts'. On 4 August, in view of his highly efficient handling of the 2nd S-flotilla, Kptlt Rudolf Petersen was awarded the Knight's Cross.

Meanwhile, the 1st S-flotilla continued torpedo patrols. Thick fog and strong defence from British patrol vessels firing star-shells and putting up fierce machine-gun fire foiled an attack near the Isle of Wight on 4 August. It was not until 7 August that they again achieved success against the first westbound convoy to traverse the English Channel since CW8. Convoy CW9 consisted of twenty-five heavily laden merchants and nine escorts, sailing from Southend at 1400hrs in order to pass through the Dover Strait under cover of darkness. Detected by Luftwaffe reconnaissance and radar, the convoy's path was accurately tracked and passed on to Birnbacher in Cherbourg. *S20*, *S21*, *S25* and *S27* departed Cherbourg at 2100hrs to lie in wait for the approaching ships. They were sighted by four MTBs from Dover Command, the Germans in turn glimpsing the MTBs. The MTBs refrained from engaging, however, considering their mission of recon-noitring German movements along the French coast to take precedence. The S-boats drifted on the swell while waiting for the convoy, the first ship sighted at 0300hrs.

Mirbach in *S21* was first to attack, torpedoing 1,216-ton SS *Holme Force*; the sixty-year-old master, William Cousins, two crewmen and three gunners lost as she sank with her cargo of coal. Mirbach mistook the steamer for a tanker and reported her as '6 8,000 tons'. The noise of the S-boats' diesels momentarily confused the British ships' crews who mistook them for aero engines. Klug's *S27* struck next, one torpedo missing the 1,042-ton SS *Empire Crusader* and hitting instead the small motor vessel *Fife Coast* in the stern, the cargo of refined sugar lost with four crewmen and a naval gunner as she sank.[34] As the battle intensified, shipwrecked Second Officer A Davis remembered: 'When I was swimming in the water ... I saw both red and white tracers in the darkness and the sound of the E-boats was like that of a fast sports car, they stopped, then accelerated, then stopped again.'[35]

Both of Klug's torpedoes, the first that had missed the stern of a ship estimated at '2,000 tons', and that which had destroyed the *Fife Coast*, had been 'surface runners'.[36] ObltzS Büchting aboard *S20* singled out the coal carrier SS *Ouse* and claimed a hit on the 1,004-ton ship, although it actually swerved to avoid *S20*'s torpedo, collided with SS *Rye* and was fatally holed. The ship, claimed as '5,000 tons', sank with twenty-three survivors rescued later.

Obltzs Siegfried Wuppermann in *S25* attacked two small freighters – 380-ton SS *Polly M* and 500-ton MV *John M* – with cannon and machine-gun fire after missing with torpedoes, damaging both though they remained afloat.[37] As the convoy scattered in confusion the S-boats came under heavy fire from the escort, the *Rotte* comprising *S21* and *S27* receiving particularly accurate fire from HMS *Bulldog* and being forced to retreat. With dawn fast approaching, the 1st S-flotilla boats laid course for Cherbourg. Blenheims scrambled from 59 Squadron based on Thorney Island hunted for the S-boats, but failed to make contact. The S-boats claimed 17,000 tons of enemy shipping sunk, the reality accruing only 2,587 tons. SKL echoed the triumphant note of the young commanders: 'An excellent success. The British Admiralty falsely reported one S-boat sunk and another damaged.'[38]

The tribulations of CW9 were far from over, however, as 8 August marked what is generally considered as the beginning of Germany's aerial assault on Britain, commemorated today as Battle of Britain Day. Massed Stukas of the VIII Fliegerkorps based at Abbeville, escorted by Bf109s and slower Bf110s, attacked the scattered ships in three waves throughout the day. The RAF rose to the challenge, losing thirteen Hurricanes and one Spitfire for eight Bf109s, a Bf110 and seven Ju87s. However, only four of the convoy's ships managed to limp into either Poole or Portsmouth harbours without significant damage. Drifting burning ships continued to be seen in the Channel, three boats of Birnbacher's flotilla sighting one that night as they prowled uneventfully in worsening weather off the Isle of Wight.

It was a disaster for the British, but one almost overshadowed by the impending Battle of Britain. German naval command was also acutely aware that the estimation of the size of ships destroyed by their S-boats was quite probably inaccurate, while also recognising that British figures were, in turn, likely understating the German success.

> The Admiralty admits the loss of a total of five ships as a result of combined attacks by S-boats and aircraft on convoys in the Channel on 8 August. Three coastal vessels totalling 1,500 tons were, it is stated, sunk by S-boats and two totalling 2,540 tons by air attack, while seven other ships were damaged. The convoy reportedly consisted of about 20 ships totalling 18,000 tons. Verification of statements as to the size of enemy ships in the Channel is impossible. Naval Intelligence Division, however, considers that at present only rather small ships are employed in Channel coastal traffic. It is therefore not unlikely that S-boats as well as planes may have been mistaken regarding the sizes of vessels.[39]

Nonetheless, ObltzS Kurt Fimmen and Götz Frhr von Mirbach became the fourth and fifth recipients of the Knight's Cross within the S-boat arm, presented on 14 August by KK Hans Bütow for their actions the previous May against French ships *Sirocco* and *Jaguar* respectively.

An additional task was now allotted to all available S-boats. As the Luftwaffe grappled with the RAF, S-boats joined *Räumboote* in search and rescue missions for downed pilots, code-named *Rosengarten*. As the Luftwaffe raids were by day, there was little room for night missions, although the effort of *Adlertag* (the initial assault on the RAF – 'Eagle Day') had so stretched the Luftwaffe that there was little activity on 14 August and 1st S-flotilla mounted its next torpedo patrol that night. However, *S20* and *S27* ran afoul of British destroyers after suffering yet more 'surface runners' while trying to launch a surprise attack. The boats retreated at speed behind smoke as the destroyers unsuccessfully chased them toward France. The 2nd S-flotilla had taken part in no operations that night due to bad weather, and on the afternoon of 15 August Petersen played host to Generaladmiral Alfred Saalwächter, chief of MGK West. After touring the installed Kriegsmarine facilities in Ostend, Petersen and his adjutant ObltzS Causemann were standing watching *S35* loading fresh torpedoes when the torpedo store barely ten metres away exploded. In what was presumably an act of sabotage, the entire storehouse and torpedo maintenance room was destroyed, along with forty-two stored torpedoes. The resulting damage was disastrous to Petersen's flotilla: the wheelhouses of both *S24* and *S35* were flattened, the upper decks of both boats and *S31*

Taking on torpedoes in harbour, the torpedo firing pistol not yet in place.

also badly damaged. Camouflaging tarpaulin covering several of the S-boats caught fire, although *S37* escaped with relatively light damage and personnel casualties amounted to only light wounds, including injuries to Kptlt Herbert Max Schultz, adjutant to FdT.

> The loss of the torpedo store is especially serious in view of the present shortage; also, with three S-boats out of action for some time, operational plans will be badly upset, as there is a shortage of boats in the Channel. The S-boats and motor minesweepers lying in readiness for air-sea rescue are doing valuable work picking up the crews of aircraft shot down. Nevertheless, the rescue service can be carried out only as a secondary service whenever possible.[40]

The explosion heralded an investigation by the Abwehr into what was suspected sabotage, but it also spelt the temporary end of the 2nd S-flotilla as a functioning strike force. All four boats were despatched to Wilhelmshaven for repair, *S31* grounding en route and taken under tow by escorting Vorpostenboot *V205*. In the early hours of the morning of 19 August, the two slowly moving vessels were attacked by a submarine west of Schiermonnikoog, but the torpedoes missed.

With Birnbacher's 1st S-flotilla the only combat-ready unit, MGK West ordered it to transfer to Rotterdam and operate against convoy traffic north of the Thames Estuary as soon as the depot ship *Tsingtau* arrived in the Dutch harbour. Until then, minelaying from Cherbourg was to be given priority, barrages to be sown off Beachy Head and the approaches to Southampton.

Bad weather delayed their first minelaying sortie, which finally took place on 24 August, the lead boat *S27* carrying a reporter from the Propaganda Kompanie who filmed the experience for the German weekly news. It was an unfortunate mission to choose. *S21* was forced to abort the operation only minutes after sailing due to rudder damage, the remaining five boats proceeding first to Boulogne where they loaded the cumbersome EMD mines aboard and then slipping back into the Channel at 2114hrs. Aboard *S20* two mines came loose and fell overboard one and a half hours into the voyage. Another mine also slipped off its rails and crashed onto the after deck, where the crew, unable to move it, lashed it in place. With the boat unstable, Birnbacher aborted the mission and at 0335hrs the flotilla entered Cherbourg harbour.

The next minelaying enterprise was more successful. *S27* and *S21*, carrying a full complement of torpedoes, escorted the other four boats armed with two torpedoes and four mines each on the night of 25 August. The sixteen mines were laid east of the Isle of Wight, though no results are recorded from them. The following day *Tsingtau* arrived in Rotterdam and the flotilla sailed from Cherbourg to meet her, apart from *S20* stranded in Cherbourg with engine trouble. The five other S-boats passed across Beachy Head in search of targets during their transit journey, but sighted only a patrol ship.

The next mission would prove even worse when *S18*, *S21*, *S25*, *S26*, *S27* and *S54* (attached from 3rd S-flotilla after commissioning on 9 August) put to sea from Rotterdam to intercept a convoy sighted east of Great Yarmouth. They were to rendezvous with *S19* and *S22* who had both sailed previously from Wilhelmshaven to Cherbourg, radioed attempts to divert them to Rotterdam having failed. The S-boats sailed as planned, when a mine exploded against the stern of *S19*. Severely damaged and with Chief Engineer StObMasch Karl Langner badly wounded in the foot and spine, *S19* was taken in tow by *S22* – the pair slowly headed to Calais harbour. Meanwhile, the weather worsened and the operation was scrubbed, all remaining S-boats returning to Rotterdam where *S26* accidentally rammed the pier while avoiding manoeuvring tanker *Brösen*.

For *S19*, the event marked the beginning of a seven-day journey to Kiel. From Calais she was towed by Räumboot first to Ostend, then by trawler to Ijmuiden and eventually patched up enough to be towed by tug through canals to Emden and then Kiel. The crew had already gone ahead by train.

Meanwhile, the 2nd S-flotilla had been made operationally ready once more. On 22 August the Dutch MTB *TM52*, captured almost completed at the Gusto shipyard at Schiedam (Rotterdam), had been finished and commissioned into the Kriegsmarine as *S201*. Commanded by LzS Ullrich Roeder and attached to the strength of the 2nd S-flotilla, she was taken to Wilhelmshaven for testing.[41] The following day the brand new *S55* was taken by ObltzS Opdenhoff from the shipyard to join the repaired *S37* in journeying back to Ostend. By the end of August *S36* and *S33* were also back in service and the flotilla front-line strength stood at four. *S201* remained in Germany as would *S202* (ex-*TM53*), *S31* and *S35* after repair, the latter two relegated to reserve. By the end of September *S30*, *S34* and *S56* were also on strength at Ostend.

6
The Channel

September 1940 – July 1941

OPERATIONS in the English Channel began inauspiciously in September. As the Luftwaffe struggled for dominance of English airspace, barges and transport craft of every description were being gathered in France and Belgium's Channel ports for the invasion of England: Operation *Seelöwe* (Sealion). The conglomeration of invasion craft attracted British aerial minelaying and bombing, causing problems within French harbours. In reality it was a forlorn hope for the Kriegsmarine. They lacked the specialised landing equipment required by such an invasion, as well as the tactical doctrine to successfully implement it. Perhaps most importantly, they lacked the strength in surface vessels to escort and protect the transfer of several divisions of assault troops, let alone the follow-up forces. Under the nose of the Royal Navy, the chances of success would, at best, have been extremely slender, even had the Luftwaffe succeeded in winning aerial supremacy.

While these events played out, the first days of September yielded frustration for both the 1st and 2nd Flotillas. Torpedo operations were thwarted by bad weather, torpedo malfunction and strong enemy defence. Finally, on the night of 4 September, the 1st S-flotilla's fortunes turned. *S18*, *S20*, *S21*, *S22*, *S27* plus the attached *S54* all sailed after sunset to intercept the 35-ship convoy FS71 (Phase 3) sailing from Sunderland to London, carrying coal to the capital's power stations. Sighted near Smith's Knoll, the convoy was attacked a little before midnight. ObltzS Klug's *S21* reported two steamers hit and sunk, estimated at 6,000 and 8,000 tons respectively; in fact the 1,729-ton SS *Corbrook* and 2,709-ton collier SS *New Lambton* of the London Power Company, both sinking with no loss of life, despite heavy machine-gun fire from the S-boat. ObltzS Christiansen in *S18* also claimed two hits from his torpedo salvo, freighters estimated at

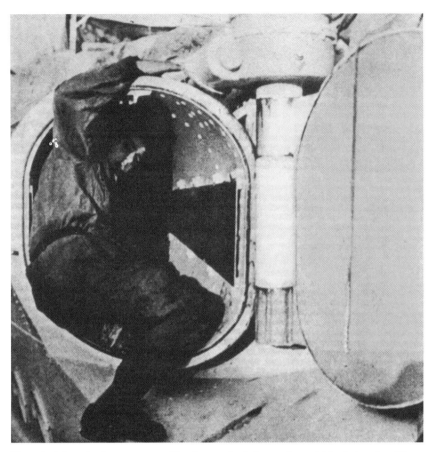

Torpedo firing pistols were screwed in place on loaded torpedoes within their tubes. This photograph originally appeared in *Die Kriegsmarine* magazine.

5,000 and 8,000 tons sent to the bottom. He had indeed destroyed two colliers: 1,571-ton SS *Joseph Swan* – also of the London Power Company – going to the bottom with seventeen of her eighteen crew and 1,075-ton Dutch freighter *Nieuwland* sinking with eight dead aboard. ObltzS Georg Grund in *S22* claimed a 12,000-ton tanker destroyed, torpedoing and sinking 1,562-ton 'flat-iron' collier SS *Fulham V* with its load of coal. Finally, the 3rd S-flotilla's 'on-loan' LzS Herbert Wagner in *S54* claimed a British *Imogen*-class destroyer sunk, in reality hitting and damaging 1,350-ton SS *Ewell*.[42]

Despite the over-claiming, it was a successful night for the S-boats, more following in the early hours of 7 September when the 2nd S-flotilla out of Ostend found convoy FS73 (Phase 3). The *Rotte* comprising *S33* and *S36* both attacked the large 5,750-ton Dutch steamer SS *Stad Alkmaar*, ObltzS

Babbel's *S36* damaging the ship and ObltzS Poppe's *S33* finishing her off, while the entire crew were rescued by fellow convoy ships. British destroyers soon managed to deter the attackers, who returned to Ostend later that morning. Babbel's triumph was relatively short-lived, however. As the RAF escalated its bombing of Channel ports, Ostend was attacked on the night of 8 September, *S36* being heavily damaged and two men badly wounded. *S33* and *S37* also received some splinter damage.

The Royal Navy soon added their weight to the anti-invasion measures when destroyers HM Ships *Malcolm*, *Venomous* and *Wild Swan* bombarded German invasion barges under tow near Ostend during their second offensive sweep of that month along the French coast. *S55* gamely put to sea in an effort to intercept the attackers and engaged the British in a short, sharp firefight. While no torpedo strikes were made on the destroyers, *S55* was hit over twenty times by 20mm and 40mm cannon fire, and 21-year-old MaschGefr Hans Hinrichs killed by the gunfire. One engine was

On 10 September 1940, *S13* rammed the stern of *S1* in Vlissingen. Accidents such as this could take weeks of repair before the boat was seaworthy once more.

knocked out and diesel poured into the bilge from the ruptured engine piping (the fuel tanks were self-sealing). MaschObGefr Helmut Gölitz managed to extinguish a fire in the forward engine room before collapsing unconscious. Severely injured, he eventually died on 25 May 1943. Two other crewmen were wounded during that battle before *S55* broke away, taken for repairs in Rotterdam on 12 September.

Meanwhile, the 3rd S-flotilla returned to the front as the boats of the 1st Flotilla put in to Cherbourg for engine overhauls; heavy equipment and spare parts were still stored in the Norman port. Still comprised largely of the oldest boats – *S1*, *S10*, *S11* and *S13* accompanied by the depot ship *Adolf Lüderitz* – Kemnade's flotilla sailed from Brunsbüttel through a night of deteriorating weather toward Vlissingen. Entering harbour at 1100hrs on 10 September, the swell caused *S1* and *S13* to briefly collide, the oldest boat coming off worst with a damaged stem. To add insult to injury, *S10* was rammed in the stern by a barge piloted by Wehrmacht infantrymen practising for *Seelöwe*. From four operational boats, Kemnade was immediately down to two: *S11* and *S13*. Kemnade travelled by car to Rotterdam to be operationally briefed by FdT aboard the *Tsingtau*. His orders were for *S11* and *S13* to patrol the waters east of Orfordness where convoy traffic had been reported.

As Kemnade returned to Vlissingen, air-raid sirens heralded the beginning of an RAF bombing raid, eleven 101 Squadron Blenheims bombing the concentration of invasion barges in harbour. Although only five aircraft actually bombed on or near target, *Adolf Lüderitz* and *S13* (the flotilla *Führerboot*) received some bomb splinter damage, the latter to its hull and starboard engine from a near-miss. More devastating, Kemnade was badly wounded, along with seven other men. The flotilla was in disarray and the injured Kemnade recommended that the boats be taken from Vlissingen and put under the tactical control of Petersen's 2nd S-flotilla in Rotterdam. This they duly were, sailing with their tender at 1330hrs the next day, while the wounded were treated at the Kriegsmarine hospital established in Bergen op Zoom. In Kemnade's enforced absence, Kptlt Hans Trummer took charge of the 3rd S-flotilla on 18 September. Bad weather prevented further S-boat operations until 21 September, which at least gave a chance to rest and repair before once again facing the enemy. Following the confusion of the attack on Vlissingen, the 3rd S-flotilla was now reoriented and ready for service. During this period the Luftwaffe admitted failure in their bid to destroy the RAF and instead turned to bombing British cities by night. Operation *Seelöwe* was

Putting to sea in travel formation line astern.

postponed and the accumulated invasion barges were beginning to disperse rather than suffer continual depredation by British air and sea forces.

During the night of 22 September boats of all three flotillas put to sea. 1st S-flotilla was directed west to Start Point, Devon; the other two flotillas headed for east-coast convoy traffic between Cromer and Harwich. The latter clashed with escorts, with *S13* claiming a 3,000-ton freighter sunk – probably in fact the 670-ton trawler HMT *Loch Inver* – and both *S13* and *S54* missed the trawler *Edwina* with a torpedo, but lashed at least ninety rounds of 20mm gunfire into the small auxiliary ship, which returned fire with 12pdr cannon and Lewis gun. The combat was broken off with no damage to the Germans, although *Edwina*'s crew claimed to have hit and sunk an 'E-boat' with their third 12pdr shot. The boats of the 3rd S-flotilla were then directed back to Rotterdam where their depot ship already lay.

An operation by the same boats was scrubbed due to bad weather the following night, although Petersen's 2nd S-flotilla put to sea to hunt a convoy of nine freighters and three destroyers sighted earlier near Smith's Knoll. *S30*, *S33*, *S34*, *S37* and *S55* all sailed, finding in bright moonlight the convoy FN89 (Phase 3) which had departed Southend that day. *S34* fired first and missed, and *S55* also experienced a double torpedo failure. Finally, ObltzS Klaus Feldt's *S30* launched a single torpedo and hit what he estimated to be a 2,000-ton freighter. It was in fact the 555-ton SS *Continental Coaster* which went to the bottom with four crewmen. It was to be the S-boats' sole success that night and the last for September as torpedo failures, misses and strong escorts foiled the next two missions. On the final day of September the brand new *S56* sailed from Emden to join the 2nd S-flotilla in Ostend, raising their front-line strength to seven boats.

In Rotterdam the reported presence of British submarines in the Channel had prompted the formation of a small *Schnelle U-Jagdgruppe* comprised of the older *S8*, *S9*, *S14*, *S15* and *S16* and independently controlled by FdT. This small unit was bedevilled by machinery problems and almost never sailed; eventually the elderly boats were consigned to training roles in Germany.

S-boats manoeuvring in harbour.

October brought unsettled weather sweeping over the English Channel from eastern France. Operations were cancelled in the face of alternating fog and storms until 11 October when 1st S-flotilla put to sea in a fruitless search for sighted steamers near Falmouth and Portsmouth. Newly promoted KK Petersen's 2nd S-flotilla resumed minelaying, sowing a field of twelve M/08 contact mines, four EMD mines, twelve explosive buoys and four *Reissbojen* – conical floats trailing a mooring wire supporting static cutters – east of Felixstowe. Although the operation ran smoothly, during the return voyage *S37* hit an enemy mine. The impact was devastating, exploding alongside the wheelhouse: the entire hull was torn in two. The stern sank within fifteen minutes, while the bow remained afloat, kept watertight by the collision bulkheads. Aboard the shattered boat there was utter pandemonium. The young skipper ObltzS Hans Schultze-Jena was killed outright along with twelve of his men. *S30* rescued eleven crewmen from a lifeboat, two of them lightly wounded and two so severely that they would later succumb to their injuries. The floating bow section refused to sink and was finally blown up with explosives before *S30* left the scene, bound for France.

The flotilla returned to lay mines again on the night of 15 October: twelve M/08s, four EMD, four *Reissbojen* and twelve explosive buoys dropped east of Orfordness. Once again, disaster seemed to overtake the mission when the new *S56* also hit a mine during the return voyage. However, damage was slight and ObltzS Meentzen was able to take his boat back to Rotterdam for shipyard repair. A third minelaying mission on 18 October near Shipwash broke the pattern, uneventful apart from the successful laying of yet another German field.

Not until that night of 18 October was a torpedo patrol successfully completed once more. With offensive S-boat operations now squarely targeting the British east coast, Birnbacher's 1st S-flotilla had been moved by FdT from Cherbourg to Rotterdam. The flotilla had experienced two failed missions in October before finding northbound convoy FN11 (Phase 4). ObltzS Christiansen in *S18* was first into the attack, firing a full salvo at a 6,000-ton freighter and 12,000-ton tanker, claiming the freighter hit and broken in two, the tanker also hit and sinking by the stern. He had in fact hit 1,595-ton ss *Hauxley* travelling in ballast from London to Warkworth; one crewman was killed in the attack. The battered wreck was taken in tow but sank the following day. Aboard *S24* ObltzS Töniges recorded a double hit on a 12,000-ton tanker, badly damaging 2,942-ton freighter ss *Gasfire* by blowing the stern completely off and killing eleven

ObltzS Georg Christiansen, Klaus
Feldt and Kurt Fimmen, 1940.

crew. The ship, however, remained afloat and was later beached at Spurn
Head, towed away to Hull and repaired.[43] The final hit was recorded by
ObltzS Büchting in *S27* who claimed an 8,000-ton freighter torpedoed:
3,754-ton French coal carrier *PLM14* travelling in ballast toward the Tyne
was badly damaged and ten of her thirty-nine crew killed. The ship was at
first abandoned, before the crew reboarded her and beached her on Haile
Sands for later repair. Aboard the collier SS *Brian*, DEMS gunners sighted
what they took to be an attacking S-boat described as 'greyish white in
colour and look[ing] like a large motor launch'. They opened fire with three
hundred rounds from their Lewis gun, after which the boat disappeared as
cries for help were heard from the water. Unfortunately, it had been a motor
launch despatched by an escorting destroyer to locate survivors. The hit-
and-run attack was over before escorting destroyers could respond and the
S-boats made their way back to Rotterdam unscathed.

With the postponement of Operation *Seelöwe*, Kriegsmarine command
took stock of their situation. Their ultimate goal was twofold: the
disruption of Britain's maritime supply and communication lines and the
preservation of German ones, notably coastal traffic from Norway. While
U-boats and capital ships roved into the Atlantic, aerial mining had taken
a more prominent role in the attempts to shut down British ports and
coastal convoy routes. Mines laid by surface craft added to the barrages;

there were destroyers in the west of the English Channel, the middle was handled by torpedo boats and the southeast by S-boats. MGK West held responsibility for these actions, their operational boundary line with MGK Nord stretching from Cromer to Den Helder. For their part, the latter naval command was chiefly defensive in nature: control over the German, Danish and Norwegian coastline and existing supply routes. They did, however, also intend to help maintain control over the North Sea by offensive operations against the British east coast, and strongly urged the relocation of a flotilla of S-boats to their area of control.

There then began a 'tug of war' between the two naval commands, FdT Hans Bütow firmly resisting any dividing of S-boat strength from the *Schwerpunkt* of operations, the southeast coast, their presence so noted by the enemy that the area had become known as 'E-boat Alley'. Torpedo boats, he argued, lacked the shallow draught to enable an approach inshore over enemy minefields. They were thus better suited in the western reaches of the Channel, rather than plugging gaps left by transferring S-boat ranks from his command. Unfortunately, he was overruled and the 1st S-flotilla was transferred to the control of Generaladmiral Carls' MGK Nord.

On 27 October, five days after a minelaying mission north of Shipwash, Birnbacher's unit sailed with *Carl Peters* from Rotterdam to escort *Admiral Scheer* from Brünsbuttel to Bergen. The cruiser was due to begin its first combat mission into the Atlantic via the Denmark Strait. There then

S-boats manoeuvring in harbour.

followed escort duty between Denmark and Norway that drew further protest from Bütow, the S-boats fulfilling a role better suited to *Vorpostenboote* ('outpost', or patrol boats) and other escort vessels. Carls proposed an anti-shipping strike against Scotland's east coast using S-boats against the Moray Firth in the Shetlands, but the sheer distance involved promised little tangible reward for the wear and tear on S-boat diesels. Raeder eventually agreed with Bütow and the 1st S-flotilla was returned to MGK West's control, although engine overhauls meant that the boats would not be on station and combat-ready in Rotterdam until mid December. By this stage – and much to the concern of Raeder amongst others – Hitler was already outlining his ambition to attack east: Russia.

On 19 November three boats of Kemnade's 3rd S-flotilla put to sea from Rotterdam. Oberleutnant zur See Hans Detlefsen had brought the newly commissioned *S38* from Germany. Departing Kiel on Saturday, 9 November, the boat passed through the Kiel Canal for Borkum, towed through the North Sea Canal, via Delfzijl and Groningen, into the Zuider Zee and on to Amsterdam, through the canal system to Rotterdam, arriving on Thursday. When S-boats traversed canals they required towing, as the minimum speed available on only one engine was 9 knots, the wash caused even at this speed being considered damaging for canal banks.

S38 marked the beginning of a new class of S-boat. A continuation of the *S26* series, it contained some modifications garnered as a result of combat experience. The engine ventilation arrangement had finally been perfected, using three large trunk type ventilators, one over each engine. Perhaps more fundamentally was the requested increase in bow-mounted firepower: the machine gun replaced by a 20mm flak weapon mounted within a *Scarff Ring*, a ring mounted on an elevated U-shaped frame, based upon a British aircraft design from World War One. Recessed into the enclosed forecastle, the weapon carried a low silhouette but would be invaluable, particularly against increasingly effective Royal Navy MTB and MGBs.

Attached to the 1st S-flotilla, *S38* was tactically under the control of Kemnade's flotilla until Birnbacher's return from Norway was complete. The weather had moderated to a gentle SSW breeze when *S38* accompanied *S54* and *S57* on her first patrol close inshore to Lowestoft, slipping from harbour at 1700hrs and proceeding in company for three hours before separating. *S38* reached her destined patrol zone at 2130hrs beneath bright moonlight punctuated by strips of drifting mist. Unfortunately for Detlefsen and his men, the same mist that obscured him from convoy traffic allowed two free-ranging destroyers to approach under cover and attack. At 0158hrs (BST) on 20 November, HM Ships *Campbell* and *Garth* sighted the S-boat at a distance of two miles, approximately twelve miles east of Southwold. The first indication the Germans had of the British warships was the sight of a destroyer to starboard, indistinct due to bands of mist masking its distance.

Suddenly, as the noise of the approaching ship drifted over the sea the Germans realised the ship was close, approximately 400m (440yds) distant and steaming straight towards them. An immediate contact message was transmitted to the other two S-boats as Detlefsen ordered *S38* turned towards the destroyer and the starboard torpedo (No 1 tube) fired. However, the man at the torpedo tube was either unready, or safety gear had been damaged preventing the torpedo from firing. *S38* then turned hurriedly to port to make off into the night as dictated by the tactical doctrine. At that moment the tardy torpedo was fired, aimlessly into the night as German lookouts saw the second destroyer, of whose presence they had been unaware, at close quarters to port.

HM Ships *Campbell* and *Garth* opened fire with close-range weapons; *S38* was hit on the port side seven or eight times, where steering gear, lighting system and engine-room telegraph were wrecked. A shell hit the fuel tank which caught fire, and the bow of the boat and starboard torpedo tube were damaged. Despite laying a smokescreen, ruined steering gear rendered escape impossible as the boat began to circle, one engine cutting out.

A German seaman ran aft with the intention of dropping depth charges in the course of the pursuing destroyer, but a burst of machine-gun fire discouraged this attempt. The Germans threw themselves flat on the deck, taking what cover they could behind their two spare torpedoes as HMS *Campbell* passed immediately ahead of *S38*'s bow at only 20m (65ft), continuing to fire. Pinned in the destroyer's searchlight, Detlefsen ordered the Kriegsmarine ensign hauled down as *S38* began sinking by the bow; the wounded were dragged aft until at 0225hrs *S38*, burning fiercely, finally sank. The destroyers picked up eighteen survivors including all three officers: they and seven other men were wounded, Detlefsen and officer under instruction LzS Georg-Robert Ratsch, severely. Five crewmen lost their lives.

The Allied interrogation report of the survivors stated that:

Detlefsen made a better impression than most German naval officers captured during recent months and seemed well educated and polite ... [He] is married, has been in England before on short visits, and speaks some English. He expressed appreciation for his treatment in England and his most sincere gratitude for the medical skill, patience, and care which has been expended on him. He was very seriously wounded, and the surgeons stated that his recovery was a triumph for them as well as a tribute to Detlefsen's constitution. The officer under instruction as a prospective E-Boat captain was Leutnant zur See Georg-Robert Ratsch ... [who] in 1939 served in the pocket battleship *Admiral Graf Spee* at the Battle of the River Plate. He was subsequently interned in Montevideo but escaped and returned to Germany. He then trained for E-Boats and was under instruction when captured. During the action in which *S38* was sunk Ratsch was very seriously wounded. He speaks both French and English quite well, is intelligent and also expressed his gratitude for the medical skill and care that had been expended on him. The third officer captured was the Flotilla doctor, who was not interrogated. He sustained burns but no serious injury in the action. He was reported to be an ardent and rather aggressive Nazi.[44]

All three officers were later repatriated to Germany in October 1943 in the agreement brokered by the Red Cross for severely wounded or disabled POWs.

It was a notable success for the British: their first prisoners from the S-boat service. On the German side, there was some level of concern that the boat may have been captured carrying a complete set of code books, despite standing orders that only those relevant to that day's action be taken aboard. As a precaution, codes were changed and a new system of embedding seemingly innocuous phrases within prisoner-of-war correspondence enabled the passing of information regarding their capture.

Six boats of the 2nd S-flotilla had put to sea during the same night, but apart from skirmishing with MTBs, the patrol dissipated amidst fog banks and bad weather. The pattern of storms, rain and fog carried into a dreary December that allowed few patrols and no success for the first fortnight. Newly commissioned *S58* and *S59* had arrived to join the 3rd S-flotilla during November and when the weather broke on 13 December both the 2nd and 3rd flotillas put to sea to assault shipping between Cromer and Great Yarmouth. *S24* and *S25* of Birnbacher's 1st S-flotilla were also involved, tactically attached to Kemnade's unit. As the boats sailed, reconnaissance reports of an enemy destroyer were received and the boats vectored towards it in an attempt to regain the initiative from the Royal Navy. *S59* was forced to abort with engine trouble in the middle engine,

Off-duty crewmen posing for a snapshot on their starboard torpedo tube. The darker paint used on the upper surface of the tube matched that used for the decking.

returning to Rotterdam as the other boat from its *Rotte* continued as *Führerboot* for the attack. However, radio messages were soon received from *S58* that instead of the expected target, they had appeared to stumble upon an entire destroyer flotilla. The hunter was now the hunted and in growing fog, the S-boats broke off the operation and returned empty-handed once again.

Two nights later, 15 December, four boats of the 3rd S-flotilla – *S54*, *S57*, *S58* and *S24* (still attached from the 1st S-flotilla) – sailed once again, the seas slight and light cloud covering the full moon that provided just enough light to be useful. Their target was a convoy of seventeen steamers reported by FdT heading north near Great Yarmouth. Instead, they found the convoy FS60 (Phase 4), southbound from Methil to Southend. Both *S58* and *S25* fired at 2158hrs, targeting a steamer and defending destroyer, HMS *Woolston*, who immediately began to shell the attackers, already withdrawing at speed, zigzagging and laying smoke. Both torpedoes passed beneath the destroyer and hit 2,301-ton Danish cargo ship *N C Monberg*, the collier exploding and going rapidly to the bottom with twelve of her complement of twenty-two.

On 17 December fog prevented three 2nd S-flotilla boats from sailing far from harbour, prompting FdT to ask for the construction of so-called 'fog buoys' using fire and smoke to guide the S-boats to and from harbour. These were to be interspersed with clearly marked decoy buoys loaded with small explosive charges designed to fool and potentially damage the enemy. Meanwhile, *S33*, *S34* and *S56* were slightly damaged by Wellingtons of RAF 40 Squadron on the morning of 21 December during a raid on Ostend, *S33* requiring shipyard time for repair.

The final successful patrol for 1940 took place on the night of 23 December, when all three flotillas put to sea to attack merchant shipping between Cromer and Orfordness. Gone were the long days and warmth of summer, *S34* and *S56* of 2nd S-flotilla both expecting severe icing and therefore only carrying two torpedoes each, no reloads. At 2035hrs *S58* reported passing through the wake of an enemy destroyer and eight minutes later the first torpedoes were fired when *S34* attacked a tanker, missing the target. Half an hour later ObltzS Klug aboard 1st S-flotilla's *S28* reported contact with a convoy near Great Yarmouth and fired torpedoes at what he estimated to be a 2,500-ton steamer. He hit and sank 358-ton minesweeping trawler HMT *Pelton*, she and her twenty crew all going under in weather worsening by the minute. New boat *S101*, which had joined 1st S-flotilla at the end of November, reported fierce defensive fire from destroyers escorting convoy FS66 (Phase 4), and *S26* and *S29* both reported torpedo failures during the confused action. As the sea state rose, the S-boats broke away and began their return, *S59* of the 3rd S-flotilla blundering into northbound convoy FN67 (Phase 4) and firing both loaded torpedoes. Oberleutnant zur See Albert Müller reported hitting both a 10,000-ton tanker and a 6,000-ton steamer. As he ploughed through heavy seas, retreating into darkness under fire from escorting destroyers, his torpedoes hit 6,552-ton steamer *Stad Maastricht*. The steamer was badly damaged and taken in tow by tugs but sank shortly thereafter. Escorting destroyer HMS *Verdun* reported hitting and sinking an S-boat during the action, but all boats reached harbour safely, ending their war in 1940 as the bad weather prevented any more operations.

It was a time to rest and reorganise: Kemnade's flotilla transferred for a short period from Ostend to Boulogne and new boats were taken on strength for both the 1st and 3rd flotillas, *S102* and *S60* respectively. Elsewhere, the 4th S-flotilla had already begun training in the Baltic, having been established on the first day of October. Illustrating the dearth of experienced S-boat officers available, Kapitänleutnant Niels Bätge was transferred from the torpedo boat service to command the new flotilla, having previously captained *T2*. The demand for S-boat men within an expanding service was increasing dramatically.

7

E-Boat Alley

January 1941 – June 1941

THE impact achieved by S-boats on the British military and civilian public psyche almost eclipsed their actual achievements. Torpedo attacks had sunk twenty-eight ships in the last seven months of 1940 and combined Luftwaffe and Kriegsmarine minelaying had destroyed 201 ships during the entire year. As U-boats had discovered during the same period, mines were actually more effective than torpedoes, although minelaying was still considered a dangerous and largely inconclusive task.

On the other side of the hill, while Luftwaffe and Kriegsmarine co-operation was relatively feeble beyond the local level, the Royal Navy and Royal Air Force were far more attuned to each other. While some inter-office and inter-service wrangling marred British forces, it paled in comparison to the levels that bedevilled the Third Reich throughout its existence, both militarily and politically.

The Royal Navy's first motor launches that fought the S-boats had proved wholly inadequate for the task, and strengthening coastal forces became an urgent priority. Modern Hunt-class coastal destroyers were put into service as quickly as they could be commissioned and improved Fairmile C 'Long' MGB and MTB models were developed, capable of not only holding their own defensively against the S-boats, but also of taking the war into German coastal waters. RAF Coastal Command soon began flying systematic reconnaissance operations over predicted S-boat routes, while shore radar stations concentrated on detecting incoming boats. So-called 'Headache' operators became more prevalent both ashore and aboard Royal Navy ships – fluent German speakers who would listen in to radio chatter between S-boats and gather intelligence. Minesweeping was also stepped up along coastal convoy routes and harbours, the number of minesweepers in service more than doubling between February 1940 and September 1941. British defences were stiffening as 1941 dawned.

Loading mines in Ostend. Mine warfare became one of the most potent weapons in the S–boat arsenal, even if it remained an unpopular assignment.

Reorganised, the S-boats waited for weather conditions to improve. In Germany tests had been completed on the new quick-firing 20mm cannon for all boats with an enclosed forecastle. Likewise, the existing stern-

As well as torpedo patrols, S-boats were frequently loaded with a mixed payload of mines and torpedoes, seen here taking the latter aboard in Ostend.

mounted flak weapon was to be changed for either a more reliable type of the same calibre, or in some cases up-gunned to a quick-firing 40mm. Elderly boats that had been gathered in Rotterdam as part of the Schnelle U-Jagdgruppe were transferred to MGK Nord for use in the fjords. There they were gathered into a 'Special Flotilla for Defensive Purposes' (*Sonderflottille für Defensivzwecke*), soon to be joined by the inferior petrol-driven Dutch boats *S201* and *S202* which had been put through their paces in Baltic trials.

Finally, after several false starts terminated by bad weather, *S26* and *S101* of the 1st S-flotilla put to sea against convoy traffic east of Southwold. Evading detection by the escort, *S26* managed to achieve firing position but suffered two torpedo failures, while ObltzS Christiansen's *S101* hit

Helmsman at his station within the wheelhouse, the voice-pipe allowing audible commands from the bridge above.

and sank the small freighter *H H Petersen*. The attack had been so sudden that the S-boats went unnoticed, the rescued British crew reporting their ship sunk by a mine.

On the afternoon of 16 January, all three flotillas were ordered to sea once more, the 1st and 2nd aborting their missions in miserable weather while *S54*, *S57*, *S59* and *S60* from the 3rd Flotilla pressed on toward Lowestoft. With temperatures plummeting and high seas, spray crashed over the S-boats' decks and caused icing problems on weapons and machinery. The S-boats slowly crept into their patrol area and found convoy FN85 (Phase 4) which had departed Southend earlier, bound for Methil. As the S-boats began their attack, their high-speed engines were detected by hydrophone operators aboard HMS *Woolston*, visual contact following shortly thereafter.

It was ObltzS Wuppermann's *S60* that led the charge, but ice had frozen his torpedoes in place and all he could do was race beneath the guns of the British destroyer, getting so close that they were unable to bring their weapons to bear before Wuppermann made off into the night. Lieutenant Commander Walter John Phipps remembered:

I thought I was bound to ram, he was right under my bow but he just saw me in time and was away in a flurry of foam just as I was on him. Pity we did not hit one … but we put the fear of God into them and they ran like hell.[45]

The technique of close quarter attacking had become a staple of S-boat offensive doctrine, remembered from the other side of the guns by Fred Bailey aboard HMS *Gleaner:*

We escorted ships to and from the Firth of Forth via the Pentland Firth, Northern Scotland. Sometimes we did East Coast convoys … as far south as the Thames through 'E-Boat Alley'. On one occasion a torpedoed stricken tanker was ablaze like a waterfall of fire, the sea was on fire as well. There were obviously no survivors. The E-Boats found that if they got close enough to a ship's side the machine guns couldn't depress sufficiently to fire. We moved the machine guns to where they could be used from the bridge. This went well until one gunner swept the gun across his own bridge.[46]

The S-flotilla returned empty-handed to Boulogne and the remainder of January continued in that vein. What few patrols were mounted during the period of heavy winter gales generally ended in torpedo failure through icing or malfunction, with tussles against destroyers ending in light damage to both sides from machine-gun and cannon fire. A second inshore convoy track running parallel to the existing FN and FS routes brought the vital merchant traffic closer to land-based radar and guns and limited any attacker's room for manoeuvre. The S-boats all returned to Ostend, moored and secured against the elements. During February the bomb damaged *S31* returned to service and, as the 2nd S-flotilla had taken *S55* and *S56* upon commissioning to replace those lost to bombing and mines, ObltzS Hans-Jürgen Meyer's repaired boat was taken into the 3rd S-flotilla along with newly commissioned *S61*, raising the unit strength to seven. The damaged and repaired *S36* returned to Petersen's 2nd Flotilla that same month. It was unfortunate timing, as the RAF raided Ostend during the night of 5 February, lightly damaging *S54* and *S58* with splinters.

The following night a break in the gales allowed boats of the 2nd and 3rd Flotillas to put to sea: *S30* and *S34* from Petersen's command, *S54*, *S58* and *S59* from Kemnade's. The S-boats had learnt how to interpret the 'tun' buoys marking convoy channels swept for mines, often tying up to them as they switched off engines and waited on the swell for target indications, slipping their lines from the buoys and moving into attack position as the merchant ships drew near. This night, hampered by flurries of sleet and snow, *S30* focused on what the skipper, ObltzS Feldt, believed was a 2,000-ton freighter or tanker. It was in fact the 501-ton British MV *Angularity* straggling from convoy FN01 (Phase 5) with an overloaded cargo of phosphate making the ship bow-heavy and sluggish. A single torpedo hit the motor ship which broke apart and sank in two minutes. Eight men went to the bottom with her, although crew member William Lind was more fortunate:

> There was a muffled explosion. I was in my cabin, having just come off watch. I opened my door to see what had happened but … a solid wall of water drove me back … The next thing I knew I was trapped in my cabin under water. Fortunately my cabin got airlocked through the vessel going down bow first. I reckon the whole thing happened within ten seconds. Strangely enough I did not panic. I was swimming in circles in my waterlogged cabin with just enough air space to keep the water below my nose. My head was bumping the bulkhead. I took one deep breath and dived through the open doorway. It seemed ages before I broke surface. The seas were high and the water was bitterly cold.

Clinging to a hatch cover, Lind was swept away from *Angularity*'s stern, which still protruded above the seawater, the wreck having hit the shallow bottom. As the cold began to take its toll and Lind faced certain death, Feldt's crew spied the lone man and *S30* eased alongside.

> With some difficulty they hauled me on board. I could not help myself owing to my numbed legs. They bundled me in blankets when I got below. I was laid in one of the crew's bunks then three sailors sat on top of me to impart the warmth of their legs. They offered me a bowl of hot soup and a glass of schnapps. After that I fell into a deep sleep and did not wake till the E-boat arrived at her base.

Feldt interrogated Lind, the British seaman learning that the ship's second engineer, 'Jimmy', had been similarly rescued by *S34*, though they were the only survivors. After a few days in Ostend being well treated by the Kriegsmarine, he was transferred to the Gestapo for a six-hour interrogation before they in turn handed him to the French police:

S-boats at sea, probably not expecting immediate action with the life raft lying unsecured to port.

> For five days and nights we slept on damp palliasses, we were never even allowed to go to the lavatory, everything had to be done on the floor of our cells … to me the French were worse than the Germans. On the fifth day I was seized with violent shivering and a high temperature [and] I collapsed.[47]

Once again, weather conditions deteriorated to the level where S-boats couldn't leave port until the early hours of 19 February. Oberleutnant zur See Töniges' *S102* found convoy FN11 (Phase 5) in the drifting fog near Sheringham Buoy. Operating at creep speed, Töniges torpedoed two ships estimated at 6,000 and 4,000 tons. The former, 1,355-ton ss *Algarve*, a Danish ship impounded into service by the British War Ministry, was hit beneath its smokestack, sinking in minutes with all twenty-one crew. The second ship had stopped and the stern lamp could be dimly seen through the fog when Töniges fired his starboard torpedo, detonation clearly heard above defensive machine-gun fire from the steamer, once again obscured by fog. *S102* withdrew, claiming the ship as sunk, although no further losses were reported that night from the convoy. All S-boats returned to Ijmuiden at the end of their patrol, *S39* running aground in the murk not far from port. On 25 February, after having skippered eighty-eight war patrols, Töniges was presented with the Knight's Cross from FdT KzS Hans Bütow.

During February, ObltzS Siegfried Wuppermann became acting commander of the 3rd S-flotilla when Kptlt Kemnade took advantage of the bad weather and returned to Germany on leave. Temperatures gradually rose, reducing the danger of drifting ice on the Scheldt river and Wuppermann took the flotilla from Ostend to Rotterdam. From there *S31*, *S54*, *S58*, *S59*, *S60* and *S61* put to sea during the afternoon of 25 February. They were joined by two 2nd S-flotilla boats, *S30* and *S33*. East of Lowestoft, the S-boats lay stopped on the swell awaiting expected northbound shipping from FN17 (Phase 5). The sound of foghorns and marine engines heralded the convoy's arrival and the Germans began their attack, the S-boats' propeller noise detected by hydrophone operators aboard HMS *Woolston*. At 2156hrs ObltzS Feldt fired one torpedo from *S33* at escorting Hunt-class destroyer HMS *Exmoor*, hitting her in the stern and causing considerable structural damage, rupturing fuel lines and spraying burning fuel oil over the surface of the sea. The ship began to blaze fiercely and within minutes had capsized. Three of the ship's officers, including her captain, and 101 crewmen perished; thirty-two survivors were rescued by HMS *Shearwater* and HMT *Commander Evans*. The burning ship had immediately alerted the remainder of the convoy to imminent danger and they swiftly altered course, escaping the other S-boats. HMS *Exmoor* was the first Hunt-class destroyer to be lost in action.

Further north two nights later, seven boats from the 1st S-flotilla prowled off Cromer. Detected by escorting destroyers, ObltzS Klug's *S28* was still able to torpedo and sink the 1,123-ton British steamer SS *Minorca*, killing seventeen crew and two passengers, with only three survivors rescued later by the Royal Navy.

The following sortie was foiled by strong defensive destroyer activity and bright moonlight, denying the S-boats the cloaking darkness that made their hit-and-run technique so formidable. This, coupled with seven torpedo failures, conspired to defeat the German attack. Weather continued to moderate as the month ended and during mid-afternoon on 7 March, Luftwaffe reconnaissance reports of a southbound convoy estimated at forty-six ships in Quadrant 7317 were received, the Luftwaffe already having attacked the convoy and sunk one collier. This was the opportunity that the S-boats had awaited and provided a clear example of the potential of inter-service co-operation between them and the Luftwaffe. In fact, the presence of the Luftwaffe's recurring reconnaissance mission over the east coast had become noted by local residents, the distant aircraft christened 'Flamborough Freddie'.

All three flotillas were mobilised, a formidable force of sixteen S-boats con-verging on what was in fact two convoys. FS29 (Phase 5) and FN26 (Phase 5) were due to pass each other during the night. This in itself was not unusual, but it was perilous, with more than seventy ships gathered in the relatively constricted mineswept convoy lane. The night was ideal for S-boats: light seas, good visibility with a moon high in the southeast, largely obscured by clouds. A dark cloud bank lay on the western horizon, clear to the east.

The S-boats fanned out and attacked the steamers passing before them, singling out the northbound ships using the inner convoy lane. First to attack was ObltzS Götz von Mirbach in *S29*. The speeding S-boat was spotted to starboard by the chief engineer aboard 1,385-ton freighter SS *Dotterel* as it closed to fire a torpedo, the resulting impact blowing apart all electric lamps within the engine room, releasing the ship's anchor and destroying steam piping. Water gushed through the jagged hole torn in the side and the steamer began to slump bow-first into the water. Escorting corvette HMS *Sheldrake* came alongside and lifted survivors off the crippled steamer. Once abandoned, a boarding party led by the merchant ship's chief officer, William Nash, and including *Sheldrake*'s first lieutenant, Lt Cdr Cecil Checcucci, two naval ratings and seven other rescued volunteers struggled through the derelict ship when a second torpedo hit the port side, exploding in a blue sheet of flame visible miles inland and killing all but two of the merchant seamen.

The next to strike was ObltzS Büchting in *S27* who torpedoed the 1,049-ton SS *Rye* travelling north in ballast. All twenty-two crewmen and six DEMS gunners died, six of their bodies later found in a drifting, damaged

Clad in black leather and wearing a kapok lifejacket, this engine-room crewman works the throttle lever for his engine; the engine room was relatively spacious and well ventilated. Prompt response to engine commands was crucial for high-speed missions, often undertaken in scant visibility.

lifeboat and another two on a life raft. ObltzS Klug in *S28* pursued the 2,345-ton freighter SS *Corduff* for nearly an hour, and was frequently glimpsed running at high speed parallel to the convoy, as gunners aboard *Corduff* and other ships blazed away into the darkness. Finally, at 2137hrs, Klug landed a torpedo on the freighter's starboard side, blowing the gun and its crew overboard and sending the ship down stern first. Klug approached survivors as they huddled in their lifeboat, enquiring about details of the ship he had sunk. He had already rescued two injured merchant seamen and with a cheery, 'Well, I am off to Germany now! Cheerio and good luck,' he began the trek back to base with his two injured prisoners.

Meanwhile, Oberleutnant zur See Christiansen in *S101* had torpedoed and sunk the small 957-ton coaster SS *Norman Queen*, on passage from London to Boston, Lincolnshire, with a cargo of wood. Twelve crewmen and two passengers were killed, with the sole survivor, Captain Horn, taken prisoner aboard the S-boat and later interned in Milag Nord.

The six boats of the 3rd S-flotilla stumbled upon more freighters and escorting destroyers, ObltzS Hans-Jürgen Meyer attacking the 1,047-ton SS *Kenton* at 2210hrs, torpedoed and sinking within one minute with four of her crew. The new boat *S61*, skippered by ObltzS Axel von Gernet, also successfully torpedoed a freighter, hitting the port side of 4,805-ton SS *Boulderpool* immediately forward of the bridge. Taking half an hour to settle on the shallow seabed, all the crew were able to abandon ship and be rescued. The final ship destroyed during this night of carnage was from southbound FS29. Escorting destroyers HM Ships *Whitshed* and *Worcester* were successfully lured away from the convoy chasing *S26*, allowing ObltzS Töniges in *S102* to torpedo 1,547-ton SS *Togston* en route from Blyth to London with a full cargo of coal. Two 'eels' sent the ship under in less than two minutes, with nine crewmen killed in the attack.

Elsewhere, the four boats of the 2nd S-flotilla seem to have borne the brunt of the defensive actions of sloops HM Ships *Sheldrake* and *Puffin*, accurate gunfire and dogged pursuit driving them empty-handed from the battle as the weather deteriorated once again. With rain lashing across the horizon and torpedoes expended aboard many of the S-boats, the Germans laid course for home. It had been the most successful single night attack for the S-boat service.

Having won their laurels that night, the S-boats were back in the fray two nights later, five boats from the 2nd S-flotilla driven off by HMS *Worcester* and HMS *Southdown* after attempting to repeat the previous success by attacking FN28 (Phase 5) and FS29A (Phase 5) off the Norfolk coast. The combination of bright moonlight and stiff defence foiled them. Another two nights later the 1st S-flotilla managed to briefly penetrate the escort screen of FS32 (Phase 5) east of Orfordness, Kptlt Klug's *S28* hitting and sinking the 5,257-ton MV *Trevethoe* laden with a cargo of wheat. One gunner was lost in the sinking, and Klug and his flotilla mates were driven away by escorting destroyer HMS *Worcester*. Klug fired a 'forlorn hope' torpedo at the attacking warship from 4,000m (4,300yds), later admonished by FdT: 'completely pointless, wastes torpedoes unnecessarily and offers no prospect of success'. The S-boats had begun to use the G7e electric torpedoes in combat, leaving no visible trail of bubbles behind the electrically driven propeller, although the torpedo's speed was less than its steam-powered counterpart and therefore fast-moving targets such as warships would require close-range launching. Nonetheless, Klug had completed dozens of war patrols and achieved an enviable record of successful attacks, and he was awarded the Knight's Cross on 12 March 1941.

The remainder of the month passed in general frustration for the S-boats. Only Töniges aboard *S102* claimed a successfully destroyed merchant ship on 18 March: French steamer SS *Daphne II* from convoy FN34 (Phase 5). The 1,970-ton collier travelling in ballast was hit by a single torpedo and, badly damaged, towed toward shore, but she broke in two and sank off the Humber. Both *S61* and *S31* became embroiled in a pitched battle with HMS *Worcester* as they attempted to attack FS41 (Phase 5) near Great Yarmouth in company with *S57*. During the cannon and machine-gun fire, both S-boats launched torpedoes at the destroyer, claiming her hit and damaged, though in reality both shots missed.

It had been a disappointing end to the month, made worse by the weather deteriorating across the English Channel and North Sea. The Germans had come to believe that enemy destroyers had been equipped with radar as they homed so accurately on the small S-boats, but this was not yet the case and still depended on sharp eyes and land-based radar guidance. The S-boats were all harbour-bound for the first half of April and a change in strategy had been decided by FdT. Instead of resuming torpedo patrols as soon as possible, all three S-flotillas would once again undertake minelaying, the aim being to block the inner British convoy lane and force ships seaward, where there was greater room for attack. On 17 April the operations by the three flotillas were completed, Birnbacher's boats laying forty-two TMB mines near Cromer, Kemnade's boats dropping thirty-two TMBs off Haisborough Sands and Petersen's boats laying twenty-six TMBs off the Cross Sands lightship.

After the 2nd S-flotilla boats had finished the delicate task of sowing their minefield, *S41*, *S42*, *S43*, *S55* and *S104*, the latter freshly commissioned and commanded by ObltzS Ullrich Roeder, hunted for convoy FS64 (Phase 5), which was found in the early hours of morning. Escort destroyers HM Ships *Eglington*, *Wallace* and *Cotswold* put up a spirited defence of the convoy and (incorrectly) claimed several hits on the attackers, while two steamers were sunk and another pair damaged. ObltzS Feldt in *S43* torpedoed and sank 1,446-ton SS *Effra*, with two of her crew killed, and ObltzS Roeder in *S104* destroyed 1,298-ton Dutch freighter SS *Nereus*, the entire crew rescued. Both SS *Eskburn* and *Ethel Radcliffe* were damaged by *S55* and *S42* respectively, and two crewmen aboard *Eskburn* killed by machine-gun fire. The 5,673-ton *Ethel Radcliffe* was towed to Yarmouth by ASW trawler HMT *Sapphire*, but was later sunk by Luftwaffe bombing.

Minelaying carried out by 3rd S-flotilla had gone without a hitch and the boats *S31*, *S34*, *S35*, *S58*, *S60* and *S61* had also pressed on in the hunt for enemy convoy traffic, clashing with the motor gunboats *MGB59*, *60* and *64* that had sailed as part of Operation QE. One of *S58*'s *Maschinenmaat* was lightly wounded by cannon and machine-gun fire which penetrated the boat's engine room. Kemnade's men sailed once again for minelaying in

Oberleutnant zur See Klaus Feldt receives his Knight's Cross from Führer der Torpedoboote KzS Hans Bütow on 25 April 1941.

April, dropping twenty-four TMB mines off Hammond Knoll on 29 April, and once again clashing with British coastal forces when the *Rotte* comprising *S58* and *S61* spent twenty minutes in a fast running battle with *MGB59* and *61*, during which *S61* fired more than eight hundred 20mm rounds, claiming several hits.

That same night, six boats of the 1st S-flotilla attacked convoy EC13, fifty-seven ships which had sailed from Southend bound for the Clyde. A new EC series of convoys had been introduced to speed the return of empty vessels to the coalfields. In the face of ferocious fire from four destroyers escorting, ObltzS Mirbach in *S29* made the only sinking when he hit and destroyed 1,555-ton SS *Ambrose Fleming*, ten crew and one gunner going down with the vessel. During the chaotic fight *S39* and *S40* collided, though all the S-boats managed to return without further mishap.

Although the success of the attacks against FN28 and FS29A had not been repeated, the S-boats had more than made their mark on Britain's maritime trade, tying down considerable naval and aerial resources in an attempt to defeat them. In fact, the combined effect of S-boats and aircraft was such that in the period March to May 1941 more ships were lost off the east coast than in the Atlantic. Another Knight's Cross was awarded when Feldt received his on 25 April, Christiansen's following on 8 May. Gales lashed France during May, keeping all S-boats in harbour; a single attempt at a minelaying was cancelled when stored mines came loose and fell from their tracks, damaging the boats that carried them.

It was the end of the first phase of concerted operations against the British east coast, something that the commanders of all three flotillas learned when they were summoned to a conference with FdT in Boulogne. There they were briefed on the next gamble that Adolf Hitler would undertake. During May all three flotillas transferred out of the English Channel and North Sea. Their place was taken by the newly formed 4th S-flotilla, training in the Baltic since the previous October under the command of Kptlt Bätge. Bätge's unit, comprising a small number of the most elderly boats, would have the unenviable task of appearing to be in several places at once, operating from both Rotterdam and Cherbourg in an attempt to keep an alert enemy off balance and mask the absence of the veteran flotillas of newer and faster boats. Meanwhile, those veterans transferred to the Baltic to face their new enemy: Russia.

8

Barbarossa

May 1941 – November 1941

O N 23 May 1941 both the 1st and 2nd S-flotillas transferred to Germany in preparation for Barbarossa, while Kemnade's 3rd S-flotilla tied up in Kiel harbour on 28 May, receiving the sobering news that afternoon of the sinking of the battleship *Bismarck* in the North Atlantic. In Kiel and Wilhelmshaven the S-boats underwent refit to prepare for the coming offensive. The FdT staff had also relocated to Germany (moving on to Helsinki at the beginning of the invasion). Bütow's position in France was held by a small staff based at The Hague, headed by FdT's operations officer ObltzS Rebensburg, who reported directly to, and received orders from, MGK West. The units transferring to the Baltic continued to receive orders from FdT, but now under the auspices of Admiral Hubert Schmundt, cruiser commander-in-chief (*Befehlshaber der Kreuzer*), who exercised operational command of all Baltic Kriegsmarine forces, in turn answering to Admiral Claasen, MGK Nord.

With war against Britain's commerce still the focus of German naval effort, only light and training units supported by two obsolete *Deutschland*-class battleships built at the turn of the century were to face the Russians. The Kriegsmarine's plan was defensive in nature and largely independent of activities on land – quite possibly a missed opportunity to instigate a combined services operation that might have eased German advances into the Soviet Union.

During the war with Soviet Russia it will be the task of the navy to protect the German coast line and to prevent any hostile naval force from breaking out of the Baltic. Since once Leningrad has been reached the Russian Baltic fleet will have lost its last base and will thus be in a hopeless position, major naval operations are to be previously avoided. After the destruction of the

Russian fleet it will be the responsibility of the navy to make the Baltic fully available to carrying sea traffic, including supplies by sea to the northern wing of the army. (The sweeping of minefields!)[48]

Geographically, the inner shores of the Gulf of Finland were 600km (370 miles) from Moscow, as opposed to a thousand from the eastern frontiers of Poland. With bolder use of amphibious assault and major Kriegsmarine surface units, Hitler's invasion of Russia could have been markedly different. However, he never saw the Baltic as a potential primary attack and supply route. Rather, it was seen as a battle to contain the formidable Soviet Baltic fleet, which included two battleships, two cruisers, twenty-three destroyers, sixty-five submarines and forty-eight MTBs, as well as annexed Latvian, Lithuanian and Estonian vessels.

For their part in Barbarossa, S-boats from five flotillas were drawn up in preparation. Birnbacher's 1st S-flotilla rendezvoused with depot ship *Carl Peters* in Danzig. *S26*, *S27*, *S28*, *S29*, *S39*, *S40*, *S101* and *S103* arrived on 15 June. The following day three boats – *S27*, *S28* and *S29* – detached and moved on to neighbouring Gotenhafen where they formed the nucleus of a new unit. Alongside two boats of the 2nd S-flotilla (*S45* and *S47*) they formed the first (and temporary) incarnation of the 5th S-flotilla, commanded by veteran Knight's Cross holder Kptlt Bernd Klug, who handed the captaincy of *S28* over to LzS Hans-Joachim Wrampe. Klug's boats moored in Gotenhafen, earmarked for minelaying. The remainder of the 2nd S-flotilla moved onward to Finland, with eight boats plus the *Tsingtau* anchored off the island of Pensar south of Turku on the eve of Barbarossa. Finland had been subjected to months of Russian demands for resources and military access following the end of the 1940 Winter War, pushing the nation further under German influence with each fresh demand.

Likewise, the Baltic States were being plundered by Soviet Russian occupation. On 14 June 1940, while German forces occupied Paris and the world's attention focused on the war in France, the Red Army had occupied Estonia, Latvia, and Lithuania, forcing their legal governments to step down, to be replaced by Soviet puppet regimes. 'Elections' were eventually held from which all non-Communist candidates had been removed. Mass deportations followed, with thousands shipped to almost certain death in Siberia. In August 1940, the Soviet Union completed the takeover by annexing all three states, officially making them a part of the USSR.

Finland's direct role in Barbarossa was at first covert, although the access

S-boats of the 1st S-flotilla lying alongside their tender *Carl Peters* in Finnish waters. The camouflage applied to both tender and S-boats appears to have been used for the first time within the Baltic during Operation Barbarossa.

granted to Kriegsmarine forces provided an ideal jumping-off point for minelaying. Three days after the attack had begun, Finnish forces moved into open action, the start of their so-called 'Continuation War'. The remaining boats of the 1st S-flotilla also moved into Finnish waters, they and their depot ship moored beneath the centuries-old Fort Suomenlinna near Helsinki. The ten boats of the 3rd S-flotilla waited at Pillau, minelaying orders received days previously from Admiral Schmundt in Swinemünde.[49]

Beginning on the night of 19 June, Kriegsmarine minelayers began sowing three huge barrages (Wartburg I–III) stretching from the northernmost East Prussian port Memel to the Swedish island of Öland. Russian light cruiser *Kirov* observed the ships of the 1st Minelaying Group west of Libau (known as Liepāja in Latvian), but did not intervene; Soviet standing instructions denied anything that could be construed as offensive action. The 3rd Minelaying Group of three ships was escorted by six boats of the 1st S-flotilla during the night of 21 June, once again observed by silent Russian warships as they created the barrage code-named Corbetha, comprising four hundred EMC and seven hundred floating mines. Klug's newly convened 5th S-flotilla dropped thirty TMB torpedo mines in the Irben Strait (Eisenach field) and the 3rd S-flotilla despatched five boats each carrying six TMB mines to lay small fields in the shallow waters off the Latvian ports of Libau (Weimar field) and Windau (Erfurth field).

During their return from minelaying, *S59* and *S60* attempted to stop the 3,077-ton Soviet-controlled Latvian freighter SS *Gaisma* with machine-gun fire across her bow. Carrying timber, the freighter increased speed in an attempt to escape, but was hit by a single torpedo from ObltzS Albert Müller's *S59*. Holed but not sinking, a second torpedo from ObltzS Wuppermann's *S60* finished the ship off. Barbarossa was only minutes old when the torpedoes hit at 0345hrs, a frantic radio message transmitted before the ship sank: 'Torpedoed ... *Gaisma* is sinking ... Goodbye.' From the crew of thirty-two, two were pulled aboard *S60* and six lost. Survivors recounted that machine-gun fire had killed all six in the water – however, this is unlikely. It is entirely possible that *S60* may have opened fire in an attempt to silence the radio transmission, for if their intention was to kill all survivors they failed badly. They also would probably have killed their two captives who were taken ashore as POWs. The Germans were carefully manoeuvring through floating wooden beams and debris to pull more men from the sea when they were ordered to break off further rescue attempts, alerted to potential Russian air attack. The two S-boats moved on, while the remaining men from *Gaisma*, under the command of mate Jan Balodis, reached the Latvian shore fourteen hours later near the Uzava Lighthouse. Their mortally wounded captain was buried there shortly afterwards, after succumbing to his wounds. Thanks to the *Gaisma*'s transmission at 0500hrs Soviet authorities ordered all ships within the Baltic Sea to return to their home ports immediately. Barbarossa was well and truly underway.

At 0745hrs the 3rd S-flotilla boats intercepted Soviet trawler *RT-24 Shchuka* off Windau (known as Ventspils in Latvian), guided to the small ship by a Luftwaffe pilot. The Soviet crew abandoned ship, whereupon men from LzS Heinz Haag's *S31* boarded and sank her with explosives. Fishing four Soviet crewmen from the water, the S-boats made way for Pillau, arriving in the early afternoon.[50]

Elsewhere, LzS Hans-Joachim Wrampe in *S28* brought the 1,181-ton passenger ship SS *Estonia* to a halt with warning shots. The 5th S-flotilla boat then placed a small prize crew aboard the steamer travelling from Stockholm to Reval (known as Tallinn in Estonian), taking the master, Captain A I Adamson, and his twenty-nine crew prisoner and bringing the ship into harbour.

The dazzle camouflage peculiar to the Baltic Sea during 1941.

Later that day, four boats of the 2nd S-flotilla put out to sea once more. *S43*, *S44*, *S104* and *S106* patrolled the waters off Estonia, stopping a Dutch motor yacht heading to Sweden before letting them proceed unmolested. Nearby, the 782-ton Estonian steamer *Liisa* was headed to Paldiski with a cargo of cement and barbed wire. The freighter had put to sea on 21 June, the crew noting large amounts of smoke coming from Windau as they passed during the following day. Later that day they heard of the outbreak of war via Radio Moscow, having already unwittingly passed through the Wartburg minefields. Towards midnight on 23 June, *Liisa* was nearing the tip of Hiiumaa Island, as the *Hiiumadal* lightship was raising anchor. The two vessels sailed a parallel course when, shortly afterwards, the 2nd S-flotilla found them, ObltzS Opdenhoff's *S44* hitting the 409-ton *Hiiumadal* with a torpedo near Hangö, sinking her with all five crew aboard. Leutnant zur See Peter Block's *S106* fired a single torpedo at *Liisa*, missing, as he overestimated the target's speed, but bringing the ship to a stop. Block ordered all fourteen people aboard into a lifeboat and then fired a second torpedo which sent the ship to the bottom. The overloaded lifeboat was turned over by a large wave, one crewman drowning before *S106* pulled the rest from the water. The S-boat made high speed to the area where the *Hiiumadal* had gone down to look for any survivors, finding none, and returning to Finland where the shipwrecked survivors were interned by the Finnish 5th Coastal Police Brigade.[51]

The initial Russian naval response was to begin laying defensive minefields across the entrance to the Gulf of Finland during the night of

22 June. Providing cover for the minelayers, the heavy cruiser *Maxim Gorky* and three destroyers left the Gulf of Riga and blundered into German mines, the cruiser losing her forecastle and the destroyer *Gnevnyj* sinking. *Maxim Gorky* was towed to Reval, made seaworthy and moved to Kronstadt a few days later. Both sides appeared willing to joust in a defensive manner.

On 23 June the 3rd S-flotilla – joined by ObltzS Babbel's *S45* on attachment from Petersen's 2nd Flotilla – sailed after refuelling at Memel to lay more mines in the Irben Strait, the main exit channel from the Gulf of Riga into the Baltic Sea. Between them they carried the last available TMB mines specially modified for S-boat use. The mission was beset by problems, *S58* aborting with bearing damage, leading to boat *S55* finding water in the diesel, which forced a half-hour delay as the problem was rectified. To the east they could hear explosions and a pall of thick smoke hanging over Libau, where heavy fighting had begun, with S-boats exhorted to sail in support of the Wehrmacht's 291st Infantry Division. Prowling the coastline, the S-boats were unable to engage the enemy, but laid eighteen mines on target before they returned to Pillau.

Torpedoes lowered aboard an S-boat from her depot ship.

During the return voyage the *Rotte S35* and *S60* sighted a shadow almost dead ahead. It was Russian submarine *S3* of the 1st Submarine Battle Fleet.[52] With the fall of Libau almost inevitable, the unseaworthy *S1* had been blown up in the shipyard to prevent capture, her crew taken aboard Captain Nikolaj A Komstromicew's *S3* which attempted to break out and reach Riga. With the additional crew and some dock workers aboard, the submarine hosted nearly a hundred people and was incapable of submerging. Both S-boats only carried a single torpedo and as they engaged the surfaced submarine both shots failed; *S60*'s torpedo sank without trace (an *Absacker*) while *S35* fired a surface runner. Undeterred, the S-boats opened fire with their 20mm flak weapons, observing numerous hits as they zigzagged furiously around the submarine. The Russians returned fire with the conning tower's 45mm flak weapon as well as hastily mounted machine guns and rifles. Although the German 20mm was a faster-firing weapon, its reach was below that of the main Russian gun, and both S-boats were momentarily forced away as guns jammed. It took twelve minutes to clear *S35*'s gun as the submarine raced northward, attempting to escape in the dim light of early morning. With ObltzS Wuppermann's men aboard *S60* unable to clear their ammunition blockage, the young captain radioed *S35* to continue firing as they closed in on the enemy and attempted to attack with hand grenades. Three shallow-fused depth charges were added to the chaos and within minutes some of the Russian crew were seen to abandon ship while it continued running at high speed. At 0324hrs a single grenade from *S60* landed on the conning tower and exploded, killing the captain as *S3* began to burn. A depth charge dropped in its path by *S60* damaged the Russian's stern and slowly she began to sink. Twenty shocked Russian survivors were rescued, and four of *S35*'s crew were wounded during the battle. The two S-boats – both showing enough battle damage to require repair – returned with their prisoners, the 3rd S-flotilla moving its home port to Memel shortly afterward.

As minelaying continued by both navies, Kemnade's boats tangled once again with the enemy in the early morning of 26 June. All five operational boats laid course for Windau where they attempted to torpedo two steamers entering harbour. Five torpedoes were fired in total and several detonations were heard, although some were considered most likely to have hit the nearby harbour mole. Nonetheless, a steamer estimated at 2,000 tons was claimed as hit and sunk, later listed as the Estonian ship SS *Lidaza*, although proof remains sketchy at best.

The S-boats came under artillery fire from the shore and retreated, *S61* suffering engine bearing damage. With too many coincidental problems within the flotilla, an investigation was already underway. Flotilla engineer Kptlt (Ing) Johannes-Martin Döpner quickly realised that all of the damage was suffered after more than three hundred hours' service of motors using roller bearings, and the conversion to motors using sleeve bearings was placed at top priority.

Meanwhile, during the following night four boats from Kemnade's flotilla sailed into the Irben Strait in search of a reported Soviet troop convoy. Two *Rotten* – *S31* and *S59*; *S35* and *S60* – approached the Irben Strait and instead found Soviet minesweepers, MTBs and destroyers embarked on defensive minelaying, with a pair of MBR2 flying boats providing overhead cover. Believing her an enemy torpedo boat, S-boats fired and missed minesweeper *T-204 Fugas* before running into destroyers *Stojkij*, *Serdityj*, *Storoževoj* and *Engels*. Oberleutnant zur See Müller's *S59* and LzS Haag's *S31* each fired a double shot, hitting *Storoževoj* sailing third in the Russian column. At least one torpedo hit the port side of the destroyer near the bridge, detonating stored ammunition and blowing the entire forepart of the ship away as far back as the 58th frame. The bow superstructure, including two guns, sank immediately and the destroyer commander Kapitan 3 Ranga I F Lomakin and eighty-four crew members were killed. Fortunately for those still alive, no torpedo hit the stern where armed mines were stacked awaiting deployment.

The S-boats continued their attack, *Stojkij* managing to repel them three times with heavy fire. The S-boats had laid a smokescreen from which they darted at high speed for every fresh attack. One torpedo launched from *S59* was only avoided after the target destroyer increased speed to full and flung the wheel to port until the rudder could go no further. The torpedo passed at less than a metre and the destroyer circled back to her original heading, unable to bring any weapons to bear while heeling violently.[53]

With fierce defensive fire from the destroyers and all torpedoes fired, the S-boats vanished behind another smokescreen, making way for home. They skirmished once more with two enemy MTBs, exchanging fire with *TKA* (*Torpedny Kater*) *17* and *47*, the latter hit and abandoned by her crew while *S35* suffered five wounded crewmen. The Russians had been in the midst of evacuating the headquarters staff from their naval base at Libau. Drifting but still seaworthy, *TKA47* was taken in tow by *S35* and brought into harbour. Once again more bearing damage was found aboard *S59*, which prompted a flotilla-wide examination of all engine oil filters. Steel shavings that could not be traced to any obvious source were found in the oil aboard *S31*, *S34*, *S35* and *S60*, leading to the highly probable conclusion of sabotage. This reduced the 3rd S-flotilla to only four combat-ready boats: *S17, S45, S54* and *S55*.

However, the damage inflicted on Kemnade's unit was not as dramatic as that suffered by Petersen's 2nd and Klug's 5th S-flotillas. That same night, boats from both units had been involved in providing cover for the minelayer *Brummer* between the Apolda and Corbetha fields, when, in the early morning hours during their return journey, *S43* detonated a Russian mine midway between Finland and Estonia. Casualties were heavy and nineteen minutes later, as *S106* and *S46* gently eased toward the sinking vessel to assist survivors, *S106* also detonated a mine. Both boats sank. Eleven men from the crew of *S43* were killed. Among the wounded was the captain, ObltzS Feldt. *S106* lost eight men dead, the engineering crew having taken the majority of casualties.

Operation Barbarossa was experiencing stunning success on land, despite pockets of dogged Russian resistance. The Wehrmacht rapidly advanced through the Baltic states and, on 29 June, Libau was occupied by elements of the 291st Infantry Division. Although Soviet naval units had been evacuated two days previously, the German infantrymen found

On 25 August 1941, *S28* collided with small Finnish submarine *Saukko* at Harmaja near Helsinki. In danger of capsizing, *Saukko* was lashed to *S28* and returned to port safely.

Captured Soviet MTB *TKA47* in German hands. Fast and agile, she underwent trials by the Kriegsmarine as part of the 1st S-flotilla, but was never committed to action under the German flag.

themselves engaged in arduous street fighting that raged for several days. Windau had also been abandoned while Daugavgriva and Riga were on the verge of evacuation before the German onslaught. The loss of Libau was particularly acute for the Russians as they had significantly reinforced the port for primary use by the Soviet Baltic Sea fleet.

On the morning of 4 July the 3rd S-flotilla, including the tender *Adolf Lüderitz*, sailed from Memel to their new base at Libau before continuing minelaying operations, frequently under fire from Russian shore artillery, the final bout of minelaying completed that night by *Brummer* under S-boat escort. The stock of mines had been exhausted and until replenishment from Germany the S-boats would be otherwise engaged. Two nights later they covered minesweeping in the approaches to Riga by *MRS11 Osnabrück* and *M31*, clashing with Soviet surface forces, the destroyer *Serdityj* expending 115 130mm shells in a battle in which nobody suffered serious damage.[54] Once the enemy had retreated, the Germans completed their task and sailed for Riga, half of the 3rd S-flotilla (*S54*, *S57*, *S58* and *Führerboot S59*) using the captured port as their new base, and torpedo transport ship *Mosel* as de facto depot vessel, the small tanker *Oleum* arriving later to provide fuel.

Meanwhile, the 1st S-flotilla had been engaged on missions at the behest of the Abwehr. Operating alongside Finnish MTBS, five S-boats began dropping small Estonian battle groups behind Soviet lines. The so-called 'Erna' groups (under the military jurisdiction of the Wehrmacht's 18th Army) were ferried from exile in Finland to the Salmistu Beach, from where they headed inland to Estonia's heavily wooded interior to link up with anti-Soviet partisans known as the Forest Brothers.

Birnbacher's unit also attempted to attack enemy convoy traffic on 10 July, but failed in all torpedo strikes, plagued by misfires, while the brightness of Baltic summer night allowed targets to follow and out-manoeuvre incoming torpedoes. Soviet-operated Latvian steamer *Rasma* was the sole loss; the 3,204-ton ship carrying a cargo of flour and grain was already disabled by Finnish mines and ran aground on Mochni Island. Between Luftwaffe attack and torpedoes from *S26* and *S28*, the beached and abandoned ship was finally sunk.

For their part, Soviet surface forces launched an offensive against Axis transport lines within the Gulf of Riga. Vitze Admiral Valentin Petrovich Drozd marshalled his forces and the first Russian MTB attack took place on 13 July, four MTBs attacking a German convoy of ten supply ships and transports under escort by minesweepers, four ASW trawlers and *S54* and *S58*, reinforced by *S47* and *S57* once battle had been joined. Russian aircraft added their weight to the attack, as did the cruiser *Kirov* and elements of the Soviet 1st Destroyer Squadron. Once fighting began, further Russian MTBs joined the fray, drawing the S-boats into fast-moving running battles, while larger Soviet ships attempted to attack the convoy. Ultimately, only the landing ship *Deutschland* was sunk with minimal loss of life, and only light damage suffered by other ships as the Germans withdrew behind smokescreens and under Luftwaffe Stuka cover. Although Kriegsmarine loss had been relatively light, the new impetus of Russian naval attacks served to delay attempts to force the Irbe Strait and build up troops by maritime transport for an assault against Estonia.

S-boats continued to act as escort for troop transport, Kemnade meeting with Fliegerführer Ostsee Oberst Wolfgang von Wild to achieve the kind of local Luftwaffe co-operation that could yield greater results for the S-boats. With no darkness to cloak operations, accurate and timely aerial reconnaissance would vastly increase any chance of success. During the afternoon of 21 July, Kemnade's headquarters received Luftwaffe reports of Soviet destroyers, four S-boats sailing from Riga to intercept. The *Rotte S54* and *S58* sighted what they reported as a 'small barge' towing an MTB off Abruk Island, but opted to continue hunting larger targets, *S54* briefly opening fire with its 20mm on the towed MTB. Trailing behind was the second *Rotte* of *S29* and *S58*, which attacked the two Russian vessels, setting *TK71* on fire and damaging the towing icebreaker, 253-ton *Lacplesis*. Both crews abandoned ship. The S-boats closed to pick up survivors, rescuing fourteen Latvians, one Russian captain and three Russian sailors. One German sailor attempted to swim to reach wounded Russians while tethered to the S-boat, but pistol fire from other survivors swimming away deterred him.

The fighting against Russian forces in Estonia continued, with Kemnade's 3rd Flotilla S-boats battling in the northern reaches of the Gulf of Riga. *S54* and *S55* intercepted minelaying destroyers and attacked the destroyer *Smelyj*, Wagner's *S54* hitting the ship's bow with a torpedo, severely damaging her and throwing one steam boiler off its foundations, causing extensive flooding. She was later sunk by a Russian *coup de grâce* torpedo shot.

By this stage of the Baltic fighting, flotilla organisations became little more than a vague administrative framework. The potential sabotage of many boats' oil supply had put more than normal numbers in shipyards for overhaul and repair. Upon emerging ready to fight once more, they were generally allocated to whichever unit was deemed to be running at the lowest combat strength. The 5th S-flotilla was disbanded and its boats shared amongst the remaining flotillas, MGK Nord even going so far as to request the meagre strength of the 4th S-flotilla, continuing the fight in the English Channel, be transferred to the Baltic, though the request was denied.

On 25 July Raeder informed Hitler of increased Soviet naval operations in the Gulf of Riga and around the Estonian islands, due in large part to resistance to the Wehrmacht's advance on land.

> The Army's thrust along the eastern edge of Lake Peipus towards Narva to the north and Leningrad to the northeast, during which the left wing weakened and fell back, afforded the enemy sufficient time to sweep enough mines to be able to operate in the area between Reval and the Baltic Islands with disturbing effect, and to attack our supply lines by sea and our right wing.[55]

Minelaying by S-boat continued. By 13 August the 2nd and 5th S-flotillas had laid another 153 mines, a combination of TMB and EMC types, in the Gulf and elsewhere offshore the Estonian coast. These augmented a formidable and complicated array of Kriegsmarine minefields blockading Reval. When not engaged on minelaying, S-boats were frequently assigned escort duties, only the 1st S-flotilla making any combat sinkings during that period when *S26*, *S28*, *S39* and *S40* clashed with enemy minesweepers, sinking *R101* by gunfire and *Tszcz-41* with torpedo, rescuing twenty-three survivors. In turn, *S39* was damaged by Russian gunfire. The minefields themselves accounted for 1,251-ton transport ship *Vodnik*, 542-ton Lithuanian steamer *Utena* and 441-ton Russian minesweeper *T-202 Buj*.

Leutnant zur See Eberhard Geiger in *S58* claimed responsibility for sinking the last two Russian vessels by torpedo in the Barbarossa campaign, small minesweeper *No 80* hit and sunk while at anchor on 17 August, and 210-ton minesweeper *T51 Pirmunas* torpedoed two days later. A final minelaying mission by Kemnade's 3rd S-flotilla deposited thirty TMB mines off Cape Rista on 25 August, by which time Russian defences in Estonia were on the verge of collapse.

On 26 August, Moscow gave Admiral Vladimir Tributs permission to evacuate all naval forces from Reval. By then over two hundred Soviet civilian and military vessels had been assembled in the harbour, planned to depart in seven staggered sailings: one primary battle fleet, four smaller convoys, a screening squadron, and a rearguard squadron. On the morning of 28 August the first thirty-two ships sailed, Luftwaffe forces attacking relentlessly and the already established minefields claiming a grim tally of ships. S-boats of Birnbacher's 1st Flotilla from Helsinki that attempted to intercept were repulsed three times by heavy defensive gunfire. It was left to mines and aircraft to destroy over fifty ships, killing in excess of fourteen thousand people. The survivors reached Leningrad two days later.

The S-boats' role in Operation Barbarossa was all but over by the beginning of September, the 3rd S-flotilla already slated for transfer to a new theatre of combat. At the end of August, Kptlt Kemnade, his flotilla engineer Kptlt (Ing) Johannes-Martin Döpner and flotilla administrative officer LzS Horst Weber (skipper of *S35* which was laid up in the shipyard due to oil contamination) travelled to Swinemünde to begin preparations for the flotilla's transfer to the Mediterranean. Kemnade temporarily passed the flotilla reins to ObltzS Wuppermann, commanding officer of *S60* and the most recent Schnellboot recipient of the Knight's Cross awarded on 3 August. Bordering the Mediterranean Sea, Mussolini's ill-judged 1940 adventure in North Africa had floundered, triggering the deployment of Erwin Rommel and his newly created Deutsche Afrika Korps in February 1941. As early as March 1941 the idea of S-boat deployment to the region had been put forward:

The question of using German S-boats in the Mediterranean, as requested by General Rommel, has been examined by the Naval Staff on a previous occasion. In view of the tasks anticipated in connection with Operation Barbarossa, S-boats cannot be transferred until this operation is completed. Until that time Italian MTBs will have to suffice for the tasks in the Mediterranean.[56]

By September, with the Baltic nearly secure, the time had come to re-evaluate this position. However, before this could be done, the remnants of Soviet resistance on the Estonian islands Ösel and Dagö needed conquering through Operation Beowulf II. Handled as if it were a large river crossing, troops from Estonia's west coast would be landed on the islands while diversionary attacks were made elsewhere. The first such diversion was code-named *Südwind*, the second, against the western coast of the island of Saaremaa, code-named *Westwind*. It was to this latter operation that new boat *S53* and *S104* of the 2nd and *S55*, *S57*, *S59* and *S60* of 3rd S-flotilla were assigned. A third diversion, *Nordwind*, was also directed against the Estonian island of Hiiumaa from Finnish bases. Beowulf II was launched on 8 September, *Westwind* not beginning until five nights later. For their part, the S-boats attacked Russian coastal units, the sole casualty being the lead machinist aboard *S57*, lightly injured by shell splinters from Russian coastal batteries. By 20 September the islands were secure. From that point, the boats of the 2nd and 3rd S-flotillas that remained in the Baltic carried out escort operations for the so-called *Baltenflotte* centred on the new battleship *Tirpitz* and cruisers *Admiral Scheer*, *Köln*, *Nürnberg*, *Leipzig* and *Emden*, as well as supporting destroyers and torpedo boats. They had gathered to prevent the Soviet Baltic fleet from breaking through from Kronstadt to Sweden.

On 24 September Kemnade received orders to return to Swinemünde and prepare for impending transfer to the Mediterranean. Petersen's 2nd S-flotilla was transferred back to Germany on the first day of October before overhaul and a return to the western front. Only Birnbacher's 1st S-flotilla remained in Finland, escorting convoys and attempting to interfere with Soviet traffic to and from the port of Hangö. Once the latter fell to Wehrmacht invaders on 26 October, the flotilla remained in Finland to cover minelaying operations. Finally, during November 1941 when winter ice threatened to trap the S-boats in the Gulf of Finland, Birnbacher led his unit comprising *S26*, *S27*, *S39*, *S40*, *S101* and *S102* back to Germany.

9
The Channel

May 1941 – December 1941

F OLLOWING withdrawal of three flotillas to the Baltic in early 1941, it was left to Kaptlt Niels Bätge's 4th S-flotilla to wage war against Britain's coastal merchant shipping. His flotilla engineer Oblt (Ing) Günther Hilbig, severely tested by keeping their meagre force of older boats in action, had previously served as a chief engineer within the 1st S-flotilla between July 1939 and February 1940. On 1 June Bätge was able to marshal five boats: *S19*, *S20*, *S22*, *S24* and *S25*. During May, the 4th S-flotilla had received orders to sail for the French port of Lorient to provide

S-boats in Ostend. Note the application of rudimentary camouflage to the foreground boat, as opposed to the uniform differing shades of grey on the rest.

coastal support for the expected arrival of *Bismarck*. However, while bad weather delayed departure, the German battleship was sunk in action and the move cancelled. Bätge's men would remain in the English Channel, their first mission the laying of six mines east of Great Yarmouth by *S19*, *S22* and *S24* on 30 May.

Throughout June, the 4th S-flotilla concentrated on patrolling the seas along England's east coast between Lowestoft and the Humber Estuary, engine unreliability in the older boats often reducing numbers to three at any one time. Bad weather dogged the S-boats, though Luftwaffe reconnaissance reported a prime target already disabled by Luftwaffe torpedo attack southeast of the Humber: a Royal Navy aircraft carrier. Identified as HMS *Hermes*, the carrier had been evading a Heinkel He111 torpedo attack when she struck the wreck of the steam tanker SS *Ahamo*, sunk by mine during the previous April. *S19*, *S20*, *S22* and *S24* were despatched to finish the job, sighting the great ship in the early hours of 3 June. As defending minesweeper and sloop HMS *Kittiwake* opened fire on the approaching S-boats, ObltzS Karcher's *S22* fired a single torpedo and ObltzS Mirbach's *S24* made a double shot, all three hitting the large target and sinking what was reported as '6,000 tons, presumably a Sperrbrecher', while the S-boats retreated behind smokescreens. In fact they had attacked and sunk 7,924-ton SS *Marmari*, a large freighter commandeered by the Admiralty in 1939 along with two others and converted into decoy ships, in this case a plywood-panelled replica of HMS *Hermes*. Known for security reasons as *Tender C*, *Marmari* had been part of Force W, designed to fool German aerial reconnaissance into chasing phantom capital ships.

Minelaying off East Anglia occupied the flotilla for the remainder of June. Three ships were sunk as a result: 3,001-ton SS *Gasfire* and 1,546-ton SS *Kenneth Hawksfield* (which lost a crewman in the sinking) of convoy EC36 on 21 June, and 717-ton SS *Hull Trader* on 23 June, only three of the fourteen crew being rescued.[57] The S-boats had also encountered increasingly effective Royal Navy MGB activity, although the weakness of the British forward-firing machine guns meant minimal damage was inflicted. *S20* and *S22* encountered *MGB58*, *59* and *65* during a return from minelaying on 21 June, both S-boats outpacing their pursuit, but also suffering from jamming of the 20mm Flak C/30 cannon on the boat's afterdeck. Concern grew that the weapon, whose limited magazine capacity enforced frequent change and corresponding diminished rate of fire, was outdated. Orders were passed that they be replaced by the newer Flak C/38, or in some cases a 40mm Bofors.

Meanwhile, despite Raeder's initial refusal to allow the construction of S-boat shelters, FdT had doggedly persisted with his request, which was finally put into action during 1940. The Organisation Todt began constructing sheltered docks and associated workshops and weaponry stores in Ijmuiden, Rotterdam, Ostend, Boulogne and Cherbourg. The threat from enemy air attack had increased since the end of the Battle of Britain and finally, on 10 June, the first four berths in Ostend were declared operational. Eleven days later Boulogne's bunker was also operational; Rotterdam followed in October and Ijmuiden early in 1942. In Cherbourg, existing berths were covered with a vault of steel-reinforced concrete and had been declared useable at the beginning of 1941. The bunker in Boulogne was designed to accommodate twelve S-boats, a torpedo bunker situated immediately to the rear, with access by railway track which connected it to both incoming transport and S-boat berths. Unlike the U-boat bunkers which had taken priority along the Atlantic coast, those that would house the S-boats (and often R-boats) had a roof thickness of only 200cm (6ft 6in), felt to be sufficient against enemy bombing at that stage of the war; the consequence of neglecting to strengthen these defences would only become tragically obvious years later.

S-boats moored alongside Ostend's quay. The vulnerability of the boat to air attack while in unsheltered harbours is obvious.

On 24 June Bätge's boats relocated to the Boulogne bunker and shifted their attention to the Channel, attempting to maintain the illusion of greater S-boat strength. A single fruitless mission was sailed before two boats of the flotilla moved on to Cherbourg, operating around Portland Bill, but achieving nothing. Engine problems reduced available boats to ludicrously low levels, until on 6 July the first new S-boat arrived from Germany. Oberleutnant zur See Friedrich Wilhelm Wilcke took command of *S107*, relinquishing *S25* for a return to Germany and relegation to a training unit. Likewise the new *S50* was taken over by LzS Karl-Erhart Karcher, passing his previous *S22* to ObltzS Friedrich Hüsig. *S49* also arrived from Germany, commanded by LzS Max Günther.

The Royal Air Force had increased its strength along the Channel coast in 1941, countering much of what Luftwaffe reconnaissance was available. The corresponding lack of Luftwaffe intelligence regarding convoy movements hampered S-boat mission planning: the few boats available were too thinly spread to trust to luck in finding targets. The emphasis therefore remained minelaying, 155 TMA mines and twenty *Reissbojen* being laid over the course of eight missions between Portland and Portsmouth. Frequently under fire from coastal batteries, the S-boats suffered no loss, but neither did they achieve any discernible results.

On 29 July the flotilla returned to Boulogne where they began torpedo missions into the Channel, guided by radar (*Funkmeßstelle*) situated at Cap Gris Nez. On the night of 6 August *S19*, *S20*, *S48* and *S49* sailed for contacts detected near Folkestone, finding five freighters, five patrol boats and two destroyers. Only ObltzS von Mirbach of the newly commissioned *S48* claimed success with the torpedoing and sinking of a '4,000-ton freighter', though this was never substantiated. During her return to Boulogne, *S19* was attacked by a British fighter, one seaman shot in the lung and the attacker shot down and seen to crash into the sea. The RAF had stepped up its 'anti-E-boat' missions, newly inaugurated Whirlwinds of 263 Squadron in particular focused on 'chameleon patrols' and already claiming (incorrectly) to have severely damaged several S-boats during the first days of August.

Fresh boats were arriving to replace the worn older models. In early August newly commissioned *S50*, *S51* and *S107* were all taken on strength, although the latter suffered rudder damage in transit and was towed by Vorpostenboot *V1512* to Calais for repair. On 10 August *S20*, *S48* and *S49* put to sea from Boulogne to attack a westbound convoy detected near

Folkestone. At 0149hrs LzS Max Günther made his first sinking when he torpedoed 1,548-ton steamer SS *Sir Russell* amidships, *S20* also claiming a hit on a 4,000-ton freighter.

In order to try and keep the British off-balance, the 4th S-flotilla moved once more, this time to Rotterdam on 18 August, Bätge establishing his headquarters at Scheveningen. Four boats sailed against a convoy reported near Orfordness and von Mirbach in *S48* hit and sank 1,971-ton Polish SS *Czestochowa* headed to Reykjavik, the captain being killed during the sinking. He also hit 2,774-ton tanker SS *Dalewood* in the stern causing severe damage and killing three crewmen and a naval gunner, though the ship was towed into the Humber for repair. *S20* fired a double shot at an escorting destroyer but missed. It was the last combat mission for the elderly boat, *S20* sailing for Kiel on 22 August and transferring to the 6th S-flotilla in Baltic training. New boat *S52* arrived and ObltzS Karl Müller took command, his previous boat *S19* already transferred to training duties in Kiel after its clash with the RAF.

The next mission on 2 September for the refreshed and modernised flotilla proved fruitless, Luftwaffe sighting reports too slow in reaching Bätge to enable convoy interception. However, Luftwaffe bombing of EC70 on the evening of 6 September triggered radio chatter between the beleaguered ships, intercepted by the German's excellent B-Dienst listening service. The target convoy's position triangulated swiftly, Bätge's boats sailed and found the Allied ships in the early morning darkness, the short nights of summer perceptibly lengthening. Oberleutnant zur See Karl-Erhart Karcher's *S50* hit and sank the small 478-ton collier SS *Duncarron*. Going under in seconds, only four of the thirteen men aboard survived, the master swept out of his enclosed bridge by the deluge of water and nearly run down by the freighter following as he struggled to stay afloat. The new *S52* also hit and sank 1,436-ton Norwegian freighter SS *Eikshaug*, seventeen of the twenty-one crew going to the bottom with her. The end was so swift that survivor Able Seaman Olaf Henrik Lagerstedt was not even aware they were under attack.

We were bound from Southend to Grangemouth with a cargo of 2,000 tons of cement. We were armed with 4 machine guns ... left Southend at 0600 GMT on September 6th and formed up in Convoy EC70. The convoy was in two columns and we were the third ship in the port column. During the afternoon of the 6th two German planes attacked the convoy for about an hour and dropped some bombs, no ship in the convoy sustained damage.

At 0230 GMT on the 7th in position 3 miles East of Sheringham Buoy there was an explosion in the stern of our ship. The sea at the time was slight, wind light, weather was fine and visibility good. It was moonlight at the time. We were making 7 knots on a north-westerly course. I was asleep in my bunk at the time and did not hear the explosion, and am unable to say whether the explosion was on the starboard or the port side or whether there was any flame. Another man, who was in bed in the same room as I was, awakened me and I immediately went up on deck. The stern of the ship was then under water and as I reached the deck I saw a wall of water coming towards me and I jumped into the sea. I was not wearing a life-jacket but I managed to catch hold of one of the hatches, and after 1/4 of an hour in the water our Escorting vessel picked me up.

Our ship sank about 30/40 seconds after the explosion. I did not hear the engines of an E-boat and thought the ship had struck a mine. I did not see any rafts in the water.[58]

Despite over-claiming that five freighters totalling 13,500-tons had been sunk, the attack was still a welcome success for the S-boats after difficult weeks of nothing. The diversion of Luftwaffe strength to the war in the east was as telling as the lack of other Kriegsmarine surface forces, not only in striking power, but also invaluable reconnaissance.

Inclement weather limited possible sailings, a minelaying mission on 8 September successfully dropping ten TMB mines along what the Kriegsmarine had designated convoy route Cäsar, clashing with a British

S-boat travelling at speed with starboard torpedo door open, filmed for the weekly newsreel *Die Deutsche Wochenschau*.

destroyer before outpacing pursuit. Not until 17 September did the flotilla experience any further triumph, vectored on to convoy EC74 near Cromer. *S51* torpedoed the 4,762-ton freighter SS *Teddington* carrying nickel ingots and mixed cargo, ultimately bound for Calcutta. The ship caught fire but stubbornly refused to sink; it was taken in tow but ran aground and was wrecked. The entire crew were successfully evacuated. Captain Woodhouse, skipper of the 5,389-ton refrigerated cargo ship SS *Tetela* heard the explosion that spelt disaster for *Teddington*, and stepped out on to the wing of his bridge in time to see the incoming bubble trail left by a G7a torpedo fired by ObltzS Karcher's *S50*. The torpedo hit below the waterline and punctured the hull, though once again the ship refused to sink. This time attempts to tow her to safety were more successful: beached at Haile Sand Flat the steamer was refloated the following day, and berthed at Hull for repair.

It was to be the final success story for the 4th S-flotilla during September. Further missions were thwarted by bad weather, enemy destroyers, MTBs and aircraft. A near-miss by an RAF bomb on 29 September against *S50* shattered an engine mounting; the boat limped to base and was later towed to shipyard for repairs. On 3 October Bomber Command attacked Rotterdam harbour, causing heavy damage to *S107* that required eight weeks to repair, as well as light splinter damage to *S51* and *S52*. Three Vorpostenboote were also badly damaged. The attack served to highlight the necessity for S-boat bunkers; those under construction at Rotterdam were nearing completion, the first of the planned sixteen individual covered docking bays being finished on 11 October. By that time the flotilla was barely operational after carrying the Channel war alone. Newly commissioned *S109* came on strength, skippered by LzS Walter Bosse and sailing into action with *S49* and *S52* on 12 October, stumbling upon British destroyers and retreating under heavy fire. A shell splinter landed squarely on the deck of *S52* but caused no damage.

While Bätge's flotilla had achieved the near impossible by keeping an offensive S-boat presence within English waters, the Kriegsmarine had in reality allowed the Royal Navy and Royal Air Force breathing space to re-arm and reorganise coastal and anti-shipping strike forces. During October 1941 they used radar-controlled aircraft for the first time in convoy defence, with six Beaufort torpedo bombers dedicated to the task. The number of German-speaking Headache operators was dramatically increased in order to take advantage of the S-boats' Achilles' heel: their reliance on clear language VHF transmissions to co-ordinate torpedo attacks.

On 9 October, after shipyard overhaul at the end of Baltic operations, reinforcement by six 2nd S-flotilla boats arrived in the English Channel. Korvettenkapitän Rudolf Petersen had been transferred from command of the 2nd S-flotilla to the staff of FdT. Petersen had suffered minor injuries in a car accident and been declared unfit for sea duties, his future instead as a staff officer ultimately leading to the future post of *Führer der Schnellboote* in 1942. In his stead was Kptlt Klaus Feldt, previously captain of *S30*. While *S42*, *S44*, *S45* and *S46* were being overhauled and would not be in service until the end of the month, *S41*, *S47*, *S53*, *S62*, *S104* and *S105* all entered Rotterdam harbour and began preparing for their first mission three days later.

It was a successful return to the Channel, the S-boats finding northbound convoy traffic off the Norfolk coast. Oberleutnant zur See Peter Block's *S53* torpedoed 1,768-ton Norwegian freighter SS *Roy* travelling in ballast from London to Blyth. The explosion blew away the entire poop above the waterline and badly holed the freighter, which began to sink. As *Roy* settled into the water, 1,537-ton SS *Chevington* was also hit, this time by LzS Hans Victor Howaldt's *S105*. The British steamer was hauling cement bound from London to Grangemouth and sank rapidly with nine men killed. Survivors were heard in the water and two lifeboats launched from the sinking SS *Roy* rowed toward them; one was almost pulled under by suction from the sinking ship as Norwegian helmsman Helmer Ditlefsen boarded *Chevington* to assist wounded men to safety. Three men died as the ship went down, including Trimmer Jack Wauby who had been found alive and conscious by Ditlefsen, but trapped in his cabin. Unable to free him as the ship flooded, the Norwegian had been forced to abandon ship without him.

Though the S-boats over-claimed six ships sunk for 18,000 tons, they had nonetheless re-established the S-boat threat to east-coast convoys and escaped without serious damage, returning to Rotterdam where they were now able to shelter within bombproof enclosures.

Bad weather prevented any further sorties and it was not until the night of 19 November that both the 4th and 2nd S-flotillas was able to put to sea, the latter successfully intercepting FS50 (Phase 7) near Great Yarmouth. Howaldt's *S105* made its second successful attack, hitting and sinking 1,159-ton collier SS *Aruba*, killing one gunner aboard ship. A second collier, 2,462-ton SS *Waldinge* was hit by Peter Block's *S53* with another gunner killed. *Waldinge* was immediately abandoned but later reboarded. Though flooding badly, the merchant crew requested a tug as they hoped she could

A boat of the 2nd S-flotilla (denoted by the flotilla insignia of a diamond on the side of the bridge) putting to sea.

yet be saved. Retiring to escorting gunboat *MGB87*, they awaited morning light to find that *Waldinge* had gone down, a tethered barrage balloon still floating above the shallow wreck site. A third ship, 5,502-ton Fleet Auxiliary tanker RFA *War Mehtar* was hit by ObltzS Ullrich Roeder's *S104*. Captain S M Woodward had seen the S-boats streaking out of the darkness, and already ordered his ship swung to port to avoid torpedo trails sighted. It was a second salvo fired that hit the ship astern, the fuel oil cargo destined for Harwich's destroyer force bursting into flames that rapidly engulfed the ship. Woodward ordered the blazing tanker abandoned; one lifeboat was almost run down by SS *Greenwood* following behind, before survivors were rescued. Aflame and abandoned, *War Mehtar* was taken in tow by tug *Superman*, a volunteer skeleton crew placed aboard before the ship's back finally broke and she went under.

However, the six attacking S-boats did not have everything their own way. The escort was formidable, comprising destroyers, HM Ships *Wolsey*, *Verdun*, *Widgeon* and *Kittiwake*, gunboat *MGB87*, and trawler HMT *Kinston Olivine*; the destroyers HM Ships *Vesper*, *Garth* and *Campbell* were nearby in support. In the confusion of the night attack, *S53* took some damage from gunfire as the S-boats withdrew to prepare for a second attack. Aboard *S105*, LzS Howaldt misinterpreted an order received by radio, believing an immediate stop was ordered after the lead S-boat sighted a shadow ahead. Number three in the column, *S105* abruptly throttled down, *S62* following closely behind, narrowly avoiding collision by throwing the wheel hard over and passing close by. However, the next boat in line, *S47*, ran straight into the side of Howaldt's boat, tearing away the railing and caving in the hull. Although *S105* remained watertight, aboard *S47* LzS Hans Joachim Stöve received reports of severe damage to compartments 7 and 8 as he slewed to a stop. In murky visibility the next boat in line, ObltzS Paul Poppe's *S41*, had no chance and ran straight into the stern of Stöve's already damaged boat. The impact tore a rudder away and damaged *S47*'s screws, while mangling the bow aboard *S41*. What had begun as a counter-attack on an already depleted and confused convoy had ended in disaster. By radio, flotilla chief Feldt ordered *S62* to take *S47* in tow and both *S105* and *S53* to jointly take the more severely damaged *S41* in tow by the stern. Their pace was tortuously slow and *S62* was forced to use its life raft as a large fender between the two boats as they made way for Rotterdam. There still remained a final obstacle.

In Felixstowe the Royal Navy's 6th Motor Gunboat Flotilla had been waiting for an opportunity to test their up-gunned boats. The flotilla's Lieutenant Commander Robert 'Hitch' Hitchens had lobbied long and hard to have his boats equipped with more impressive firepower, including 20mm Oerlikons and 2pdr pom-poms. As the 2nd S-flotilla retreated on 20 November, a nearby Headache station intercepted transmissions from the S-boats, Hitchens immediately sailing with *MGB63*, 64 and 67 to intercept, though *MGB63* was forced to abort with engine trouble. Using the S-boats' own tactics against them, Hitchens lay in wait silently along the Germans' expected route with engines off. At 0445hrs BST the sound of S-boat diesels was heard and both MGBs raced into the attack, catching their slowly moving target completely off guard and opening fire. Aboard *S104* one seaman was badly wounded, the bridge of *S47* also hit and ObltzS Stöve shot in the thigh. The Germans returned fire, though relatively ineffectually, with only *MGB64* hit sporadically. In the confusion Poppe's damaged *S41* was hit again, towing the deadweight no longer feasible as the MGBs continued to make three high-speed strafing runs. Code books and papers were thrown overboard and the entire crew evacuated aboard *S105* and *S53*. Attempts to vector nearby 4th S-flotilla units into the action failed and Feldt's boats attempted to throw off their attackers. Orders were received from flotilla headquarters to scuttle *S41*, though a hasty attempt to set charges was badly handled before she was abandoned, the tow dropped and the remaining S-boats made off for home.

Despite breaking free from the MGBs, the trials of the 2nd S-flotilla were not yet over. A pair of Spitfires intercepted them near the Dutch coast at 0915hrs, strafing *S104* and killing MaschMt Hans Röttger, as well as scoring hits on *S62* and *S47*. Three men were severely wounded and eight lightly injured, and the tow was dropped on *S47* to allow faster retreat. The 4th S-flotilla boats hove into view, *S110* picking up the tow for *S47* and bringing her into port. Every one of Feldt's boats had taken damage; the next pair of two newly commissioned S-boats scheduled for the 6th S-flotilla – *S111* from Travemünde and *S70* from Bremen – were instead diverted to Feldt's battered command lest it be unable to field any operational units.

Meanwhile, Hitchens on *MGB64* had come upon the drifting hulk of *S41* as he led his two gunboats back to base, an opportunity too good to pass up.

> The E-boat was lying two hundred yards to the eastward, black and silent. The first of the dawn was by this time taking effect. She was clearly silhouetted against the growing light in the eastern sky. The moment was exhilarating in the extreme. 'We must board!' I shouted.
>
> She was obviously hopelessly crippled: there was no fear of her suddenly departing. It was, therefore, worth taking what precautions we could. We got all our tommy-guns and revolvers, we arranged to approach one on either side, with Boffin [Lt L G R Campbell, *MGB67*] to starboard, in such a way that we should not fire across the E-boat at each other ... A brilliant finger of light shot out from Boffin's boat, played on the decks of the E-boat. A deserted shambles. Bullet-holes everywhere, gear lying about, no signs of life; at the yardarm of her diminutive mast the ugly German naval flag with the swastika and iron cross hung lifeless in the still air.[59]

The British boarded the shattered boat, momentary confusion caused by the first of their number tripping as he landed on the German deck, inadvertently pulling the trigger of his submachine-gun and sending a stream of bullets perilously close to Hitchens's bridge, causing momentary alarm at the possibility of a German trap.

Investigating the abandoned boat, they found seacocks open and scuttling charges set, though the detonator was unprimed. Nonetheless, water was flooding the engine room and other compartments and there was clearly no way to find and close the stopcocks. With no heavy-duty pumping gear carried, there was clearly no chance of taking the captured boat intact to England and Hitchens ordered her ransacked for anything they could find.

> Sailors swarmed all over her, appearing from the hatches with arms full of equipment. Roberts removed all the W/T equipment, gunners took what guns they could detach and pans of ammunition. Charts, books, logs, compasses, searchlights, revolvers, even pictures of Hitler were bundled into the gunboats. Someone came up waving a long German sausage. They had found it all spread out, half eaten, on the mess-deck table for'ard: sausage, black bread, sauerkraut.
>
> 'Abandon the E-boat. Get back to your boats.'
>
> The order was quickly though reluctantly obeyed. We let go and stood off fifty yards to watch her end. Only just in time! She was going rapidly by the stern. Her bows were lifting, lifting, until for a few moments she hung vertical, her stern underwater, her bows pointed upwards, as if in supplication to the sky. Then quickly she sank and disappeared from view.[60]

Despite sinking three ships, it had been a disastrous night for Feldt's 2nd S-flotilla and, though they could not know it yet, marked their last torpedo sinkings for 1941. Once again the 4th S-flotilla was left to carry the battle, making their next successful attack on 24 November. Five boats lay silently in wait east of Orfordness until convoy FS54 (Phase 7) sailed slowly into view. Attacking at 0113hrs, LzS Bosse torpedoed 5,723-ton tanker SS *Virgilia*, setting the cargo of fuel oil and kerosene alight as the great ship sank by the stern. The burning cargo spilled into the sea and the ship's master, Captain N R Caird, piloted an asbestos-coated lifeboat into the flames to attempt to rescue survivors. A pair of escorting motor launches, *ML150* and *152*, joined in the rescue, but twenty-three of the tanker's crew still perished in the flames. Three minutes after *Virgilia* was hit, 1,984-ton Dutch collier SS *Groenlo* was torpedoed by ObltzS Karl Müller's *S52*, one crewman killed in the sinking and nine listed as missing. British freighter SS *Blairnevis* was hit by ObltzS Hans-Jürgen Meyer's *S51*, though the ship was successfully beached at Great Yarmouth roads, and later refloated and towed to London for repair. The S-boats broke away and returned individually to Rotterdam.

At the end of that same week, *S50*, *S51*, *S52* and *S64* returned to the sea area north of Cromer and laid eighteen TMB mines, lying in wait for convoy traffic once the mines had been fired and tubes reloaded with torpedoes. This time it was northbound FN64 (Phase 6) and Meyer's *S51* torpedoed 2,848-ton freighter SS *Cormarsh*, her entire crew rescued before she went down. Müller's *S52* hit and sank 2,840-ton SS *Empire Newcomen* five miles south of Dudgeon Light, the ship going down in only thirty seconds with eleven of her thirty-three crew still aboard. The final sinking was made by ObltzS Wilcke's *S64* when he hit the small 644-ton tanker SS *Asperity* travelling in ballast to Hull. Though the stricken tanker took minutes to sink, only four of her fourteen crewmen survived. Using their tried and tested tactics, the S-boats retreated behind smoke into the darkness, although they clashed with *MGB86* and *89* as they broke away, the latter taking damage and *S51* being hit, with one man lightly wounded after bullets struck the wheelhouse.

During December the weather deteriorated once more. The first of the damaged 2nd S-flotilla boats to return to operations, *S62* joined with *S50*, *S51* and *S64* of the 4th Flotilla to lay thirty LMA mines east of Orfordness. They were almost immediately successful as recorded by SKL on 3 December:

> According to a report by FdT radio monitoring seems to have confirmed success of the mines laid at buoy '54' by the 4th S-flotilla. Busy minesweeping could be observed along this part, of the convoy route during 2 Dec.[61]

It was in fact 6,968-ton tanker SS *British Captain* which had activated the mine, the ship recently arrived in British waters at the end of a voyage that had begun in Corpus Christi, via Halifax (as part of convoy SC53) to Methil Roads and bound ultimately to Shellhaven with 9,000 tons of motor spirits and fuel oil. From the crew of forty-four and ten gunners, one man was killed.

Minelaying thus became the focus of December's S-boat effort, though its regularity was dictated by the vagaries of winter weather. Although both flotillas sailed with combined mine and torpedo weapon loads, the combination of strong escorting forces and bad weather rendered them unable to launch any successful torpedo attacks. The mines, however, proved devastating. Over eight separate missions during December, thirty LMA, 110 LMB and thirty-two TMB mines were laid along the east-coast convoy routes and twelve merchant ships totalling 50,396 tons were sunk and forty-nine men killed. The Royal Navy's minesweeper HMT *Henriette* was also sunk near Spurn Point off the Humber, though with no casualties. During a minelaying mission on 22 December, LzS Walter Bosse's *S109* was part of a *Rotte* with *S24*, the two boats losing their way in the winter darkness and returning to harbour. Navigational problems were subsequently deemed regrettable, though acceptable to FdT, but the fact that Bosse returned with his mines unlaid was characterised as a 'lack of initiative' and he was relieved of his command.

The last month of the year saw the war waged by the Schnellboote widen as the newly inaugurated 8th S-flotilla headed north for the Norwegian Arctic and the 3rd S-flotilla deployed into the balmy waters of the Mediterranean. Requests were also recorded in SKL's War Diary on 16 December for the presence of S-boats in the new battleground of the Black Sea:

It is planned to transfer a number of vessels from their home bases in Germany to the southeastern theatre. Additionally, Group South requests action as follows:

a. Transfer of an experienced S-flotilla to the Black Sea as soon as ice conditions in the Danube permit. The Russian situation leads us to expect a continuation of operations in the spring, in which case the Army will be very much dependent on Navy support. Group South considers an S-flotilla of at least ten boats best suited to render such support in the most effective manner. Naval support will be indispensable to Army operations. However, without such a flotilla such support will be as inadequate as it was this year because of lack of sufficient forces. We might try to transfer the flotilla to the Aegean Sea as soon as the naval situation in the Black Sea has been brought under control in the course of the next year. If this is still impossible, the flotilla can always be withdrawn to the northern theatre of war via the Danube.[62]

Grossadmiral Raeder had been completely won over to the effectiveness and potential of the S-boats. On the basis of observations made during an inspection tour of flotillas in the Channel, he ordered plans to be instigated for an acceleration of Schnellboot construction which was to be put on a par with the building of U-boats. Correspondingly, they were to have equal emphasis as U-boats when it came to recruitment. On 15 December the chief of OKW's quartermaster division reported that, at the current rate of production, there would likely be a 50 per cent reserve stock of S-boat engines available by summer 1942. Finally, Raeder also ordered an

S115 leaving Kiel harbour in the wake of the light cruiser *Nürnberg*. Both the naval memorial and U-boat memorial are visible in the distance.

investigation into the S-boats' organisational hierarchy, deeming the service to be sufficiently important as to merit creation of an independent fleet command.

However, although Germany's military star appeared still to be in the ascendant, there were many who considered the war raging against the Soviet Union as barely winnable. The dreaded 'war on two fronts' had been wilfully opened by the gambler in the Reich's Chancellery while Britain remained far from defeated. Raeder had already known he was woefully unprepared for war in 1939 – regrettably believing Hitler's assurances that there would be no war before 1944. On 7 December 1941 the SKL War Diary made bitter reading.

This evening it became known that Japanese Armed Forces have opened hostilities against the USA and Britain. The attacks on the US bases in the Pacific and against Singapore were a complete surprise ... It remains to be seen what immediate repercussions this event will bring about. Undoubtedly few nations will stay out of this war in which all the great powers are now involved. The new order of things can therefore become a general one; this depends entirely on the success of the weapons, the ability of the various leaderships and the stamina of the peoples involved.

Therefore the day of 7 December 1941 marks not only the beginning of a new chapter in the history of war, but also opens an unobstructed global and supra-continental view of the future world order. The extension of this struggle to the seven seas and the participation in it of a third great sea power will cause every last European to realise the importance of overseas communications and sea power. It is that much more painful for the Naval Staff that the German Navy cannot be the one to deal the decisive blows whose historical significance is being felt already. For the Navy, the war with England began five years too soon in regard to materiel. For this reason the Navy is not even in a position to exploit decisively in the Atlantic and the Mediterranean the great advantage which the war in the Pacific brings.

The general sense of despondency emanating from those passages in the official SKL log were perhaps more relevant to the 'blue-water navies', but did sketch the same picture facing S-boats in the English Channel. While strength had been diverted east, pressure had relaxed somewhat on Great Britain. Correspondingly, a British build-up was well underway. By the beginning of 1942, as S-boats were diverted to more combat areas, the Royal Navy were able to field seven MTB flotillas, nine MGB flotillas and eighteen ML flotillas. Facing them were twelve serviceable S-boats.[63]

10
The Arctic

November 1941 – August 1942

T HE German invasion of Norway secured access to the vital Arctic iron ore mines on which wartime production depended. Despite severe losses to the Kriegsmarine, the Norwegian invasion had been a stunning coup involving the highest co-operation between the Wehrmacht's three service branches. However, once secured, defence of the region became an increasing problem for OKW as fears rose of a potential British offensive to recapture the northern Norwegian territories. On 4 March 1941 troops from the newly established British No 3 and 4 Commando as well as Royal Engineers and fifty-two men of the Royal Norwegian Navy completed Operation Claymore, a successful attack against factories on the Lofoten Islands which produced fish oil for use in the German armaments industry.[64] Claymore was the first of twelve Allied raids on Norwegian soil, four of them in 1941 alone.

Militarily, the Allied forces achieved results from these attacks, but psychologically they actually achieved far more. Hitler, supreme commander of Germany's armed forces, developed an increasing paranoia that Norway would fall to Allied invasion, stating during a naval conference on 22 January 1942 that he was convinced Britain and the United States, with assistance from Sweden, would make landings on northern Norway between Trondheim and Kirkenes. He declared that Norway was the 'zone of destiny' for Germany's war and demanded 'unconditional obedience to all his commands and wishes concerning the defence of this area.'[65] The SKL War Diary recorded:

> The Army and Luftwaffe have been ordered to strengthen their forces in Norway. The Führer demands also that the Kriegsmarine exert the utmost efforts to nip British plans in the bud. Naval vessels are to patrol approach

routes during non-flying weather. In case of an enemy landing all available naval forces are to be committed to the defence of Norway at the expense of operations in all other theatres except the Mediterranean. The Führer demands that each and every vessel be employed in Norway. He approves of the Naval Staff's plans for the use of battleships, pocket battleships, heavy cruisers, light naval forces, and S-boats; he insists on intensified submarine operations. The Führer shares the opinion of the Naval Staff concerning the improbability of an enemy landing in western France ... The Führer expressed his deep concern about the possibility that events in northern Norway might have catastrophic consequences, repeatedly <u>emphasising the need for utmost speed and extreme measures</u> [original emphasis].[66]

Hitler had already been frustrated in attempts to secure the northern extremities of the Arctic front line. As Barbarossa had begun, a three-stage attack code-named Operation Silverfox (*Silberfuchs*) had been launched by Generaloberst Eduard Dietl's German Alpine Corps Norway (*Gebirgskorps Norwegen*) supported by XXXVI Gebirgs Korps and Finnish III Corps against the Russian port of Murmansk. A distance of only 120km (75 miles) separated the German front line in Norway from Russia's only year-round ice-free port, but it was over some of the most inhospitable terrain on earth and the German advance soon stalled in the face of stubborn Soviet army resistance with naval support. In turn, the Germans required supply by sea, a route attacked by freshly deployed Royal Navy forces within the Barents Sea. The land attack devolved into trench warfare that would see no real movement until 1944.

The sole part of Silverfox that had proceeded according to plan was the occupation of the Petsamo nickel mines by German forces and by September 1941 Hitler ordered coastal defences strengthened in the region to help hold the mines against any counter-attack. Amongst the provisions for such increased forces was the attachment of an S-boat unit to light forces already based at Kirkenes. To this end, the 8th S-flotilla was established on 19 September 1941 under the command of Knight's Cross winner Kptlt Georg Christiansen and placed under the control of Admiral Norway just under a month later. Freshly overhauled, *S42*, *S44*, *S45* and *S46* gathered in Kiel on the first day of November and eleven days later began their trek northward, motoring first to Bergen, from where they were taken under tow in order to spare the S-boats' engines. By 2 December the flotilla and tender *Adolf Lüderitz* departed Aalesund, arriving in Trondheim two days later. There they were joined by the depot ship *Tanga*, also headed to Kirkenes to act as command ship and transporting torpedoes, depth charges and supplies for use by Christiansen's unit. Supporting units also sailed to Norway: freighter *Larsen* to Trondheim where it underwent conversion to a workshop ship; the steamer *Herösand* arriving for transformation to torpedo arsenal and balancing station. Both vessels would join the Arctic S-boats. *Tanga* proceeded ahead of the 8th S-flotilla, sailing in company with destroyers despatched to reinforce the Arctic front. Christiansen's flotilla experienced frequent delays due to bad weather, arriving in Tromsø on 15 December under escort by destroyers *Z25* and *Z27* where they remained during weeks of heavy weather.

Boats of the 8th S-flotilla with their tender *Adolf Lüderitz* in Semske Fjord during January 1942, part of what would ultimately be a pointless deployment.

On Boxing Day, British commandos attacked the Lofoten Islands as part of Operation Anklet, more commandos landing the next day at Vågsøy in Operation Archery. Local Kriegsmarine forces were immediately placed on high alert and ordered to intercept supporting British naval units. At 1206hrs the 8th Destroyer Flotilla and the 8th S-flotilla received orders to patrol west of the Lofoten Islands, although the S-boats were not underway until four hours later, by which time enemy contact was thought unlikely and the flotilla recalled. The sum total of their commitment was *S45* scraping the shallow fjord bottom and sustaining enough damage to necessitate shipyard work in Harstad. The following day, after British landings in Vågsøy, Commanding Admiral, Norway, posted the 8th S-flotilla to Narvik in readiness for potential action.

> The Commanding Admiral, Norway as well as Group North analyse the situation as follows:
>
> The foregoing events do not point to a large scale operation. They are, rather, a series of larger raids directed against the focal points of our trade routes off Narvik and near Bergen. It is their aim to destroy our outposts and batteries, hamper and temporarily disrupt our trade. These raids are staged for propaganda and prestige reasons, as well as for the purpose of reconnoitring the terrain, the state of the defences, and of alertness, with view to a subsequent establishment of bridgeheads from which to disrupt and cut the supply routes. The Naval Staff agrees with this analysis.[67]

S42, *S44* and *S46* arrived in Narvik with their tender at 1600hrs on 28 December, refuelling before the S-boats headed to sea once more to operate against four British destroyers reported in Ofotenfjord. However, bad weather closed in once more and the hunt was abandoned, *S42* and *S44* colliding, damaging the former's forecastle and lowering the flotilla's fully operational strength to two boats.

Hitler then made a momentous decision for the Kriegsmarine. Fears of further blows to German national prestige should any more capital ships be lost in the Atlantic had increased dramatically following the sinking of the *Bismarck*. Now, with absolute certainty that Norway was targeted for invasion, he ordered Raeder to bring the battleships *Scharnhorst* and *Gneisenau*, as well as the heavy cruiser *Prinz Eugen*, back to Norway from their current location in Brest, France. Their commitment in the defence of the Norwegian coast was of paramount importance, according to Hitler, therefore they were ordered to attempt a breakthrough of the English Channel. If this was rendered unfeasible, then he threatened to have them decommissioned and their weapons dismounted for use in establishing coastal batteries in Norway, an incensed Raeder arguing forcefully against the idea. Operation Cerberus the celebrated 'Channel Dash' – was the result.

The beginning of 1942 brought fresh instructions for the 8th S-flotilla to proceed in company with the 8th Destroyer Flotilla to Vardø, the easternmost town in Norway. This was to be the S-boats' Arctic base.

Tender *Adolf Lüderitz* began the voyage on the afternoon of 3 January, both operational S-boats already sailing from Tromsø to Honningsvaag and then onwards the following morning. *S44* and *S46* reached Vardø in Finnmark on 6 January, laid up for two days for maintenance and were then forced to remain in harbour by high winds sweeping across the barren Varanger Peninsula. A high sea ran directly into the unsheltered harbour and it quickly became apparent that, although the port was ice-free all year round due to the North Atlantic drift, it was totally unsuitable as a flotilla base. Additionally, they also attracted the attention of Russian bombers who, though relatively ineffectual, added to an already moribund atmosphere amongst the S-boat men. On 12 January they relocated to the port of Vadsø on the southern coast of the Varanger Peninsula and more sheltered from the elements, evidenced by birch forests that dominated the surrounding countryside.

Elsewhere in Norway, the elderly *S15* was despatched from Bergen in company with torpedo boat *Zick* (*V5501*, ex-Norwegian *Trygg*) to hunt for the cruiser HMS *Sheffield* and destroyers HM Ships *Inglefield* and *Intrepid* which had shelled the town of Floeröy as part of the raiding Operation Kitbag, again destroying fish-oil processing plants. The German search was unsuccessful.

S-boats put out for another fruitless mission in Norwegian waters. The war largely bypassed the boats committed in defence of phantom invasions of Scandinavia by the Allies, who were grinding down the S-boats within the English Channel.

By this stage MGK North (Generaladmiral Carls) had requested the permanent stationing of twelve S-boats within the Arctic Circle, a request refused on the grounds that there simply weren't enough S-boats to go round. Carls' justification remained that, even if hampered by the kind of ice that inhibited peacetime shipping, merchant vessels laden with supplies for Russia could still pass through the White Sea and an extensive minelaying programme was planned by Commanding Admiral Norway (Generaladmiral Boehm) which included six offensive mine fields off Kola Bay, three to be laid by destroyers, three by S-boats.

By 28 January the sea at Vadsø had frozen over and the 8th S-flotilla was forced to relocate once more, this time to Semske Fjord near Kirkenes. Two fruitless torpedo operations had been mounted in the perpetual darkness of polar winter, neither sighting any enemy units. Conditions aboard the boats at sea were barely tolerable: flak weapons, depth charges and mine rails all totally iced over and unserviceable, and men forced to frequently change watches in the sub-zero temperatures. Aboard the tender *Adolf Lüderitz* things were at least comfortable, but the interminable darkness and lack of diversions ashore when off-duty did little to improve spirits among Christiansen's men. Even their diet began to suffer as supplies from Germany dried up and convoys bringing fresh produce were increasingly intercepted by the British. Bartering fresh fish locally in exchange for schnapps at least kept a portion of their menu away from reconstituted dried rations, but a lack of fruit and vegetables contributed to a general decline in health.

Reinforcing failure, Hitler's implacable desire to have more surface units transferred to Norway resulted in a recommendation that 1st S-flotilla be sent there upon completion of Operation Korsika (one of a confusing array of code names for what would become known under the umbrella term Operation Cerberus), rather than the planned flotilla assignment to the Black Sea. Meanwhile the 8th S-flotilla was to be reinforced to eight boats. Lying completely idle until 15 March, the first mission was minelaying off the Arctic coast, abandoned after four hours in storm conditions. Four boats successfully escorted minelayer *Ulm* on 19 March to the Bantos A minefield sown near Helnes Lighthouse on the North Cape. Finally, on 15 February, the decision was made not to divert the 1st S-flotilla, but rather Kptlt Albrecht Obermaier's 6th S-flotilla, engaged at that time in Channel operations. Obermaier's unit was withdrawn from the battle and ordered to transfer with tender *Tsingtau* to the Lofoten–Narvik area. Harstad was, at first, considered the optimal flotilla berth until Commanding Admiral

S-boat engine rooms were incredibly noisy environments for crewmen, although in the harsh weather of the Arctic the resultant heat from the diesel engines would no doubt have been welcome.

Norway designated the port at Svolvær on Austvågøya Island as flotilla base. Obermaier's flotilla was ordered to remain on constant alert, anchorages changing periodically so as to diminish the chance of enemy interference.

On 16 March the first four boats from 6th S-flotilla put to sea from Heligoland bound for Stavanger, where they joined torpedo boats and three U-boats in an attempted interception of ten Norwegian ships breaking out of the Baltic, following months of sheltering in the Swedish port of Gothenburg, the subject of bitter international diplomatic wrangles.[68] Although Obermaier's boats put to sea during the early morning of 1 April to join the blockading forces, they were forced back to Stavanger by bad weather. Following this Norwegian attempt to break out of the Baltic, the 6th S-flotilla was transferred to Kristiansand South to patrol the Skagerrak, half of the boats constantly kept at two hours' alert while in harbour. By 16 April orders were received to resume the march north, the first four boats arriving in Svolvær on 27 April. By 14 May the flotilla comprised *S69, S71, S73, S74, S75, S76, S113* (*S114* absent although on the flotilla strength, commissioned on 23 April) and were detailed to make an initial reconnaissance mission from their new home port. Oberleutnant zur See Walter Schnebel's *S113* ran aground on rocks and was towed to Trondheim for shipyard repair. It was an inauspicious start that set the pattern for their deployment in the Narvik region.

In Kirkenes, Kptlt Christiansen repeatedly reported the unsuitability of S-boats within the Arctic circle. What few missions they had been able to sail had been completely ineffectual, not a single torpedo fired or mine laid as the boats wrestled with conditions beyond their capabilities. Their use as convoy escorts and harbour protection harkened back to the war's early days when the role of the fast attack craft was little understood; the wear and tear on engine parts and crews far outweighed what meagre use they were, tasks far better suited to converted trawlers of the Vorpostenboot flotillas and U-Boot Jäger. Finally, his views found an ally as the newly created Führer der Schnellboote, KK Rudolf Petersen, added his weight to the argument.[69] On 18 May Petersen proposed the withdrawal of all four boats of the 8th S-flotilla (which had never been brought up to their planned strength of eight) and the tender *Adolf Lüderitz*, and their return to the war in the Channel that was currently being fought by only seven serviceable S-boats. Eventually, Admiral Polar Seas relented, noting in a study submitted to SKL that 'their use is greatly restricted during the period of the polar day; there is an urgent need for S-boats in other theatres of war; the training of S-boats in home waters depends on S-boat tenders.'[70] SKL nonetheless maintained that the boats of 6th S-flotilla remain where they were as a defensive weapon against the spectre of Allied invasion.

To keep an S-boat presence alive in the far north, MGK Nord were authorised to split the deployment of 6th S-flotilla, five boats transferring to Semske Fjord to take over the post left by the departing 8th S-flotilla. They also swapped tenders, as *Adolf Lüderitz* was equipped with powerful radio gear needed as a repeat station for short-wave traffic from Arctic U-boats until an equivalent radio station could be built ashore. *Tanga* was scheduled to replace *Lüderitz* at some point, to allow the ship to return to Germany for overhaul, *Carl Peters* the only dedicated S-boat tender available to boats of the 5th and 7th S-flotillas training in German waters at that time. On 20 June *S71*, *S73*, *S74*, *S75* and *S114* accompanied *Tsingtau* to Kirkenes, *Adolf Lüderitz* officially being taken on the 6th S-flotilla strength and *Tsingtau* released for the return to Germany. *S69*, *S113* (still in the shipyard undergoing repair) and *S76* remained near Narvik, the latter designated *Führerboot* for the trio. The four 8th S-flotilla boats arrived in Kiel on 6 July where they were placed into shipyards for repairs and overhaul that lasted six weeks and included the installation of 40mm Bofors cannon on the stern platform. The flotilla was disbanded on 12 July, *S42* and *S45* transferred to the 4th S-flotilla, *S46* to the 2nd S-flotilla and *S44* to the 6th whose tenure in Norway was also coming to an end.

On 23 July SKL put forward the return of 6th S-flotilla to the west, no objections raised by MGK Nord other than keeping *Adolf Lüderitz* and its radio capabilities until a suitable replacement was found. An expected operation, involving the S-boats, to land Wehrmacht troops on the Rybachy Peninsula and kick-start the land attack against Murmansk (Operation *Wiesengrund*) had been postponed to March and gradually edged towards

S-boats moving along the rugged Norwegian coast. Impossible to secure against British commando operations, S-boats reacted too late to intervene in any actions in Norway. Only one ship was torpedoed by the sole weapon fired by Norwegian-based S-boats, and this was an accident.

final cancellation in 1944. With no useful role left, the flotilla was transferred back to Germany, arriving on 16 August and beginning weeks of overhaul. Designated already for operations in the Channel, MGK Nord appealed for the flotilla to be deployed in the Baltic to frustrate a feared Soviet naval breakout, though ultimately the request was denied. The battle in the English Channel was raging and Germany's S-boats had lost the upper hand. The deployment of S-boats in northern Norway had tied up valuable resources which could have been better used in just about any other theatre of action. Not a single weapon had been fired by the twelve boats, which had remained penned in harbour for most of their time. Unfortunately for Petersen's hard-pressed S-boats, it was not the last time that Norway would feature on their list of priorities.

11
The Channel

January 1942 – December 1942

NEW Year's Eve 1941 in the North Sea found the 2nd S-flotilla laying mines west of Cromer Knoll. In poor visibility no torpedo operations were possible, although two S-boats were unsuccessfully chased by free-ranging enemy destroyers. By 0730hrs all boats were home. Twice more during January Kptlt Klaus Feldt's flotilla was engaged in minelaying, uneventfully on 2 January and again on 18 January, split into three groups, the third dropping their LMB-3 mines under fire from patrolling destroyers. *S39* was narrowly missed by the falling shells, the attacker's muzzle flashes not even visible in the limited visibility of a foggy night.

It was a clear indication to the Germans of the presence of radar aboard British destroyers, heralding difficulties for the S-boats. Radar-equipped Whitley bombers had also been added to British patrols along the east coast. Wing Commander J Constable-Roberts was RAF Liaison Officer to Admiral Ramsay's Dover Command, as part of the staff of 16 (Reconnaissance) Group. In October 1941 he had initiated the first use of radar-controlled aircraft to defend convoy traffic, when six Bristol Beaufort torpedo bombers had been directed by the Chain Home radar station at Swingate. Now he had escalated his armoury to airborne radar which, in British eyes, resulted in a marked decrease in German minelaying. Nevertheless, in total, seventy-eight mines were sown near Cromer during January, February adding another 131 to this number, laid by the 2nd and Kptlt Niels Bätge's 4th S-flotilla.

On 18 January the 6th S-flotilla transferred to Ostend, the 4th to Boulogne and the 2nd from the iced waters of the Meuse River to the incomplete base at Ijmuiden. Torpedo operations were carried out when weather permitted during January, but with no success; brief brushes with

Admiral Otto Schniewind (SKL chief of staff) decorates S-boat men with the Iron Cross, first class, in Boulogne.

MTBs, an unsuccessful attack on a destroyer and a failed attack on convoy traffic near Great Yarmouth made for a poor start to the year.

On 1 February the 2nd and 6th S-flotillas made a torpedo patrol in difficult weather, ObltzS Opdenhoff's *S62* intercepting a darkened Dutch steam trawler and sinking her with artillery fire after taking eleven crew prisoner. Five nights later boats of the 4th S-flotilla reported detection by British radar eleven miles off South Foreland, the crews startled by what they perceived to be 'radiations of enemy origin causing our boats to emit a clearly visible, glaring, phosphorescent glow from aerials, rails, and other wet protrusions', later explained as the natural atmospheric phenomenon, St Elmo's fire.[71]

Kapitänleutnant Bätge's 4th S-flotilla was earmarked for a more audacious Kriegsmarine plan during February. Bätge, who had become the latest recipient of a Knight's Cross within the S-boat service on 4 January 1942, had his flotilla bolstered by *S39* and *S108* from 2nd S-flotilla and *S69* from the 6th to reach an operational strength of ten boats. They were ordered to provide flank coverage for Operation Cerberus, the dash through the English Channel by capital ships *Scharnhorst*, *Gneisenau* and *Prinz Eugen* in response to Hitler's command for the ships to return from France to Norway. The three capital ships were shepherded from Brest harbour at 2114hrs on 11 February by an impressive covering force. As well as a flotilla of destroyers, they were accompanied at different stages of the voyage by three torpedo-boat flotillas, minesweepers and a total of 252 fighter aircraft and thirty-two twin-engine night fighters. The 4th S-flotilla sailed to join the armada on 12 February and 2nd S-flotilla were put on instant readiness in harbour, while 6th S-flotilla sortied in two groups on unsuccessful torpedo missions off Folkestone and Beachy Head in an attempted distraction. Bätge's boats put to sea from Boulogne on the code words 'Aurora 123' in sea state 5–6, each boat fully armed with torpedoes and extra flak ammunition. Their forepeaks had been painted bright yellow to aid identification by the strong Luftwaffe presence. For their part, the British response to the bold German plan was late and badly co-ordinated. German forces weren't detected until they had already steamed for twelve hours, coastal artillery finally opening fire but blindly as they were unable to observe and adjust their fall of shot, all of which went wide. Poorly co-ordinated attacks by RAF aircraft achieved nothing, although a Spitfire badly wounded two men aboard *S64*, lightly injuring one other. The forward tank room was set on fire and ObltzS Friedrich Wilhelm Wilcke was ordered to take *S64* back to port.

Six obsolete Swordfish torpedo aircraft attempted to attack the capital ships; Vizeadmiral Otto Ciliax – in overall command of the operation from the bridge of the *Scharnhorst* – was quoted as saying that they were 'piloted by men whose bravery surpasses any other action by either side that day.' All six were shot down long before they posed any threat, one by the flak gunners aboard *S69*. Five British MTBs tried to break through the S-boat shield at 1344hrs but were all forced away with gunfire damage, launching torpedoes at extreme range more in hope than trust.

Cerberus was successful: *Scharnhorst* and *Gneisenau* were both damaged by mines in German waters, but otherwise untouched by the British. It was a major blow to British prestige, *The Times* newspaper editorial trumpeting that 'Vice Admiral Ciliax has succeeded where the Duke of Medina Sidonia failed. Nothing more mortifying to the pride of our seapower has happened since the seventeenth century.' However, although it was a tactical victory for the Germans, it was a strategic defeat. The threat posed by capital ships capable of Atlantic raiding had been removed as they sailed into ignominious unemployment in Norwegian waters and, ultimately, inglorious ends.

An alternating routine of torpedo missions and minelaying began almost as soon as Cerberus was completed. The waters from Dover to Dungeness and North Sea convoy route within the Smith's Knoll–Ordfordness area were targeted, using timer-equipped mines for the first time. The S-boats faced stormy weather and increasingly active and accurate defences, continuously spotted and illuminated with star-shells.

An operation mounted by two groups of boats from the 2nd S-flotilla took place on the night of 19 February. The first group of two *Rotten* (*S70* and *S105* in the first, *S104* and *S111* in the second) laid twenty-four mines before encountering destroyers – missed by a snapped double torpedo shot as the boats laid smoke and broke for home. The destroyers had been ready and waiting for the S-boats after detection and translation of their radio transmissions by onboard Headache operators. The second group comprised *S39*, *S53* and *S108*, likewise engaged on laying eighteen mines, before they too were surprised by three enemy destroyers. HM Ships *Mendip*, *Pytchley* and *Holderness* had been convoy escort but homed in using Headache intelligence. The S-boats immediately began laying smoke as they attempted to escape the glare of star-shells. As the trio turned to speed away, Kptlt Felix Zymalkowski's *S39* was rammed by ObltzS Peter Block's *S53*, both boats momentarily locked together and tracing an arc through the water before they broke apart. *S39* was badly damaged, the hull side smashed in and compartment IV flooded. To minimise further flooding, Zymalkowski fired both torpedoes and jettisoned smoke buoys, auxiliary machinery and radio equipment as *S39* set course for home, finally reaching Ijmuiden at 0930hrs after a nerve-wracking 10-knot journey.

In the meantime, Block's *S53* had lost the majority of its bow in the collision and was unable to restart stalled engines. Disabled and left wallowing in the swell, the S-boat was approached by HMS *Holderness*, with guns trained and ready to fire until the British crew saw the Kriegsmarine ensign being lowered. A boarding party led by Midshipman Ditcham leapt across the gap between destroyer and S-boat, making their way towards the bridge when ObltzS Peter Block and his wheelhouse disintegrated in a sheet of flame. Scuttling charges had exploded, Ditcham and his party narrowly escaping injury. With little time before the remaining ammunition and stored torpedoes exploded in the spreading flames, they transferred surviving prisoners to *Holderness*; hose pipes from the destroyer trained on the torpedo tubes as flames licked around them. Finally, she backed away as flak rounds exploded, *S53* disappearing in a final blast as torpedoes ignited. Ditcham later recalled his impressions of the German prisoners:

We found that we had eighteen prisoners including one officer, Otto, who was very glum and would eat nothing. He had probably told his girlfriend that he would be back in the morning. Their uniforms were very inferior serge but they had good leather sea boots and soft leather wind-proof greatcoats.[72]

The remaining seven of the crew, including the skipper, were lost with their boat, German listening service, B-Dienst, intercepting a radio message from HMS *Holderness* confirming the loss.

Peter Block's death started a small storm within the Kriegsmarine recruiting service. The U-boat arm had long held dominance in the recruitment of young officers. However, S-boat action required extreme physical and mental fortitude and ability, frequently taking place at high speeds in darkness. The question had vexed FdT whether to relieve those commanders deemed inferior (as had been the case with *S109*'s LzS Walter Bosse during December) and therefore run the risk of an inactive boat, as the availability of trained skippers always lagged behind required numbers, or to let the commander in question continue and risk not only his boat and crew, but also the fighting cohesion of the flotilla. Requests made to the Kriegsmarine's personnel department to forward only experienced destroyer or torpedo boat men for training as potential S-boat commanders were unable to be met, the casualty rate within the U-boats already a steady drain on available candidates. On operations, new commanders were generally monitored by the flotilla commander who would sail aboard the *Führerboot*, but the exigencies of wartime rendered this practice difficult to continue when those skippers judged of average ability would require years of training to fully master the skills attained by the early S-boat captains. It was, of course, no different within the U-boat service, as surviving veterans rotated ashore to attempt to pass on their hard-won knowledge. Sadly, Kptlt Klaus Feldt, commander of 2nd S-flotilla, had already perceived weaknesses in Peter Block's abilities while sailing in his instructional capacity. However, circumstances had forced Feldt to let fate play its part in Block's future.

These circumstances played a pivotal role in the creation of the *Schnellbootsschulflottille*, established at Swinemünde in July 1942 under the command of Kptlt Opdenhoff. There, using older boats withdrawn from combat, veteran instructors would take on the training of commanders and replacement personnel for all skills aboard the S-boats, the priority not being the creation of a complete crew, but the accumulation of a pool of individual replacements who could be despatched to the front as required. Eventually, the training flotilla would comprise sixteen boats – *S19*, *S20*, *S21*, *S22*, *S24*, *S25*, *S50*, *S95*, *S103*, *S105*, *S107*, *S108*, *S109*, *S115*, *S118*, *S123* – and the three tenders *Tanga*, *Adolf Lüderitz* and *Carl Peters*.

During February and into March S-boat mines took a steady toll on enemy shipping: 1,796-ton Swede SS *Thyra* sunk near Great Yarmouth on 28 February, 589-ton tanker *Audacity* on 1 March, 6,675-ton tanker *Frumention* from convoy FS40 (Phase 8) on 4 March near Orfordness and 4,270-ton steamer SS *Cressdene* twelve days later. However, torpedo attacks had yielded nothing as the Royal Navy was able to keep the S-boats at bay. As pressure mounted on the Channel flotillas, Hitler's obsession with defending Norway against a phantom attack weakened an already difficult position. On 15 February Kptlt Albrecht Obermaier's 6th S-flotilla was ordered to the Narvik region, sailing from Ostend to Heligoland on 28 February before moving onward for overhaul and the voyage north.

Alternating mine and torpedo missions continued unsuccessfully until well into March. British MTBs and MGBs had become bolder in their efforts to interdict German coastal convoys, particularly tanker traffic from the west. Consideration was given to redirecting some of the scant S-boat strength to escort and protection duties, resisted by FdT, who reasoned that pressure on British merchant shipping was of greater importance, requesting instead that the Luftwaffe increase the tempo of their attacks against British MTB bases. On the night of 9 March the 2nd S-flotilla operated against convoys off Lowestoft while the 4th S-flotilla prowled the Dungeness convoy route, also providing escort for German supply ships. Neither flotilla sighted targets. The boats of Bätge's 4th S-flotilla were unsuccessfully shelled by British coastal artillery while escorting a German tanker and, more gallingly, were also fired on by German patrol vessels off Gris Nez without having been asked for a recognition signal. ObltzS Götz Frhr von Mirbach's *S48* was hit four times in the port side, though without injury to any crewmen, before the ceasefire order was received aboard the Vorpostenboote.

The following night Feldt's 2nd S-flotilla was once again patrolling with torpedoes, finding southbound FS46 (Phase 8) in the early hours of 11 March. The *Rotte S70* and *S105* launched double torpedo shots at what they took to be a '3,000 and another 2,000-ton freighter' respectively, as escorting destroyers and gunboats fired star-shells overhead. Claiming both ships hit and sunk, the S-boats retreated under smokescreen and successfully returned to base. The only confirmed casualty was the

951-ton steamer ss *Horseferry*, hit by ObltzS Hans Helmut Klose's *S70* while carrying coal from Tyne to London. Eleven men went down with their ship.

Both flotillas were in operation on the night of 14 March. The 4th S-flotilla unsuccessfully attacked northbound convoy FN7 (Phase 8) at buoy 54E. Surrounded by an imposing force of seven destroyers as they attempted to attack before midnight, ObltzS Hans Jürgen Meyer's *S51* was hit several times by 40mm pom-pom rounds, wounding five men severely and several more lightly. ObltzS Albert Causemann's crew on *S110* also suffered some minor injuries from the same fire, the unusually low visibility at that time probably saving both S-boats from more significant damage.

Simultaneously, the 2nd S-flotilla attacked southbound convoy FS49 (Phase 8) at buoy 57E, two of the S-boats blundering into the convoy in the early morning fog. ObltzS Ullrich Roeder's *S104* was quickest off the mark and fired two torpedo shots at a 'two-stack enemy destroyer', hitting and sinking HMS *Vortigern*. The V-class destroyer, a veteran of this and the previous world war, sank with 110 of her crew, the highest Royal Navy loss of life while escorting east-coast convoys. Her escort partner, corvette HMS *Guillemot*, rescued only fourteen survivors. Roeder's boat had received a direct 5in shell hit on the bridge, though miraculously it had failed to detonate. One German crewman was injured by machine-gun fire before the S-boats disappeared into the darkness.

Making their way either in *Rotten* or individually back to Ostend, all boats except *S111* had been accounted for by 0900hrs. Due to the proximity of their base to the enemy, the boats of the 2nd S-flotilla were particularly vulnerable to aggressive British attacks. So it was that intercepted radio communications from British MGBs scrambled to head off the returning S-boats revealed a battle between *S111* and *MGB88*, *87* and *91* of the Royal Navy's 7th MGB Flotilla. Initially mistaking the MGBs for German air-sea rescue boats, ObltzS Paul Poppe and his crew were caught off-guard as the British attacked at speed with all guns blazing. Poppe and his bridge crew, including a commander under instruction, ObltzS Friedrich-Wilhelm Joppig, were killed by the intense gunfire that penetrated all compartments, fourteen men dead in total and the boat disabled and drifting. Three compartments were flooded as a British boarding party immediately rushed aboard *S111* and proceeded to take the remaining sixteen crew captive, six of them wounded, three severely. The Royal Navy ensign was hoisted above the Kriegsmarine flag and *MGB88* took the boat in tow as they tried to return their prize to England.

Meanwhile, Kptlt Feldt led *S104*, *S62* and *S29* back to sea in search of their missing flotilla-mate. By 1100hrs the three MGBs and their captive were sighted and the S-boats laid on maximum speed to attack. Knowing they were outgunned, the British boats cut the tow and abandoned *S111*, having already stripped it of every valuable piece of equipment and intelligence they could find, including maps, weapons, torpedo targeting gear and signal books.

Shots were seen to hit at least one of the MGBs before pursuit was abandoned because of engine failure. Feldt led his own boarding party, which found the seven dead men still aboard and the boat emptied. *S111* was taken in tow as *S105* and *S108* arrived as reinforcements. With no Luftwaffe cover, the slow-moving entourage was attacked by eleven Spitfires, all S-boats taking damage during the half-hour battle that ensued, wounding five sailors badly and another eight lightly, before Feldt opted to abandon the tow and *S111* sank in 23m (75ft) of turbid water. The Spitfires withdrew as Luftwaffe fighters put in a belated appearance, covering the S-boats during the last stage of their return to harbour. It would be four weeks before any of the boats were repaired and declared operational once more.

The increased offensive activity by British coastal forces within the English Channel was acutely felt by the Kriegsmarine in the first months of 1942. MTBs and destroyers were attacking German convoys and laying more minefields than at any point thus far. S-boats became vulnerable to ambush along approach and return routes from operations. It became evident that the intensifying of Luftwaffe harbour raids was having no discernible effect at sea. Providing cover for S-boats became a distinct problem. A proposal to provide torpedo boats as S-boat protection was turned down by MGK West, who judged them not only vulnerable to mines, but also outgunned by British destroyers. Räumboote were also considered, the new R-boats bristling with flak weapons. Although there were already too few of them available to escort 'exceptionally vital convoys' from the west, Führer der Schnellboote agreed that R-boats were ideal to rendezvous with returning S-boats and provide flak coverage, either kept at immediate readiness in harbour or on station along the S-boats' planned routes.

Minelaying was also called into question during February and March. As boats of the 4th S-flotilla laid mines between Dover and Dungeness, their own radio intelligence (*Funkaufklärung*) determined that British radar stations were accurately plotting the locations of the sown minefields, not only allowing them to be effectively swept but also rerouting convoy traffic to clear waters. On 23 February SKL noted that 'to judge from radar location of a British convoy on the evening of 22 February, the route from the mouth of the Thames River to the west which was used up until now has been shifted farther south, evidently due to our mine operations.'[73] FdT temporarily suspended further minelaying, although MGK West disagreed with his judgement, reasoning that even if the minefields were detected they would force merchant traffic wide of the coast, rendering them vulnerable to torpedo attack. It was only a brief respite in any case. Although operations by S-boats were severely limited due to bad weather, the sowing of mines was resumed on 3 April by both flotillas, sailing with combined torpedo and mine loads.

It had been one of the last major decisions made on behalf of the S-boats by Führer der Torpedoboote; the post abolished in April and amalgamated within the post of Führer der Zerstörer. Kapitän zur See Hans Bütow, who had been FdT since November 1939, became Chief of Staff at Marineoberkommando Öst. On 20 April KK Rudolf Petersen was named Führer der Schnellboote and the S-boat arm finally became autonomous. The FdS headquarters remained at Scheveningen from where FdT had operated and Petersen's chief of operations remained Kptlt Bernd Rebensburg who had fulfilled the role with FdT. It was unusual for a man

Korvettenkapitän Rudolf Petersen, Führer der Schnellboote.

of Petersen's relatively junior rank to hold this level of staff position within the Kriegsmarine, but his diligence and efficiency were exactly what the S-boat service required. He also attracted the ire of other naval departments – as well as that of future Oberbefehlshaber der Kriegsmarine Karl Dönitz – by his supreme commitment to the welfare of men within his command, even at the expense of perceived operational necessity. While Petersen exercised an overall say in all of the operational S-boats, his tactical control only concerned those deployed in the west – though still within the command sphere of MGK West; other theatres were directly controlled by regional naval commands.

During April the 2nd and 4th S-flotillas undertook four minelaying operations, an unfortunate Matrosengefreiter lost overboard when he became entangled in a mine on the night of 11 April. On 19 April Feldt's 2nd S-flotilla skirmished with destroyers, one boat slightly damaged, while two nights later it was the turn of Bätge's 4th S-flotilla to exchange fire with the enemy, three MGBs attacking the S-boats at close range off Nord-Hinder. One MGB took multiple hits while *S52* was also damaged before the action ended amidst drifting fog.

Bätge's flotilla transferred between ports four times during April and May, moving finally to Boulogne on a limited assignment to escort for the raider *Stier*. The day of the escort rendezvous Bätge's flotilla sailed in three *Rotten* from Ijmuiden and laid thirty-six UMB and LMB mines off Orfordness without incident, although radio monitoring aboard *S105* noted that the boats were continuously tracked by enemy radar, confirming fears that British forces were able to pinpoint and avoid or clear minefields.

In Germany, the auxiliary cruiser *Stier* known as Ship 23, had been readied for departure on a raiding mission into the South Atlantic. The last raider to break out from Germany, *Stier*, sailed under escort into the English Channel in stages. On 13 May, 4th S-flotilla served as remote escort after having completed its minelaying mission. Between 0200hrs and 0300hrs *Stier* and its close escort of torpedo boats *Kondor*, *Falke*, *Seeadler* and *Iltis* and ships of the 2nd Minesweeping Flotilla came under long-range coastal artillery fire, located and tracked by British radar which homed numerous MGB and MTBs on to the small convoy within the Dover Strait. In driving rain and heavy seas the British made the best use of their radar advantage, and torpedoed and sank both *Seeadler* and *Iltis*, though not before *MTB219* was sighted by *Iltis* and destroyed. German minesweepers reported scoring several hits on attacking craft before the action ended. Bätge's S-boats arrived too late to take part in the fighting, though they rescued eighty-three German and three British survivors. *Stier* reached Boulogne unscathed, proceeding onward to Royan and ultimately the South Atlantic.[74]

For the remainder of May and early June, both flotillas continued minelaying operations from Rotterdam and then Boulogne. As nights grew shorter, there were insufficient hours of darkness for S-boats to travel to their east-coast hunting grounds and so the focus shifted west into the Channel. Although the British were able to pinpoint German minelaying, MGK West still considered the task valuable, if only to divert British efforts to minesweeping rather than the interdiction of German supply convoys. By mid June, both flotillas were only able to field seven operational S-boats; the remainder were under repair or unable to sail due to a shortage of trained skippers. Petersen and his staff moved from Scheveningen to Wimereux on 6 June to exercise closer control over the combat boats, as well as strengthen communications with local Luftwaffe units.

At FdS headquarters a refined tactic had been developed for convoy location and engagement. Known as *Stichansatz* (the stitch), it relied on current and accurate B-Dienst or Luftwaffe reports of a convoy's co-ordinates, or expected location. A small B-Dienst unit was permanently stationed at FdS headquarters from 1 August. Proceeding towards calculated target area, S-boats would deploy in *Rotten*, dispersing approximately ten miles from and parallel to the convoy's path, keeping a two-mile gap between each *Rotte*. Creeping toward the convoy lane, the S-boats would then cut engines and lay adrift waiting for targets. If nothing was seen within a predetermined time period, the S-boats would carry out search patterns in either direction of the convoy's line of travel. The tactic was not profoundly different from previously developed methods, but entailed a higher level of organisation and improved co-ordination with reconnaissance and intelligence sources.

Minelaying continued throughout June, newly commissioned *S78* sailing as reinforcement for the Channel boats from Rotterdam on the night of 26 June. At 0208hrs the following morning, the boat was attacked by a British night-fighter, with two men killed and eleven wounded. The boat itself was only lightly damaged and continued to Boulogne for minor repairs, one of the severely wounded men, FkGefr Gerhard Kröck, later dying of his injuries.

By the end of June both flotillas had relocated to Cherbourg to attack the Channel convoys streaming west and east. Kptlt Feldt took overall command of all five operational boats temporarily merged under the banner of 2nd S-flotilla, the number soon bolstered by others returning to action following repair. On 6 July the first use of the *Stichansatz* failed to locate the reported convoy as the few boats available had been spaced too close together and had therefore not covered enough search area. However, two nights later, a long-overdue success was achieved when they intercepted convoy WP183 travelling from Milford Haven to Portsmouth.

The eastbound convoy had been detected at 1715hrs by Junkers Ju88s of Aufklärungsgruppe (Reconnaissance Group) 123, lookouts aboard the convoy commodore's ship, SS *Kongshaug*, observing the distant aircraft, though unable to determine its type or nationality. However, intercepted convoy radio transmissions reporting the aircraft's presence gave B-Dienst confirmation of WP183's position and course, and by 2230hrs eight S-boats were headed at speed to lie in wait along the convoy's route. The Luftwaffe began harrying WP183, dropping flares and drawing anti-aircraft fire from the escorts as the S-boats homed in below. Kptlt Mirbach's *S48* was the first to fire, hitting 1,156-ton Norwegian freighter SS *Kongshaug*. The ship carried 1,250 tons of patent fuel and was torpedoed forward of the bridge on the port side. Although the skipper, Einar Apeland, ordered boats swung out and the ship abandoned, she sank so fast that the crew barely had time to jump overboard, eight of them going down with her, and the remainder later rescued by escorting destroyer HMS *Brocklesby*. Kapitänleutnant Zymalkowski's *S67* shot next. A single torpedo arced toward 6,766-ton tanker SS *Pomella* laden with crude oil, hitting the ship on the port side and killing six aboard as she listed over and settled onto the seabed of Lyme Bay, a second torpedo in her starboard hull making sure the tanker would sink. The 698-ton freighter SS *Bokn* was torpedoed by ObltzS Hans Helmut Klose's *S70*, the Norwegian freighter forced to sail past shipwrecked survivors before Klose's torpedo hit. Twelve men died with the ship as *Bokn* and its cargo of coal went to the bottom. Large 2,836-ton Dutch ship SS *Reggestrom*, crewed predominantly by Chinese merchantmen, was hit by two torpedoes and sunk by ObltzS Karl-Erhard Karcher's *S50*. The last merchant ship to be hit was 736-ton Norwegian collier SS *Rosten*, torpedoed by ObltzS Helmut Dross' *S109* and sinking immediately, the crew leaping overboard, to be rescued by SS *Gripfast*, which had narrowly avoided a torpedo-shot across her bow. ObltzS Peter Block, now skippering *S63*, also sank what he identified as a '1,100-ton tanker', but was in reality 314-ton escorting trawler HMT *Manor*; only one of the twenty crewmen survived, later rescued by HMT *Ruby*. Cyril Foale's small ship had gone under so fast that he had escaped through a submerged bridge window, becoming entangled in the wireless aerial before managing to break free and reach the surface, clinging to wreckage until pulled from the sea.

The attack had come as a surprise, the Luftwaffe not only successfully guiding the S-boats to WP183, but also acting as distraction. For the Allies it was a disastrous night, the convoy suffering severe casualties and completely scattered by morning. However, it did not end there, for the Luftwaffe returned the following day and six more ships were sent to the bottom. For Feldt's men it was a welcome break in weeks of meagre results from both mine and torpedo missions. However, it was only a brief respite from minelaying, with a dearth of Luftwaffe reconnaissance reports during following weeks. The Channel S-boats were at least returning to stronger numbers, the 5th S-flotilla confirmed for Channel commitment in July, rather than the originally planned deployment in Norway. Kapitänleutnant Bernd Klug's new flotilla had been training in German waters, and were in Boulogne by the month's end.

Meanwhile, Feldt was ordered to despatch three S-boats from Cherbourg to Guernsey for reconnaissance duties, temporarily stationed in St Peter Port. The mission was uneventful before their return to Cherbourg, twelve vessels of both the 4th and 5th S-flotilla taking their place in Guernsey. St Peter Port was considered for potential construction of another S-boat shelter, Petersen expressing a preference for the island port over MGK West's proffered St Malo. Ultimately, a compromise between FdT and MGK West was reached, with planned expansion of the Cherbourg bunker to be capable of accommodating thirty-four boats at any one time.

By the first week of August, Petersen had nineteen operational S-boats spread between three flotillas. An attempted attack on WP196 during the night of 3 August using the *Stichansatz* found the convoy, but failed to penetrate the strong escort force. Despite claims of three ships hit by *S63*, *S104* and *S110* totalling 5,000 tons, Allied records show no torpedo strikes on any of the freighters. Three nights later, twelve boats of 2nd and 4th S-flotillas put to sea to intercept WP197 reported by Luftwaffe reconnaissance aircraft, but failed to make contact, both *S64* and *S66* retiring with engine problems and *S110* suffering rudder damage.

As summer gave way to autumn and the nights lengthened, Petersen transferred the flotillas eastward once again, to refocus attention on the thicker convoy traffic flowing along England's east coast. Bätge's 4th S-flotilla transferred to Rotterdam on 13 August, while Feldt's 2nd S-flotilla began moving in stages to Ijmuiden during the following day. Kptlt Albrecht Obermaier's 5th S-flotilla remained spread between Cherbourg, St Peter Port and Boulogne. Petersen and his staff returned to Scheveningen in order to maintain close contact with the focus of the S-boat offensive in 'E-boat Alley'. Initially, the S-boats laid more mines: 5th S-flotilla in Lyme Bay, the 2nd and 4th S-flotillas east of Southwold, a single steamer, 2,820-ton ss *Kyloe* damaged by the latter on 25 August.

Meanwhile, German intelligence had reported a perceived build-up of radio traffic and landing craft in England's southern ports, with aircraft concentrating in the south and southeast. Fears of an attempted Allied landing on the French coast grew in August, until it materialised on the morning of 19 August. The 5th S-flotilla had carried out a minelaying mission, dropping twenty-four UMB mines in Lyme Bay, and returned to Guernsey when reports of Allied troops storming ashore at Dieppe were received. The S-boats played no part in the defeat of the Allied landing, boats of 2nd and 4th S-flotillas sailing a torpedo mission in British coastal waters, with *S48* hit in the bow by destroyer gunfire before retreating. S-boat commanders had been ordered to avoid contact, where possible, with enemy military vessels and to save their ammunition for merchants. During the return voyage *S81* rescued a Polish Spitfire pilot who had been shot down by a Bf109 during the heavy aerial fighting that accompanied Operation Jubilee at Dieppe, the Allied landing defeated by the afternoon of 19 August with heavy Canadian and British casualties.

During September Kptlt Albrecht Obermaier's 6th S-flotilla returned from its pointless diversion to Norway. With additional boats and crews urgently requested for the 1st S-flotilla fighting in the Black Sea and the 5th S-flotilla remaining in the Cherbourg area, at first it appeared that Obermaier's unit would be plundered for reserves. However, FdS Petersen requested that the flotilla remain intact and be based in the principal zone of S-boat operations, the Hoofden area. So it was that Obermaier's first two refitted boats were operational in Ijmuiden during the beginning of September, the remainder following shortly as they left German shipyards. On 7 September those two boats, alongside four 4th S-flotilla boats and seven from 2nd S-flotilla, launched a torpedo mission against the east coast, although they failed to sight their target and instead tangled with four British motor launches during their return to base. *S117* reported at least one ML hit with her heavy 40mm flak weapon, ObltzS Dietrich Bludau's newly commissioned reinforcement for 4th S-flotilla the first to carry the weapon on the stern flak platform.

Three nights later and Bludau's boat would again be at the forefront of action. During the afternoon, fourteen boats from the 4th, 2nd and 6th S-flotillas sailed for a *Stichansatz* attack against a northbound convoy. However, the strong S-boat force failed to make contact with their target, a British bomber machine-gunning several of them as they began their return journeys. West of Den Helder three British MGBs of 16th Flotilla – *MGB329*, *334* and *335* – intercepted some of the Germans and a running battle commenced. Lieutenant J A 'Tufty' Forbes in *MGB335* attempted to close the enemy but his boat was hit in the engine room and seriously damaged, wallowing to a halt as the S-boats concentrated their fire upon it. Quickly realising they were vastly outnumbered, the British senior officer, Lt E M 'Mickey' Thorpe, brought *MGB334* alongside to rescue survivors while under heavy fire, pulling ten of the fifteen crew aboard before being forced to retreat. Thorpe ordered pom-poms fired at the disabled MGB's waterline in an attempt to sink her as he sped away, but failed as *S80* and *S105* swiftly came alongside and boarded the drifting MGB. Three British sailors had been killed in the sharp exchange, and two others were rescued by the boarding party after becoming trapped by fire in the telegraph station. The boat was severely damaged, but was a treasure trove of intelligence material, including a functioning radar, signals material, maps, identification books and detailed plots of German minefields that revealed the extent of British awareness of German minelaying and pointed to potential weaknesses in German codes. Despite great difficulty, including the tow line parting more than once, the captured MGB was taken to the Netherlands and passed over to a tug off Den Helder. Once again, *S117*'s armament had shown its worth, several hits from the 40mm having penetrated *MGB335*'s armoured bridge. Each S-boat showed gunfire damage, *S62* and *S80* having five badly wounded and several with minor injuries, two more aboard *S78*, while the 6th S-flotilla reported only one injury.

The capture added fresh impetus for Petersen to push for several upgrades for the S-boats. First, the 40mm flak had more than proved its worth and was to become standard equipment aboard the S-boats. Secondly, both radar and radar detection equipment were desperately needed. The completion of a belt of British coastal radars, confirmed by interrogation of a prisoner from *MGB335*, robbed S-boats of their protective cloak of darkness. Periods of poor visibility, previously useful for surprise attacks, were now detrimental to the S-boats, unable to detect the enemy while still harried by radar-equipped destroyers and units guided from shore. The S-boats required radar detectors to reveal potential threats (*Funkmessbeobachtungsgeräte*) and their own radars to enable swift location of enemy targets. The former would soon be issued as standard in the shape of the primitive (and flawed) Metox receiver, already tested in the Mediterranean and English Channel. Priority was given to equipping U-boats with the device and it wasn't until August that S-flotillas had begun receiving them. For the latter problem of radar equipment, *S112* had conducted trials of modified Luftwaffe FuMo 71 Lichtenstein radar, but results had been deemed unsatisfactory, a limited range and arc of detection rendering them unacceptable for mass installation. Finally, Petersen pushed for the addition of bridge armour, the wooden wheelhouse proving extremely vulnerable to cannon fire.

Initial experiments with fitting an 8mm-thick Plexiglass dome to *S67* was found unsatisfactory due to the material's high reflectivity; *S68* was given a metal alloy dome instead which proved vastly superior. Its construction was, however, difficult and an alternative made of faceted sheet metal plates was made. This comprised a 10–12mm (0.47in) thick centre section of Wotan armoured steel, 10mm (0.4in) thick front bulkhead and 8mm (0.31in) thick rear bulkhead, adding enough weight to reduce the boat's speed by 3 knots. However, the increased protection was deemed completely necessary and production of what became known as the 'skullcap' (*Kalotte*) was begun, fitted as standard to all new boats from late

S67 sporting the experimental plexiglass bridge armour. Imperfect due to its high reflectivity, research ended with the armoured *Kalottenbrücke* (skullcap).

1942 including new *S38*-class boats (designated *S38b*) and the 1943 *S100* class. They were also retrofitted to boats undergoing shipyard overhaul. Amidships, all S-boats were also fitted with double-barrelled machine guns, the quick firing 20mm still present amidst the enclosed forecastle. New boat *S208* was used in trials for the installation of the more powerful MB518 diesels after the fitting of a *Kalotte* and a subsequent desire to raise maximum speed. However, developmental problems and bombing of factories led to an abandonment of the new engines.

During September and October, as S-boats continued rotating in and out of shipyards with minor damage or for scheduled refits and engine changes, the 5th S-flotilla mounted alternating minelaying and torpedo missions. Tragedy struck on 29 September when ObltzS Gerhard Rebensburg was accidently shot by an MP40 sub-machine gun in an accident aboard *S82* while the flotilla laid mines and explosive buoys in Lyme Bay. Severely wounded, the young skipper died, despite the presence of the senior medical officer aboard. The flotilla sank only one ship during October: the escort trawler HMT *Lord Stonehaven*, torpedoed on 2 October while part of convoy PW226 by ObltzS Karl Müller's *S112* and sinking off Eddystone Light with eighteen men killed. Müller reported the destruction of a '1,500-ton freighter', while ObltzS Walter Sobbotka also claimed to have hit and sunk another. The attack on the convoy had once again originated from Luftwaffe sightings, but strong escort and skilful manoeuvring by merchant ships avoided all other torpedo shots.

The remaining three Channel flotillas alternated between minelaying and torpedo missions, but with greater effect. On 6 October a combined force of seventeen S-boats put to sea against convoy FN32 (Phase 9) escorted by destroyers HMS *Westminster* and *Vanity* and coastal forces.

Obermaier's 6th S-flotilla fielded *S71*, *S114*, *S74*, *S75*, *S76*, *S73*, *S113* and *S69*; Feldt's 2nd S-flotilla *S101*, *S62*, *S108*, *S105*, *S46* and *S80* while Bätge's 4th put *S117*, *S63* and *S69* to sea. The S-boats opened fire at 0436hrs the next morning. ObltzS Bludau's *S117* hit 2,730-ton SS *Sheafwater* travelling north in ballast and abandoned by all of her crew before going down. The 2,844-ton SS *Ilse* was next, hit by torpedoes from ObltzS Block's *S63*, the merchant lurching to port with her back broken. Unable to stop engines, the crippled ship careered out of station, the crew abandoning her while still underway. Danish coaster, 1,972-ton SS *Jessie Maersk* was hit and sunk by *S79*, with twenty of the thirty-man crew killed. Royal Navy motor launch *ML339* raced in to the attack, witnessed by the captain of the Danish steamer as he abandoned ship:

We did not see the E-boat but there was a British Motor Launch in the vicinity which gave chase and attacked one at a comparatively short distance from us. Later this motorboat passed us again but she was burning fiercely … I could see tracer bullets while she was fighting with the E-boat and gather she had been badly hit and caught fire.[75]

The gallant *ML339* was riddled with gunfire by *S62* and sank, her skipper and thirteen surviving crew rescued by *ML207*. The final convoy member to go down was rescue ship *Caroline Moller*, the 444-ton requisitioned tug hit by a torpedo from *S80* and sinking with the loss of sixteen lives. The sloop HMS *Sheldrake* and minesweeping trawler HMT *Monimia* were both damaged during the attack which had been the most successful single action for the S-boats since July. One other ship was lost from FN32, somewhat ironically to a mine laid previously by the S-boats. Attempting to avoid torpedo attack, 1,337-ton SS *Ightham* travelling in ballast from London to Sunderland struck two mines, the entire crew managing to abandon ship as the ship wallowed in the swell, finally striking a third mine as she went under.

Predominantly a merchant shipping tonnage war, like that waged by the U-boats, this S-boat officer strings victory pennants from his boat's radio aerial.

It would be another week before the S-boats put to sea once again, bad weather hemming them into their Channel ports. On 13 October eight boats of 5th S-flotilla hunted near Eddystone Rocks for reported convoy traffic but failed to find anything. Instead they were diverted to search for survivors from the merchant raider *Komet* sunk by *MTB236* after travelling under heavy escort from Le Havre towards the Atlantic on its second war patrol. No survivors of the 251 crew were ever found.

That same night to the east all three flotillas put to sea with a combined seventeen boats to attack FN38 (Phase 9) north of Cromer. Only the 6th S-flotilla managed to penetrate the escort screen in the early morning and reported sinking four freighters totalling 8,000 tons. In fact they had hit 1,335-ton Norwegian SS *Lysland* laden with coal. Although set ablaze, the crew fought the fires and she was towed to Immingham later that day and eventually repaired. The second confirmed victim was 1,570-ton SS *George Balfour*, hit and blown in half, though both halves were later towed into Yarmouth.

The remainder of October into November passed with little activity as winter approached and the Channel was lashed with storms. When the S-boats were able to infrequently venture from harbour they lacked any Luftwaffe reports, the aircraft grounded by bad weather. Several times S-boats returned with engine damage caused by the heightened strain such conditions put on the boats. Not until 8 November did Luftwaffe reconnaissance reports of a convoy between Lyme Bay and Start Point send the 5th S-flotilla on what appeared a worthwhile chase, yet they still came up empty-handed. The following night seven boats of the 6th S-flotilla and eight each from the 2nd and 4th sailed to intercept FN61 (Phase 9). *S114* was forced to abort with engine damage, and both *S78* and *S109* with rudder problems as the remainder pressed onward, FdS Petersen aboard *S83* as *Führerboot* in order to get a more direct picture of the situation at sea. An enemy destroyer was sighted at 2134hrs, the rest of FN61 creeping into view east of Lowestoft shortly afterward. In the hectic action that followed, the S-boats fired at least fourteen torpedoes, claiming six steamers hit and sunk aggregating 16,000 tons. In fact, they sank 1,843-ton SS *Fidelio*, her stern hit and exploding, killing seven men in their cabins. The twenty surviving crew were able to get a lifeboat clear before the freighter sank. The only other confirmed hit was on 1,482-ton British SS *Brite Wandle*, though she was later towed into harbour by a French tugboat and salvaged. The attackers also took damage, *S112* hit by 40mm fire along the waterline, *S113* badly hit in the foreship and three men wounded as compartment III flooded, *S48* and *S66* towing the severely damaged boat back to harbour.

While several more boats were consigned to the shipyard for repairs, an Fw190 of Luftwaffe Reconnaissance Group 123 reported a large convoy of forty freighters escorted by three destroyers headed south from Grimsby on 14 November. Between the three Netherlands-based flotillas, twenty-three S-boats sallied from port to intercept, but completely failed to break through enemy destroyer forces and reach merchant targets. Artillery hits were reported by *S64* on the bridge of HMS *Vesper*, although MatrGefr Meyer was killed by return fire that damaged the boat and wounded three others. The attack was abandoned and the S-boats returned in pairs or individually. ObltzS Ulrich Miljes' *S101* became detached from the group and approached two vessels that Miljes mistook for S-boats as they had been flashing the correct green light signals denoting friendly forces. A sudden burst of accurate gunfire from *ML201* and *MGB103* raked the unarmoured bridge, killing Miljes and everybody present, wounding men at other stations. A wounded signaller managed to order all engines to full and the boat thrown at right angles to escape, allowing *S101* to break away and reach port.

More bad weather hampered operations until 19 November when Klug's Cherbourg-based 5th S-flotilla attacked PW250 off Eddystone Lighthouse. The flotilla divided into two groups – *S82*, *S116*, *S77* the first and *S112*, *S65*, *S115* and *S81* the second – the first sweeping in at high speed and drawing the destroyer escort away from the convoy body, opening it up for attack by the second which had been lying in wait with engines silent. Oberleutnant zur See Karl Müller's *S112* fired two torpedoes and hit a '1,000-ton steamer', destroying a 555-ton escorting trawler, HMT *Ullswater*, the commander and thirty-two ratings missing after she had sunk. Almost simultaneously more torpedoes arced from the darkness, hitting 1,118-ton Norwegian SS *Lab*, 815-ton British steamer SS *Yewforest* and 1,595-ton SS *Birgitte*, all of them sinking in minutes. *Yewforest* had slowed to rescue men from the stricken trawler when the torpedo struck, only four crewmen surviving. After *Birgitte* was hit, the majority of the crew escaped in lifeboats, although the sinking steamer fouled one with its forward davit, pulling it under until it released and shot to the surface, crashing upside down on several crewmen swimming to safety, including the ship's master.

Klug's flotilla returned twice more to attack PW convoy traffic before the year was finished, the next battle centred on PW256 escorted by HMS *Glaisdale*, *ML184*, HMT *Jasper* and HMT *Cornelian* on 1 December. In four

Rotten, eight S-boats struggled to reach the merchant ships, successfully deflected by the escorting ships, though ObltzS Klocke claimed an unsubstantiated hit on a 3,000-ton steamer. Only ObltzS Wendler's *S81* sank a vessel, torpedoing HMT *Jasper* and killing four aboard, with six ratings listed as missing after the ship had gone down.

On the night of 2 December at 2200hrs eight boats of Klug's flotilla sailed once more, though *S112* aborted with engine failure, returning with *S65* to port. The remainder headed to their target area but failed to find anything. However, during their return voyage four of the six S-boats stumbled upon PW257 escorted by a single destroyer, five trawlers and three motor launches near Start Point, all four S-boats opening fire with double torpedo shots. *S81* and *S116* both claimed to hit a steamer estimated at 3,000 tons, *S82* another estimated at 2,000 tons, while ObltzS Klocke's *S115* hit new British Hunt-class destroyer HMS *Penylan*, only thirty days into her active service life. Five officers and 112 ratings were rescued after the ship went down, though five later died of their wounds. Amidst the confusion there was one other loss to the convoy: 383-ton MV *Gatinais* carrying scrap iron from Portsmouth to Llanelli torpedoed and sunk with nine crewmen killed. The attack had not, however, been one-sided; *S116* lost two men killed by gunfire and *S82* three with several

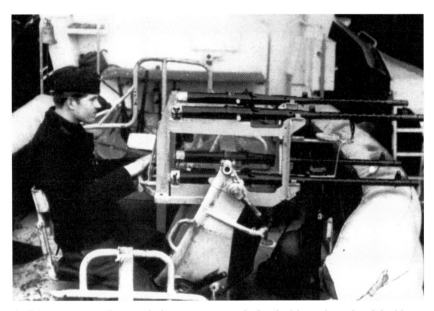

As S-boat armament increased, they were commonly fitted with a twin-pedestal double machine-gun mount amidships, though some carried this four-barrelled MG34 mount instead.

others wounded. The 5th S-flotilla returned to Cherbourg, its final successful mission for 1942 completed.

To the east, high winds prevented much activity from the three flotillas stationed in the Netherlands. A failed hunt for targets on 4 December yielded nothing other than skirmishes with British MGBs and MTBs, two men wounded aboard *S109* by machine-gun fire. Not until 12 December did reliable Luftwaffe reports lead a combined force of seventeen S-boats to FN89 (Phase 9). Once again the *Stichansatz* tactic was used to locate the enemy: the boats of the 2nd and 5th S-flotillas drew the escorts away on either flank, allowing six boats of the 4th to attack the merchant ships beyond. When Bätge's boats struck, the convoy of thirty-eight merchants straggled over five miles, an almost impossible target for the escort to protect. Destroyer HMS *Wallace* leading the convoy turned to seaward in pursuit of the 6th S-flotilla, firing star-shells but sighting nothing until the battle behind was already underway. A torpedo passed the destroyer's bow travelling east, another travelling west, indicating that the S-boats were attacking from both directions. Five were finally sighted and engaged by *Wallace* and another destroyer HMS *Meynell*, the latter hitting *S114* in the foreship with cannon fire. Behind them five ships were aflame.

The first to be hit was 1,056-ton British steamer SS *Avonwood*, blown clean in half by a torpedo hit from ObltzS von Mirbach's *S48*, survivors going into the water where a number were run down and killed by SS *Fulham* travelling immediately astern. The 999-ton SS *Lindisfarne* was also hit by a torpedo from ObltzS Block's *S63*, lurching first to port under the impact before rising vertically into the air and sinking, with sixteen men killed aboard the ship. British freighter SS *Knitsley* was hit and sunk by two torpedoes from ObltzS Bludau's *S117*, at least eleven men killed aboard, while the 871-ton SS *Glen Tilt* carrying a cargo of cement from Middlesbrough to London was torpedoed by ObltzS Graser's *S110* and sank rapidly. The last ship to be sunk from FN89 was also the last Norwegian merchant ship destroyed in 1942. The 1,915-ton SS *Marianne* was travelling in ballast when she was hit by a torpedo from ObltzS Block's *S63*, his second success of the night. The ship immediately listed to port, the wheelhouse blown away and scalding steam pouring from broken pipes. Several crewmen had been blown overboard by the explosion, the rest opting to jump as the ship capsized within a minute, rolling on top of the single lifeboat launched before sliding beneath the waves. As reinforcements arrived for the British in the shape of more MGBs, the Germans withdrew into deteriorating weather, *S105* taking a major shell hit in compartments 7 and 8, but suffering no casualties.

It was something of a triumph for the S-boats and the final one within North Sea for 1942. Worsening winter weather precluded any further operations, providing time for damaged S-boats to be repaired and crews to rest as best they could. The year had seen vindication of Petersen's tactical decisions and had yielded several notable successes for the western boats. However, on balance, the victory margin was small for the S-boats, who were engaged on a war of attrition they had no hope of winning. In total, the S-boats had sunk two destroyers, one motor launch, four trawlers and nineteen merchant ships. They had captured an MGB, damaged three merchants with torpedoes, another two destroyers and one freighter also damaged through mines, while the relentless minelaying destroyed five more freighters. Compared with the sheer volume of coastal convoy traffic – 21,552 individual passages both north and southbound along the east coast alone – the predation achieved by S-boats was almost insignificant.

While the S-boat service was being spread thinly throughout Germany's war zones, the British had steadily built up their forces in opposition. Newer, larger and better armed Fairmile D 'Dog Boats' were coming out of shipyards, a versatile design able to be fitted out as either MGB or MTB and a fearsome adversary for the S-boats. The Allies were refining inter-service co-operation to a new level of efficiency, something that Petersen's forces woefully lacked, except for local liaison with Luftwaffe units. However, even if the Luftwaffe was willing to provide the necessary support, they lacked the structure and training to use it to anything like its potential. Besides, the Luftwaffe too was overstretched as the gaping maw of war on the eastern front and the defence of the Reich itself against the rising tempo of Allied bombing swallowed more and more men and machines. Technologically the Allies had also outpaced the Kriegsmarine, something that the capture of *MGB335* showed them in no uncertain terms. Indeed, on the cusp of another new year of war, the prospects for the S-boats appeared as bleak as the winter storms that buffeted the English Channel.

12

The Mediterranean

December 1941 – November 1942

ON 27 August 1941 while the 3rd S-flotilla, numbering only four operational boats, was still engaged in Operation Barbarossa, the flotilla commander Kptlt Friedrich Kemnade, flotilla engineer Kptlt (Ing) Johannes-Martin Döpner and his administrative officer, LzS Horst Weber, had travelled to Swinemünde to meet with FdT and discuss the planned transfer of 3rd S-flotilla to the Mediterranean. Logistically, the prospect was daunting and Kemnade and his officers distilled their queries about the forthcoming plans into four questions:

1. What tasks were expected of the 3rd S-flotilla within the Mediterranean?
2. When was the flotilla expected there?
3. How can the flotilla reach the Mediterranean from the North Sea?
4. What structural changes were required for the 'march through the waterways of Europe' during the current shipyard time?

The first two questions would rest with SKL in Berlin and then with local commands in Rome and Sicily, where the three officers were flown shortly thereafter. In Rome they met with the chief of the Kriegsmarine liaison staff to the Italian Navy (Regia Marina), KA Eberhard Weichold. Weichold had held the post since Italy's entry into the war in June 1940, and his was a broad understanding of the complex relationship of the two allies' war efforts. The war aims of both nations were vastly different, mirrored perfectly by their naval ambitions. With no close alliance during the road towards war, Germany and Italy shared little common vision. Indeed, at a conference held between the two naval chiefs, Admiral Raeder and Admiral Cavignari, in Friedrichshafen on 20/21 June 1939, OKM recorded the statement '... that direct co-operation between the two navies was hardly appropriate or even possible.'[76] Kriegsmarine ambition was firmly centred on a 'blue water navy' that would fight in the Atlantic, with control also of the North, Baltic and Arctic Seas, while Italy believed that it could control the central Mediterranean, with additional spheres of influence within the Black and Red Seas. Thus the two European Axis powers were waging a 'parallel war' as opposed to that of a co-operative alliance. Unfortunately, Italy's military star waned almost immediately. The country had little appetite for the war in which they found themselves embroiled and their military fortunes declined with defeats on land, in the air and at sea. The balance of power within the Mediterranean shifted firmly in Britain's favour.

Italian forces suffered severe defeats following an ill-fated invasion of Greece and in North Africa during 1940; Germany was compelled to come to the Italians' aid in order to secure their southern flank for the coming war against Russia. Germany invaded Yugoslavia, Greece and Crete, and from February 1941 the Deutsche Afrika Korps began building up in North Africa, about to give the triumphant British forces a bloody nose. However, Rommel's Afrika Korps required vital supplies sent by convoys which were increasingly intercepted by the Royal Navy. The Germans immediately blamed Italian escort forces and also hinted at Italian intelligence leaks as the reason for an uncanny British knack for finding and destroying the ships – the secrets of ULTRA code-breaking completely beyond suspicion.

With no faith in the Regia Marina and no German units available, Hitler ordered the transfer of S-boats, R-boats and U-boats into the Mediterranean, though he continually failed to grasp the strategic possibilities of a theatre of war he judged peripheral to his ambitions. Weichold was able to explain the situation to the officers of the 3rd S-flotilla in Rome before they travelled onward to Messina, Sicily, to meet with the base commander, Admiral Pietro Barone, who was responsible also for the harbour at Augusta, earmarked as an S-boat base owing to its proximity to the British-held island fortress of Malta. The tasks already mapped for the 3rd S-flotilla were the escort and security of supply convoys travelling from Sicily to Tripoli as well as torpedo and mine operations along the North African coast.

The logistics of transporting the flotilla (as well as the 6th R-flotilla) to the Mediterranean involved using the array of canals and rivers stretching from the Netherlands and through France, at the suggestion of KzS Heinz Dietrich von Conrady who had commanded the 1st S-flotilla pre-war and was now a staff officer at OKM. He himself had taken S-boats along the

Rhine as far as Worms. Permission was granted by Vichy President Marshal Philippe Pétain for the S-boats to pass through the waterways of unoccupied France, and Kemnade began preparations in earnest. His was the only flotilla capable of the voyage, as their 16-cylinder engines and corresponding beam width allowed just enough space to pass through locks that would have prevented larger boats equipped with 20-cylinder engines.

At the cessation of the flotilla's commitment to the Baltic, the S-boats sailed in company with their depot ship *Adolf Lüderitz* for refit in Wilhelmshaven. The *Lüderitz* would be parting company with Kemnade's men after serving together for more than a year, the tender's modern facilities soon in demand within the Arctic Circle. Once all ten flotilla boats had been overhauled, they sailed on the evening of 7 October in two groups to Rotterdam, docking inside the bunkers, where their super-structures were altered to disguise their identity. Torpedo tube doors were covered over with sheet-metal plating and all deck weapons dismounted. While the wheelhouse was reduced to half its height, a dummy funnel was fitted above the forward engine room fanlight and the S-boats painted black, transformed into apparently harmless barges plying their trade along the canal system. All crewmen wore civilian clothes as the first three boats began their journey on 9 October. *S31*, *S35* and *S61* entered the Rhine river and reached Nijmegen by 1830hrs. Travelling slowly, the voyage took them south in daily stages, briefly delayed at Mannheim where *S61* was docked to repair bent propellers. Every effort was made to lighten the boats, including emptying fuel bunkers for the next stage of the voyage. Once they had reached Strasbourg, their route led into the Rhine–Rhône canal, through 167 narrow locks, down to the Belfort Gap in the Vosges Mountains, west along the Doubs to the Saône, reaching the border of Vichy France on 12 November. From there they followed the river into the Rhône at Lyon and along that river to the Mediterranean. The two remaining boats from the first half-flotilla, *S33* and *S34*, trailed two days behind.

Once in the Mediterranean, deck weapons were remounted and crews donned uniforms; the S-boats rejoined the Kriegsmarine and sailed onwards, the first entering the Italian naval base at La Spezia on 18 October for seven days of refitting and repainting. On 3 December the first five 3rd S-flotilla boats arrived at the Sicilian port of Augusta, visited that day by Italian King Victor Emanuel III in company with Weichold. Following engine overhaul and torpedo loading, the flotilla was reported operational on 11 December 1941.

Changing S-boat engines in Palermo, Italy.

The second group of five boats took longer to complete the journey, delayed by six weeks due to the low water level in the Rhône river. Not until 10 January 1942 were they able to continue their voyage, reaching La Spezia for overhaul on 15 January 1942, continuing on to Augusta to reunite with the rest of the 3rd S-flotilla, which had already begun operations against Malta.

Malta was the thorn in the side of Axis supply missions to North Africa. Lightly defended in June 1940 when Italy had entered the war, Mussolini's military strategists had failed to capitalise on that weakness and conquer the island that soon became home to air and naval units, including the Royal Navy's 10th Submarine Flotilla. Despite coming under fierce and effective aerial bombardment by Italian and German aircraft, the diversion of Luftwaffe force to the eastern front in June 1941 had given beleaguered RAF defenders enough space to build up their forces, and during the second half of 1941 Fleet Air Arm, Royal Air Force and Navy forces based in Malta began offensive operations against Axis supply routes to North Africa. Between June and September they sank 108 ships, totalling approximately 300,000 tons. Rommel's advance was stalled and he was unable to capture the port of Tobruk, still under supply by sea. The first available S-boats were thrown immediately into action against Malta.

At 1630hrs on 12 December the 3rd S-flotilla sailed to intercept enemy warships departing Malta, waiting with engines off three miles from Valletta. The men of the S-boats witnessed an air raid on the darkened island before them, searchlights and flak mixing with the high-explosive bombardment, but neither sighted nor heard any enemy ships and broke for home in the early hours as instructed. Vizeadmiral Weichold was their operational chief in his new role as Befehlshaber des Deutschen Marinekommandos Italie, a post created in November with the arrival of Kriegsmarine surface forces. The following night a repeat mission with four boats yielded the same result and the decision was made to switch to minelaying.

The four S-boats allocated – *S31*, *S33*, *S35* and *S61* – each collected three TMA and one UMA mines as well as four explosive buoys and one cutter buoy (*Reissbojen*) from the depot, before departing at 1700hrs on 16 December. They deposited the deadly cargo just over half a nautical mile from Saint Elmo Point, Valletta, the noise of the slow-moving boats covered by co-ordinating their approach with an intruder air raid. All four boats successfully dropped their cargo and returned to base by 0900hrs the next morning.

A second minelaying expedition was mounted on 22 December after several days of inclement weather, with *S55* added as a fifth boat. This time they were detected by British listening stations, and searchlights probed the darkness as the S-boats began dropping the first of thirteen TMA mines in the field designated MT2. Another Luftwaffe intruder raid was mounted, covering the sound of the S-boats, although four prematurely exploding mines alerted British defences and triggered an eighteen-minute barrage from ashore. The mines had detonated some distance from each carrier S-boat, but the flotilla was fortunate to evade an RAF night fighter briefly seen overhead. The next mission took place on Christmas Day, *S34*, *S35* and *S61* sailing at 2100hrs, Kemnade aboard *S35* as *Führerboot*. Two hours from port a cracked cylinder head forced *S35* to abort and return to Sicily, Kemnade, his adjutant and flotilla navigation officer transferring aboard *S61* and the remaining S-boat pair continuing their mission as planned. This time the boats laid nine TMA mines in field MT4, another mine prematurely detonating on the seabed twenty-eight minutes after being fired from its tube, a second thirty seconds later. Defective depth mechanism was suspected and no more minelaying was planned until the New Year.

The month ended in little activity for 3rd S-flotilla. A search and rescue operation was mounted for a downed Luftwaffe bomber by two boats on 28 December; minelaying resumed shortly afterward. The remaining five S-boats of the flotilla were still en route and the first four would not actually arrive in Augusta until 5 February; four more small *S30*-class boats were earmarked during January for transfer to the Mediterranean to act as flotilla reserves. Meanwhile, *S58* sailed to Gaeta, where it conducted experiments with LMF mines (an influence mine weighing 1,050kg that could be moored in water up to 300m deep). Designed for aerial minelaying, it was undergoing adaptation for S-boat use, and would see first active use as such in 1943, designated type LMF/S.

In North Africa, Rommel's military fortunes improved. On 21 January 1942 he had launched a surprise counter-offensive at El Agheila and by February had reached El Gazala, Libya, near the border with Egypt. An intensified air campaign by the Italian Air Force began in early February and once again victory appeared to loom on the Mediterranean horizon. In Berlin, SKL considered requests to use the 3rd S-flotilla in more direct support of the land battle raging in North Africa.

The present successes of the Rommel offensive indicate the possibility that the Panzer Group, recognising the operational and tactical inadequacy of the defeated enemy and the comparatively weak enemy forces behind the front, will not be satisfied with its present gains. Therefore a surprise attack on Tobruk is not altogether out of the question. It is interesting to note that the British press is already mentioning a new threat to Egypt. In surveying all potentialities of this situation, it should be considered whether it is still justifiable to continue holding our S-boats in reserve for operations in the area around Sicily or Malta, or whether transferring them at once to Derna for fighting light enemy naval forces and transports in the Tobruk-Bardia area would be more important. In the latter case we would have to abandon some of our current plans for mining the Malta area ... The German Admiral, Rome is being informed of these conclusions by the following telegram: 'The unexpectedly favourable development of the military situation in Africa suggests the expediency of temporarily using even single S-boats based in the Benghazi and Derna areas. The Naval Staff believes that a surprise attack holds promise of success and will have a particularly deterring effect on the enemy. Opinion and plans are requested.'[77]

In answer, the German Naval Command, Italy, reports that the suggested S-boat operations as well as operations by S-boats based in the Gulf of Suda had been investigated some time ago and were rejected for the following reasons:

1. Weather will greatly limit S-boat operations until the end of spring.
2. The fuel shortage will permit the use of only three S-boats.
3. No repair or overhaul facilities are available in Africa.
4. Only Benghazi can be used as a base.
5. In all African ports the S-boats are very much exposed to air raids.
6. Participation in the offensive against Malta is still the principal task of the 3rd S-flotilla.[78]

Weichold held firm to the commitment of minelaying around Valletta, which the flotilla continued until May 1942.

Kemnade's flotilla moved station from Augusta on 20 February, seven boats sailing to Porto Empedocle on Sicily's south coast, from where they acted as distant escort for convoy traffic to Tripoli, while reconnoitring Pantellaria, midway between Sicily and Tunisia and soon to boast a Luftwaffe airfield. From their new flotilla base they were equally able to patrol the Straits of Sicily while maintaining the Malta mine barrage. Bad weather frequently halted plans, as the boats required a period of no moon and sea state of 2 or less, owing to their heavy loading, and so the 3rd S-flotilla was frequently harbour-bound, camouflaged with draped sheets of canvas as they lay pierside. Once at sea, weather conditions could change with unexpected speed: on 20 March the flotilla was caught out while sailing as weather conditions deteriorated rapidly, leading to all mines being jettisoned and the mission being abandoned.

Despite Weichold's stated reservations, he received an explicit directive that Kemnade's flotilla would shortly commence operations in the Tobruk area, using Derna as the main operational port, reserve and resting boats stationed in Suda Bay, Crete. Weichold acquiesced and planned to transfer four boats of the 3rd S-flotilla to Suda under Kemnade's direct control, leaving three boats available for ongoing mining operations against Malta. The remainder were in shipyards undergoing minor repairs.

On 24 March the first success attributed to the flotilla's mines was the sinking of British Hunt-class destroyer HMS *Southwold* in mine barrage MT7 north of Valletta harbour. Fast-moving supply convoy MW10, four freighters with destroyer and cruiser escort, had attempted to reach Malta from Alexandria, but suffered severe Luftwaffe attacks, one freighter sunk and SS *Breconshire* disabled and drifting before the crew managed to anchor the ship off Zonqor Point, where she remained under Luftwaffe attack. During the morning of 24 March the anchor was found to be dragging along the sandy bottom and destroyer HMS *Southwold* was ordered to tow the freighter and its crucial supplies into port. While trying to pass a line to the disabled ship, a mine exploded under *Southwold*'s engine room, killing one officer and four ratings. Flooding was severe, but damage parties raced to bring it under control as the tug *Ancient* attached a tow to the destroyer. As the crippled ship began moving again, the engine room hull split completely through to the upper deck, *Southwold* listing violently to starboard. Abandoned, she sank soon after in two pieces. That night, *Breconshire* was towed into Marsaxlokk by tugs *Ancient* and *Robust*.

Mines continued to be laid by the 3rd S-flotilla boats in Sicily, *S31*, *S34* and *S61* successfully adding to the thickening fields on the night of 6 May. At 0126hrs German lookouts sighted shadows off the port bow, four and a half miles from Valletta, all three boats turning to the pursuit. It was in fact British motor launch *ML130*, commanded by Lieutenant David Robert Hamilton Jolly RNVR. Engaged primarily in escorting submarines in and out of harbour, the motor launches had also begun sweeps in conjunction with land-based searchlights against suspected S-boat incursions. *ML130* was returning to Valletta when the three S-boats

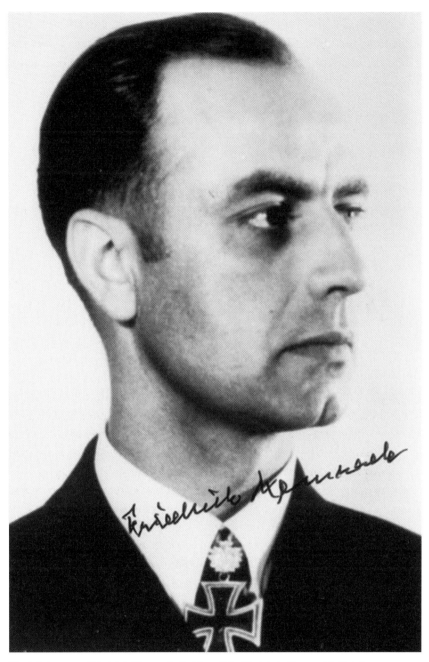

Kapitänleutnant Friedrich Kemnade, holder of the Knight's Cross with Oak Leaves, commander of the 3rd S-flotilla until wounded on 29 June 1943 and transferred to OKM staff.

opened fire with deck weapons at a range of only 300m (328yds). Despite returning fire with its superior weaponry of a 76mm and two 20mm cannon, the British vessel was battered into submission by four separate attacks. Eventually, four German sailors boarded the shattered and burning boat and captured the crew, five of whom had been wounded – including Jolly who had been shot in the knee. Three British sailors had been killed, the eleven survivors taken prisoner. One German had been lightly wounded aboard *S31*, his head grazed by a bullet. After retrieving the motor launch's ensign, maps and whatever useful material they could find, the Germans scuttled the wrecked boat by placing explosives among stored depth charges. The battle was seen ashore and the following day an RAF rescue launch searched for survivors, finding only wreckage and a Carley float to mark the end of *ML130*. Meanwhile, the S-boats continued minelaying that night.

On 9 May Luftwaffe reconnaissance aircraft of Luftflotte 2 reported a possible enemy cruiser in the Straits of Sicily, bound for Malta. *S54*, *S56*, *S57* and *S58* of the so-called 'Africa boats' were despatched to intercept, along with the three Sicilian minelayers carrying a mixed load of mines and torpedoes. The 'Africa boats' lay in wait northeast of Marsascala, the others proceeding close inshore of Valletta harbour's entrance to lay a triangular field off Sliema Point by 0421hrs. Less than a minute after completion, and only 700m (765yds) from shore, *S31* detonated a drifting surface mine alongside the engine room. *Führerboot S61* closed on the shattered wreck, which had been broken in half, and lifted off survivors, including the skipper ObltzS Haag, flotilla medical officer MarSttArzt Dr Mehnen, and two Italian liaison officers. Two men had been severely wounded and behind them in the burning wreckage were eight dead, all within the engine rooms.

Ironically, it was at that time that the vague outline of the approaching 'cruiser' – the fast minelayer HMS *Welshman* – was detected, and both *S61* and *S34* broke away from the still floating bow section of *S31* and attempted torpedo attacks, both failing as they underestimated the *Welshman*'s speed. The British ship reached Valletta under a smokescreen, though suffered slight damage after her paravanes detonated two mines. The other S-boats waiting nearby failed to sight the incoming target, instead opening fire on trawler HMS *Beryl* and minesweeper HMD *Trusty Star* before returning to base. Aware that the remains of *S31* were still afloat, four Messerschmitt Bf109s of JG53 strafed and bombed what was left until the sea was clear.[79]

While HMS *Welshman* had avoided the minefields and torpedoes, 1,475-ton *Odin*-class submarine HMS *Olympus* was not so lucky. After running surfaced from Valletta at 0430hrs on 8 May, she detonated a mine half an hour later, seven miles from the coast. The targeted submarine was en route to Gibraltar and overfilled with people, carrying her own fifty-five crew plus forty-three crewmen from submarines HMS *Pandora*, *P36* and *P39*, which had been sunk by air raids. As the submarine sank, survivors began the long swim to shore, only twelve later making landfall, three of them wounded. The area where *Olympus* went down was searched and three bodies recovered. Minesweepers *C308* and *St Angelo* were sent to repeatedly sweep the entrance channel to Valletta's Grand Harbour again, escorted by HMS *Beryl* and *ML126*. On 11 May all sweepers had returned to harbour by 0230hrs, except for 154-ton *C308*, which struck a mine and sank. Seven survivors were picked up by the boom patrol picket boat, but the skipper and eight of the crew were lost.

The minefields were still considered highest priority for S-boat operations against Malta. The Luftwaffe and Regia Aeronautica intensified their air assault on the beleaguered island, where defeat always appeared perilously close. *S35* and *S34* laid twelve mines in MT23 on 13 May and three nights later were back alongside *S58* and *S59* to sow more mines in MT24. However, during this latter operation disaster struck the S-boats when they were detected by searchlights. British radio direction finders had traced the S-boats at 0150hrs, their engines heard north of Fort Saint Elmo. Searchlights swept the sea but revealed nothing at first as the 6in guns at Fort Campbell fired two rounds, guided by map plot with no discernible effect. However, at 0204hrs all four S-boats were picked up by the searchlights and engaged by Tigne Battery at a range of 10,000yds (9,100m). Laying smoke, the S-boats attempted to retreat, but within minutes *S34* was hit to starboard above the engine room. Three men were killed immediately, one badly wounded and three others lightly injured. The enemy searchlights followed the other zigzagging boats as they attempted to evacuate survivors from *S34*. More shells from both Tigne and Rocco forts fell, although a thickening smokescreen helped obscure Kemnade's boats as they retrieved survivors and set scuttling charges. At 0235hrs *S34* exploded, the three surviving boats already retreating to Sicily.

However, the total destruction of *S34* could not be guaranteed by Kemnade, who communicated with II Fliegerkorps the need to investigate, and if necessary destroy any floating remains. Kemnade's assessment was correct, and daybreak revealed the smoking shell of *S34* still afloat. Four

229 Squadron Hurricanes scrambled from Hal Far to attack *S34*, strafing the boat and reporting 'return fire', though the only men left aboard were those who had died. Three-quarters of an hour later a Dornier Do24 flying boat approached the smouldering wreck, its escort of four Bf109s attacking, setting her on fire until she finally sank.

It was a bitter blow for the 3rd S-flotilla: a second boat lost in less than a week. The dangers of inshore minelaying were immense, and on 17 May Kemnade received instructions that there were to be no more such missions, the complex mosaic of mine barrages completed. Ultimately, despite the unreliability of the TMA mines that resulted in occasional detonation, 557 mines had been laid in twenty-eight different minefields.[80] On 26 May HMD *Eddy* was engaged on minesweeping operations in Valletta's main entrance channel when the drifter struck a mine and sank with the loss of eight hands. The sweep was abandoned with only one mine having been swept. Four days later, 150-ton tug HMS *St Angelo* also struck a mine and sank three-quarters of a mile from the harbour entrance. Four crewmen were lost.

During this period Malta had ceased to be an effective naval base for the Royal Navy. With harbour installations reduced to rubble by constant aerial bombardment and shrinking supplies for whichever ships were serviceable, the decision was taken to evacuate all operational surface warships to Alexandria. While this relieved the pressure on Axis supply convoys for North Africa, it still did not convince the vacillating leaders of Italy and Germany to attempt their planned invasion of the island. Operation Hercules would have destroyed the British outpost once and for all, but instead they decreed the capture of the besieged harbour at Tobruk must come first, and so the Kriegsmarine's attention was refocused to the southeast.

While *S33*, *S35* and *S61* were dry-docked in Palermo for engine overhauls, on 21 May *S54*, *S56*, *S57*, *S58* and *S59* sailed from Augusta bound for Navarino Bay, Greece, before heading south to Crete's Suda Bay and ultimately onward to North Africa, arriving at the port of Ra's al Hilal, Libya, on 27 May. There the German crews refuelled using hand pumps, before transferring east to Derna. The S-boats anchored offshore while stationed in North Africa, all supplies brought to the boats using infantry lighters.

In the small town of Derna two engineering officers, Oblt (Ing) Lührs and Bielitzer, with the help of Army pioneers, had established a torpedo workshop, fuel dump and basic workshops; a nearby Luftwaffe repair hangar was also available when needed. Engine overhauls would still require the boats' return to Augusta. The pioneers had also constructed a pair of bunkers, one for torpedo storage, the other for other munitions. The former were in shorter supply than expected after 6,500-ton Italian steamer SS *Allegri* was sunk by submarine and air attack while proceeding from Brindisi to Benghazi. Amongst the cargo lost were ninety vehicles, 1,663 tons of Wehrmacht supplies and twenty-three torpedoes for the 3rd S-flotilla. Derna had already proved a valuable supply head for the Wehrmacht, 42,849 tons of supplies being unloaded there between 7 March and 26 May when Operation Theseus – the resumption of Rommel's offensive in North Africa – was scheduled to begin. The Commanding General of North African Italian Forces handed over responsibility for the control and protection of Axis supply traffic, interdiction of Allied supply traffic and the organisation, execution and protection of landings behind the enemy lines to VA Weichold.

On 30 May *S55* and *S60* also arrived in Derna, seven boats now present, and *S30* and *S36* following soon afterward. Reinforcements were already planned for Kemnade's flotilla following the loss of two boats in action. Owing to the size of the Rhine–Rhône canal locks, only the boats *S151* to *S158* were considered for the transfer journey. These were a unique class of S-boat, built on the unfinished Dutch MTB hulls *TM54* to *TM61*, captured at the Gusto Werke in Schiedam in 1940. Completed by both Dutch and German workers, the first had been commissioned into the Kriegsmarine on 19 December 1941.[81] Their small size rendered them unable to carry mines on the stern deck, equipped with the standard German torpedoes and flak weapons. The *S151*-class boats were 28.3m (92ft 10in) in length, with a beam of 4.46m (14ft 7in), displacing only 57 tons and capable of 34 knots. Originally scheduled for sale to Bulgaria, the need for them within the Mediterranean took precedence. Those commissioned by June 1942 were attached to the 7th S-flotilla, undergoing Baltic training as SKL dithered over the decision to despatch the boats to the Mediterranean, demanding assurances that Rhine–Rhône water levels during summer would allow use of the route. Under time pressure for a decision – 15 July considered the last possible day of despatch – SKL postponed their verdict until that date, when they relented and ordered the despatch of boats *S151* to *S158*. Rather than add them to the complement of 3rd S-flotilla, they would travel as the 7th S-flotilla, their journey scheduled to begin during September.

Meanwhile, the assault on Tobruk began. An initial operation involving five boats led by *S57* – with VA Eberhard Weichold aboard as observer – began on the afternoon of 28 May. Their task was to act as escort for

Operation Hecker, an amphibious landing, Kampfgruppe Hecker (led by Oberst Hermann-Hans Hecker, Pionier Führer Afrika), comprising men of the 13th Brandenburger Company, 33rd and 39th Panzerjäger Battalion, 778th Pioneer Landing Company and Italian 3rd San Marco Marine Battalion. Their plan was to cut the main British supply route by landing 30km (19 miles) east of Tobruk, while Rommel's forces attacked the Gazala Line. The troops were embarked on *Marinefahrpräms*, accompanied by minesweepers and escorted by Kemnade's S-boats. However, after only a few hours at sea the operation was cancelled by radio and all boats returned to Derna.

On the night of 3 June, four boats led by *S54* began their first torpedo patrol east toward Tobruk. The shadow of a steamship estimated at 5,000 tons was sighted and attacked by *S54* and *S56*, both missing due to a combination of torpedo failure and defensive zigzagging. However, ObltzS Gunter Erdmann's *S57* successfully torpedoed what he reported as an 'enemy destroyer' a little past midnight, actually hitting escort ship HMS *Cocker*, engaged in an ASDIC sweep off Tobruk Harbour during the departure of freighter SS *Hanna Møller* for Alexandria. Taking station as seaward escort for the Danish freighter, *Cocker* was hit on the port side by a single torpedo below the bridge, which detonated the magazine and sent her to the bottom. As the survivors struggled amidst oil and debris, corvette HMS *Gloxinia* followed orders when under presumed U-boat attack and steamed through the men to drop depth charges nearby. Fifteen of the thirty-one crew were lost.

For the 3rd S-flotilla this had been an important victory: the first torpedo success for the Mediterranean S-boats. Despite the failures reported by accompanying boats, the sinking of what was presumed to be a destroyer was gratifying. However, there were few confirmed successes to follow. A patrol sweep between Tobruk and Ras Azzaz on the night of 6 June by four boats yielded nothing, despite two boats reporting that they had penetrated Tobruk Bay and attacked two freighters riding at anchor with a pair of torpedoes each. Three detonations were heard, but results unseen. The garrison reported three torpedoes fired into the harbour by a suspected U-boat, damage to the harbour boom soon being repaired. The following night four boats returned to the same area: a torpedo fired by *S60* at corvette HMS *Gloxinia* missed, as she attacked what was thought to be an enemy U-boat in the darkness. A third mission off Tobruk on the night of 7 June again proved fruitless.

As Rommel advanced through Libya, Malta was nearing the end of its tether. Despite increasing numbers of aircraft being brought to the island,

Generalfeldmarschall Erwin Rommel visits the 3rd S-flotilla at Mersa Matruh, pictured here with flotilla commander Kptlt Friedrich Kemnade.

supplies for both the military and civilians had dwindled to almost nothing. In a desperate attempt to forestall their collapse, two convoys were despatched, one from Gibraltar in the west, the other from Alexandria to the east, in an attempt to split Axis forces and break through the siege. From Gibraltar, Operation Harpoon comprised five freighters (convoy WS19Z) and an American tanker carrying 39,000 tons of cargo and oil. Their escort was the anti-aircraft cruiser HMS *Cairo*, HMS *Welshman*, nine destroyers and four minesweepers. Distant cover was provided by battleship HMS *Malaya*, two aircraft carriers, two cruisers and eight destroyers. In the east, Operation Vigorous sailed from Alexandria with eleven freighters (convoy MW11), escorted by 'decoy battleship' HMS *Centurion*, twelve destroyers, four corvettes and two minesweepers. Distant cover comprised eight cruisers and fourteen destroyers.

Almost upon departing Alexandria, Vigorous came under air attack, and by 14 June two ships had been lost and two damaged. All available

Kriegsmarine and Italian forces in the eastern Mediterranean were vectored onto the convoy and at 1420hrs *S36*, *S54*, *S55*, *S56*, *S58* and *S59* sailed from Derna to join the attack, *S36* kept apprised of Luftwaffe reconnaissance reports. The S-boats carried a test version of the radar detector Metox, later made famous aboard U-boats as the 'Biscay Cross'. By early evening flak and aircraft were visible on the horizon, a Junkers Ju88 mistakenly dropping three bombs near *S58*, though too far away for damage. At 2025hrs the first pair of destroyers came into *S54*'s view, trailed by three large freighters. At that moment the Luftwaffe unwittingly came to the aid of the Royal Navy, dropping brilliant flares designed to help pilots attack, but illuminating both the convoy and the waiting S-boats. Hurried radio requests transmitted to the S-boat headquarters at Derna to cease dropping flares yielded no result: the advantage of surprise was lost.

The S-boats had divided into two groups: 1 Gruppe comprising *S54*, *S55*, *S58* headed the northern flank of the oncoming enemy and the most experienced commander ObltzS Siegfried Wuppermann led 2 Gruppe – *S56*, *S36* and *S59* – to the southern fringe of the convoy's track. As each new Luftwaffe attack illuminated the sea ahead of Vigorous, 1 Gruppe came under direct attack from oncoming destroyers, travelling at full speed in the artificial light as they attempted to attack the convoy. Kemnade desperately contacted Weichold at 2345hrs: 'Please no more bombing attacks, torpedo attacks impossible due to flares,' while the S-boats launched repeated unsuccessful torpedo attacks, experiencing several torpedo failures in the process. They withdrew to the edge of contact range, probing for the chance to attack the precious merchant ships. The onboard Metox had also proved its worth, detecting beams of British radar as it hunted the S-boats. Wuppermann had already declared by radio that if the Luftwaffe continued to drop flares, then the S-boat attack would be broken off completely and at 0400hrs 1 Gruppe began the return trek to Derna. As they broke away, ObltzS Horst Weber reported four destroyers sighted from *S55* and a final belated twin torpedo attack before departing.

However, 2 Gruppe had experienced a breakthrough. The British commander of 15th Cruiser Squadron, Rear Admiral Philip Vian, was aware via his own reconnaissance aircraft that the convoy was likely to meet the Italian battle fleet that had sailed to intercept Vigorous. At that time they dominated the eastern Mediterranean and Vian ordered the convoy turned east to delay the clash until after daybreak. During the turn manoeuvre, cruiser HMS *Newcastle* and several other ships became separated and despite five destroyers harrying the attacking S-boats,

Wuppermann's *S56* was able to hit the cruiser with two torpedoes, a hole 30ft (9m) in diameter blown in her bow with serious damage to the ship's structure and machinery. The forward turret was put out of action but, almost miraculously, there were no casualties. Nonetheless, *Newcastle* was forced to retreat to Alexandria.

The success against a cruiser was some consolation for 3rd S-flotilla as they docked in Libya during the morning. What they did not realise was that Weber's torpedoes had also found a target. After *Newcastle* had been hit, H-class destroyer HMS *Hasty* gave chase to the S-boats before returning to provide protection for the damaged cruiser. A torpedo from *S55* hit the port side bow: the structure was completely destroyed and fire broke out in the forward boiler room. The destroyer began rapid flooding and was dead in the water. With no option left, the crew abandoned ship, the floating hulk torpedoed by HMS *Hotspur*. Thirteen British sailors were lost.

The S-boats were rapidly refuelled and rearmed, and sailed again for a second night attack on the convoy.[82] Vian meanwhile deliberated between proceeding east or west. Heavy air attacks continued to take their toll and the Italian fleet appeared still to be on interception course. The British ships sailed to and fro until it became clear at 1900hrs that, although the Italian battle fleet appeared to have broken off their interception, fuel and ammunition supplies within the surviving Vigorous ships were so low that they would be unable to reach Malta. The convoy turned for Alexandria for the final time.

Ironically, after the successful appeals of Weichold on behalf of 3rd S-flotilla to General Albert Kesselring of Luftlotte II for a cessation of Luftwaffe flares, the S-boats were shrouded in darkness and unable to find the main convoy. They briefly brushed with destroyers before returning empty-handed to Derna.

Meanwhile, the Harpoon convoy closed on Malta from the west. The procession had already been severely battered by Italian warships and air attack, and as the exhausted survivors made their final approach to Valletta, Polish destroyer ORP *Kujawiak* detonated one of the S-boats' mines and sank with thirteen dead and twenty injured. HMS *Badsworth* detonated another, killing nine sailors and five merchantmen rescued from ships sunk earlier by bombing. The destroyer had a huge gash torn below the waterline and required temporary repairs, taking until August, before it was able to leave the island. Destroyer HMS *Matchless* was likewise damaged by a mine and forced to remain in the rubble-strewn port for repair, likewise for minesweeper HMS *Hebe*. Of the two merchant ships that survived to reach Malta, the largest freighter of the convoy, 10,400-ton SS *Orari* detonated a mine near the harbour entrance and, though managing to limp to a berth, lost much cargo outside of the breakwater through the damaged hull. Malta, already on starvation rations, had its life prolonged for eight weeks.

Vizeadmiral Weichold waited until the end of the attack on Vigorous to request that OKM rescind their instructions to keep 'secret' the presence of S-boats within the Mediterranean. The British already suspected the 'E-boats' they were battling were not Italian, and now the time had come to include Kemnade's men and their achievements within regular Wehrmacht bulletins. The apparent success of the Metox installation had also come to the attention of FdS, who immediately requested an investigation into the possibility of mass production and installation on all S-boats. As events transpired, Metox would be prioritised for U-boats and ultimately prove of limited value.

On 20 June Rommel's Afrika Korps, along with their Italian allies, finally entered Tobruk. The port officially surrendered the following morning with 33,000 Allied prisoners taken, as well as 2,000 tons of fuel, 5,000 tons of supplies, 2,000 vehicles and a working water filtration plant. The SKL War Diary recorded the event and its major ramifications for the entire war within the Mediterranean:

> The town and harbour of Tobruk was taken by German panzer forces at 1842hrs. The Admiral, German Naval Command, Italy thereupon immediately ordered the 3rd S-flotilla and the 6th R-flotilla to leave Derna. The task of the S-flotilla will be to intercept any enemy ships that may have been left in Tobruk and that now may attempt to flee. Subsequently the flotilla will form a patrol line north of Has Azzaz in order to protect the 6th R-flotilla. The task of the latter will be to sweep a lane into Tobruk. Three U-boats are on their way to Tobruk.
>
> The significance of this brilliant victory of the forces in North Africa is tremendous. Quite apart from its political importance and the prestige gained through this victory, together with its potential effect on the enemy and on all neutrals, the fact that we now hold this coastal fortress and excellent harbour has definite tactical and strategic implications requiring very quick military and naval decisions. The fall of Tobruk leaves the route to Egypt open and Operation Aida [Rommel's advance on Egypt] has suddenly moved into the realm of possibility. It is obvious that the primary task for the time being is to exploit fully the defeat of the enemy 8th Army.

This will create the basis for later carrying out operations with the Nile Delta as their ultimate goal. This victory will also extend the task of the Naval Staff, since the Naval Staff now will have to assume responsibility for transporting and convoying increased troop and supply shipments, together with the Luftwaffe. It will no longer be possible to delay carrying out Operation Herkules [the planned invasion of Malta] now, if the victory at Tobruk is not to remain a mere episode but is to be the beginning of a large operation which may decide the outcome of the war. Recognising his critical situation, the enemy will put all of his available forces into action, particularly his air and naval forces. He will desperately attempt to prevent our conquest of the Delta by trying to smash our troops and material supply. The battle for air and sea supremacy in the Mediterranean has entered its decisive phase. The faster we are able to deal the first blows, the more effective they will be. Every delay gives the enemy the time he needs for bringing up reinforcements.[83]

Kemnade despatched *S36*, *S54*, *S55*, *S56*, *S58* and *S59* from Derna at 2045hrs. The six boats sailed east in wedge formation at 26 knots, arriving in the waters off Tobruk past midnight. The first enemy vessels spotted were three small landing craft laden with escaping troops; *S56* and *S58* detached to intercept and sink them, plucking shocked survivors from the water. Soon more vessels were sighted attempting to break out of the falling city. The 72-ton HMT *Alaisia* was set on fire by gunfire from ObltzS Schmidt's *S54* before approaching 250-ton South African minesweeper HMSAS *Parktown* was sighted. The last Allied vessel to leave harbour, coming under infantry small-arms fire and shellfire from German tanks on the dock, *Parktown* was the most heavily armed of the escaping ships with a single Bofors cannon and four-barrelled Vickers anti-aircraft machine gun. Crowded with troops and towing a barge carrying more, the minesweeper opened fire as the S-boats attacked, hitting *S58* and killing the skipper ObltzS Eberhard Geiger, as well as severely wounding seven others, including flotilla medical officer, Marinestabsarzt Dr Heinrich Mehnen, shot in the stomach. German gunfire destroyed the South African's bridge, ruptured the boiler, killed or wounded half of the men on board and led to onboard ammunition exploding, causing her to burst into flames. Commanding officer, Lieutenant Leslie James Jagger, was killed and a sub lieutenant had his leg blown off. The remaining crew and soldiers abandoned ship and clung to Carley floats as the S-boats retreated, an Allied MTB sinking the burning wreck with depth charges later that evening.[84]

It was a confusing free-for-all as the S-boats took a heavy toll on fleeing vessels. The starboard and central engines on *S58* failed and *S54* came alongside, allowing flotilla adjutant ObltzS Johannes Backhaus to jump aboard the damaged boat and take command. In company with *S36*, Backhaus took the boat at full possible speed back to Derna, where the wounded men could be placed in hospital. En route Backhaus delivered a *coup de grâce* torpedo shot on a '5000-ton freighter', which was in fact the 6,811-ton Dutch motor vessel *Aagtekerk*, which had been part of the Vigorous convoy before heading to Tobruk with mechanical damage, and sunk by the Luftwaffe in shallow water. *S36* was mistakenly attacked by a Bf109 and two men lightly wounded before they reached port. For Mehnen it would be too late and he succumbed to his painful wounds the following day.

In combat, 'often bitter and at close range', the 3rd S-flotilla claimed to have sunk one patrol steamer (HMSAS *Parktown*), a tug, auxiliary sailing vessel, three landing barges, one motorboat and a steamer of 4,000 to 5,000-tons, previously damaged by the Luftwaffe. They also captured a large motor barge and two landing barges, and 175 prisoners, including ten officers. In combat lasting from before dawn to 1300hrs, no British vessels appeared to have escaped Tobruk. All S-boats were hit repeatedly: two were relegated to shipyard repairs and out of commission for a short time. Official Kriegsmarine reports singled out the 'aggressive fighting spirit of the flotilla, its commander, and the captains of the individual vessels.'[85]

The flotilla now took station in Tobruk, once again riding at anchor while in the harbour. They took advantage of captured British supplies to obtain fresh khaki uniforms, cigarettes and even Royal Navy rum, escorting occasional Italian supply convoys between Tobruk, Derna and Benghazi. The Afrika Korps continued its eastern advance, crossing the border into Egypt and capturing the small town of Mersa Matruh, an Egyptian fishing port sheltered from high seas by a natural rocky promontory shielding El Gharam Bay. Mersa Matruh fell to Axis troops on 29 June, and at 1700hrs on the first day of July *S54*, *S59* and *S56* departed Tobruk to establish a new forward base in Egypt. A single concrete pier was available, all port facilities, pontoons and water installations destroyed by the retreating British. From Mersa Matruh the Allies' main naval base, Alexandria, was a mere 139 nautical miles distant, S-boats planning offensive operations immediately. Twelve torpedoes were shipped to Mersa Matruh aboard an infantry landing ship, while a Greek coaster carrying fuel soon arrived; torpedo-balancing gear was shuttled from Tobruk aboard captured British trucks, the senior flotilla torpedo mechanic Obertorpedomechaniker Pusak accompanying them. By 3 July the new forward base was pronounced operational; *S61*, *S60* and *S33* were en route from Augusta and arrived the following day.

The flotilla's first mission into the waters off Alexandria began at night on 4 July, the port visible beneath Luftwaffe bombs. The S-boats sighted no targets aside from three small patrol vessels which faded into the darkness, and detected no defensive minefields as they passed close inshore.

In the early hours of 7 July the RAF bombed Tobruk, Benghazi and Mersa Matruh, damaging the anchored *S61* with bomb fragments, killing one man and injuring ObltzS Axel von Gernet. The boat was so seriously damaged that it required repair at Palermo, almost swamped by leaks in the hull in transit. The following day both *S56* and *S57* were also forced to leave the front as they had exhausted their engines' running time, sailing from Tobruk via Suda, Navarino and Augusta to Palermo for engine replacement. The flotilla was whittled down to two operational boats. Two others were ready for action in Augusta by 8 July, but lacked skippers. At S-boat headquarters, Petersen planned to transfer one new officer to Kemnade on 10 July; the shortage of trained officers was felt in nearly all Kriegsmarine branches.

The pressure on Kemnade's boats in their forward Egyptian base intensified with air attacks during 11 July by eight Fleet Air Arm 830 Squadron Albacores; the German steamer SS *Brook* was sunk after her fuel cargo ignited following a bomb hit. A little after midnight, shellfire from destroyers HM Ships *Beaufort*, *Dulverton*, *Eridge* and *Hurworth* began landing in and around the harbour, although no S-boats were damaged. Italian freighter SS *Sturla* was approaching the port under R-boat escort, and sank offshore. Both *S55* and *S60* immediately put to sea to rescue survivors, plucking forty-six men, including the captain, from the sea. A second attempted destroyer attack was foiled by *S33*, *S55* and *S60* who had been forewarned of the enemy's approach by their Metox radar detector. Waiting outside the harbour, the S-boat trio attempted their own torpedo attacks, but were thwarted by enemy flares and gunfire. *S60* suffered a hit in the central machine room and two men aboard *S33* were lightly wounded by another Albacore attack, while Italian supply ship MV *Citta di Agrigento* was hit four times and sank by the stern, although later refloated and successfully unloaded in harbour. It was a difficult end to the month of July as victory hung tantalisingly close for Axis forces in North Africa. On 23 July Kptlt Friedrich Kemnade was officially awarded the Knight's Cross.

Of the first ten nights of August, five were disturbed by bombing raids on Mersa Matruh. Despite the small target area, somewhat miraculously the flotilla suffered no casualties. Kemnade journeyed to Rome for a conference with Weichold. The flotilla was spread thinly: in Mersa Metruh the North African *Rotte* of *S33* and *S55* remained operational (under the command of ObltzS von Gernet during Kemnade's absence); in Suda Bay, Crete, *S35* and *S36* exercised under new commanders (ObltzS Klaus-Degenhard Schmidt and Günther Brauns respectively); in Augusta *S58* and *S59* were somewhat limited in their operational readiness, due to personnel shortages through enemy action, tropical disease and overdue leave granted to some crewmen. Even the flotilla reserve boat *S30*, also in Augusta, was uncrewed. The remainder of the flotilla boats were still in Palermo's shipyards.

Nonetheless, full commitment, bar the two African *Rotte*, was required, as another convoy attempted to reach Malta. The island's survival hung precariously in the balance and despite Hitler's earlier assertion that he would order invasion once Tobruk fell, Malta remained only under bombardment. The new effort, Operation Pedestal, was a huge undertaking by the British: a convoy of fourteen merchant ships escorted by four aircraft carriers, two battleships, seven light cruisers and thirty-two destroyers. Passing Gibraltar on 10 August, the first major loss had been the sinking of carrier HMS *Eagle* by *U81* the following day. Aircraft and submarine attacks then whittled the convoy down, while the Italian cruiser division sailed to intercept. Amongst the Axis forces, 3rd S-flotilla was to launch its own attacks from Porto Empedocle, beginning on the night of 12 August. The five boats gathered in harbour – *S58*, *S59*, *S35*, *S36* and *S30* (sailing with a composite crew commanded by ObltzS Weber and assembled from men whose boats were in the shipyard) – put to sea at 1600hrs. Oberleutnant zur See Günter Brauns' *S36* acted as *Führerboot*, but the young captain who was new to command was not in tactical control; Kptlt Kemnade came aboard, along with his adjutant and chief flotilla navigation and radio officers to take charge of the impending operation. Once within the Straits of Sicily they waited for Pedestal's approach. At 0308hrs the convoy came into view and 3rd S-flotilla attacked.

The confused battle that followed took place in an arena of flares, gunfire and burning ships, as the S-boats twisted and turned to avoid escorts and assault the vital merchant ships. Italian MAS boats joined the fray and, although various sources quote different results, by the end of the night German S-boats had sunk four merchant ships and damaged a fifth: ObltzS

The small port at Mersa Matruh became an ad hoc forward outpost for the 3rd S-flotilla sailing against British forces in Egypt. Their deployment here marked the high point of S-boat operations within the Mediterranean, soon to begin an irreversible slide towards defeat.

Müller's *S59* torpedoed 8,892-ton SS *Glenorchy* (eight seamen and a gunner killed, eight survivors rescued as prisoners of war); ObltzS Brauns' *S36* sank 8,379-ton SS *Santa Eliza* (four army gunners killed as the ship's aviation fuel caught fire); ObltzS Weber's *S30* successfully torpedoed 7,723-ton SS *Almeria Lykes* and 12,436-ton SS *Wairangi*, both ships being abandoned and later sunk. One other ship, 7,795-ton MV *Rochester Castle* was hit in the bow by *S30* but ploughed onward to Malta.

The casualty list for Operation Pedestal was daunting, and only five of the merchant ships reached Valletta's Grand Harbour, with hundreds of lives lost while battering the convoy through. The Italian cruiser division failed to engage the enemy, an undoubted tactical blunder on Mussolini's behalf. In the end, although the convoy was a debacle comparable to such disasters as PQ17 within the Arctic, it resupplied Malta to such a degree that the island no longer faced starvation. Fighter cover above Malta was secured with the arrival of aviation fuel and machine parts and, ultimately, Malta was revived as a functional military base. Once again Axis convoys supplying the Afrika Korps came under attack during August 1942 – 35 per cent destroyed that month and the figure rising in September. As

Rommel appeared poised to strike a decisive blow in Egypt, his supply lines were severely depleted once again.

For the 3rd S-flotilla it had been a triumphant attack although, seen through history's prism, it appears more akin to failure. A hunt for stragglers the following night was uneventful and by the end of August *S36* and *S61* had returned to Mersa Matruh to join the *Afrika Rotte* supporting Rommel, whose victorious advance had been halted at El Alamein. However, with Alexandria temporarily evacuated by the Royal Navy and the 8th Army's overland supply lines short and effective, there were no targets of opportunity, the flotilla leaving Mersa Matruh and returning to Sicily on the evening of 7 September. After a brief stay in Augusta, the 3rd S-flotilla moved to Porto Empedocle by the middle of September to make space for the incoming boats of 7th S-flotilla, which had begun its journey south on 10 September. The 3rd S-flotilla returned to its old hunting ground of Malta.

After a period of relative inactivity, the strength of the flotilla rested at twelve boats, including two reserves without commanders. Back to rude

Kapitänleutnant Albert Müller (commanding officer of the 3rd S-flotilla) and ObltzS Horst Weber, celebrating their recent awards of a Knight's Cross each, July 1943.

health, the flotilla once again began minelaying off Malta in November. This time, however, things had changed on the island. Morale was high following the Pedestal resupply and at El Alamein a second battle had been fought and won by the Allies, their counteroffensive forcing Rommel's slow retreat east. Cairo was no longer likely ever to see German rule. New radar and searchlight installations had been established on Malta and Gozo, able to detect the incoming S-boats and allow searchlights and artillery to keep them further offshore than planned, also allowing targeted sweeping to take place each day after the S-boats had departed. The balance had shifted within the Mediterranean and on 5 November seven boats of the 3rd S-flotilla laid the field MT27 to the south of Malta. It was to be their last Maltese minelaying operation.

During the previous day, 4 November, intelligence reports were received of another huge convoy in the Gibraltar region and the ten operational boats of 3rd S-flotilla were moved to Trapani on Sicily's west coast in expectation of another Malta convoy. However, this time they were wrong. The massive conglomeration of shipping was not bound for Malta but instead swung south to approach the shores of Algeria and Morocco, outside of the S-boats' range: Operation Torch had begun.

13
The Mediterranean

November 1942 – November 1943

THE 7th S-flotilla had begun formation in October 1941, originally under the control of Kptlt Bernd Klug, fresh from the temporary 5th S-flotilla during Barbarossa. Kapitänleutnant Hans Trummer, who held pre-war command of *S13* and had also served on Kemnade's staff in the Baltic, took charge of the new flotilla in June 1942. During early Swinemünde training the flotilla had used older boats *S18*, *S19*, *S20*, *S21*, *S22* and *S24* stationed with the tenders *Estonia* and *Hecht*. For transfer to the Mediterranean, they took charge of the eight Dutch boats commissioned in Schiedam; a further eight under construction were never completed. Training was still incomplete as they began their transit through the same waterways taken by Kemnade's flotilla, time being allocated to finish training within the Mediterranean after the boats refitted in Italy. On 10 September the first six began their journey, the remaining pair following shortly afterward. Once again the S-boats were disguised as much as possible and all crewmen dressed in civilian clothes, taking aboard Vichy liaison officers for the transit through France. They reached the Mediterranean on 8 October, and transferred for refit to La Spezia before the final training period was completed. On 15 December 1942 the 7th S-flotilla arrived in Augusta and was declared operational.

In the meantime, Allied forces had landed on Vichy French-held Morocco and Algeria in Operation Torch. The invasion was partially a sop to demands from Josef Stalin for the Western Allies to open a second front, but also held the strategic aim of crushing the retreating Afrika Korps from east and west, while establishing possible rapprochement with Vichy France. Allied strategists did not expect Vichy forces to fight, but several sharp battles occurred before Allied forces accomplished their objectives. Clearly, Vichy loyalties were confused and once the Allies' political manoeuvring with some Vichy officials became known to Hitler's government, the Germans moved to occupy Vichy France itself, the regime having been guaranteed nominal sovereignty over French territories as agreed in the 1940 Armistice. Germany now held all of France and, although the Vichy fleet in Toulon had scuttled itself rather than be captured by the Wehrmacht, the French Mediterranean coast opened itself for Kriegsmarine bases. The 3rd S-flotilla despatched their chief engineering officer to study the feasibility of basing S-boats in Toulon.

The 3rd S-flotilla lay in Trapani when news of Torch landings arrived, swiftly returning to Porto Empedocle. From there *S60*, *S35*, *S57*, *S56* and *S30* sailed immediately to Vichy-controlled Tunisia, making landfall at La Goulette in Tunis, where they were instructed to blockade all Vichy vessels and take control of the port installations.[86] Tunis boasted a deep-water harbour, crucial to any German defence in the west. The minesweeper *Canard* and three other smaller craft were found and disarmed. On 12 November Luftwaffe Oberst Harlinghausen arrived at the head of a makeshift Luftwaffe ground unit to take control of the city, supported by 5th Fallschirmjäger Regiment with fighter and dive bomber aircraft.

The city of Tunis was not to be the flotilla's base of operations and while the port was secured Kemnade despatched *S56* and *S60* northwest to Bizerte, Tunisia's other deep-water port, where the S-boats established a temporary headquarters. There they helped take control of the harbour alongside Wehrmacht troops, capturing in the process three small torpedo boats, nine submarines and nine minesweepers moored in the harbour and Lac de Bizerte. The Allies' failure to risk more with Operation Torch and make landings at both Tunisian ports undoubtedly prolonged German resistance in Africa. A new local command – Deutsche Marinekommando Tunisien – was established, exercising immediate operational control of the S-boats, KzS Otto Loycke occupying the new post until December, when he was replaced by KA Wilhelm Meendsen-Bohlken.

The S-boats sailed on the night of 16 November against expected Allied convoy traffic to the west, but nothing was sighted and the boats returned to Bizerte by 0500hrs. Later that day, an Italian motor vessel carrying 75,000 litres (16,500 gallons) of fuel, four weeks of supplies, ammunition and eight torpedoes reached Bizerta, although with no torpedo-regulating station they were not battle-ready. The crews spent the next few days establishing a base infrastructure from which to operate while unloading the Italian ship.

On the night of 24 November, Allied bombers began the first of a series of heavy air raids on Bizerte, Kemnade distributing his camouflaged boats between Cape Bizerte, the small offshore island of Cani, and Cape Rad Zebib; no casualties or damage ensued. Two days later the hard-pressed base personnel from Mersa Matruh arrived under the leadership of Leutnant (V) Max Jensen aboard four captured British trucks, after nearly 1,500 miles (2,400km) of driving. With them they brought the torpedo-balancing station – although, unfortunately, with no ability to carry ammunition from Egypt, Jensen had been forced to blow up eighty torpedoes before Mersa Matruh was abandoned.

The classic S-boat profile.

On the afternoon of 1 December, the 3rd S-flotilla sailed from Bizerte to rendezvous and help protect a supply convoy of one German and three Italian freighters under Italian warship escort heading for Bizerte. Detected by the Allies, the convoy was attacked by the Royal Navy cruisers and destroyers of Force Q, newly based in Bône, Algeria. They and a newly-established cruiser force in Malta took turns at intercepting Axis convoys bound for North Africa. The British attack was a triumph: every freighter sunk, as well as Italian ships *Folgore*, *Nicoloso da Recco* and *Procione* badly damaged. The British, in turn, suffered no damage until returning to Bône when they were attacked by the Luftwaffe with HMS *Quentin* sunk. By the time that 3rd S-flotilla reached the scene of the convoy disaster, there was nothing to be seen except the badly damaged *Procione* limping to port.

The following day the flotilla again sailed to meet a supply convoy, this time four steamers escorted by four torpedo boats. Rendezvousing with the incoming ships, the S-boats remained with them until the convoy split, two merchants and torpedo boats bound for Tunis, SS *Caupania* and SS

Menes and the remaining torpedo boats and S-boats heading west to Bizerte. A mine was seen and detonated by gunfire, although a second mine was not detected and SS *Menes* exploded east of Cani Island, sinking in 80m (260ft) of water. From a crew and passenger complement of 350, *S59* rescued thirty-three German soldiers, while *S57* found only five.

German troops had established an effective defensive line against the Torch forces, as the chaos of the first few weeks gave way to some semblance of order. French crewmen aboard the captured Vichy vessels in Bizerte were removed by 3rd S-flotilla, the French tricolour ceremonially taken down and the men interned. The flotilla continued to operate as convoy security, *S33*, *S57*, *S58* and *S61* sailing on the night of 12 December to meet fast Italian motor ship MV *Foscolo* escorted by the destroyer *Freccia*. The 4,500-ton freighter carried munitions and cans of petrol bound for the Afrika Korps, but was torpedoed by Albacores of 828 Squadron FAA from Malta. The S-boats arrived in time to rescue fifty Italian and thirty-one German troops from a sea covered with a burning layer of petrol.

That same day *S59* had begun the voyage to Palermo's shipyard for scheduled engine overhaul, *S54* accompanying her as far as Porto Empedocle. The remainder of the flotilla moved into Lac de Bizerte and transferred their headquarters to the naval basin at Ferryville, now vacated by the Vichy ships. There the boats took full advantage of the long pier and crews were stationed in nearby Fort Leoch as Allied aerial bombardment of Bizerte continued. Mines were transported from Tunis, and on 17 December the flotilla undertook a minelaying mission southeast of Cape de Garde and in the Bône Bight. The following night they repeated the task, this time north of the cape, returning to Bizerte as yet more bombers pounded the city. A third mission planned for 30 December was scrubbed due to bad weather.

The beginning of 1943 found Kemnade's 3rd S-flotilla in a poor state. Although on paper the unit's strength was formidable, in reality it possessed only four serviceable boats. In Palermo's shipyard *S30*, *S35*, *S36*, and *S59* were all undergoing overhaul, while *S54* and *S56* were being refitted in Augusta.[87] Only *S60*, *S56*, *S57* and *S61* were combat-ready in Ferryville. Friedrich Kemnade himself took command of the reserve boat *S58*, raising flotilla numbers, and he sailed with the others on their first mission of the New Year, laying mines from the stern rails near Bône once more. Radio interception betrayed the presence of the S-boats, although Allied naval command failed to notify minesweeping trawler HMT *Horatio* patrolling off Cape de Garde. The trawler was spotted by Kemnade's *S58* and two torpedoes were fired, both hitting the 545-ton ship and sinking her immediately. Only two survivors of the thirty-four crew were rescued by Kemnade and taken back to Bizerte.

The following day, Kptlt Trummer arrived in Bizerte with seven boats from 7th S-flotilla, *S155* still in an Augusta shipyard. Now, while 3rd S-flotilla continued minelaying, the smaller boats of 7th S-flotilla provided flanking torpedo support or ran distraction missions. Both flotillas were capable of carrying torpedo mines, thus the roles could be reversed when such mines were available. Minelaying continued wherever possible, constrained only by the supply of mines and weather conditions. The S-boats clashed for the first time with three enemy MTBs on the night of 29 January and in a brief, but fierce, gun battle, mines were jettisoned and the Germans returned to harbour.

The combat-readiness of 3rd S-flotilla deteriorated yet further with the losses and damage inflicted by Allied bombing in Sicily as well as North Africa. The S-boats relied on camouflage for protection in harbour; however, an American attack on Augusta on 23 January killed one man from the crew of *S57*. Two nights later the navigator from *S60* was also killed by bombing in Porto Empedocle where his boat was undergoing an overhaul. More followed on 30 January, when *S155* was hit by bombs in Augusta, with two men killed and another two severely wounded. With Palermo's facilities severely hampered and increased bombing of Sicily and mainland Italy, an alternative destination for S-boats requiring repair was sought. Meanwhile, *S56* was sunk by bombs in Augusta, later refloated and taken under tow to the French naval base at Toulon. The Allies had so far paid no attention to the French harbour and by the end of February *S33*, *S58*, and *S61* from 3rd S-flotilla had all followed, *S151*, *S152* and *S155* not far behind.

On 4 February the harbour entrance to Algeria's Philippeville was mined by the 3rd S-flotilla. The next mission on 27 February entailed *S36* and three boats of the 7th S-flotilla laying eight TMA torpedo mines in Bône's entrance channels. Three boats of the 3rd S-flotilla were to provide cover, *S35*, *S54* and *S55* standing out to sea. Rain and hailstones descended on the outbound boats, causing the mine carriers to return to harbour, while the three torpedo boats formed a loose picket line in the western Sicilian Strait. As they rode the swell, a strong phosphorescence wake was seen moving fast to port. Assuming it to be enemy MTBs, the S-boats opened fire, gunning their engines to give chase as the enemy began to return fire.

The S-boat crews made out what appeared to be three smokestacks in the muzzle flash of heavy weapons before the enemy ship faded into the bad visibility, the S-boats beginning their return to Ferryville. At 0650hrs *S54* tied up to the pier, followed an hour later by *S55*. There was no sign of the third boat and no communication had been received. By 0945hrs *S35* was considered missing and the two S-boats retraced their steps looking for ObltzS Stolzenburg's boat, *S55* finding floating wreckage including 5m-long planking amongst the debris field, as well as an empty lifeboat. The entire crew were missing: *S35* had blundered into a large minefield sown that night by the fast minelayer HMS *Abdiel* – the same ship that the S-boats had been chasing. ObltzS Karl-Heinz Stolzenburg and his twenty-one crewmen were killed.

The first Allied casualty to recently laid S-boat mines was recorded on 5 February when 545-ton HMT *Stronsay* was sunk. Bad weather delayed further minelaying until 11 March. The following night three boats from each flotilla sailed, KK Trummer recording in his War Diary that: 'Due to our own large convoy travelling from Sicily and Sardinia to Bizerte, the 7th S-flotilla is ordered by Marinekommando to take up position at the Western Patrol Line'.

Opposite the S-boats, Force Q had shipped from Bône to intercept the same convoy. Destroyers HMS *Lightning* and *Loyal* provided flanking cover to cruisers HMS *Aurora* and *Sirius*. While the S-boat crews were weary after constant alerts both at sea and under the bombs in harbour, Allied crews were equally tired and suffering from ration deficiencies, resulting in ships operating far from peak efficiency. Royal Navy crewman Jack Hall recalled what followed:

As usual we were at action stations on leaving Bône and damage control continued to plug the shrapnel holes ... The plan was to attack a German convoy out of Sicily bound for Tunisia. We heard later that the convoy returned to harbour when they realised that we had left port. German intelligence must have been good as we were attacked by twelve torpedo bombers at 1851hrs ... After the air attack ceased ... we pressed on in formation. At about 2200hrs our [Headache] interpreters on board intercepted a radio message, in German saying that they were about to attack the *Lightning*.

We had been at action stations all evening and I was closed up in 'A' turret. I was tired, hungry and frightened as we were so close to the enemy. At about 2215hrs, through my sights, I clearly saw the pale grey E-boat on the port beam when it fired the first torpedo. We were not operating RDF, ASDIC or HFDF and had no time to return fire – perhaps if we had all been fighting fit we may have opened fire in time – who knows? The skipper turned the ship hard to port to comb the track of the torpedo as he had done on so many previous occasions, but she was just too slow this time and we were hit fine on the port bow, blowing it clean off 'as if cut by a knife'.

Even though I was very near the point of impact I heard no loud explosion, just a sickening heavy thud that jarred my bones. The ship shuddered from the blow and everything went dead. Realising what had happened and with no electrical power to operate the gun we had no choice but to abandon the turret. We could not escape from the door as it was jammed. Instead, we had to escape onto the deck by sliding down the chute for ejected shell cases ... Upon emerging from the gun turret I was amazed at the enormity of the damage and how near we had been to being killed outright. About fifty feet of the ship had been blown clean away and our turret was leaning over onto the deck ... Everything was still and quiet – there was no return of fire and no rushing about. The only other ship visible was the E-boat. We just waited for the inevitable, like a rabbit hypnotised in a car's headlights.

The stricken ship quickly lost way and became a sitting target. In a desperate attempt to save her, the skipper gave orders to go astern to relieve pressure on the forward bulkheads that were still holding. But I could only watch as our attacker slowly circled the dead ship and came round to the starboard side. I heard his engines speed up as he turned to run in towards us. He came straight for us and fired a second, fatal, tin fish. It was carefully aimed and hit us square amidships beneath the funnel. This caused terrible damage, destroying both boiler rooms, pom pom and for'ard torpedo tubes on the upper deck, and breaking the poor ship's back. I watched in disbelief and horror as a huge plume of water and steam rose high above us as the torpedo plunged into our lovely ship. Men and machinery were blown to oblivion. I felt very sorry for my good mates on the pom pom, they never stood a chance and must have watched helplessly as the fateful torpedo sped straight for them. With her back broken she immediately began to founder.[88]

The first torpedo had been fired by ObltzS Claus Schultze-Jena's *S158* hitting the port bow. The second was Kptlt Horst Weber's *S55*, hitting below the funnel. *S157* had also fired a double salvo on the leading destroyer but missed, the S-boat turning away and slowly running northeast on one engine while reloading when *Lightning* was hit, skipper

LzS Hans-Wulf Heckel radioing the sight of 'a torpedo detonation with an unusually high, very pointed detonation mushroom'. Rain began to obscure the battlefield, *S158* moving slowly among the survivors asking for the captain and for anybody who wanted rescuing. A single wounded man was passed aboard and the S-boat left the scene as the rest of Force Q loomed out of the murk to rescue survivors. Two officers and forty-three ratings went down with their ship. A shell hit on *S158* had killed one man, another was severely wounded aboard *S55* and one lightly injured on *S60* by shell splinters. Oberleutnant zur See Weber in *S55* claimed two destroyers hit, ObltzS Thomsen in *S156* a cruiser damaged, and S60's ObltzS Haag an unknown ship also hit. HMS *Lightning* was the sole casualty of Force Q. On 5 July 1943, ObltzS Horst Weber was awarded the Knight's Cross.

By the middle of March the 3rd S-flotilla had laid 404 mines and 195 explosive and cutter buoys. The 4,636-ton British freighter SS *Beckenham* was damaged by one of the mines, but other than that results were poor. A period of full moon prevented minelaying until the beginning of April when the next planned mission was aborted due to the presence of British destroyers.

By the beginning of March Allied troops had advanced in the east as far as the Tunisian border, while Torch forces in the west were pressing hard, though periodically stunned into inaction by the experienced and still dangerous Heeresgruppe Afrika. However, the Axis grip on North Africa was untenable and defeat inevitable. The 7th S-flotilla received brief reinforcement during April with the attachment of *RA10*, the ex-British *MTB314* captured off Tobruk harbour during the heady days of German success. Commanded by LzS Brusgatis, the small MTB rescued nine Luftwaffe troops from a downed Me323 Gigant evacuating troops to Sicily. Three other soldiers and one body were later retrieved from the same area. However, Brusgatis' command was cut short when *RA10* was attacked and sunk by British Spitfires at La Goulette, six of the twenty-one crew killed and eight wounded.

On 14 April ObltzS Siegfried Wuppermann was awarded the coveted Oak Leaves to his Knight's Cross. His was the 226th such award issued and only the second for the S-boat service. As was often the case for such highly-decorated men, Wuppermann was transferred back to Germany to take charge of the 21st and 22nd S-boat training flotillas, his place as skipper of *S56* left vacant as the boat went into reserve. The Oak Leaves also followed on 27 May for KK Friedrich Kemnade.

The post of Marinekommando Tunisien, held since March 1943 by KzS Dr Paul Meixner, was dissolved in May 1943 and control of the flotillas reverted to MGK Italy. There too the commander had changed: Weichold moved out by Dönitz and replaced by VA Friedrich Ruge. In bad weather during early May, MGK Italy ordered all S-boats to leave Tunisia. The majority of both flotillas' boats were already in French shipyards and on 5 May *S57* and *S60* embarked as many headquarters personnel and soldiers as they could and departed for Porto Empedocle. *S33* and *S36* laid a last round of mines in front of Bizerte harbour before returning to Ferryville and destroying as many port installations as possible. On 7 May *S33*, *S36*, *S153* and *S158* left Bizerte for the last time with 100 soldiers aboard, including Paul Meixner and his staff officers,. Bad weather forced the small 7th S-flotilla boats to divert to Trapani before later proceeding also to Porto Empedocle.

As the final dramatic moments of Heeresgruppe Afrika played out around Tunis, three boats of the 3rd S-flotilla put out for Cape Bon on the evening of 9 May. They were attempting to evacuate more men but kept from approaching shore by a high sea state and lack of disembarkation facilities. The boats put in to Empedocle the next morning of 10 May, all seaborne and evacuation transport suspended immediately by OKW. The Kriegsmarine's small vessels were switched over to carrying supplies to Pantelleria Island, midway between Sicily and Tunisia, S-boats providing flanking cover. Axis forces in Tunisia finally surrendered on 13 May and 275,000 men went into captivity.

The final mine barriers that had been laid by the S-boats in Tunisia reaped a grim tally of victims including *MTB264*, minesweeper *MMS89*, *ML1154* and the 850-ton minesweeper HMS *Fantome*, severely damaged and later written off. The 8,046-ton American tanker SS *Yankee Arrow* was also damaged on 3 August off Cap Bône, with seven crewmen killed.

The two S-flotillas were spread across the western Mediterranean. Trummer's 7th S-flotilla possessed five combat-ready boats: *S152*, *S155*, *S156*, *S157* and *S158*; flotilla headquarters moved to Porto Vesme in southern Sardinia. In Augusta's shipyard lay *S153* and *S154* while *S151* was in Toulon. From Kemnade's 3rd S-flotilla four boats were in the Toulon yards – *S54*, *S58*, *S60* and *S61* – *S36* in Augusta and *S56* in Palermo. His flotilla could muster only five operational boats: *S30*, *S33*, *S55*, *S57* and *S59*. *S55* was disabled on the night of 17 May by Allied bombs that killed one man and wounded three others, after having laid the first of several defensive minefields before Porto Empedocle. The damaged boat was towed home by *S57*.

Porto Empedocle came under sustained attack on the afternoon of 25 May by thirty-six B-26 bombers of the USAAF 320th Bombardment Group. They demolished buildings and installations, splitting the small quayside apart. Twenty-four P-38 Lightning escorts were superfluous as only light flak greeted them and the Luftwaffe were nowhere to be seen. *S55* was hit once more and two men wounded. It was during those difficult days for the Mediterranean boats that KK Friedrich Kemnade was awarded the Oak Leaves to his Knight's Cross on 27 May, the third such award for the S-boat service.

Increasing Allied bombing caused Kemnade to request MGK Italy for new flotilla bases on the more easily defended mainland. In reply, 3rd S-flotilla was ordered to abandon Porto Empedocle and Augusta, and transfer men and equipment to Marseilles. The dismantling of the base equipment would take some time, and efforts were made to reduce the stock of torpedoes, munitions and spare parts before the remainder were shipped with all residual headquarters personnel and equipment to the harbours of Salerno and Viareggio, considered relatively safe, for the time being at least.

However, the use of Marseilles was already causing some concern in Kriegsmarine command circles. MGK West, under whose jurisdiction the port fell, reported that only Toulon and Marseilles were suitable for S-boat deployment. However, the personnel and equipment requirements to establish such primary bases exceeded MGK West's limited means. Instead, the Aegean Sea was put forward as a better location, operational S-boats remaining in Italian waters pending a decision.

The day following an inspection by the Regia Marina's Chief of Staff, Admiral Arturo Riccardi, the 3rd S-flotilla departed, proceeding first to Trapani, where the men were quartered under canvas, while four of the boats sailed onward to the small island of Pantelleria, also heavily bombed by Allied aircraft. Bad weather prevented further movement to Portovesma until 8 June. From there, the two flotillas were tasked with patrolling the Sicilian Strait into the Gulf of Hammamet as flanking escorts for evacuation transports from Pantelleria to Sicily. Pantelleria capitulated on 11 June as British troops of 1st Infantry Division stormed ashore in Operation Corkscrew, the Allies now with a foothold and airfield in the middle of the Strait. Operations by both Sicilian S-flotillas against potential invasion were hamstrung by order delays from the island's Italian headquarters. Listening posts detected increasing MTB activity, as well as the presence of American PT boats and during the following night six S-boats sighted what they believed to be a convoy of Hunt-class destroyers, every boat firing a double torpedo salvo and each torpedo missing, as the targets were in fact six shallow-draught MTBs. A full moon period was approaching, which meant minimal operations. Attempted evacuation of Luftwaffe troops from tiny Lampione Island west of Malta was undertaken by two boats on 14 June, but ended in failure when the island was found already occupied by the Allies. The flotilla's dealings with the Luftwaffe were more successful two nights later when Oberleutnant H Müller was rescued from the sea by *S59* after his fighter plane had been shot down.

Both flotillas were frequently kept at immediate readiness over the ensuing days, sailing to intercept enemy shipping and returning empty-handed each time with little more than engine wear and tear to show for their efforts. Both units had briefly been put under the direct command of

Aerial photograph of the USAAF bombing of Porto Empedocle on 25 May 1943, by thirty-six B26 bombers of the 320th Bombardment Group. *S55* was damaged during the attack.

the Regia Marina's Messina district in order to provide a more homogeneous defence against any Allied invasion, although language difficulties and fundamentally different operational doctrine brought the S-boats back under MGK Italy's control. Meanwhile, Allied bombing continued and on 29 June Kemnade himself was badly injured in an automobile accident during a British night raid. With flares dropping over the harbour, his car, travelling from the flotilla accommodation to the harbour, rammed the crew bus travelling in the opposite direction. Kemnade's head went through his car's windscreen and he also suffered a fractured knee. The flotilla was subsequently handed over to his most experienced S-boat commander, ObltzS Albert Müller, acting as temporary chief while Kemnade recuperated in Catania's Luftwaffe hospital; he was later transferred to a staff position within OKM.

By the time of his ascension to flotilla command, Müller's boat *S59* had been sunk. Eight RAF Hurricane fighter bombers had attacked the harbour at Porto Empedocle on 6 July, hitting *S59* with a bomb and sinking her in flames. Two men were killed during the attack and the boats *S55* and *S61* damaged by bomb splinters. Under such direct pressure, the decision was taken for 3rd S-flotilla to break out of the beleaguered port and travel to Palermo, with a planned onward voyage to Augusta, all seven boats reaching Palermo at 0830hrs on 10 July. They had been ordered to engage any enemy forces encountered, although after brushing with a superior force of seventeen American PT boats and the destroyer USS *Ordronaux* the flotilla withdrew to the west. The Americans had been despatched to patrol Porto Empedocle, forcing any S-boats or Italian MAS boats into action and neutralising them. The 7th S-flotilla still lay in Cagliari, Sardinia, at immediate readiness as Wehrmacht command in Italy attempted to guess their enemy's intentions. By the time the 3rd S-flotilla reached Palermo, Allied landings in Sicily – Operation Husky – were underway.

The 3rd S-flotilla was ordered immediately to the Straits of Messina near Syracuse, two boats dropping out due to damaged steering gear, the remainder finding nothing. This left the flotilla strength at five boats ready for action at Palermo, and two more in limited operational status, while three others lay in Toulon shipyards. Five boats of 7th S-flotilla were ready for action at Cagliari and three boats also non-operational at Toulon. The 3rd S-flotilla made another thrust into the southern reaches of the Straits of Messina, but again found nothing, putting in to the mainland harbour of Naples to refuel and take on torpedoes. MGK Italy planned to employ the flotilla off the southeastern tip of Sicily, reasoning that with the presence of an entire invasion fleet there should be targets aplenty, even during the short darkness hours of the Mediterranean summer. However, the Allied beaches were protected by a huge naval commitment and at no point could the S-boats begin offensive action.

Confusion dogged the flotilla as it found itself divided between small Italian harbours with little or no facilities for the S-boats to refuel or re-arm. A permanent replacement for Kemnade was still en route from Germany, as they continued operating in the growing welter of confusion. Skirmishes by all available S-boats with enemy MGBs and MTBs further eroded German striking power, without any tangible success in return. Indeed, immediately following one confused night action, all seven available vessels from both flotillas put into Salerno where they were declared out of action due to combat damage or engine trouble. To compound an already difficult situation, the commanders of *S33* and *S61* (ObltzS Günther Brauns and ObltZS Axel von Gernet) were hospitalised with jaundice, and by 15 July the 3rd S-flotilla had only *S55* combat-ready.

The following day the new commander arrived from Germany. Korvettenkapitän Herbert Max Schultz, previously FdS Chief of Staff, arrived not only as commander of the 3rd S-flotilla, but also in a new role designed to reunify the scattered S-boats within the Mediterranean theatre. At the request of FdS, as a new organisational step the 1st Schnellboots-division was created, tasked with the co-ordination of all S-boat activities within the Mediterranean, Tyrrhenian, Adriatic, Aegean and Ionian Seas. With boats scattered far and wide, the new post would allow a more complete overview for those responsible for handling operations. Initial estimation of the striking power available to the 1st S-division did not make happy reading.

3rd S-flotilla:
   Combat-ready in Salerno only *S55*. *S30* and *S36* out of service.
   In Naples out of service: *S33* and *S54*.
   In Castellamare out of service: *S61* and *S58*
   In Toulon out of service: *S56* and *S57*.

7th S-flotilla:
   Combat-ready in Salerno: *S151*, *S152*, *S154* and *S155*.
   In Toulon out of service: *S153*, *S156*, *S157* and *S158*.

Potential bases within the Aegean had already been offered by SKL, Thessaloniki, Suda, Kalamata and Patras deemed suitable for S-boats as the Germans feared an Allied invasion of Greece, as well as Italian territories. The harbours were designated as future S-boat bases with planned torpedo stocks and torpedo-regulating equipment, while Argostoli, Prevesa and Navarino were named as bases with fuel dumps only. Construction work began immediately.

Five boats of the 7th S-flotilla clashed in an artillery duel with four MGBs on the night of 15 July, twenty miles south of Messina. The Germans claimed two MGBs hit and one probably sunk; a combined torpedo attack made later on a tanker or LST with two escort vessels was unsuccessful due to a phosphorescent bubble track. While returning to base the S-boats were heavily engaged by a superior force of eight MTBs; *S156* was temporarily immobilised by engine failure during the action, one man wounded by gunfire before the boat was underway once more. By the time the flotilla returned to Paradiso, four boats were deemed out of service by combined shell hits and engine trouble, placed on inactive duty until the larger boats of 3rd S-flotilla were ready once more, the *S151* type that comprised Trummer's command considered 'very unreliable' by MGK Italy, and 'in spite of the new engines, can make only 28 knots maximum speed, and barely 24 knots, cruising speed.' Both *S154* and *S157* were despatched to Toulon for engine overhauls.

Finally, on 19 July six boats were able to make a combat sortie that appeared to reap dividends for the newly established division. *S30*, *S33*, *S54*, *S61*, *S152* and *S155* sailed from Salerno for Sicily's east coast. Between 0032hrs and 0140hrs they attacked in broad formation a convoy of three steamers, two LSTs and four escorts steaming from the south toward Syracuse, which had been in Allied hands for seven days. *S30* fired a torpedo at an LST and a steamer estimated at 5–8,000 tons, though both shots missed. *S61* in turn claimed a destroyer hit and sunk, before return fire from the third escorting destroyer killed a junior officer. *S33* also radioed a hit on a 'single-funnelled' destroyer. Finally, *S152* reported sinking a 3,000-ton steamer before the S-boats returned to Crotone, ammunition expended. The attack brought swift retaliation by the Allies, the cruiser HMS *Aurora* leading a naval bombardment of the port and its railway junction. Forewarned of the Allies' approach by radar, the S-boats had already put to sea and escaped damage, unable to intervene through fuel shortage and a lack of torpedo reloads in the port: 112 Eto-type electric torpedoes were captured intact by the Allied advance through Augusta. Allied records show nothing related to the S-boats' claimed successes. The following day, 22 July, Palermo fell to the Allies, six S-boats sailing to

Taranto where they found neither available fuel nor ammunition.

It would be a week before supplies reached the S-boats, by which time the Italian dictator Benito Mussolini had been deposed and arrested. German fears that Italy would conclude a separate peace with the Allies led to pre-emptive instructions for Operation Achse: German disarmament of local Italian units to be carried out upon receipt of further orders.

The beginning of August found both flotillas at an operational readiness of three boats each. The 3rd S-flotilla had *S30*, *S33* and *S61* in Crotone, where there were now torpedoes and fuel available, the port damaged by British cruisers' bombardment on 2 August. The remainder of unserviceable boats were spread between Taranto (*S54* and *S60*), Vibo Valentina (*S36* which had no crew), Salamis (*S55*), Castellamare (*S58*) and Toulon (*S57* and *S56*, the latter also lacking crew). The 7th S-flotilla mustered *S152*, *S154* and *S155* operationally ready in Taranto, while *S151*, *S153*, *S156*, *S157* and *S158* remained in Toulon's yards.

Meanwhile, the Allied invasion of Sicily neared its climax. Casualties aboard S-boats rose under Allied bombs and in action at sea. On land, German and Italian forces began to evacuate Sicily across the narrow Straits of Messina, protected by a formidable array of coastal artillery and flak weapons that successfully kept Allied interference to a minimum. By 17 August the evacuation was complete and Sicily fell to the Allies the following day. There was little doubt that the Allies would press their advantage and assault Italy itself, begun on the morning of 3 September when British troops crossed the Straits of Messina onto the toe of Italy in Operation Baytown. Five days later, as the British advanced with painful sluggishness over obstacles and inhospitable terrain, Eisenhower announced the negotiated surrender of Italy. Those naval forces that remained loyal to the deposed Mussolini became known as Marina Nazionale Repubblicana, while Mussolini himself was liberated from incarceration by German paratroopers on 12 September, flown to Germany and browbeaten into forming a new Fascist regime, the Italian Social Republic established on 18 September 1943.

Meanwhile, German units carried out Operation Achse, as further Allied forces landed at Taranto in Operation Slapstick, executed with short notice following an Italian offer to surrender the port and its military units. Kesselring correctly surmised that neither Baytown nor Slapstick were the primary Allied invasion which landed that same day at Salerno: Operation Avalanche. During the morning the 1st S-division was informed of a large invasion force west of Palinuro and all mobile units of the 3rd S-flotilla marched north by road, transporting munitions, weapons and torpedo-regulating equipment.

As Slapstick forces approached Taranto, *S54* and *S61* prepared to depart. Unfettered by Italian forces they withdrew with artillery lighter *F478*, but not before ObltzS Klaus-Degenhard Schmidt laid thirty TMA/TMB mines from *S54* across the harbour entrance. *F478* also dropped twenty more and *S61* under temporary command of Bootsmaat Friedel Blömker (ObltzS von Gernet still recovering from jaundice in Germany) added another four. The mines accounted for two ships, including 2,650-ton minelayer HMS *Abdiel*, laden with airborne troops, exploding and sinking with fifty-eight soldiers and forty-eight crewmen killed.

The three German vessels made way for Venice, encountering 91-ton Italian auxiliary minelayer *Victoria* and, following several warning shots, persuading the crew to abandon ship and take to their lifeboat while their ship was scuttled by a German boarding party. Italian cruiser *Scipione Africano* was then spotted and Schmidt ordered the slow *F478* abandoned and scuttled, Kptlt Winkler and his crew coming aboard the S-boats as they sped north.

Travelling into the Adriatic Sea, the S-boats sighted a southbound gunboat off Ancona on 11 September. Receiving no reply to his order to stop, Schmidt fired a torpedo that failed to detonate after impact. Blömker aboard *S61* then fired a torpedo spread, one of which the Italian avoided, while the other hit and sank 935-ton *Aurora*, twenty-six men going down with the ship and sixty-two survivors rescued as prisoners of war. The two S-boats continued north, swinging east and hugging the Adriatic coast of Yugoslavia to avoid minefields. The following morning they sighted 4,572-ton Italian passenger ship MV *Leopardi*, which had departed Fiume with 1,000 troops and 500 civilians bound for Italy. The vessel's captain complied with the German order to stop and, following negotiations with Schmidt, jettisoned all arms and surrendered, Kptlt Winkler and ten of his men, late of *F478*, boarding as prize crew, following the S-boats as they headed to Venice. A short time later, 1,590-ton Italian freighter SS *Saubasia* was intercepted by Blömker's *S61* and brought to a halt, and another prize crew put aboard the captured steamer. Finally, just short of Venice lagoon, 715-ton Italian SS *Pontonia* was also stopped by Schmidt's *S61* and captured. As the latest prize was being added to the German tally, lookouts sighted the distant shape of Italian torpedo boat *Quintino Sella* travelling to Taranto to surrender to British forces. Schmidt did not hesitate and swiftly brought *S54* into the lee of SS *Pontonia*, hiding the S-boat from sight as *Quintino Sella* approached. By manipulating the steamer's engines and rudder, the two vessels were able to remain in perfect formation until the unwitting torpedo boat stopped before *Pontonia*'s bow and Schmidt opened fire, two torpedoes impacting near the bridge and in boiler room number one. As the boiler exploded, the ship broke in two, the bow sinking immediately, while the stern floated for some time before also slipping beneath the waves. Twenty-seven crewmen went down with the ship as well as at least a hundred civilian refugees, the S-boats continuing to Venice as two crewmen from *S54* directed the captured SS *Pontinia* in rescuing eighty survivors. A radioed request to the damaged *S30* and *S33* in nearby Pola for help with the rescue was unsuccessful, Italian forces preventing them leaving harbour.

At 1933hrs *S54* and the prize *Leopardi* entered Venice lagoon. The Kriegsmarine ensign had been lowered and uniform details removed so as to pass relatively unnoticed. Within two hours *S61* and the remaining prizes also entered Venice. Both S-boats had exhausted their supplies: fuel was virtually gone, as were water and provisions. While *S54* possessed no further torpedoes, *S61* had a single 'eel' left as the S-boats headed directly to the Italian naval arsenal. Schmidt's plan was simple: he was going to capture Venice.

The S-boats docked and Schmidt, accompanied by several heavily armed crewmen, disembarked and requested an audience with the senior Italian officer. Shortly thereafter, Schmidt, together with the local German consul-general and an officer of the German railways, delivered an ultimatum bluff to the Italian Commander-in Chief, Northern Adriatic Sea, Divisionadmiral Emilio Brenta, and the chief of the Venice arsenal, Contrammiraglio Franco Zannoni. Unless the city and its arsenal capitulated, it would face annihilation by Stuka and Kriegsmarine bombardment. The Italians capitulated and more than ten thousand Italian sailors, the destroyer *Sebenico*, torpedo boat *Audace*, two submarines, eight auxiliaries and thirty merchant ships surrendered to the two S-boat crews. It was, to say the least, a remarkable achievement, and later Bootsmaat Blömker was awarded the *Deutsches Kreuz in Gold* on 18 September, with Schmidt awarded the Knight's Cross on 22 December. Kapitänleutnant Albert Müller, who had taken the 3rd S-flotilla reins from an injured Kemnade, had also been awarded the Knight's Cross on 13 December for his energetic leadership.

Both ObltzS Baruns' *S33* and ObltzS Johannes Backhaus' *S30* had been prevented from assisting in the rescue of survivors from *Quintino Sella*.

Italian forces in Pola prevented them and the Type VIIC *U407* from either arming with torpedoes or putting to sea; the harbour boom was lowered and guarded by corvettes. Both S-boats had reached the Croatian harbour after transferring from threatened Taranto, bringing with them twenty-three survivors from the Italian tanker *Flegetonte*, sunk on 31 August by HMS *Unsparing*. Their original orders were to enter the Aegean as soon as possible, continuing any necessary repairs there, although the Italian armistice trapped them in Pola.

The port had been of primary importance to the Austro-Hungarian navy during the First World War and had retained its significance during the Second. Annexed by the Italians in 1918, their surrender left 18,000 sailors and 15,000 soldiers in Pola facing 160 German soldiers manning a small Kriegsmarine base. The Italians moved heavy weapons to face them, signalling their intention to hold the Germans by force if necessary. However, the Italian armistice provided few guidelines for troops regarding duties either for or against their former allies and, once again, German bluster won the day after Kriegsmarine base commandant Oblt (Ing) Erwin Pohl threatened the Italian commander, Divisionadmiral Gustavo Strazzeri, with aerial bombardment unless they ceased interference in German operations. Strazzeri deferred to German demands and Italian troops remained silent when *S30* and *S33* put to sea fully armed. They were, however, too late to assist the Venice-bound S-boats and soon returned to Pola, which was soon occupied by units of the Wehrmacht's 71st Infantry Division who proceeded to disarm their erstwhile allies and place the Istrian Peninsula firmly under German control. The two S-boats assisted in dealing with the large number of Italian troops and on 16 September *S30* escorted the prisoner of war transport ship *Vulcania* to Venice, carrying the bulk of the former Italian garrison.

However, the tribulations of the two Istrian S-boats were not yet over, as partisan activity swiftly escalated: an attack on the harbour at Rovigno on 22 September killed Steuermannsmaat Erich Wirth and wounded two others. *S30* and *S33* transferred to Venice shortly thereafter where, together with *S54* and *S61*, repairs were carried out and they sailed to the Aegean to reunite with remaining boats of 3rd S-flotilla.

As the Allies established beachheads on the Italian mainland, four S-boats sailed from Civitavecchia during the afternoon of 10 September for the waters off Salerno. *Führerboot S57* was forced to abort due to engine problems, leaving *S151*, *S152* and *S158* to continue. A little past midnight they sighted eleven steamers escorted by five destroyers outbound from

ObltzS Klaus-Degenhard Schmidt's *S54* photographed during the audacious capture of Venice.

the coast. The troop transports were empty, being shepherded back to North Africa. Escorting destroyer USS *Rowan*'s radar and sonar both remained clear of contacts, when lookouts sighted the phosphorescent track of an incoming torpedo. Alerted in time, *Rowan* was able to take evasive action, the incoming 'eel' passing harmlessly by. At that moment the radar screen showed three incoming contacts, the destroyer opening fire with small-calibre weapons, while turning to bring main batteries to bear against the incoming S-boats. Three torpedoes streaked toward target and one impacted on the ship's port quarter. The initial explosion stopped *Rowan* in her tracks before the after magazine ignited, the entire stern thrown out of the water by the blast. Within forty seconds the ship was gone, 202 American crewmen from a complement of 273 going down with their ship.

It was the sole success for S-boats that continued to sail against Salerno. Torpedo supply was swiftly exhausted, exacerbated by the sinking of a barge carrying twenty-four torpedoes by air attack on Livorno. This, combined with deteriorating weather and effective defence, foiled every attempted attack, mines laid off Sardinia and Corsica following German evacuation also yielding no immediate results.

By October 1943 the S-boats were spread thinly across the Mediterranean and achieving little. Marinekommando Italien, VA Meendsen-Bohlken, requested the allocation of two S-flotillas (and one of midget submarines) as a minimum in order to fulfil offensive requirements within the Adriatic, where partisan activity supported by Allied forces increased. On 4 October *S30* and *S33* were placed at the disposal of the newly created Kommandierender Admiral Adriatic, Vizeadmiral Joachim Lietzmann, both boats still only at limited operational readiness in Venice's naval arsenal. The decision was taken to move all S-boats from the western Mediterranean into the Adriatic and Aegean Seas. Already within the Aegean were two light S-boats (*Leicht-Schnellboote*), *LS5* and *LS6*, fitted solely with depth charges and a single deck weapon within an enclosed turret. On 15 October *LS5* was strafed by seven Allied aircraft northwest of Kos and beached, later attacked by British MTBs and destroyed. The small boats had been designed to be transported aboard raiders *Meteorit* and *Komet*, carried a crew of seven and were only 12.5m (41ft) in length and 3.46 m (11ft 4in) beam. Capable of 38 knots, they were powered by two Junkers 6-cylinder JuMo205 aircraft engines, but had proved ineffective. An enhanced model powered by reliable Daimler-Benz MB 507 diesels was already due for delivery, equipped with two rearward-firing torpedo tubes and scheduled to form the cadre of a new S-flotilla within the Aegean. Kommandierender Admiral Aegean VA Werner Lange had already expressed his opinion that a major task suitable for S-boats was the 'mopping-up of the remaining [Aegean] islands, [followed by] continuous supplies to the island occupation forces and, if necessary, evacuations.'[89]

The Italian surrender had started a scramble by German and Allied forces to occupy Greek islands within the former Italian zone of responsibility. While the Germans successfully took Rhodes and several other major islands, British troops secured the islands of Kos, Kalymnos, Samos, Leros, Symi, and Astypalaia. The resulting German invasion of Kos on 3 October was successful, setting the stage for an assault against Leros, code-named Operation Leopard (later changed to Operation Taifun). Oberleutnant zur See Horst Weber's *S55* was attached as part of the covering force for the invading Germans, before being forced to return to Salamis with severe engine damage. The German invasion began on 12 November 1943, completing four days later when 3,200 British and 5,350 Italian soldiers surrendered. Faced with this disaster, the British evacuated the remaining Greek footholds, and remaining Italian forces surrendered to approaching German units.

With continual failure off Salerno, the last S-boats within the Tyrrhenian Sea were earmarked for transport by road from Genoa to Piacenza and then along the River Po to the Adriatic. Owing to the required removal of all engines and armament before travel, they were not expected to be operationally ready within the Adriatic before December. MGK Italy objected, opining that despite weeks of failure there were still 'excellent prospects of success' for S-boats operating against Salerno invasion traffic. They further reasoned that the withdrawal of the only offensive surface weapon available on Italy's west coast would release so many enemy forces that German strength in the Adriatic and Aegean would be more than equalised. The S-boats were considered to be tying up considerable numbers of Allied light naval forces, even alleviating pressure on German coastal convoys, which MK Italy deemed essential owing to 'the peculiarity of the Italian road and railroad network', which could be paralysed 'to a great extent by systematic air raids.'

However, the latter issue applied equally to the Adriatic and Aegean; re-routing of supply transport columns from sea lanes to overland transport was entirely out of the question owing to increasing partisan pressure and difficult traffic conditions at best. The Aegean islands were extremely dependent on maritime supply. Accordingly, OKM confirmed the S-boats' transfer.

Allied bombing damaged the 7th S-flotilla's torpedo maintenance unit on 30 October in raids centred on Genoa, Savona and Albisola. The following day three S-boats at Nettuno were hit by numerous splinters in another air attack by B-25 bombers. Even Toulon, where S-boats were undergoing shipyard overhaul was coming under Allied fire, and here, on 24 November, *S56* was heavily damaged by the first American bombing raid against the port, the stern being completely blown off. While *S58* and *S155* received only minor damage, *S56* was a total loss and decom-missioned on 15 December.

Meanwhile, the headquarters of 1st S-division and 3rd S-flotilla had relocated to Venice, Schultz intending to depart the port with four boats on 9 November and proceed to Dubrovnik after refuelling at Pola. The boats *S30* and *S33* would remain in Pola for Adriatic operations (though their engine state rendered them only suitable for three missions before requiring shipyard maintenance), while Schultz, *S54* and *S61* continued to Patras in order to play a supporting role in Operation Taifun. Unfor-tunately, their departure was delayed by bad weather. *S61* was then forced to abort with a broken crankshaft, the transit to the Aegean cancelled and

S54 returning to Dubrovnik until 12 November, by which time Taifun was underway. The four boats remained in the Adriatic, where all, bar *S54*, were soon non-operational with the required engine changes.

In the interim, another flotilla had been formed within the Aegean, coming onto the Kriegsmarine roll at the beginning of November. The 24th S-flotilla was commanded by the experienced skipper Kptlt Hans-Jürgen Meyer, with Oblt (Ing) Heinrich Lehmann as his chief flotilla engineer. The unit was created to take advantage of a number of craft that had fallen into German hands following the Italian surrender; many were cannibalised for spare parts while six boats formed the nucleus of the new flotilla.

Ironically, four of the six had originated in the Lürssen yards, built between 1936 and 1938 for the Yugoslavian Navy and modelled on the *S2* design. Their primary differences were slight changes in dimensions – the Yugoslavian boats 20cm (8in) shorter, 10cm (4in) wider and with a draught 45cm (18in) deeper – and the addition of a 40mm gun on the stern platform. They were powered by three Daimler-Benz twelve-cylinder four-stroke gasoline engines, with one 100 HP Maybach cruising engine. Upon Yugoslavia's defeat by the Germans in 1941, the four boats – *Velebit*, *Dinara*, *Triglav* and *Rudnik* – had passed under Italian control and been redesignated *MS42*, *MS43*, *MS44* and *MS46* respectively. Now they were

The 'light S-boats' (*Leicht-Schnellboote*) *LS5* and *LS6*, fitted solely with depth charges and a single turret weapon, were based within the Aegean. *LS5* was strafed by seven Allied aircraft northwest of Kos and beached; later it was attacked and destroyed by British MTBs in October 1943.

back in German hands and were given fresh nomenclature: *S601* (ex-*MS42*), *S602* (ex-*MS43*), *S603* (ex-*MS44*) and *S604* (ex-*MS46*). Two other smaller boats – the Italian built *MAS557* and *MAS553* – were also taken on strength as *S511* and *S512* respectively, but proved less than successful. *S511* had actually deserted the Regia Marina to continue serving alongside the Kriegsmarine, but was sunk on 4 December by RAF Beaufighters while en route from Piraeus to Leros, survivors rescued by two auxiliary sailing vessels who in turn were also strafed the following day, killing *S511*'s German commander before the remaining crew were landed in Portolago (now Lakki) on Leros.

S-boats had already visited the reconquered Dodecanese islands. On the evening of 16 November *S54* brought into Calino, Kalymnos, a captured motorboat carrying Italian officers and men escaping from Leros. Shortly after Leros' capitulation to German invaders, KK Schultz put into Portolago, above which the white flag of surrender still flew. The Germans had captured one large tug, one 500-ton steamer, two auxiliary sailing vessels, one fuel barge, 330 Italian mines and a food dump in Parteni Bay on the island's northern tip, and Schultz reported to FdS Petersen that the bay had excellent potential as an S-boat base. During the night of 18 November *S54* penetrated into Vathi harbour on the north coast of Samos to probe British defences. The boat received small-arms fire from a British

Italian *MAS557*, later taken into Kriegsmarine service as *S511* following Italian capitulation. She was sunk on 4 December 1943 by RAF Beaufighters while en route from Piraeus to Leros.

officer ashore, but otherwise no other Allied units were seen. A further reconnaissance thrust into Tigani Harbour was undertaken during the following night. No ships were seen and refugees reported only 100 British troops still present, alongside an Italian garrison willing to negotiate surrender. *S55* and *S54* were both put on patrol routes nearby as part of the planned occupation of Samos: Operation Damokles. The two boats transported a Wehrmacht officer with surrender terms on 21 November; the offer was refused, with both boats coming under fire, thus triggering orders for the Luftwaffe-led invasion. However, a final attempt at averting Damokles was made the following morning, the senior Italian officer agreeing surrender terms that came into effect at 1000hrs on 22 November. The majority of British soldiers had already evacuated the island, but 4,000 Italian troops passed into captivity. The capture of the Dodecanese Islands was the last major German success within the Mediterranean region.

Oberleutnant zur See Horst Weber, commander of *S55* (*centre*) and ObltzS Klaus-Degenhard Schmidt, commander of *S54* (*right*) share a drink with an infantry officer after the successful recapture of Samos, 1943.

14

The Adriatic, Ionian and Aegean Seas

November 1943 – May 1944

BY the end of 1943, the German logistical and organisational situation within the Tyrrhenian, Adriatic, Ionian and Aegean Seas was confused and difficult, to say the least. As commander of the 1st S-division, KK Herbert Max Schultz attempted to match his forces to tasks not always suitable and although minelaying was continued, it was more often than not cancelled due to weather conditions. On 7 December the Kriegsmarine attempted to clarify the Mediterranean S-boat command hierarchy.

1. Along with the transfer of the 3rd S-flotilla to the Command of Naval Group, South, the 1st S-boat Division is also attached to Naval Group, South.

2. Naval Group will assign the 1st S-boat Division in such a way that it is always subordinate to the Commanding Admiral of that area where S-boat operations are concentrated. The 1st S-boat Division will then be operationally under that command and administratively detached. Before detachment the FdS will be the authority in command.

3. The following regulations apply to S-flotillas under the command of Naval Group, South:

   a. Flotillas in the area of the Commanding Admiral, which are under command of the 1st S-boat Division, as in paragraph two, will be fully subordinate to the 1st S-boat Division.

   b. Flotillas assigned to the other Commanding Admiral will be subordinate to him operationally as well as administratively detached. In this case the authority in command before detachment will be the 1st S-Boat Division.

[Additionally]

1. Of the former Italian S-boats, only the minesweepers will be taken over. With the exception of those boats just captured in the Aegean, all Italian S-

boats already commissioned by the 1st S-boat Division are to be decommissioned.

2. The minesweepers in the Adriatic and six minesweepers in the western Mediterranean are to be seized and taken over. The six boats in the Mediterranean will be transferred to the command of Naval Group, South and formed, with the boats already there, into the 24th S-flotilla.

3. The minesweeper which is equipped with special devices for assault boats is to be detached and transferred to the 10th Italian S-boat Flotilla, Commander Borghese, so that the 24th S-flotilla eventually consists of eight boats.'

Schultz requested that two Italian minesweepers also equipped for torpedo operations be assigned to the 24th S-flotilla, but was denied and they were allocated to the 10th MAS Flotilla, an Italian unit loyal to Mussolini and under Kriegsmarine control. The transfer of S-boats from Genoa to the Adriatic was still in progress by early January, expected to be complete by late February. Meanwhile, the 7th S-flotilla had also begun its journey east; however, the extremely low water levels in the River Po caused delays – travel resumed following dredging at Piacenzia.

Although S-boats were initially tasked with safeguarding maritime supply lines, the advance of Tito's partisans and their use of small vessels of their own led to S-boats intercepting partisan ships running supplies to island outposts, as well as bombardment of those islands already controlled by Tito's forces. At the end of December ObltzS Horst Weber's *S55* and ObltzS Hans-Georg Buschmann's *S36* bombarded partisan units in Lagosta Harbour, going into action on the night of 8 January 1944 against Yugoslavian supply shipping, and sinking two small motor yachts carrying fuel and ammunition between Hvar and Brač islands south of Split. Both were stopped, boarded and sunk with scuttling charges. The harbour at Vis was then shelled, defensive partisan fire falling around the S-boats but causing no damage. The following night they repeated the attack, this time against Komiža Harbour on the island's west coast. Following their successful artillery attack they stopped and took as prize another small sailing vessel carrying three Italian artillery pieces, provisions and ammunition, heading the yacht toward German-occupied harbour Vela Luka. Short of their destination they were attacked by two British fighter bombers that strafed all three vessels: *S55* was hit in the port engine which immediately seized. Aboard *S36* two men were killed in the attack and half an hour later further aircraft appeared and also attacked. The captured motor yacht caught fire, stored ammunition exploding and sending it to the bottom. Weber's *S55* took more hits, a reserve torpedo exploding into the air and wrecking what remained of the boat. The crew, some of whom had been wounded, were evacuated to *S36* and *S55* sank soon after. Once the survivors from the prize vessel had been rescued, Buschmann set course for Cattaro on two remaining undamaged engines, one of the more seriously wounded men from *S55* later dying in hospital. Repairs were urgently needed for Buschmann's *S36* and the boat sailed for Pola's shipyard soon afterward.[90]

The newly appropriated ex-Italian boats *S601* and *S603* of 24th S-flotilla were also caught out by Allied fighter bombers during a passage from Piraeus to Cattaro. *S603* had suffered a failure of main engines and was reduced to sailing on the 'march motor' when they were attacked by Spitfires. Both boats were damaged and put into Corfu, one of the four attackers shot down by *S601*, aboard which two torpedo mechanics were killed and the navigator wounded and knocked unconscious during the brief engagement. *S603* also carried two severely wounded men; the skipper, ObltzS Hermann Bollenhagen, was slightly injured.

During February there were no S-boat sorties, fighting strength having fallen to its lowest ebb. The Tyrrhenian Sea was now clear of S-boats, the 7th S-flotilla arriving in Venice on 7 March where they began refitting. Three 3rd S-flotilla boats were also in Venice following their transit from the west. *S30*, *S33* and *S36* were under repair in Pola, *S61* in Venice and *S54* in Thessaloniki. The first six boats of the 24th S-flotilla were also in Venice for refit before officially commissioning into service.

With Hermann Bollenhagen wounded, ObStrm Wernecke had taken command of *S603*, which had been dogged by mechanical failure during its first voyage under the Kriegsmarine ensign. Attempting to complete the curtailed voyage, *S603* departed Corfu on 22 February in company with *S601* again. Shortly after clearing the harbour boom, the engine carburettor caught fire twice forcing another return. Days of repairs followed before *S603* undertook a test voyage. However, yet another fire began, burning three men badly. Further repairs delayed the two boats' departure until 14 March, this time the 'march motor' exploding and injuring two crewmen. Both boats were scheduled to transfer to Salamis for repair, weather conditions in the central Adriatic Sea forcing the diversion east, which was completed by 29 February, *S601* towing her disabled flotilla-mate. By the end of March *S601* was involved in anti-partisan and commando operations following a British Special Boat Service raid on Stampalia. Kptlt (MA)

Walter Bünsch of Seekomandant Westgriechenland requested ObStrm Swoboda's *S601* for help against the commandos and on 29 March the S-boat intercepted a 60-ton sailing vessel near Oxia carrying fuel to the enemy, two crewmen boarding and scuttling the boat with charges.[91] During the afternoon of 30 March Swoboda carried twenty Wehrmacht troops and towed the artillery lighter *MAL12* to the island of Oxia to assist in mopping-up operations. By the time the Germans landed, their enemy had already gone.

The remaining pair of 24th S-flotilla boats – *S604* and *S602* – were in Salamis, joined by *S603* at the end of March. Stocked with ammunition and supplies, the trio travelled to Thessaloniki, *S603* still under tow with engine damage, and arrived on 18 April 1944. Four additional flotilla boats were hit by Allied bombs in Monfalcone as their refitting neared completion: *S622* and *S624* were destroyed, *S623* and *S626* badly damaged.

War and peace: this seemingly idyllic scene is actually shooting practice; the starboard torpedo tube is open after firing.

Within the Adriatic Sea the Allies exercised almost complete aerial superiority, severely disrupting German naval movement. With only piecemeal commitment to action possible for any part of 1st S-division, successes were small and sparse within both the Adriatic and Aegean. The *Rotte* comprising *S36* and *S61* sailed from Pola to Cattaro with flotilla commander KK Schultz aboard, intercepting a small 80-ton partisan supply trawler between the islands of Mljet and Lagosta and sinking it with artillery fire on 17 March.

By the middle of April 1944 the paper strength of the 1st S-boat Division seemed formidable: 3rd S-flotilla with eight boats, 7th S-flotilla with eight boats, 24th S-flotilla with twelve boats and the newly established 21st S-flotilla with six boats. In reality only a single boat was operational: *S30*. The remainder were in shipyards either damaged or being refitted, the Italian power plants of the 24th S-flotilla being particularly problematic. The 21st S-flotilla was an ambitious attempt at using light S-boats originally designed for merchant raiders. Built at the Dornier Werft in Friedrichshafen, the first four boats numbered *LS7* to *LS10* were 12.5m (41ft) long, 3.46m (11ft 4in) wide and had a draught of 0.8m (2ft 7in). Crewed by nine men, the 11.5-ton vessels mounted a single 20mm MG151/20 Flak weapon in a plexiglass domed, hydraulically operated Luftwaffe HD151 turret behind the bridge. The primary armament was a pair of stern-firing 45cm torpedoes and the craft was powered by two 850hp Daimler-Benz MB507 engines capable of 42.5 knots. Small enough for rail transport from Germany, the first four had arrived at the beginning of May. The flotilla was commanded by experienced skipper Kptlt Ludwig Graser and each boat was captained by a senior non-commissioned officer. At the end of July the last boats arrived in Athens.

On 22 April OblzS Klaus-Degenhard Schmidt was taking *S54* from Saloniki's shipyard towards Cattaro when his boat struck a mine off Lefkada, the stern tore away and three men were killed in the blast. With five wounded men aboard, the boat was towed to Salamis and into the shipyard. In recognition of the time it would take to repair, and the lack of trained skippers, Schmidt was posted back to Swinemünde to join the 10th S-flotilla.

During May *S30*, *S36* and *S61* made several sorties from Cattaro in rotating pairs, claiming an enemy destroyer hit by torpedo on 3 May, although never confirmed. On 11 May *S61* and *S30* sank a 250-ton coastal ferry with artillery fire, and another partisan cutter was sunk on 21 May with four survivors rescued and taken prisoner. An attempt to escort minesweepers of the 12th R-flotilla through the Otranto Strait into the Ionian Sea was foiled by a strong enemy destroyer presence under a full moon. At the beginning of June the *Rotte* was operating in support of German counter-attacks against the joint British-Yugoslavian assault on the Croatian island of Brač. Strafed by aircraft, both boats were forced away with splinter damage and three men wounded – bound once again for shipyard repairs.

The first refitted 7th S-flotilla boats finally left Venice for Split, *S153*, *S155*, *S156*, *S157* and *S158* cleared for action, although faulty oil pumps aboard *S153* and *S158* forced a brief return. On the last night of May the flotilla intercepted a small convoy and sank six fully loaded coastal motorboats and motor fishing vessels, as well as one small tanker, SS *Oalma*. Unable to take them as prizes, they were sunk by artillery fire southwest of Žirje: 159 men in uniform, including English, Croatians, Serbs and Italians, as well as a downed American Lightning pilot, were taken prisoner along with thirty-seven women and five children. The following afternoon they repeated the success, sinking one empty and two full motor cutters by artillery fire with seventy-seven partisans, two British paratroopers, fifty women and twenty-four children rescued and taken prisoner. However, all five of the 7th S-flotilla boats suffered damage from return fire, three suffering engine failures, and, at a stroke, the entire flotilla was out of commission pending several days of repair. Two men aboard the *Führerboot* were wounded and KK Hans Trummer departed as flotilla commander during July, hospitalised in Germany and replaced by Kptlt Günther Schulz.

During the night of 11 June the boats left Split to protect a tanker convoy in the area of Zlarin, making unexpected contact with destroyers HMS *Blackmore* and *Eggesford* of the 5th Destroyer Flotilla near the island of Hvar. The British opened fire, bracketing ObltzS Sven Rautenberg's *S153* and completely destroying it along with most of her crew, the flotilla medical officer, Marineoberassistenzart Klotski being amongst the fourteen men killed.

On 24 June *S154* and *S157* were attached as escort to the small, though well-armed, 240-ton Yugoslavian torpedo boat *T7* (which had begun life as Austrian *96F* in 1916) sailing between Šibenik and Rijeka, tasked with safeguarding German maritime communication and supply lines within the Adriatic. During the evening three British 'Dog' boats *MGB659*, *662* and *670* attacked near the island of Kukuljari, firing two torpedoes at the torpedo boat, both missing and exploding on nearby rocks. The three attackers then pummelled *T7* with artillery fire and set her ablaze; the ship beached while the S-boats rescued twenty-one crewmen. British sailors from the three MGBs later examined the wreck and captured five other crewmen before British demolition teams destroyed it.

The first few Italian-built ex-MAS boats were commissioned into the 24th S-flotilla on 1 July from their Grado shipyard. *S621* (ex-*MAS561*), *S627* (ex-*MAS504*), *S628* (ex-*MAS505*) and *S629* (ex-*MAS558*) raised the

Köhler's *Flotten-Kalender* – a yearly international naval review that functioned as the Kriegsmarine's yearbook during the war, 1944.

operational level of the flotilla to seven boats. Considerably smaller than their German counterparts, the MAS boats were 18.7m (61ft 4in) long with a displacement of 28.3 tons. Pushed by two Isotta Fraschini engines capable of 43 knots, a 140hp Alfa Romeo auxiliary engine provided a march speed of 8.5 knots. Their primary armament was a pair of 45cm lateral thrust torpedoes; no reloads were carried aboard the small boats. A 20mm Breda 20/65 rapid fire cannon provided air defence and six 50kg (110lbs) depth charges could be carried astern. The crew complement was thirteen.

The reinforcement was, however, too little too late: the tide had irrevocably turned against the Kriegsmarine. Allied troops had landed at Anzio during January 1944 and, despite a startling reluctance to advance, finally broke out of their beachhead and captured Rome. The grinding battle for Monte Cassino was over and Allied troops were slowly advancing on the Gothic Line in northern Italy. To the east in Yugoslavia, Tito's partisans were gaining strength and coherence, winning control of several Adriatic islands by July. Greece was soon directly threatened and Allied air and naval forces vastly outnumbered German, even including the minor units of the fascist Italian Navy. British destroyers, MGBs and MTBs operated in concert within the Adriatic and the S-boats were under a pressure that they could no longer bear.

On 24 July the six boats of the 7th S-flotilla were escorting a supply convoy when they were attacked by three MTBs a little past midnight, four torpedoes appearing from the darkness. During the frenetic action that followed, LzS der Reserve Marxen's *S155* rammed ObFhnrzS Gunnar Kelm's *S154* while taking evasive action, although German gunfire managed to hit and destroy the Vosper-built *MTB372*, ablaze and heard to explode as the Germans retreated. German infantrymen ashore reported British fighter bombers later sinking the burning wreck. The S-boats returned to Split with *S154* out of commission for repairs.

On 26 July LzS Werner Pankow's *S151* and two other S-boats were escorting the 333-ton German motor ship MV *Vega*, which had been heavily armed with flak weapons, when they were attacked by the Royal Navy's *MGB651*, *667* and *670* of the 60th MGB/MTB Flotilla. This type of coastal boat – the Fairmile D – had been specifically designed to battle S-boats, the so-called 'Dog Boats' able to be fitted out in either torpedo carrier or gunboat role and carrying a formidable array of weaponry comprising two single 6pdr guns, four 20mm Oerlikon (two single, one twin), two twin .303 Vickers K guns and four depth charges. The three MGBs heavily damaged MV *Vega* which was set on fire and sent to the bottom. The S-boats withdrew to seaward of the crippled ship, firing torpedoes at the attackers, though missing with each shot. In the gunfire that followed, *MGB651* was hit in the engine room and temporarily disabled, but *S151* was also severely damaged, with five crewmen killed and a further five wounded before Pankow was able to escape.

On 9 August *S623* and *S626* were attacked south of Venice by three fighter bombers, both S-boats taking damage and two men killed aboard *S623*, a third man later dying of his injuries in a Venetian hospital. Between the two boats there were three other severely wounded men and eleven with minor injuries. Perhaps ironically, two passengers, both of them Luftwaffe flak officers, were also wounded, the pair hitching a lift from Grado to Venice aboard the S-boats.

As well as increasing aerial pressure, during July another 'Dog Boat' flotilla, the 56th, had been transferred by the Royal Navy into the Adriatic, quartered on the recently conquered island of Vis. These most formidable of opponents clashed with the 3rd S-flotilla near Mljet on the night of 17 August. *MGB657*, *658* and *663* had landed two Royal Marine commandos on the island when they detected fast-moving S-boats. Attempting to give chase, they were outclassed by the Germans' speed. Shortly after midnight, following contact being lost, the three MGBs detected and attacked a convoy code-named Hammer, comprising schooners *Jota* and *Dora*, armed with several 37mm and 20mm guns, and lighters *Helga* and *Peter*, as well as two infantry boats, *I68* and *I48*, all travelling from Carcula to Dubrovnik. The British sank *Jota*, *Dora* and *Peter*, but also took several shell hits from the well-armed schooners, *MGB658* being temporarily disabled. One infantry boat capsized, though the second later arrived with the survivors at Doli. Four S-boats, *S30*, *S57*, *S58* and *S60*, were acting as distant escort, but curiously failed to assist other than desultory gunfire from great range. They were later sharply criticised by MGK Süd for their lack of aggression, perhaps indicating that S-boat morale had finally cracked in the face of overwhelming odds. The SKL War Diary states that the S-boats 'reported the situation was so incalculable that no possibilities to attack were available. When fire was opened against two gun boats, they turned off without defence under a smokescreen.'[92] Meanwhile, the convoy was sandwiched between the island shore and the attacking MGBs as they attempted a second run, bush fires started by ricochets silhouetting the German convoy as the British scattered them and hunted each vessel individually.

The following night the S-boats had an opportunity for redemption as *S30*, *S33*, *S57*, *S58* and *S60* sailed from Dubrovnik escorting infantry lighters tasked with searching for survivors from the previous night. They clashed with *MGB659*, *663* and *643* expecting further convoys. During the fierce gun-battle that ensued, ObltzS Hans-Georg Buschmann's *S57* was hit several times and damaged beyond saving, with two men killed before the crew, including nine wounded men, were evacuated and *S57* scuttled to prevent capture. The S-boats withdrew, *S30* losing another man to gunfire.

A brief curiosity of September 1944 was the deployment of the 22nd S-flotilla, comprised entirely of LS and captured Italian MAS boats. Originally formed in Surendorf, Germany, during December 1943, and equipped with small coastal S-boats (KS-boats), the flotilla had trained under Kptlt Siegfried Wuppermann's command, before it was transported during May 1944 by train to Lignano. While German flotilla personnel were used to fill the depleted ranks of other Adriatic combat flotillas, Croatian crews were recruited and began training under the command of Kptlt Friedrich Hüsig. The five boats were handed over to the Croatian Navy on 9 September, transferred from Lignano to Rijeka where they formed the Croatian KKS Flottille (Kroatische Küsten-Schnellbootsflottille) subordinate to the German 11th Security Division (Sicherungsdivision); the 22nd S-flotilla subsequently dissolved. None of the boats saw action after they attempted to desert to the partisans in December 1944; all crews were arrested and court-martialled.

Major reorganisation for S-boats within the Adriatic and Aegean occurred in September. Once again attempting to gather scattered units beneath a centralised command structure, all boats were amalgamated beneath the umbrella of KK Schultze's 1st S-division and its immediate subordinate, 3rd S-flotilla. On 1 September veteran Kptlt Albert Müller took command of the 3rd S-flotilla, replaced one month later by Kptlt Günther Schulz, recently of the 7th S-flotilla. The 3rd S-flotilla now comprised three groups:

Group 1
Commander: ObltzS Johannes Backhaus
(Formerly the boats of the 3rd S-flotilla) *S30, S33, S36, S58, S60, S61*

Group 2
Commander: ObltzS Hans-Georg Buschmann
(Formerly the boats of 7th S-flotilla) *S151, S152, S154, S155, S156, S157, S158*

Group 3
Commander: ObltzSdRes Hermann Bollenhagen
(Formerly the boats of 24th S-flotilla) *S621, S623, S626, S627, S628, S629, S630*

Subsequently, the 7th and 24th S-flotillas were officially dissolved during October 1944. For the LS boats of the 21st S-flotilla, the writing was also on the wall. Originally earmarked for offensive action against Allied convoys in the Otranto Strait between the heel of Italy and Albania, a shortage of escort vessels kept them within the Aegean, stationed between Rhodes, Leros and Phaleron while a base was planned for Corfu. However, frequent damage through heavy weather resulted in *LS8*, *LS9* and *LS11* being in an Athens shipyard when the general evacuation of German forces from Greece began. The advance of Russian forces in southeastern Europe threatened to isolate Greece, and Hitler had granted Generaloberst Alexander Löhr, commander of Army Group F, permission to withdraw. During August Bulgaria withdrew from the Axis and declared its neutrality, further weakening the eastern flank. The evacuation of the Aegean Islands began at the beginning of September, though the last would not surrender until May 1945. Rhodes was evacuated on 12 September, Allied troops advancing into the power vacuum. Nine days later, Löhr began the evacuation of the Peloponnese peninsula, western Greece following soon afterward. The LS boats in Athens were destroyed with explosives, while ObStrm Breitschuh's *LS10* was sunk by aircraft on 12 October while escorting a convoy to Saloniki that lost thirteen other ships to the carrier-borne aircraft from the newly deployed, powerful British Aegean Force.

Remaining 21st S-flotilla personnel joined the march north out of Greece, taking part in land battles alongside elements of XXII Gebirgskorps. Rudolf Petersen ordered the immediate return of skilled S-boat men and seventy-four were flown to Germany by Ju52 aircraft, the remaining 200 fighting against advancing Allied forces and partisans. The last seaworthy boat, *LS7*, sailed solo into the north Adriatic, running aground near Grado while skirting a minefield. Obersteuermann Erwin Schipke took his six men ashore and fought their way inland to the Axis base at Palmanova, the stranded boat destroyed by Allied aircraft. On 15 December Petersen officially disbanded the 21st S-flotilla.

Meanwhile, the restructured 3rd S-flotilla battled onward. On 9 October *S158* intercepted a small sailing vessel and captured five partisans, destroying the craft with explosives. The following night, eight S-boats from 1 and 2 Groups joined Operation Dacapo alongside torpedo boat *TA40* and *UJ202* and *UJ208* for an attack on suspected enemy vessels and a radio station on Molat Island. The radio station was successfully destroyed by gunfire, though no ships were sighted. All bar one of the torpedoes fired into the harbour to destroy the docks failed to detonate, though a concrete pier elsewhere on the island was demolished. *S626* suffered a hit below the waterline from enemy fire and was towed to safety by *UJ202*, the forward bulkhead keeping the remainder of the S-boat watertight.

Group 3 received fresh orders on 18 October when Linsen explosive motorboats of the Kleinkampfverbände's Lehrkommando 700 arrived in the Adriatic.[93] New flotilla addition, Italian-crewed *S630* (ex-*MS75*) was already equipped to carry and launch a Linsen from the stern deck. However, bad weather prevented any operations with the Kleinkampf-verbände men until November, whereupon two attempted missions failed, *S628* ramming *S627*'s forecastle after dropping commandos on the island of Silba, the latter taken for shipyard repair.

The attritional battle waged by the 1st S-division in 1944 was doomed to defeat. *S158* was lost to an attack by RAF Mosquitoes on the harbour at Šibenik on 25 October, with two men killed, two others including the skipper, StObStrm Hertwig, severely wounded. The same attack so badly damaged *S156* that she was declared non-operational pending weeks of repair. As German forces were driven north both on land and sea, the Italian port of Ancona fell to the Allies, and was immediately used as an MGB base, thus putting the furthest reaches of the Adriatic within striking distance of Royal Navy coastal forces. Sporadic minelaying by S-boats may have accounted for the loss of *MGB657* on 12 September; the boat was towed back to Ancona but written off. Likewise, *MGB663* exploded on a mine on 10 October, and three men were killed and eight injured. On 14 December the destroyer HMS *Aldenham* also detonated a mine and sank after a bombardment mission of Pag Island. The ship broke in two, 126 crewmen and a wounded partisan aboard were killed in the cold water, with only sixty-three men rescued. She was the final Royal Navy destroyer loss of World War Two. During April both *MTB710* and *MTB697* were also destroyed by mines, and *ML558* and HMT *Coriolanus* lost on 5 May 1945.

Four S-boats mounted a sortie from Pola against shipping suspected off Ancona on 19 November, with *S58* and *S30* as *Rotte 1*, *S60* and *S61*, *Rotte 2*. Sighting a small coastal tanker, *S60* fired its port torpedo, which missed and exploded against the shore, *S61* similarly failing to hit the ship with a surface-runner. As the target melted into the darkness, they continued south to San Benedetto del Tronto where an anchored schooner, 162-ton *Stella*, was torpedoed by *S60* and sank immediately. A second two-master, 148-ton *Adua*, was attacked using *S61*'s 40mm cannon, stopped, boarded and sunk with explosives. They were small victories for the final days of the war within the Adriatic. On 25 November veteran commander ObltzS Heinz Haag received the Knight's Cross.

Small localised actions involving minelaying, supporting of commando and infantry raids and covering German convoys punctuated the final month of 1944. S-boats also played an important role in evacuating Wehrmacht troops from Adriatic islands and transporting them to the Italian mainland. *S623*, *S626*, *S627*, *S628* and *S629* of Group 3 all put into Monfalcone's shipyard on 3 December for overhaul, frequent air attacks delaying completion of the work until the New Year. On 17 December three Royal Navy destroyers and supporting MGBs attacked the harbour on Lussin Island, damaging *S152* and wounding two men. Fortunately, stored EMB mines on the quayside failed to explode.

By the year's end the 1st S-division comprised fourteen operational S-boats:

Group 1: *S30*, *S33*, *S36*, *S58* ready for action at Pola, with *S60* and *S61* in the shipyard;
Group 2: *S151*, *S152*, *S154*, *S156* and *S157* ready for action at Venice, *S155* in Pola's shipyard;
Group 3: *S621*, *S623*, *S626*, *S628* and *S630* ready for action at Grado, *S627* and *S629* in the Mofalcone shipyard.

On 4 January 1945 four boats from Group 1 sortied against Molat Island. There, at the entrance to Brgulje Bay, they sighted the harbour defence vessel *HDML1163*, commanded by Sub-Lt Kenyon Howden SANVR. Howden's task was to guard the Macnare Channel, an artery of munitions supply for the Allied campaign. The S-boats surprised the small vessel, *S33* firing a single torpedo which struck *HDML1163* amidships and exploded in a blinding sheet of flame, killing all nine men aboard. *S61* fired two torpedoes into the harbour to demolish piers, but they were caught in an anti-torpedo net. The sinking of *HDML1163* was the final torpedo success for an S-boat within the Adriatic Sea.

During January, 1st S-division co-operated several times with commandos of the Kleinkampfverbände, particularly the frogmen of the Marine Einsatz Kommando (MEK), who went ashore behind enemy lines to destroy bridges, railways and other installations. During the night of 10 January *S30*, *S33*, *S58* and *S60* transported MEK men for Operation Gustav, an attack on Isto Island. Group 3 commander, ObltzSdRes Hermann Bollenhagen, sailed aboard *S60* to oversee the mission. However, due to poor visibility and a compass malfunction, all except *S30* grounded on a sandbank near Unije Island. Stuck firmly in glutinous sand, the three boats attempted to lighten their loads, while *S30* attached tow lines which failed to break any free. Two naval barges also tried and failed, as did the tugboat *Chirone* despatched from Pola. The situation grew more perilous when four Allied aircraft passed overhead the following day, albeit without attacking.

The three boats remained trapped for four days, despite the Germans' best efforts and, eventually, attempted recovery was cancelled. All salvageable material was being removed, when on the morning of 16 January *MTB699*, *706* and *698* attacked. A single torpedo missed *S33*, exploding on nearby cliffs as the remaining crew abandoned the vessel under artillery fire that touched off a reserve torpedo. The resulting explosion destroyed *S33*. *S58* and *S60* were also under heavy bombardment, with three German crewmen wounded and the boats completely wrecked. What remained after the British had departed was demolished with explosives.

During the night of 18 January the last three boats of Group 1 – *S30*, *S36* and *S61* – joined *S151*, *S152*, *S154*, *S155* and *S157* in an offensive against Zadar, clashing with British gunboats, which left *S30*, *S151* and *S152* heavily damaged and one man badly wounded. Land-based search-lights lit up the chaotic battle before the S-boats broke away for Pola behind a smokescreen, having failed to inflict significant damage on the enemy. Once in Pola they were no more secure, six British fighter bombers strafing the harbour, followed by thirteen P51 Mustangs; ObStrm Erwin Schipke's *S154* was so badly damaged that it was written off.

January ended with sporadic minelaying, punctuated by boats held in harbour by bad weather and an acute shortage of fuel. The three Group 1 boats attempted a minelaying mission on the night of 4 February, but instead were forced to jettison their cargo unprimed after running into two groups of British MGBs. A second attempt by the three S-boats also resulted in fighting with British MGBs, no mines laid and *S36* colliding with *S61*, causing enough damage to render both capable of only light service until proper repairs could be made – no longer possible as Pola was severely bombed by the RAF on 7 February and the USAAF six days later. Two more raids on the port that month destroyed the Sperrwaffenkommando, responsible for storage and maintenance of mines. The shipyard at Monfalcone was also heavily bombed and damaged beyond any further use.

During March 1945 Kptlt Siegfried Wuppermann had the somewhat unenviable task of taking command of the 1st S-division, his boats battered, low on fuel and ammunition, and their crews exhausted in every way. The war had only weeks left to run and during that time no records were kept by the Adriatic S-boats. On land the 2nd New Zealand Infantry Division, together with Tito's partisans, had taken Monfalcone on 1 May. Mortar fire from the partisans hit ObltzS HansUlrich Liebholt's *S157* that evening west of Trieste and sank it, killing three men. In Trieste – under attack and about to fall – ObStrm Elksneit scuttled *S623*, LzS Müller having done the same to *S629* the previous day.

On the afternoon of 2 May the 9th Brigade of the New Zealand Division entered Trieste city centre. German troops began surrendering to them rather than to the Yugoslavian partisans; brutality had been part of the Balkans land war, the partisans being no different in this respect. Though small isolated pockets of fighting continued, Pola surrendered on the evening of 7 May. From the port Kptlt Wuppermann had led his last boats – *S30, S36, S61, S151, S152, S155* and *S156* – to Ancona to surrender to the Allies. Aboard they carried as many flotilla personnel as possible and the commander of 3rd S-flotilla, Kptlt Schultz.

The arrival at Ancona of the seven S-boats caught the Allies by surprise, the Germans heaving-to near the harbour entrance. Wuppermann flew a white flag from his S-boat's bridge, British forces scrambling to surround them with MTBs. Wuppermann was taken aboard *MTB658*, where he explained that he had brought troops from Pola to surrender them as prisoners of war, rather than leave them in the hands of the partisans. He requested permission to return to Pola and collect more men before surrendering his boats: the request was denied. With their surrender, the war of the S-boats in the Mediterranean basin ended.

15
The Black Sea

December 1941 – September 1944

OPERATION Barbarossa sent Army Group South into the Ukraine and towards the Black Sea. Undoubtedly weakened by the diversion of forces used for invading Yugoslavia and Greece in April 1941, Army Group South faced stiffer Soviet defence than anticipated. The port city of Odessa held out for two months under siege before Soviet forces successfully evacuated. The Crimea then became the scene of some of the fiercest fighting on the eastern front during 1941. The prize, Sevastopol, was placed under German siege on 30 October 1941 and stubbornly refused to crack. Key to Soviet ability to hold both cities was the Black Sea fleet, comprising one battleship, five cruisers, three destroyer leaders, eleven modern destroyers, four old destroyers, forty-four submarines, two gunboats, eighteen minesweepers and eighty-four MTBs. Opposing them was the Royal Romanian Navy comprising four destroyers, six fleet torpedo boats,

A surrendered S-boat moored alongside a British MTB within the Adriatic, 1945.

one submarine (two more launched in 1944 but never proceeding past sea trials), five midget submarines, two minelayers and seven MTBs. The Germans for their part could field only the six small riverine vessels of the Danube Flotilla.

On 26 December Soviet troops made seaborne landings on the northern coast of the Kerch Peninsula, establishing five bridgeheads up to one battalion in strength each. While huge resources were still engaged in battered Sevastopol, the Germans were momentarily thrown off-balance by Soviet ability to land troops in force, supported by naval artillery.[94] Sevastopol continued to be supplied by freighters supported and protected by the Black Sea fleet, who also used their artillery to great effect on the besieging Axis troops. Typical supply convoys were small, generally one or two steamers with one or two destroyers and MTBs and minesweepers. In Berlin OKW recognised the dominance of the Soviet Navy within the Black Sea and both U-boats and S-boats were ordered to the region. The six large S-boats of Birnbacher's 1st S-flotilla, the last to be released from action in the Baltic Sea before refit, were earmarked for the transfer, dependent upon ice conditions along inland waterways. The Romanian naval base at Constanta was planned as operational hub for 1st S-flotilla, although it quickly became apparent that Sevastopol and the eastern edge of the Crimean Peninsula would be the focal point for operations, over two hundred nautical miles distant from the Romanian port. Odessa was put forward as an alternative, the Kriegsmarine hoping to establish a new base before the S-boats arrived. Italian MAS boats and midget submarines were also transferred from the Mediterranean to the Black Sea, their operational zones later strictly segregated from those of the S-boats lest mistaken identification caused friendly fire casualties.

Transporting six S-boats from Germany to Romania was an impressive logistical feat. After their scheduled refit, they were reorganised slightly so as to provide uniformity in S-boat type, easing potential supply and maintenance problems during a posting so far from Germany. The superstructure and all weapons were removed leaving only the hull, which was then towed along the Elbe to Dresden, from where they were lifted from the water and carried by Kuhlmeier eight-axle trailers on a 450km (280 miles) overland transfer via autobahn to Ingolstadt in southern Germany. This took nearly sixty hours, engineering teams travelling ahead to remove potential obstacles. Once in Ingolstad, the boats were transferred back to the water and towed onward to Linz along the Danube. Railway cars carrying the S-boats' equipment rendezvoused with them within the

Austrian city and the superstructure was rebuilt, before the journey continued along the Danube, each boat lashed to barges until Galatz, where the main engines were installed. The S-boats then proceeded under their own power to Constanta where refitting was completed. The first two boats, *S26* and *S28*, arrived in Constanta on 24 May 1942, the second pair, *S72* and *S102* on 3 June, and the final pair, *S27* and *S40*, ten days later.

On 1 June Birnbacher reported his first two boats as available for urgent use, though not fully operational. German radio interception units had identified the formidable Soviet naval presence at Sevastopol and so both boats were ordered by MGK Süd's Admiral Black Sea (Kommandierender Admiral Schwarzes Meer) VA Hans-Heinrich Wurmbach to stand west and southwest of Sevastopol during the night of 2 June, in order to interdict Russian supply convoys off Cape Khersones. Once completed, the boats

The 1st S-flotilla's *S28* being towed along the river Rhine near Dresden.

were to proceed to Yalta or Ak Mechet rather than trek back to Romania. Engine failure forced a premature return, as faulty packing allowed water to leak into the fuel system, the mission rescheduled for one night later. Although the boats succeeded in reaching their allotted area, they sighted nothing in the bright moonlight, and were nonetheless forced to return to Constanta after Kriegsmarine ferry barge 145 was sunk by mine whilst en route to Ak Mechet with diesel for the S-boats.

Once again on 6 June they sailed for Sevastopol without sighting anything other than two patrol boats, which they avoided rather than waste ammunition. Their target was the supply shipping that traversed the route. *S72* and *S102* also made their first foray following an urgent request from the Luftwaffe to rescue the downed crew of a BV138 flying boat.

Relations with the Black Sea Italian MAS unit quickly soured following the arrival of the S-boats. Italian MTB commanders complained to MGK Süd that they were being deliberately placed away from the main Russian convoy routes; this was flatly refuted by the Germans. This, combined with difficulties in finding the elusive enemy in so vast an area, led Wurmbach to

An S-boat loaded aboard a Kuhlmeier eight-axle trailer during the 450km (280-mile) overland transfer via autobahn between Dresden and Ingolstadt while headed to the Black Sea.

decree that Yalta would remain the operational base for Italian forces, while Birnbacher's flotilla would occupy Ak Mechet on Crimea's west coast. Co-operation between Birnbacher and Capitano di Fregata Francesco Maria Mimbelli subsequently improved, with the establishment of a common operational headquarters at Sadki.

All four S-boats sailed on 9 June to the Sevastopol area, barren of enemy shipping. While entering Ak Mechet the following morning, a reserve torpedo warhead aboard *S26* caught fire, destroying some of the light metal construction work in the engine rooms, the deck over the engine room and central tank area. Pipes and electrical wires in the side engine room and the air compressor were damaged, while the starboard engine was itself damaged by the flow of liquefied metal. Extensive repairs were required in the dockyard at Linz, with assistance from Lürssen dockyard workers. Sabotage was suspected and both a torpedo specialist and counter-intelligence officer were despatched to investigate as *S26* underwent repair.

The three operational boats sailed again on 11 June, finally engaging the enemy. They sighted three lurking submarines and then a southbound convoy of one steamer, one torpedo boat and three MTBs. *S28* and *S72* both fired at the torpedo boat and missed, betrayed by a natural peculiarity of the Black Sea. The enclosed sea receives an unusually high level of river discharge, reducing salinity and raising the level of phosphorescent phytoplankton. In practical terms, this meant that torpedoes could frequently be tracked by the naked eye at night, owing to the phosphorescent wake trailing behind.

Torpedoes were shipped by barge to Ak Mechet, though S-boats were forbidden to overnight in harbour until anti-torpedo nets could be installed. A recent Soviet MTB attack on Italian forces in Yalta, also lacking nets, had resulted in Italian casualties. Up to a thousand metres of net was required to protect Ak Mechet, S-boats diverted to spend nights in the protected harbour at Skadovs'k, periodically returning to Constanta. By 16 June the final pair of Birnbacher's boats was operational, and the 1st S-flotilla combat strength raised to five.

Finally, after several torpedo failures and missed shots, on 19 June ObltzS Werner Töniges's *S102* torpedoed 2,034-ton passenger steamer SS *Belostok* evacuating wounded troops from Sevastopol. Töniges saw the ship sink as three Russian torpedo boats and three destroyers arrived on the scene. *S102* fired a second torpedo at an incoming destroyer, *S27* fired three at enemy warships and *S72* shot another at a steamer, all of which were avoided as the phosphorescent trails betrayed the incoming torpedoes.

Further patrols resulted in little until July, torpedo misses and bad weather causing intense frustration. Rough seas shipped water into the captains' cabins and radio rooms on all boats during the night of 21 June, *S40* losing two depth charges overboard in the turbulence. When the weather moderated, bright nights also prevented S-boat approaches close enough to fire with any real hope of success. Instead, S-boats were diverted to minelaying, dropping thirty FMC mines five miles from the coastline south of Cape Khersonese. *S72* and *S102* also took part in a feint landing by Wehrmacht troops in the same region on 27 June, designed to pin Soviet troops to coastal defence rather than the frontline facing Germany's besieging troops inland. The two S-boats cruised the waters while army radiomen transmitted messages to nonexistent landings troops and fired periodic star-shells into the sky. Finally, bad weather forced the operation to be curtailed in the early morning hours.

During the night of 1 July all five operational boats of Birnbacher's flotilla encountered two Soviet MO-Class ASW motor gun boats, *SKA0124* and *SKA0112*. The battle was short and furious, with both Soviet craft sunk and thirty-six men and one female harbour pilot rescued as prisoners of war. Included in those captured was a cruiser commander, political commissar and Major General Petr Georgievich Novikov. Aboard *S40*, the port reserve torpedo had taken a direct hit from 45mm gunfire, rupturing the compressed air cylinder used for propulsion and causing severe damage. The boat's number one was killed in the explosion, new skipper Kptlt Karl-Schneider-Pungs, with flotilla medical officer MStArzt Dr Haenisch and eight other men wounded. Aboard *S28* one crewman was killed. Men from *S102* managed to salvage a bag containing secret documents including maps and radio keys from the sinking boats. The damaged *S40* was towed to Yalta, and later taken to Linz for extensive repair, whittling the flotilla strength down to four which returned to Constanta.

The presence of Novikov, who was hospitalised with injuries, pointed to the imminent collapse of Sevastopol. A veteran of Spain and the early battles of Barbarossa, he had arrived in the city as commanding officer of the 109th Rifle Division and overall commander of Defensive Sector 1 northeast of Sevastopol on the Crimean Peninsula. With Sevastopol about to fall, the commander of the Black Sea fleet and director of Sevastopol's defence, Vice Admiral Filip Oktyabrsky, left the city by submarine under orders from Moscow. Novikov briefly took over command of the city before also attempting to escape as capitulation loomed.[95] On 3 July the Soviet defences were breached and all resistance collapsed the following day. Although sporadic fighting by isolated Soviet pockets continued for a week, Sevastopol was now in German hands, though its valuable port was completely destroyed. The far-reaching consequence of the Wehrmacht's 11th Army having been bogged down for 250 days of siege and unable to support the 6th Army's march on Stalingrad was yet to be seen. SKL recorded on 2 July:

> Even though naval forces could do but little so far as direct participation in the capture of the fortress of Sevastopol is concerned, the employment of light naval forces resulted in considerable interference with enemy supply

movements, It has been pointed out once before that lately ships plying in and out of Sevastopol did so only during the night and that the use of larger ships for the delivery of supplies had been completely abandoned. The co-operation of the German and Italian naval forces undoubtedly hastened the collapse of enemy resistance against the units of the 11th Army Command and the VIII Air Corps which deserve the highest admiration for their outstanding achievements.[96]

The fall of Sevastopol provided respite in which to have the S-boats' engines' 300-hour overhaul. The centre of operations moved east to the Caucasian coast, requiring a closer flotilla harbour base. On 5 June the head of SKL Naval Intelligence (*Abteilung 3/Skl Marine-Nachrichten-auswertung*), KzS Norbert von Baumbach, reported a small port at Ordzhonikidze, known to the Germans as Ivan Baba, as a suitable location for an advance S-boat base and other small Kriegsmarine units. Birnbacher agreed, the port already boasting enough buildings to accommodate the flotilla, two moles on which to load fuel and torpedoes and a torpedo testing station. Soon trucks carrying the flotilla base personnel and all required munitions and supplies began arriving on site. Luftwaffe flak units, ranging from quick-firing 20mm to 88mm cannon, as well as captured Russian weapons manned by Kriegsmarine artillery men were situated around Ivan Baba – soon to prove their worth as a bombing raid two days after the S-flotilla occupied the port was successfully foiled. However, Soviet destroyers and light units began a series of attacks against the harbour and its environs, though with negligible effect. Torpedo nets soon protected the boats in harbour and a Kriegsmarine meteorological station was also established nearby to assist in the planning of S-boat operations.

On 31 July the first four flotilla boats put into their new base from Constanta with the Commanding Admiral, Black Sea on board, he and his operations staff moving onward to Kerch. Four S-boats laid a defensive barrier of Type C river mines south of the Kerch Straight during the first night of August, the same day that Kptlt Georg Christiansen transferred in and relieved Birnbacher as flotilla commander, the latter transferring to captain of destroyer *Z23*.

The flotilla was now targeted against Soviet shipping along the supply route that stretched between Tuapse and Sochi. Orders were given to avoid military vessels smaller than torpedo boats unless absolutely necessary, maximising the effect on Soviet supply shipping. Wehrmacht and Romanian troops were battling into the Caucasus as part of Operation Edelweiss, their ultimate goal the oilfields at Baku. By the beginning of August, Axis forces had passed Rostov and were headed south to Novorossiysk on the coast, isolating the Taman Peninsula. The Soviet Black Sea fleet had begun evacuating troops from the Sea of Asov, as well as mounting 'nuisance attacks' on the advancing enemy.

The German plan to cross the Kerch Strait and attack the Taman Peninsula directly was code-named Operation Blücher and S-boats were ordered to provide flank support. The great distance from Ivan Baba limited the S-boats' time in the operational area, threat of air attack dictating that all voyages be timed under cover of darkness, phosphorescence once more coming to the enemy's aid. *S27*, *S28*, *S72* and *S102* sailed for the Tuapse area on the night of 7 August in an unsuccessful first mission: only patrol boats sighted and depth charges dropped on a submarine with no

Part of the impressive and effective flak defence at Ivan Baba included captured Soviet weapons such as this twin 76.2 weapon captured at Sevastopol and manned by Kriegsmarine artillery men of MAA602.

discernible result during the return trip. A mission two nights later yielded more, Kptlt Töniges' *S102* sinking 1,339-ton SS *Sevastopol* southbound near Lazarevskaya. The ship appeared to be carrying troops and ammunition, and escorting destroyers clearly believed the attacker to be a U-boat, dropping depth charges nearby. The following missions, frequently postponed due to inclement weather, resulted in little: clashes with Russian flying boats and a paucity of torpedo targets.

Another pressing problem was that all four operational boats were due for engine replacement. Demand for their commitment against the Caucasian coast allowed little time for the required maintenance and at the end of August FdS Petersen authorised the transfer of two additional S-boat crews to the 1st Flotilla, in order to permit the commissioning of two extra vessels for the unit at the expense of the flotillas in the English Channel.

During the last night of August, 1st S-flotilla operated off Sochi, Töniges claiming a 3,000-ton freighter hit and sunk, and ObltzS Karl-Friedrich Künzel in *S28* hitting and sinking 1,988-ton cargo ship SS *Jan-Tomp* from a convoy protected by MTBs and torpedo boats that dropped depth charges as the S-boats retreated unseen.

Army Group A's commander Generalfeldmarschall Wilhelm List levelled complaints at a Führer meeting on 31 August that the S-boats were not being used 'successfully enough' against shipping off Tuapse – leading to Hitler demanding that they be 'ruthlessly committed' – and the 1st S-flotilla pressed their attacks home against the enemy over the nights that followed. Kptlt Töniges led the flotilla in action along the Taman Peninsula's southern coast on the night of 3 September, Töniges claiming one 2,000-ton freighter and two 1,200-ton lighters sunk. Künzel's *S28* claimed a 2,000-ton tanker and another pair of lighters, Büchting's *S27* claimed a 4,000-ton tanker and OblzS Schneider's *S72*, one 1,000-ton freighter and two 1,000-ton lighters. The claims are difficult to substantiate, as are the claimed successes over the following nights as the S-boats proceeded to take a heavy toll on the Soviets. By 5 September they reckoned to have sunk twenty enemy ships taking part in Russian evacuation of the Taman Peninsula as Axis forces surrounded them. On 13 November 1942 Kaptlt Werner Töniges was awarded the Oak Leaves to his Knight's Cross, the first for the S-boat service.

On the night of 5 September disaster struck the S-boats when a malfunctioning torpedo fired from *S72* circled and hit *S27* in the forepeak. The blast killed twelve men aboard and sank the boat instantly, *S28* pulling shocked survivors from the sea, three severely wounded and three with minor injuries, including the commander ObltzS Hermann Büchting. Flotilla medical officer, MStArzt Dr Rolf Haenisch, later died of his wounds in hospital.

Meanwhile, four reserve boats had been despatched to the Black Sea without crews, arriving in August. *S47*, *S49*, *S51* and *S52* were made operationally ready, should they be required by the 1st S-flotilla to replace boats undergoing maintenance. The idea to bolster the S-boat presence by crewing some or all of the reserve boats with Romanian commanders and crews was dismissed, as they were felt to have neither the training nor experience to function effectively. Similarly, investigation into using Croat crews yielded the same result. In a curious turn of events two Russian MTBs – *TKA47* captured in the Baltic during 1941 and *TKA111* that had run aground off Yevpatoriya and been salvaged – were assigned to the 1st S-flotilla during 1942. The small boats displaced only 16 tons, were armed with two 53.3cm torpedoes and one 12.7mm machine gun, and were propelled by two GAM 34 BSF gasoline engines, enabling them to reach speeds in excess of 50 knots. However, they showed major corrosion problems and were never committed to action in a flotilla already short on men, not machines.

Kapitänleutnant Werner Töniges, *S102*: the first S-boat recipient of the Oak Leaves to his Knight's Cross on 13 November 1942.

Three of the remaining flotilla boats – *S28*, *S72* and *S102* – were soon relegated to the Constanta shipyard for engine replacement, leaving only *S26* operational, fresh from repairs in Linz, although Kptlt Karl Schneider-Pungs and his crew took command of newly commissioned reserve boat *S49*, leaving *S40* in the shipyard. Oberleutnant zur See Kurt Fimmen's *S26* made his first sinking in the Black Sea when he reported hitting and sinking a 1,000-ton steamer lying at anchor between Tuapse and Cape Idukopas on the night of 26 September, despite what SKL called a 'strong defence by three patrol vessels'.

In the east the German 17th Army had begun an offensive to capture Tuapse, but the advance was soon bogged down amidst fierce defence. With only two available S-boats, the sea lanes could not be effectively searched for Soviet supply convoys; those boats also needed engine overhauls in Constanta by the month's end. On 1 October *S28*, *S72* and *S102* were declared operationally ready once more in Constanta (though *S102* was forced to go to Varna with a damaged screw on 7 October), with newly added *S51* due for release from the yards four days later.

With unfavourable weather forecast for Constanta from 10 September, Admiral Black Sea despatched all operational boats to Ivan Baba to prepare for operations. A shortage of skippers plagued the flotilla, with ObltzS Walter Schneider of *S72* on sick leave and the destroyed *S27*'s skipper Büchting still in hospital. With every torpedo required, VA Wurmbach asked flotilla commander Christiansen to temporarily take the helm of *S72*, but Christiansen was already required aboard *S49* to oversee the actions of her young and inexperienced skipper.

On 14 October the four boats of the flotilla put to sea from Ivan Baba to intercept and destroy any Soviet coastal supply ships. If none were sighted, they were under orders to engage military targets and draw the Russians away from the German maritime supply routes now trailing across the Kerch Strait as Operation Blücher continued. However, deteriorating weather forced the mission to be aborted, all boats returning to Ivan Baba as six Russian bombers attempted unsuccessfully to bomb the harbour.

Bad weather continued to dog the S-boats throughout October. While Russian ships generally sailed under the lee of the coast, and were therefore afforded some protection from the elements, the S-boats were compelled to cross large swathes of open sea at the mercy of the elements. A mission against a Soviet battle group near Tuapse ended with two reported but unverified hits on an enemy destroyer and torpedoes also hitting the mole in Tuapse harbour. A simultaneous Soviet raid by bombers and MTBs on Ivan Baba resulted in no damage, S-boats skirmishing briefly with one MTB

Flotilla buildings in use by 1st S-flotilla in Ivan Baba. The anti-torpedo net has been strung across the harbour mouth.

while returning. After an hour's pursuit, several hits were seen on the speeding Russian, while return fire severely wounded skipper of *S49*, Kptlt Karl Schneider-Pungs, in the head. The MTB escaped. On 26 October *S72* and *S102* unsuccessfully engaged a Russian gunboat near Tuapse, again inconclusively.

At the end of the month the 1st S-flotilla was acting in co-operation with army units, guarding the approach to Novorossiysk Bay, whilst also feigning preparations for landings southeast of Cape Doob near Kabardinka. Close communication between the S-boats and Army Operational Command was ensured by the installation of pack radio sets aboard the S-boats, as they attempted to draw Soviet defenders away from the front line.

The stormy weather cleared on the first day of November and the boats returned to prowling the Tuapse–Soki supply route, their task complicated by Soviet installation of searchlights ashore, which swept the seas for potential intruders. On 5 November *S26*, *S28* and *S49* experienced six torpedo misses against a steamer hugging the Caucasian coastline, *S72* claiming a 500-ton ship hit and sunk in the last operation undertaken for two weeks. *S28* was disabled by collision with floating driftwood on an otherwise uneventful patrol on 18 November.

Elsewhere, German fortunes in Russia changed forever. The Russians encircled the Wehrmacht's 6th Army in Stalingrad during November, throwing German forces in the Caucasus on the defensive, with an attack against the Taman Peninsula expected imminently. The year ended miserably for 1st S-flotilla. A combination of deteriorating weather with heavy snow and ice, difficulty in locating targets and torpedo failure resulted in a single 500-ton lighter reported sunk by *S28* on 18 December. During the same action, two other boats fired torpedoes at small targets, one which missed as a surface runner, the other malfunctioned and circled, narrowly passing before the bow of *S28*.

The year 1942 had seen the high tide mark for German forces within the Black Sea. The 1st S-flotilla continued to run a succession of failed operations, most aborted mere hours from base. On 7 January 1943 VA Robert Witthoeft-Emden, Admiral Black Sea since November 1942, met with Christiansen to discuss the situation:

Kptlt Christiansen told me that present conditions in the Black Sea are particularly unfavourable owing to constant and frequently very strong winds plus rough seas and a heavy swell which hamper operations even when the winds in the operational area are still reasonably favourable. I then discussed the question of laying minefields off Feodosiya Bay. The flotilla commander reported that in an approach or return passage of 200 miles an error in fix up to 20 miles was to be expected owing to errors in steering and changing currents. This means that the return passage to Ivan Baba may be steered most inaccurately, making our own minefields off the bay very dangerous to S-boats, especially since they have to be laid as shallow minefields if they are to be of any use, S-boats cannot therefore pass over them.[97]

Ice became a major factor in the Black Sea during the freezing winter. The reserve boats *S40* and *S52*, proceeding down the Danube to Sulina, became stuck 5km (3 miles) above Braila. With drift ice a very real danger to the trapped boats' hulls, channels were cut into tributaries of the Danube to safeguard them until the passage could be resumed.

The November Soviet offensive had battered its way to the shores of the Sea of Asov; the German 1st Panzer Army pushed back to Rostov and the 17th Army towards the Taman Peninsula into what history remembers as the Kuban bridgehead. Hitler had authorised the withdrawal, not only to protect the eastern approaches to the Crimea, but also to provide a launching point for a renewed offensive against the Caucasus during 1943. Luftwaffe reconnaissance noted a build-up in Soviet forces within ports along the Black Sea and, fearing Russian seaborne landings, S-boats were committed whenever possible to patrolling the expansive coastlines stretching between Feodosija in the Crimea to Novorossiysk, south of Anapa.

By the end of January only three boats – *S26*, *S51* and *S102* – were operational and during the few times they were able to put to sea they were hampered by terrible weather and ice floes within the Kerch Strait. *S28* and *S72* were in Constanta for engine overhaul, an original deadline for completion by 5 February impossible to meet for *S72*, since the reserve driveshaft required had only just left Kiel. *S72* had suffered severe shaft damage during December after the thrust bearing collapsed following severe corrosion, the middle shaft violently vibrating as the boat aborted its mission, causing extensive damage. *S49* was also disabled at Ivan Baba with a broken shaft, due to return to Constanta for an indeterminate period when weather permitted.[98] *S47* was due to become operational by 15 February, manned by *S49*'s redundant crew. When *S47* was cleared for action at Ivan Baba, it would be the turn of *S102* to sail to Constanta for a scheduled engine overhaul. What few missions were possible resulted in no sightings of the enemy throughout January and into early February.

The feared Soviet attack across the Kuban Strait happened on 4 February, when elements of three infantry brigades landed at Cape Myshako near Novorossiysk. The 1st S-flotilla was immediately despatched to hunt for troop and supply ships within the area, but only 250-ton tugboat *Elling* was torpedoed and sunk by *S102* southeast of Gelendzhik. The missions that followed, repeating the same patrol pattern, experienced a frustrating lack of targets, despite continued Russian landings and German aircraft flares dropped over suspected Russian landing grounds. Finally, on the night of 17 February the flotilla once again claimed success, albeit a minor one. At 0200hrs they attacked a steamer, estimated at 1,000-tons, escorted by two MTBs heading northwest. Under a clear full moon, the S-boats took return fire as *S28* let loose two torpedoes that went wide. Künzel's *S28* hit and destroyed a 500-ton lighter, the S-boats then breaking off to haul ahead of the convoy track and attack again. However, the enemy evaded two torpedoes fired by *S102* and opened fire on the attacking S-boats. Before the Germans could reach another firing position, the small convoy entered Ghelenjik harbour. No other ships were seen. On 24 February *S102* departed Ivan Baba for engine overhaul in Constanta, while *S26*, *S47* and *S51* were despatched to finish off a beached Russian steamer southeast of Tuapse, reported by Luftwaffe sightings. *S51* was forced to abort after water in the fuel caused engine trouble and ObltzS Otto Erich Schlenzka's *S47* successfully torpedoed and destroyed the ship, estimated at 3,000 tons. Spotted by Russian searchlights ashore, the two boats were fired on by artillery but suffered no damage.

With torpedo success rare, three of the four operational boats were equipped with mine rails and ordered to lay a mine barrage between Myshako and Cape Tolstoy before continuing onward with torpedoes. However, the boats were forced to break off their passage to the operational area on account of increasingly heavy seas. The weight of the mines caused a very real danger that the boats might capsize, or at least the mine rails be torn from their deck sockets. On the return passage they sighted a small submarine; unequipped with depth charges and unsure of its identity they declined to attack as the submarine dived out of sight.

The following night, 26 February, they tried again as winds had dropped and the sea state calmed considerably. After proceeding by the prescribed route, immediately off the Crimean and Taman coast, the flotilla stood in their operational area between Myshako and Suchuk where they sighted and attacked Russian ships moored for unloading. Successfully surprising the Soviets, *S26* and *S47* torpedoed and sank 1,100-ton gunboat *Krasnaja*

Gruzija, *S51* sank 441-ton minesweeper *Gruz*, *S28* claimed an 800-ton steamer sunk and *S51* hit and destroyed the small motor ship MV *Racija* that exploded as if carrying munitions. The 122-ton trawler *Mius* was also sunk as the Germans left the scene to lay their cargo of UMB mines. Their instructions were to deposit the mines 50m (55yds) apart at a depth setting of less than one metre, so as to impede shallow-draught troop-carrying barges. The field was designed to run 'off Myshako parallel to and as close to the coast as possible'.[99] Upon arrival, however, the S-boats encountered strong enemy patrols attracted by their torpedo attack and were forced to lay the minefield farther east, MTBs sighted approaching from the west pushing the S-boats away, and to spread the mines at an average interval of 100m rather than 50m. Once their task was completed, the S-boats put into Feodosiya, a major Axis supply point, for refuelling at 0345hrs. Russian minesweeper *Novorossiysk/No 604* and tug *Simenz* were both sunk, probably by these mines in the first week of April.

During March the Luftwaffe began flying radar-equipped reconnaissance aircraft over the area of 1st S-flotilla operations by night, in order to attempt tracking of enemy supply convoys. To hasten S-boat acquisition of sighted targets, Luftwaffe pilots agreed to drop flares on target convoys, followed by batches of flares along the convoy's course. The system was first successfully used on 13 March when *S26* and *S47* were guided to the 6,086-ton tanker *Moskva* northeast of Tuapse, hitting her with torpedoes and reporting her sunk as the cargo of petrol poured over the sea surface and ignited. Escort vessels opened fire on the attacking S-boats, but their targeting was inaccurate and wide of the mark as the Germans withdrew. Though severely damaged, *Moskva* was towed into harbour and salvaged after burning for several days.

The remainder of March passed unsuccessfully, the Soviets running their convoy traffic during daylight hours to prevent S-boat attack. Reinforcement boats *S42*, *S45* and *S46* had begun their journey to the Black Sea, expected to be operational by mid June. A further minelaying mission was planned on the first night of April, twenty-four UMB mines to be laid near Cape Myshako, but the mission was postponed due to bad weather, the mines unloaded, and put into storage in Ivan Baba. The flotilla had been whittled down again to only four operational boats by this stage as *S26* put out from Ivan Baba for engine overhaul in Constanta.

Missions during the first two weeks of April were frequently either cancelled or broken off in severe wind and rain, the boats that did reach anywhere near their allocated search areas sighting nothing. With the

Kuban bridgehead under severe pressure on land and Soviet light naval forces making nuisance raids along the coast, MGK Süd ordered provision made to transfer some or all of the operational S-boats to a port closer to the combat. The German 17th Army had begun planning an offensive named Operation Neptune, focused upon eliminating the Soviet beachhead at Myshako. The Kriegsmarine intensified its supply convoys to Anapa, but needed Russian naval forces diverted from these vulnerable convoys, hoping to achieve this by increasing S-boat deployment in the area. The long transit from Ivan Baba not only put useless hours on labouring S-boat engines, but left little time actually within the patrol area. Anapa at the southern point of the German front line was put forward as the ideal candidate for an advanced S-boat station, and although both the prevailing weather and presence of the enemy would probably only permit temporary use, the port berths were improvised by anchoring a lighter in harbour. Anti-aircraft defences placed inland protected the anchorage from surprise attacks.

Admiral Black Sea VA Gustav Kieseritzky and Christiansen conferred regarding this proposal and made several valid points against stationing S-boats in Anapa.[100] With an estimated enemy strength in light forces of forty MTBs – many faster and better-armed, carrying heavy armour resilient to gunfire – they considered that the loss of even one S-boat would significantly cut German strength. Anapa, a port already used as a forward supply head for the Wehrmacht, was considerably more open to air attack than Ivan Baba and Feodosiya, raided almost daily by large bomber formations. This, combined with artillery bombardment from the sea, had reduced much of the small port to ruins. They reasoned that as the Russians became aware of the S-boats' presence within the confined space of the bay, they would intensify all attacks on boats that would be almost impossible to camouflage. The length of time S-boats could spend operating against shipping off the Caucasus coast was determined more by the hours of darkness than any other factor, daylight attacks out of the question in a region easily observed from the enemy-held coastline. The S-boat's greatest weapon was surprise, and enemy knowledge of their movements in and out of Anapa would provide ample warning of attack. The primary advantage, as the two officers saw it, was that Anapa had prevailing easterly winds, enabling S-boats to sail to the operational region, even in bad weather, by using the lee of the coast. Ultimately, this was considered to outweigh the problems and on the proviso that effective anti-aircraft protection could be provided, Anapa was agreed as a forward base of operations.

Four boats left Ivan Baba on the afternoon of 14 April headed east: *S72*, *S28*, *S47* and *S102*. The first *Rotte S72* and *S28* waited near Idokopas and at 0127hrs attacked a convoy headed northwest and escorted by gunboats. Künzel's *S28* hit and sank 818-ton coaster SS *Sakko i Vanzetti*, before having to break off the operation due to engine failure. The second *Rotte* sighted nothing and all four boats put in to Anapa at 0810hrs, *S28*'s engine repaired within an hour. Supplies had been rushed to the port for both S-boats and several Italian MAS boats that arrived to share the harbour. However, with no stored torpedoes, any boats with less than two on board were ordered to return to Ivan Baba for reloads. The following night the S-boats were frustrated by enemy searchlights picking them out in their hunt for targets. Christiansen arrived at Anapa aboard *S51* on 17 April as the Wehrmacht began the ground assault of Operation Neptune. The code-word *Schützenfest* had been flashed to the 1st S-flotilla, signalling them to leave harbour and make for the waters off Novorossiysk.

The first night of operations was hectic: at 2000hrs the S-boats fired eight torpedoes at three Soviet landing points between Myshako and Ostrov Sudzhuk to destroy infantry landing stages. *S47* and *S72* both torpedoed wrecks being used as a bridgehead, as well as bridging connecting them to shore. *S51* hit a coastal vessel at the landing stage and, in total, six of the eight torpedoes fired hit targets. Intercepted Russian radio reports later confirmed that two ammunition barges had been struck by the torpedoes, one sunk, one saved but severely damaged by fire. The S-boats withdrew to reload, proceeding to patrol between Cape Sdzhuk and Cape Doob. They clashed with two Russian MTBs and three patrol boats, one of the latter, *MK054*, exploding during the action, although the cause was uncertain. Sixteen Russian naval personnel and thirty-three Red Army soldiers were killed. Seven times the S-boats fought with Russian patrol ships, also coming under fire from coastal artillery as the bright moonlight and constant flares from Russian and German aircraft betrayed their position. The boats returned to Anapa, before sailing onward to Ivan Baba for torpedo loading.

On 20 April – the same day that *S49* and *S50* were commissioned in Constanta — the 1st S-flotilla repeated the operation with similar results. Increased Russian naval patrols meant more frequent firefights, though without serious damage or casualties. The Italian MAS boats were also fully committed by VA Kieseritzky against the Russian landing zones further to the southeast. On land the Wehrmacht was struggling, unable to meet daily objectives against fierce Soviet resistance. The S-boats encountered a convoy of escorted coasters and pressed home an attack during which *S28*, *S72* and

S102 each claimed a coaster of approximately 250 tons sunk. Army artillery crashed around the attacking S-boats and the escort craft put up a strong defence, foiling further attacks. Disengaging, *S47* suffered engine trouble, forcing a premature return to Ivan Baba while the remainder reached Anapa at 0445hrs. Three boats were soon in action again, shelling the Russian landing points and firing off their remaining torpedoes before also returning to Ivan Baba for reloading.

On 24 April the army suspended Operation Neptune in the face of mounting casualties and little headway. Despite this cessation, S-boats were kept attacking the landing points used by Russian troops, though they returned to Ivan Baba rather than run the risk of being stationed in the increasingly bombed and vulnerable Anapa. Suffering no casualties, *S72* narrowly missed blowing itself up with a ground runner that exploded just a hundred metres ahead of the boat in shallow water.

Weather affected S-boat sailing once again, but by the middle of May they had claimed two patrol vessels, seven coasters and a schooner destroyed by torpedoes. Enemy cruisers and destroyers had bombarded Ivan Baba at the end of April; this increasing pressure and frequently heavy swell encountered at sea during operations put an extraordinary strain on both crews and boats – *S51* was damaged and forced to return to Constanta for repair on 19 May. By this time the flotilla strength had increased, with

S-boats quayside in Ivan Baba for reloading.

reinforcements commissioned and gathered in Constanta and Ivan Baba. The flotilla now numbered *S26*, *S28*, *S40*, *S42*, *S45*, *S46*, *S47*, *S49*, *S52*, *S72* and *S102* with *S51* under repair. However, the numbers were not the full story, not least of all because new boats and crews required further training before being assigned carefully chosen operations in an attempt to let them learn their craft in advance of pitched combat.

VA Kieseritzky repeatedly requested further reinforcements for the flotilla, in view of the obvious superiority of enemy forces. Apart from six U–boats of the 30th U–flotilla, the 1st S–flotilla was the only offensive unit within the Black Sea. Russian convoy traffic had dramatically increased in the northeastern reaches, successfully supplying Russian ground forces near Novorossiysk. Almost continuous S-boat missions to interdict this supply covered the boats' maximum number of operational hours before mandatory dockyard repair, the original 300 hours raised to 500 owing to the demands of the front line, but still not sufficient to keep enough pressure on the Soviets. Concurrently, an increase in Russian Sturmovik ground attack aircraft targeting S-boats caused casualties. The flotilla war diary recorded that:

> In the approach the planes, firing two guns, come to within 25 metres of the boats and drop 15 to 20 fragmentation bombs when pulling up. They also drop four to six light bombs which are suspended under the wings ... *S72* received 15 hits, all of them 20mm armour-piercing shells. *S49* also hit, developed a big cloud of smoke. Two men slightly wounded, both 20mm AA guns hit, but remained serviceable. The radio operated only on emergency power. Hits in two tanks in compartment No 6 and holes below the waterline, repaired by damage control group.
>
> A two engine plane is hit several times by shells from the 20mm guns of *S72* while making its approach. One landing gear is extended, parts of the other fall into the water beside the S-boat. The plane steadily loses altitude and plunges into the water about 1,000 metres away.

Kieseritzky requested the transfer of four more boats equipped with 40mm flak weapons and radar to the Black Sea. On 20 May *S26*, operating with *S52*, was repeatedly attacked by ground attack aircraft in the early hours of the morning; one man was killed and another severely injured. The boat returned to Ivan Baba and remained operational although only able to take on board 15,000 litres (3,300 gallons) of fuel due to hits in the fuel bunker, limiting her radius of action until fully repaired on 23 May.

Another *Rotte* at sea near Sochi sank two ships from a convoy of a pair of towed lighters escorted by a single gunboat. *S72* fired a double shot that hit and sank a 600-ton barge, while *S49* destroyed the 170-ton tug *CF-6 Pervanš*. Accurate gunfire from the escort and shore batteries as well as searchlights sweeping the area made *S72* fumble a second attack after reloading.

On its return passage, the *Rotte* was attacked by fourteen MBR-2 flying boats, ten Il-2 Sturmoviks and six Jak-1 fighters, nearby bomb blasts and machine-gunning killing one crewman and wounding three others on *S49*, lightly injuring five aboard *S72*. The pitched battle ended with two Sturmoviks and a Jak-1 shot down, but not before *S49* suffered damage to two engines, the electrical mains, bilge connections, air plant and radio apparatus, sixty shells having penetrated the hull and causing compartment number 5 to flood. The electrical system aboard *S72* was knocked out, at least fifteen 20mm cannon shell hits damaging the hull. By cannibalising parts from two damaged engines, the third was kept running aboard *S49* and the boats proceeded at 7 knots for Ivan Baba, fighter escort requested and received by 0800hrs; *S49* and *S72* were declared non-operational pending repair at Constanta.

The last of the new arrivals, *S40* was commissioned into the Kriegsmarine on 24 May. That same month S-boat forces had been bolstered by the addition of seven MAS boats, appropriated from the Regia Marina. The Italian 101st Squadron had operated continually alongside German S-boats since their arrival in the Black Sea but Capitano di Fregata Francesco Maria Mimbelli's unit had begun to suffer from worn-out machinery and fuel shortages, prompting Italian command to repatriate their men back to Italy. The remaining MAS craft were gifted to the Kriegsmarine in a ceremony in Feodosiya. Designated the 11th S-flotilla under the command of Kptlt Hans-Jürgen Meyer, the new unit comprised seven boats, the majority skippered by senior NCOs and divided into two operational groups:

Group 1: *S503* (ex-*MAS568*), *S502* (ex-*MAS567*), *S505* (ex-*MAS570*), *S506* (ex-*MAS574*)
Group 2: *S504* (ex-*MAS569*), *S501* (ex-*MAS566*), *S507* (ex-*MAS575*).

The small boats were extremely susceptible to bad weather, problematic within the Black Sea. Displacing 29.4 tons, they were armed with two lateral thrust 45cm torpedoes and a single 20mm cannon, making them also vulnerable to air attack, although their small 18.7m by 4.7m (61ft 4in x 15ft 5in) size and a top speed of 44 knots at least made them a difficult target.

Once German crews had acclimatised to their new boats, they made few war patrols as they were found relatively unsuited to Black Sea conditions. Their first operational sailing from Feodosiya did not come until 5 June, *S501*, *S504* and *S505* employed in an ASW role to allow the crew time to familiarise themselves with the boats in action. After their first showing, they were moved on to offensive operations in support of the Kuban bridgehead. On 13 June at 0440hrs the operational boats of the 11th S-flotilla put into Feodosiya after having clashed with Russian MTBs. *S501* and *S505* had both been attacked by 40mm cannon fire from a range of 4,000m (4,300yds), breaking immediately westward, *S501* under high-speed pursuit. *S504*, *S505* and *S506* skirmished with an MTB at close range, though the latter's Breda machine gun jammed, leaving the MAS craft with no defence other than speed, none of the ex-Italian boats carrying smoke-making gear. A torpedo attack was impossible because of the broad angle on the bow and the high speed of the enemy boat. Though they escaped, the engagement demonstrated that patrol duty off the Taman coast was not at all suitable employment and they were earmarked for defensive operations from that point onward, except possibly during periods of no moon.

The 1st S-flotilla had not remained idle during the interim, although neither had they achieved notable success. On 5 June Ivan Baba was attacked twice during the morning, twenty-six bombs raining down from high altitude, destroying buildings and crew quarters, killing four men and seriously wounding another. The boats had continued to operate against the Myshako beachhead, *S26*, *S42*, *S46* and *S52* attacking and sinking one 500-ton coaster and 1,300-ton lighter lying alongside disembarkation jetties. They then attempted unsuccessfully to intercept naval forces shelling Anapa. On 8 July, Kptlt Karl 'Charlie' Müller, commander of *S52*, was awarded the Knight's Cross.

During June, elements of the 1st S-flotilla were despatched into the Sea of Asov to prevent an expected enemy landing in Temryuk Bay. German artillery barges had shelled enemy positions as far north as Primorsko-Akhtarsk and the S-boats were sent to hunt for supply ships while defending the artillery lighters. Four boats entered the new target area on the night of 13 June and clashed with Russian MTBs, S-boat artillery fire hampered by frequent jamming of the 40mm flak weapons aboard *S40*, *S46* and *S49* and only *S42* maintaining fire. The four boats returned to Kerch, repeating their mission over the ensuing three consecutive nights before a rest. They remained on patrol off Kerch until 20 June when they returned to Ivan Baba for engine repairs, sailing to the Caucasian coast six days later. On 29 June the four boats were lurking in positions off the Mezib Estuary when *S47* fired a double torpedo shot at an enemy patrol vessel, both exploding prematurely in shallow water. Following the explosion, the S-boats were picked out by numerous searchlights and shelled, returning 40mm fire while retreating under cover of smoke.

The Soviet Air Force had intensified its attacks considerably as the tide of battle turned inexorably against the Axis. During June there had been eleven raids on Crimean ports, during July there were fourteen, and another thirteen on ports within the Kuban bridgehead. Attacks on both S-boat bases at Ivan Baba and Feodosiya became more frequent and Kieseritzky recorded within the pages of his KTB that 'in Ivan Baba, where, since 1st S-flotilla was reinforced, about nine boats are stationed permanently, one accurate heavy bomb could destroy the whole flotilla. This would mean the destruction of the core of my offensive forces.' He urgently requested concrete shelters be constructed in both ports, but the situation on the Russian front deteriorated before any decision could be made regarding the matter.

Russian POWs landed in Ivan Baba after capture by S-boat.

The weeks remained barren of German success, Soviet aircraft continually harassing incoming and outgoing patrols. Finally, on the night of 6 July four boats of the 1st S-flotilla attacked an escorted convoy of lighters: *S28* torpedoed an estimated 800-ton lighter, *S47* one of 500 tons and *S40* one of 400 tons. After escaping the feeble defence put up by the escort, the boats tangled with an MGB while headed to Ivan Baba, *S28* scoring several artillery hits, but unable to verify the result as the enemy disappeared at high speed. Aboard *S47* one man had been slightly wounded by gunfire.

In good weather the following night, three simultaneous operations were carried out against Soviet supply traffic. To bolster the eight operational boats of 1st S-flotilla, Admiral Black Sea attached Räumboote of the 3rd R-Flotilla. *R33* and *R166* were ordered to accompany *S40* – chosen as she carried a 40mm gun – to attack the Myshako landing stages once more. Four other S-boats were tasked with torpedo attacks against shipping off the Vulan Valley southeast of Gelendzhik, while the final three were directed against enemy supply traffic off the Dzhubga Estuary midway between Tuapse and Gelendzhik, specifically targeting any vessels lying off the river mouths.

At 1130 hours on 8 July *S40*, *R33* and *R166* put into Kerch, having shelled jetties within the beachhead. Driven back twice by enemy patrol vessels, *S40* fired a salvo of two torpedoes at a northwest-bound convoy but missed. Under artillery fire from shore, the three boats retreated at high speed, *S40* ramming *R33* and causing considerable damage. Both remained watertight and were able to make their own way at 7 knots to Kerch for emergency repairs, escorted as far as Cape Takil' by the Vulan Valley boats, which returned to Ivan Baba after sighting nothing in drifting fog. The S-boats operating off Dzhubga were also frustrated by haze and fog; during their return to Ivan Baba *S102* struck a moored mine six miles southeast of Zheleznyy Rog. The blast killed the Chief Engineer ObMasch Helmut Menzel, two other non-commissioned officers and five sailors, the rest of the crew being only slightly wounded and rescued from their sinking boat by *S28*. The strength of the flotilla now rested at five operational S-boats: *S28*, *S42*, *S45*, *S47* and *S51*; *S40* in Kerch, *S26* out of commission in Ivan Baba and *S49*, *S52* and *S72* in the middle of overhaul in Constanta, *S28* scheduled to join them within days. Upon *S72*'s return to action, the boat was slightly damaged by splinters from fragmentation bombs under bright moonlight south of the Taman Peninsula. Two men were wounded. The S-flotillas had stopped sending boats in the standard *Rotte* pair owing to the marked increase in air attack, choosing instead to group at least three boats together for protection afforded by more flak weaponry.

A joint operation between the Army, Luftwaffe and Kriegsmarine was planned for the night of 23 July. Code-named Operation *Feuerzauber*, it was a concerted attack against the Russian beachhead and supply points at Myshako. At 1700hrs six 1st S-flotilla boats put out from Ivan Baba, when the Luftwaffe cancelled the operation. Left to Christiansen's discretion as to proceed or not, the S-boats pressed on and attacked the Soviet landing zones as planned. ObltzS Seevers' *S51* and ObltzS Silies' *S26* each claimed a lighter of 400 tons sunk, both boats using a full salvo of two torpedoes. The only recorded sinking in Russian records is of floating battery *No 627*. The boats then launched a concerted artillery attack on Russian positions before retreating under fire. The Army had launched their simultaneous attack, but the effect was minimal.

The shelling of enemy land targets was repeated in August, S-boats often creeping on one engine offshore to avoid Russian sound-guided search-lights. Torpedo missions continued, though fuel shortages had started to impede operations. Only one sinking was recorded by either flotilla during August, the 560-ton tug *Petraš* torpedoed on 7 August southeast of Betta. A patrol vessel was sighted and fired on by 40mm and 20mm cannon and sub-machine guns, hits observed until the attackers were blinded by the beams of seven searchlights in what Christiansen described as a 'dome of light like the display at the National Socialist Party's rally.' The target vessel escaped.

Soviet aircraft continually harassed the S-boats at sea, bombers and rocket-firing ground attack aircraft guided to their targets by naval reconnaissance planes that detected the S-boats on radar before firing green flares identifying the Germans. On 24 August *S46* was set aflame by a rocket that exploded 100m above the boat, showering it with a non-phosphorus incendiary material, although the crew extinguished it with water.

On land the Wehrmacht was relentlessly beaten back. The battle of Kursk had been fought and lost and now the Red Army launched counteroffensives that pushed the Germans west. On 10 September the Red Army landed in Novorossiysk; 129 landing craft carrying nearly nine thousand troops forced the German defenders to evacuate, constricting the German pocket defending the Taman Peninsula. That same night three 1st S-flotilla boats prowled the coastline until deteriorating weather forced a premature break for Ivan Baba. At 0430hrs the trio were detected by reconnaissance aircraft and within twenty minutes were under fire by heavily armoured Il-2 Sturmoviks. Their defensive flak was ineffective, several 20mm hits seen to bounce off the aircrafts' skin. The Sturmoviks dove down to an altitude of 10m and pummelled the boats with heavy cannon fire. *S46* was hit in her smoke canisters, both flak weapons and the starboard engine, which died immediately, exhaust, oil, air and water pipes completely destroyed. The aircraft concentrated their attacks on the disabled boat, setting the main engine room ablaze and knocking out the centre and auxiliary engines and main electric circuitry. The final engine was hit by cannon fire moments before shells impacted on loaded torpedoes, causing them to explode. The forecastle was completely destroyed and the boat doomed. Both remaining S-boats laid thick smoke while returning fire until the aircraft finally departed. *S49* rescued all survivors – every one of them wounded – and recovered the bodies of two men killed in the attack. Secret papers were retrieved and the burning wreck sunk by a torpedo.

Pressure on the Kuban bridgehead had become intolerable and permission was finally given for the 17th Army to withdraw across the Kerch Strait, abandoning the Taman Peninsula. The operation was not completed until October and S-boats from both flotillas continued to operate as cover, lest the Soviets attempt to land behind Kerch and isolate the Kuban Peninsula. Patrols into the Sea of Azov were periodically undertaken, frequently subject to intense air attack. Anapa was evacuated on 21 September, Soviet troops occupying the port and immediately using it as an MTB base. The dominant Soviet air force defeated Luftwaffe attempts to interfere. On 28 September the 1st S-flotilla's *S28*, *S42*, *S45* and *S49* attacked Russian shipping in Anapa. Firing at 800m (875yds) range, *S28* sank one 500-ton lighter anchored beneath the cliffs, *S42* also sank a 500-ton lighter, *S49* two coasters, one of 300 tons and the other of 500 tons, which were lying on the seaward side of the mole, and *S45* destroyed a third lighter at anchor estimated at 300 tons. Two of the vessels exploded violently, throwing fountains of water and mushroom clouds into the sky. The mole itself was also hit and damaged, leading to a temporary withdrawal of Russian naval units from the port.

During September Christiansen departed as commander of 1st S-flotilla and was replaced by Kptlt Hermann Büchting, now sporting his Knight's Cross awarded on 22 April 1943. For his part, Christiansen joined FdS Staff, awarded the Oak Leaves on 13 November 1943. As Büchting arrived, the 11th S-flotilla was officially disbanded, the boats worn beyond useful service and spare parts a major problem for the Italian petrol engines. Any personnel from the flotilla maintenance staff were transferred to the Aegean and the Italian boats of the 24th S-flotilla. *S501*, *S506* and *S507* were temporarily assigned to the 1st S-flotilla, though decommissioned on 5 October and towed to Linz. This left the beleaguered boats of Büchting's flotilla to continue the fight alone.[101]

The evacuation of the Taman Peninsula continued into October, an attack by Soviet destroyers against the evacuation transport successfully beaten away by *S28*, *S42* and *S45*, though *S45* was hit and lightly damaged. Three of the Soviet destroyers were subsequently sunk by the Luftwaffe. Temryuk fell on 27 September and finally, on 9 October, the evacuation was complete, the Taman Peninsula in Soviet hands. The maritime evacuation had lifted 239,669 soldiers, 16,311 wounded, 27,456 civilians and 115,477 tons of military equipment (primarily ammunition), 21,230 vehicles, 74 tanks, 1,815 guns and 74,657 horses from the Kuban bridgehead back to the Crimea. On 12 December 1943 ObltzS Karl-Friedrich Künzel of *S28* was awarded the Knight's Cross for his part in the pell-mell fighting around the Taman Peninsula.

With the eastern part of the Black Sea now completely under Soviet domination and land approaches to the Crimea cut by Red Army advances, Büchting urged the flotilla's relocation to Sevastopol and the evacuation of Ivan Baba. However, Admiral Black Sea denied permission, as he regarded the small harbour to be the most geographically suitable base from which the essential task of defending the Crimea could be carried out. Bombing raids became more frequent and by the New Year were a daily occurrence. Meanwhile, Soviet troops landed at Eltigen and Yenikale in November, crossing the Kerch Strait in hundreds of makeshift landing craft. The southern landing at Eltigen was blockaded by R-boats of 3rd R-flotilla, covered by S-boats.

Around midnight on 4 November the 1st S-flotilla clashed with Soviet patrol boats, damaging *TK81* with a torpedo hit and sinking *TK101*. Four nights later five S-boats found Russian Task Force F sinking patrol boat *0122*, with the Russian flotilla commander aboard, two other patrol boats hitting defensive German mines and going down. On 11 November a Russian MGB was destroyed by artillery fire and ten nights later two landing craft were set on fire by artillery attack, eight others forced to retreat from the Eltigen beachhead. The beachhead eventually collapsed, though Soviet troops reinforced the northern landing at Yenikale to strength sufficient to hold and eventually provide a jumping-off point for the 1944 liberation of the Crimea.

This *Torpedomechanikerobergefreiten* of the 1st S-flotilla carries the Iron Cross, first and second class, wound badge, S-boat badge, Crimean campaign arm shield and ribbon for the Romanian anti-Communist campaign medal.

On 1 January 1944 the 1st S-flotilla numbered six operational boats at Ivan Baba: *S26*, *S42*, *S47*, *S49*, *S52* and *S72*. In Constanta *S28*, *S40*, *S45* and S51 were all out of commission undergoing repair.[102] Meanwhile, FdS had promised six reinforcement boats sent from Germany, three already shipped down the Danube and in the process of reconstruction in Constanta. Their deployment would come too late to affect the outcome of the Black Sea campaign as it spiralled toward its conclusion. During January, with terrible weather preventing operations, only one unsuccessful torpedo mission was sailed. Another single mission on 4 March found S-boats clashing inconclusively with Russian MGBs northwest of Tuapse, the enemy hit several times by artillery fire but retreating at speed.

At 0830hrs on 11 March Ivan Baba was attacked by Russian bombers which dropped rocket fragmentation bombs and 15cm artillery shells with ad hoc tail fins, as well as 500 light and medium high-explosive bombs. One attacking plane was shot down while four S-boats sustained slight splinter damage, *S29*'s engine room waterlogged as a result. The base itself was slightly damaged and two men killed and another pair wounded. Further raids followed, wearing down the S-boats' operational capacity with frequent damage.

Finally, on 8 April 1944, the long-awaited Soviet invasion of the Crimea began when elements of 4th Ukrainian Front's 2nd Guards and 51st Armies crossed the Kerch Strait. Four days later the base at Ivan Baba was abandoned while stocks of mines, torpedoes and ammunition were blown up. Balaclava was also abandoned. The flotilla transferred to Sevastopol, which itself was under attack by the end of April. The S-boats became engaged in the evacuation of the great city, under constant and unrelenting air attack. By 8 May 90,260 soldiers and 15,435 wounded were transported

Korvettenkapitän Hermann Büchting as commander of the 1st S-flotilla at Ivan Baba within the Black Sea.

from Crimea to Constanta, 1,265 of them by S-boats. The city fell to the Soviets the following day. The Crimea was lost.

On 1 June *S28*, *S40*, *S47*, *S49*, *S72*, *S131*, *S148* and *S149* were operational in Constanta. Fuel shortage kept the boats largely penned in harbour, unless firm sightings could be guaranteed by the meagre Luftwaffe reconnaissance presence. No targets were found during the whole of June. During July *S26*, *S28*, *S40* and *S42* transferred to Sulina at the mouth of the Danube, *S42* being fitted for a new propeller. The remainder of the boats were in Constanta's shipyard, *S72* following to Sulina in early August. On 19 August *S26*, *S40* and *S72* were destroyed in a Soviet air attack on the port, *S26* losing eight crewmen killed and *S72* four. On 22 August ObltzS Hubertus von Dülong's *S148* hit a mine north of Sulima, suffering no casualties, but the boat scuttled as a result. An aircraft attack the following day against Constanta harbour destroyed *S42*, *S52* and *S131* (killing three men), and severely damaging *S28* and *S149*.

On 27 February 1934 the Nazi Party introduced the national holiday, Heldengedenktag (Day of Commemoration of Heroes) and in 1943 a set of stamps was issued to coincide with the celebration, each depicting a scene from Germany's military machine. These included an early model S-boat that graced the fifty-pfennig stamp. To commemorate Heldengedenktag in 1944, following the change that year of inscription on all stamps from 'Deutsches Reich' to 'Grossdeutsches Reich' (Greater German Empire), a second set of military themed stamps were issued and the S-boat updated accordingly.

The 1st S-flotilla had been decimated and now their erstwhile allies turned against them. On 23 August 1944, just as the Red Army was penetrating the Moldavian front, King Michael I of Romania led a successful coup that deposed the Antonescu dictatorship. Admiral Black Sea ordered Büchting to take his flotilla to operate against any Soviet units sighted, *S51*, *S49*, *S45* and *S47* sailing, while non-operational *S28* and *S149* were scuttled. The flotilla staff in Constanta took advantage of Romanian guarantees of a non-obstructed retreat and departed by truck for German lines.

With no targets, Büchting ordered his boats to Varna in Bulgaria, that country also changing allegiance on 8 September after coming under direct Soviet attack. With nowhere left to go, Büchting ordered his last four boats scuttled off Varna. The crews were interned but were soon able to 'escape' with Bulgarian assistance and travel via Sofia to Belgrade and Vienna, then ultimately to Saßnitz where they arrived on 21 September. From there they would form the nucleus of a new 1st S-flotilla; the Kriegsmarine's war in the Black Sea was over.

16
The West

January 1943 – May 1944

A T the beginning of 1943 FdS had twenty-two operational boats at his disposal from a total of thirty-nine in the west: twelve in Ijmuiden, six belonging to 2nd S-flotilla, six to the 6th S-flotilla; four 4th S-flotilla boats in Rotterdam and six 5th S-flotilla boats in Cherbourg.

January storms lashed the English Channel, curtailing operations until five days into the New Year when all flotillas sailed. In the west the 5th S-flotilla headed for Lyme Bay, but in a strong gust of wind *S116* rammed *Führerboot S82*, forced to limp slowly to St Peter Port in Guernsey, and the operation was cancelled. To the east, in extraordinary conditions of sleet and snow, S-boats found nothing of a reported FN convoy, two boats from Obermaier's 6th S-flotilla – *S76* and *S119* – colliding in snow flurries and returning damaged for shipyard repair.

On 8 January fifteen boats from the three Netherlands-based flotillas put to sea, at once facing limited visibility and atrocious weather. Midway between Ijmuiden and Lowestoft in the early hours of the morning, ObltzS Ullrich Roeder's *S104* hit a floating mine. The explosion wrecked the foreship, killing one man instantly and wounding six others. Shocked survivors were evacuated and, unable to be taken under tow, the abandoned vessel was scuttled with explosives.

On 18 January the weather moderated enough for large-scale mining northwest of Cromer. In total nineteen boats departed and laid 100 LMB mines as planned. During the return, disaster befell *S109* when it too struck a floating mine. The blast destroyed the foreship and blew the forward gunner overboard, never to be seen again. One other man was injured and the battered boat taken in tow by *S78* and *S87*, who dragged it toward Ijmuiden, passing her over to a tugboat which took *S109* into harbour. From Cherbourg, Klug's 5th S-flotilla conducted partially successful minelaying

S65 at sea.

near Dungeness on 28 January, *S68* and *S65* returning with mines intact due to defective mine carts that prevented them sliding along fitted rails.

Bad weather closed in once more and it wasn't until the middle of February that the S-boats were in action again. On 17 February, fifteen set out from the Netherlands to mine the waters north of Sheringham. Less than four hours from port a Fairey Albacore dropped five bombs, lightly wounding one man but nothing more. However, the British were clearly aware of the S-boats' movement and destroyers HM Ships *Montrose*, and *Garth* from 21st Destroyer Flotilla, supported by sloop HMS *Kittiwake* and a group of MGBs sailed to intercept. At 0051hrs HMS *Garth* sighted three S-boats eleven miles from Lowestoft and opened fire. ObltzS Rüdiger Suhr's *S71* was hit in the engine room and catching fire, radioed appeals for help intercepted by HMS *Montrose*'s Headache operator. HMS *Garth* came alongside the stricken S-boat, finding the skipper and seventeen crewmen dead, rescuing seven survivors as well as the boat's canine mascot before *S71* sank. Unaware of this, the remaining S-boats returned to base and Luftwaffe aircraft searched for the missing boat, but found no trace. In a decision that drew sharp criticism, amounting to a personal reprimand from Generaladmiral Wilhelm Marschall at MGK West, Rudolf Petersen despatched seventeen boats from three flotillas in a futile search operation. Marschall reasoned that the deployment of all combat-ready boats on anything other than an offensive operation constituted unnecessary risk. Though they later reconciled during a private meeting, the relationship between Petersen and his superiors remained uneasy.

On 26 February Luftwaffe Reconnaissance Group 123 reported twenty freighters and five destroyers near Start Point, Klug's 5th S-flotilla putting *S77*, *S65*, *S85*, *S81* and *S68* into action, sailing toward Lyme Bay. *Führerboot S77* hit rocks and was forced to abort, but the remainder made contact before Berry Head at 0119hrs, ObltzS Sobottka's *S65* firing first toward the ships of convoy WP300. His torpedo hit 445-ton ASW trawler HMT *Lord Hailsham*, sending her under with nine confirmed dead and nine missing. Norwegian minesweeping trawler *Harstad* was also hit, ObltzS Goetschke's *S68* sinking the 258-ton ship with all but one of her crew, the sole survivor wounded but later rescued. ObltzS Kolbe's *S85* hit the 625-ton tank landing craft *LCT381* with a single torpedo, bringing the vessel to halt, during which time some of Kolbe's crew boarded her with small arms and, after a brief battle, took eleven prisoners. A *coup de grâce* was fired by *S65* to put the ship under. Kolbe also claimed to have hit two more 2,000-ton freighters, but they remain unconfirmed. The largest ship of the convoy, 4,858-ton MV *Modavia* was also sunk in a combined attack by *S68* and ObltzS Wendler's *S81*; by 0600hrs the S-boats were back in Guernsey.

The next mission on 28 February ended with nothing but damage to *S110* from 40mm gunfire before poor visibility curtailed operations until 4 March. That night 5th S-flotilla was driven away from Lyme Bay by destroyers, *S68* and *S85* grounding on rocks and forced to abort to Guernsey, later requiring extensive shipyard time in Cherbourg. As the remaining four boats returned, *S81* and *S90* collided, putting both out of commission until repaired. In the North Sea, however, S-boats suffered greater casualties. ObltzS Hans Klose's *S70* of the 2nd S-flotilla struck a mine which detonated a reserve torpedo, immediately sinking the boat with five men killed. The 6th S-flotilla's *S74* and *S75* were attacked by Spitfire and Typhoon fighters, ObltzS Wolfgang Hörning's *S75* severely hit and set ablaze, sinking within forty minutes. Eleven crewmen had been killed, including the chief engineer. Kptlt Herbert Witt's *S74* was also heavily damaged, two men killed and the skipper and four others badly injured, but the boat was able to limp back to Ijmuiden under its own power – no Luftwaffe cover was available despite urgent requests. In a little over two months, Petersen's operational force had been significantly reduced. Of his four western flotillas only nineteen boats remained operational, eight out of commission due to heavy damage, ten others under scheduled refit.

On 7 March things did not improve for Petersen's flotillas, despite the inauguration of a new tactic using radar technology. In a combined operation the 2nd and 6th S-flotillas carried out a normal *Stichansatz* attack, while boats of the 4th S-flotilla hung back from the convoy route. Equipped with newly installed radars, their task was convoy detection, a tactic named *FuMB-Lauer* (radar lurking). However, British changes to the convoy lanes put the radar boats too far seaward and only a few 6th S-flotilla boats made contact, deflected by enemy escorts. The *Rotte S114* and *S119* were pursued by HMS *Mackay* and *MGB20* and *21* when *S119* rammed LzS d Res August Licht's *S114*, the former so heavily damaged that it was abandoned and scuttled. Licht returned to port with the rescued crew and was later praised by SKL for his 'initiative and foresight' during the event.

While diplomatic sources in Portugal indicated an Allied offensive within the Mediterranean was imminent, Hitler remained obsessed with a potential invasion of Norway. German intelligence reported large concentrations of troops and material along Britain's east coast and rumours of invasion reaching levels similar in proportion to that which preceded Operation Torch. With this tension permeating MGK West, Petersen placed his flotillas in defensive readiness throughout the English Channel within small groups that shifted port regularly. Gradually, following several false alarms, the threat level declined and boats returned to their original ports. Petersen, however, remained under pressure to further reduce his western combat strength. From four flotillas of a theoretical strength of forty, he stood at an operational level of fourteen S-boats by the middle of March. A gradual addition of eighteen new or repaired boats was expected within a month, but he was being asked to allow six boats to be sold to Spain and transfer reinforcement to the 1st S-flotilla in the Black Sea.[103] Petersen strongly urged against these decisions, warning of a 'great aggravation of the present catastrophic situation of operational readiness.' He requested immediate return to the Channel of the idle 8th S-flotilla from Norway, rejected immediately by Hitler.

In 'E-Boat Alley' the battle continued. During the night of 28 March S-boats encountered fierce defence of convoy FS74 (Phase 9), *S92* and *S29* battling *MGB333* and *321* and British gunfire hammering *S29*'s unarmoured bridge, killing ObltzS Hans Lemm and six of his crew. Lieutenant Donald Bradford aboard *MGB333* charged forward and rammed the disabled S-boat in the stern, slicing the aft section clean away, but was forced to retire with his own damage. German survivors were later taken aboard returning S-boats, *S29* sunk at 0714hrs with scuttling charges.

Kapitänleutnant Niels Bätge moved on from command of 4th S-flotilla in March 1943. He transferred initially to the post of first officer aboard the destroyer *Hans Lody* before taking command of torpedo boat *T20* and, subsequently, destroyer *Z35* following promotion to Korvettenkapitän.[104] In his place, KK Werner Lützow, former first officer aboard *Karl Galster* and Admiralty staff officer, arrived to take charge of the flotilla.

In early April several torpedo patrols guided by Luftwaffe reconnaissance failed to make contact with the enemy, although *S90* reported a torpedo hit on a patrol craft near Start Point. Although the Luftwaffe had provided sighting information, visibility at sea was so poor that S-boats were unable to find the convoys. Two Bf109 reconnaissance aircraft reported sixteen freighters, two tankers and four escorts in Lyme Bay during Friday, 13 April, Klug's 5th S-flotilla sailing to intercept. In order to operate further west than previously possible, Klug's unit had moved to the Breton port of Aberwrac'h, eight boats putting to sea but two aborting, *S84* with rudder damage accompanied by the other half of the *Rotte S116*.[105] The remaining six managed to find and attack PW323 off Lizard Head. ObltzS Johann Konrad Klocke's *S121* torpedoed and sank 1,742-ton SS *Stanlake*, while Norwegian destroyer HNoMS *Eskdale* was also torpedoed and sunk, twenty-five crewmen going to the bottom with their ship. It is possible the destroyer was hit and disabled first by *S90*, before being finished off by both *S65* and *S111*. Oberleutnant zur See Hans Dietrich's *S82* claimed one other unconfirmed 4,000-ton tanker sunk.

The following night 2nd and 4th S-flotillas laid mines, clashing with enemy forces led by HM Ships *Westminster* and *Widgeon* and sinking radar-equipped HMT *Adonis* in the brief battle. Rating T Roy Sparkes later recalled the attack:

> On the night of the 14th, after manoeuvring my way across the pitching deck to take over the middle-watch, I had been settled down in the radar caboose astern for about an hour when I became aware of movement on the screen. There was a blip or two at about 6,000 or 7,000 yards. With the general conditions and the hand-turned radar 'aerial' to contend with, the blip was at about 2,000 yards before I could make any really definite report. At 1.15 a.m. I whistled up the old voice-pipe to the bridge to report my suspicions, but they could see nothing. The range then closed to 1,700 yards. From the bridge I heard the muffled order given to fire star-shells, a task for our fo'c'sle gun crew with their pride of weaponry, an old Japanese 14-pounder.
>
> Then all hell was let loose. Faintly I heard the gun's report, followed almost immediately by a huge explosion – the whole ship appeared to heave her guts

and shudder. Up in my radar caboose, on its four spindly angle-iron legs, I was flung violently forward, crashing my nose into the radar tube. All the lights had gone out and I felt the floor beneath me begin to tilt.[106]

Only eleven men out of the thirty-two aboard ship survived, later plucked from the sea by an RAF rescue launch. As nights shortened, Petersen moved his flotillas west once more to operate within the Channel; Feldt's 2nd S–

S121 moving at speed.

flotilla transferred to Cherbourg, while both the 4th and 6th went first to St Peter Port, Guernsey, to load torpedoes and then onwards to Cherbourg. Petersen and his FdS staff moved back to Wimereux.

Towards the end of May minelaying took precedence, S-boats attempting to vary routes to and from target areas and use their speed advantage to throw off potential pursuit and confuse radar and radio location monitoring. Only a few inconclusive engagements with enemy aircraft or surface vessels appeared to validate their efforts: 321 mines and eighty-four explosive buoys laid along the south coast of England between 23 May and 12 June. Not one single sinking can be attributed to them. Indeed, B-Dienst interceptions showed that the British were still able to accurately pinpoint minefield locations, avoiding routing convoys through them or having them swept. With the Luftwaffe no longer on hand to interfere with British mine-sweeping, the entire minelaying offensive proved an exercise in futility.

While torpedo missions were in a lull, Petersen rotated half of his front-line Channel strength at any one time to shipyards where they were up-gunned and fitted with the new *Kalotte* armoured bridge. Sixteen S-boats were fitted with 40mm C/28 Bofors anti-aircraft guns, the remainder carrying the new fully automatic 37mm flak weapon, theoretically allowing each *Rotte* to carry one of each.

At the beginning of 1943 Raeder had resigned as head of the Kriegs-marine, Hitler's strategic decisions concerning German naval power no longer tolerable to him. He was replaced by Grossadmiral Karl Dönitz, previous head of the U-boat service, who appeared to understand the potential and requirements of the S-boats, and lobbied for increased production of them to interdict the British coastal convoys from the strategically advantageous Channel coast ports. This boded well for Petersen's Schnellboote. During 1942 thirty-four new German S-boats had been commissioned, another seven smaller Dutch boats in Schiedam. During 1943, the number remained more or less the same, peaking at thirty-eight new boats. However, in 1944 Dönitz's support and Albert Speer's genius for production raised the number of boats commissioned into service to sixty-three. Of course, the problem remained of equipping them with skilled crews.

As available combat boats slowly increased in the Channel, Petersen transferred the 2nd and 6th S-flotillas back to Ostend, planning operations within the Thames Estuary and splitting British defenders from the south coast. S-boats continued to rotate through shipyards for upgrade and refit. *S90* and *S122* were caught by radar-equipped aircraft during the early hours of 19 June while sailing from Boulogne to Rotterdam, one man killed aboard *S122*, while ObltzS Hans-Jürgen Stohwasser and seven of his crew were wounded aboard *S90*, the boat badly damaged but diverting under its own power to Dunkirk for emergency repair.

On 25 July *S77* and *S68* of Klug's 5th S-flotilla sailed from Boulogne headed for refit in Germany, running unexpectedly into four MGBs north of Dunkirk. The ensuing firefight caused an engine failure and the jamming of two machine guns aboard ObltzS Josef Ludwig's *S77*, which then came under sustained fire, igniting one of the torpedoes that engulfed the boat in flames as she began to flood. Ludwig lay dead on his shattered bridge, six other men also killed as *MGB40* and *42* rescued four survivors from the water between them as prisoners of war. The remaining twelve crewmen still aboard *S77* scuttled the boat and paddled for the French shore aboard a life raft, found on a beach near Dunkirk the following day by men of a

Luftwaffe flak battery. From *Führerboot S68*, ObltzS Helmuth Moritzen had not exchanged fire with the enemy, nor had he issued a contact report via radio, continuing on to Ostend where a furious Kptlt Obermaier immediately scrambled five S-boats and led them on a search for survivors. Moritzen's judgement was severely criticised and he was relieved of his command and court-martialled.

Seven S-boats swept into action off Orfordness during the night of 4 August, targeting a British minesweeping group. Seconds after making contact, they opened fire with machine guns and flak weapons, ObltzS Hans-Joachim Wrampe's *S86* torpedoing HMT *Red Gauntlet*, the trawler caught with her sweep gear still extended and unable to evade. The explosion blew the 338-ton vessel apart and from the seventeen crew only one body of a leading seaman was recovered by an RAF rescue launch the following day.

On the night of 7 August seven operational boats of the 4th and 5th S-flotillas were transferred to Brest in an effort to spread S-boat range further west. From the heavily defended harbour they moved to Aberwrac'h in preparation for an attack on Plymouth Sound. Moored in the outer harbour, they were vulnerable when Cornwall-based 263 Squadron Whirlwinds and a Spitfire escort screamed into the attack, raking the S-boats with cannon fire and bombs. *S121* was squarely hit by bombs that exploded stored ammunition and set the shattered hulk on fire; ObltzS Johann Konrad Klocke, two petty officers and eight men were killed and three men wounded, one of whom died shortly afterward in a Brest hospital. All of the S-boats received damage requiring repair before they could sail again, *S84* and *S136* officially put out of commission with damage to the hulls and engines and at least two weeks' repair time expected. The chief of the 4th S-flotilla, KK Werner Lützow and commander of *S110*, ObltzS Ludwig Graser, were also lightly wounded in the attack that the RAF called 'The Massacre at the Aber Vrach [*sic*] River', incorrectly claiming four S-boats sunk.

With more boats in Germany for engine replacement and overhaul and the disaster at Aberwrac'h, Petersen prepared his few S-boats for another concerted minelaying offensive using newly developed AA1 sub-sonic acoustic detonators. S-boats were kept at a state of intermittent alert as MGK West continued to fear Allied landings somewhere on the French coast, an alternating rota of crews kept at half-hour readiness into September. S-boats were also tasked with scouring inshore waters south of Cap Gris Nez for evidence of enemy activity. R-boats engaged in minelaying were also allocated S-boat escort and despite small skirmishes with enemy naval and air forces – including rocket-firing Typhoon fighter bombers for the first time – there were no losses.

New boats were also arriving, *S100*, *S138* and *S140* docking in Cherbourg on the last day of the month. *S100* marked the beginning of a new class of boat. While retaining the outward dimensions of the *S38*-class they incorporated the *Kalotte* armoured bridge as standard, with additional armour-plating for the three 2,500hp MB511 engine superchargers. The bow 20mm was retained, with an additional 37mm or 40mm on the aft platform and twin 20mm flak weapon amidships. By mid September the four western flotillas were almost at full strength once more, all boats now carrying *Kalottenbrücke* and 40mm or 37mm quick-firing guns. Additionally, Klug's 5th S-flotilla had received new 2,500hp MB 511 engines, allowing a cruising speed of 35 knots.

As the nights lengthened Petersen moved his flotillas once more, the 2nd and 6th transferring to Ijmuiden, the 4th to Boulogne and Rotterdam, while the 5th remained on station in Cherbourg. In Boulogne the 4th S-flotilla celebrated the award of the Knight's Cross to ObltzS Karl-Erhart Karcher on 13 August. On 12 September a newly formed incarnation of the 8th S-flotilla began deploying into the Channel. S-boat veteran KK Felix Zymalkowski had been promoted to take charge of the new flotilla which initially comprised *S64, S65, S68, S69, S93* and *S127*, sailing into Hoofden as they prepared for the minelaying scheduled for the night of 24 September.

At the allotted hour all four flotillas from the Netherlands carried out their assigned missions. The 2nd S-flotilla left Ijmuiden with eight boats at 2000hrs, dropping forty-two LMB mines as planned and all boats returned to the Hook of Holland by 0800hrs. Seven boats of the 4th S-flotilla had left the Hook at 2115hrs, *S39* ramming *S90* while trying to avoid an R-boat during departure. The damaged *S90* was towed back into harbour by *S39* and *S74*. From 0123hrs onwards the rest of the flotilla was within sight of the convoy route south of buoy 52 when they stumbled upon four minesweeping trawlers, ObltzS Sander's *S96* firing a torpedo that hit and sank 314-ton HMT *Franc Tireur* with half the crew killed. As the remaining trawlers tried desperately to evade the oncoming S-boats, two of them collided, sending HMT *Donna Nook* to the bottom also. The S-boats went on to lay thirty-four active mines, before withdrawing in bad visibility. As they did so, four British MGBs coming at high speed from a Z-patrol to the north suddenly blundered into the S-boats, Sander's *S96* colliding with

ObltzS Johann Konrad Klocke, skipper of *S121*, killed in action during the RAF attack on Aberwrac'h, 11 August 1943.

ML150 and *145*, damaging the British vessels but also dooming herself. [107] Sander, aware that the ruined *S96* was defenceless and going down, requested and received permission to scuttle his ship from flotilla head-quarters, sixteen survivors, including Sander, taken prisoner by the British.

Eight S-boats of the 6th Flotilla left Ijmuiden at 2000hrs and carried out their minelaying operation according to plan. Engine trouble forced the first group of *S74, S90* and *S39* to return immediately after laying ten TMB mines near Shipwash, while the second group started on its return passage after an unsuccessful search for *S96* survivors, clashing with MGBs in the swirling fog. The six newly arrived members of the 8th S-flotilla left the Hook at 2115hrs, laying thirty-four LMB mines as planned. Chancing upon a trawler group, *S69* fired two torpedoes at HMT *Corena* but missed, *S68*'s side engine room hit by return cannon fire and the starboard engine put out of action. Nonetheless, they all returned to the Hook by 0900hrs. Six of the participating S-boats were rendered non-operational by the mission, three by unexplained crankcase explosions attributed to potential sabotage.

September was something of a high-water mark for Petersen's western S-boats, able to field twenty-six operational craft. However, facing them were 324 MGBs, MTBs and MLs of the Allied coastal forces, not to mention larger warships and those of the auxiliary flotillas. The Luftwaffe had stopped its part in minelaying, diverted instead to defensive tasks or the resumed bombing of British cities. Bad weather prevented further S-boat operations until 7 October when all four flotillas laid mines once more along the east coast, *S93* damaged outbound by another mysterious explosion within the crank casing and returning to Ijmuiden with *S127* escorting. Hours later *S83* was also compelled to return with engine damage, in company with *S62*.

Intelligence reports indicated that the British were not only aware of the minefields laid by S-boats, but also had developed a counter to the new fuses being deployed, and Petersen reverted to his trusted method of alternating torpedo and minelaying patrols, not informing MGK West of his decision but trusting to the level of autonomy that he held over S-boat operations.

Following a period of bright moonlight, the first torpedo mission took place on the night of 23 October using a massed force of twenty-seven boats

Photograph from *Die Kriegsmarine* magazine, 1944, showing the 20mm C/38 gun mounted in the bow of an S-boat equipped with the *Kalottenbrücke*.

from 2nd, 4th, 6th and 8th S-flotillas, led by KK Heinrich Erdmann – FdS Chief of Staff – aboard *S94*. While once this formidable force would have seemed assured of victory, in October 1943 they ran into the overwhelming might of British convoy defence while attacking convoy FN60 (Phase 10) near Cromer. The incoming S-boats were detected by British bombers laying minefields in German waters, placing defences on high alert. The Germans arrived near the estimated convoy location, but were actually well astern of its path as FN60 was two hours ahead of schedule. The escort comprised destroyers HM Ships *Campbell*, *MacKay*, *Worcester*, *Eglington* and *Pytchley* as well as six MGBs, two ML and two MTBs. While shore radar tracked the inbound Germans, HMS *Pytchley* detected S-boat traces on shipboard radar and opened fire at 2318hrs. The sole German success was the torpedoing of straggling trawler HMT *William Stephan* by Kptlt Witt's *S74*, four survivors rescued by their attacker. The remainder of the night was a German disaster.

All nine boats of the 2nd S-flotilla, including *S94*, managed to outpace pursuit and break free. Four boats of 6th S-flotilla, led by Kptlt Obermaier aboard *Führerboot S76*, suffered severe damage in the struggle that followed. Obermaier was forced to transfer to *S114* after radio failure and, following Witt's sinking of the British trawler, several S-boats suffered torpedo failures, many crewmen wounded by British cannon fire. Likewise, the six 8th S-flotilla boats took several hits before escaping under a hail of bullets and star-shells. The eight boats of the 4th S-flotilla bore the brunt of the enemy's fury. One group – *S88*, *S63*, *S110* and *S117* – led by KK Lützow in *S88*, came under fire by HMS *Worcester*, a 4.7in shell hitting *S88* directly and badly damaging her as she slewed to a halt. The bridge was wrecked and the bodies of Lützow and skipper Obstrm Heinz Räbiger were seen lying in the wreckage, both with severe head injuries. Fire quickly spread after more British shells landed, fuel tanks exploding as survivors sprang overboard, nineteen rescued by the British, two of whom later perished. Shell splinters had also knocked out one engine aboard *S63*, which was then bracketed by fire from HMS *MacKay* while laying smoke and dropping delayed action depth charges behind them. *S63* was straddled with 6pdr fire and sank, LzS Dietrich Howaldt and twenty-three of his crew rescued, three as prisoners of the British.

There were no further missions in October as bad weather hampered a renewal of operations. Following the loss of Lützow, *S120* skipper Kptlt Albert Causemann stepped in as interim commander of 4th S-flotilla until November

A close-up of the same gunner manning his 20mm cannon.

when KK Kurt Fimmen, former commander of *S26*, and more recently captain of torpedo boat *T16*, came in to take the flotilla helm.

Kriegsmarine command proposed replacing some torpedo gear with extra guns to combat the increasingly effective British coastal forces, but Petersen strongly objected, despite recent losses. As if to confirm his faith in the torpedo, the 5th S-flotilla found convoy CW221 during the morning of 3 November and ObltzS Stohwasser's *S138* hit SS *Storaa* amidships. Heavily laden with tons of iron tank-tracks and aircraft parts, the 1,967-ton ship went straight down with twenty-two of her thirty-six-man crew killed. ObltzS Kolbe's *S100* also hit 811-ton SS *Foam Queen* carrying coal to Poole, her stern blew off as stored ammunition exploded, and she sank immediately as the engines also fell into the sea. What remained afloat was later towed to Dover and beached. ObltzS Jürgensmeyer's *S136* also torpedoed collier SS *Donna Isabel*, the torpedo hitting the engine room, but failing to explode and passing clean through the ship, before the eyes of the merchant's chief engineer. Badly holed, the ship took one hour and twenty minutes to go down, the crew abandoning her without loss of life to be rescued by *ML141*. Though the S-boats had experienced a successful night, the statistic of only four hits from twenty-three torpedoes fired was sobering. For some commanders present these had been the first live torpedoes they had ever fired, Baltic training cut short by demand for front-line crews.

The following night the four Netherlands flotillas mounted another combined minelaying mission near Orfordness. Twenty-four boats sailed, two aborting with engine damage. The first group of 2nd S-flotilla laid twenty-eight UMB mines before encountering FN70 (Phase 10), its escorts unable to detect the S-boats on radar due to atmospheric interference. *S80* and *S89* both fired double torpedo shots, hitting and damaging 2,841-ton collier SS *Firelight*, blowing away most of the ship's bow. *S62* hit and badly damaged commodore ship MV *British Progress*. This 4,581-ton tanker was the first victim of an S-boat launched FAT torpedo. The FAT (*Federapparat Torpedo*) ran a wandering course with regular 180° turns, designed as a long-distance unguided weapon for use against densely packed convoy traffic.

The second group from Feldt's flotilla unsuccessfully skirmished with escorting destroyers before breaking away from the action. Elsewhere, all minelaying was completed to plan, boats heading back to base as morning approached. The 6th S-flotilla's *S116* suffered engine failure, while *S114* had another mysterious explosion within the crankcase shortly afterward. With dawn approaching, the flotilla boats sailed at reduced speed in mutually defensive posture, inevitably attacked by six RAF Beaufighters at 0725hrs. Oberleutnant zur See Herbert Witt's *S74* took multiple hits and lost all manoeuvrability, three men killed by cannon fire before the boat was abandoned and sunk by a torpedo from *S135*. *S116* and *S91* were also damaged as urgent appeals for Luftwaffe cover were denied. Eventually, at 0830hrs, six German fighters took off to assist, by which time the Beaufighters had gone.

During February 1944 KK Klaus Feldt departed 2nd S-flotilla, replaced as commander by Kptlt Hermann Opdenhoff, the two officers exchanging roles as Feldt returned to Germany to head the S-boat training division (*Schnellbootslehrdivision*) formed under Opdenhoff's command in November 1943. Training division headquarters were established in Swinemünde, forming an administrative umbrella over all S-boat training units. Upon Feldt's arrival these comprised 1st Detachment (*Abteilung*) in Swinemünde, and 1st S-training Flotilla (*Schnellbootsschulflottille*) centred on tender *Adolf Lüderitz*. By June 1944 a second detachment was established in Kaseburg and two more flotillas with tenders *Carl Peters* and *Tsingtau*.

Bad weather prevented many more Channel operations in 1943. A foray by 5th S-flotilla near Beachy Head on 1 December sank HMT *Avanturine* with a single torpedo, ObltzS Ahrens hitting the 296-ton trawler while it was under tow by HMT *Peter Carey*. The year had seen a drastic fall in S-boat success within the Channel: twenty-six merchant ships were sunk in total.

For the S-boats, eighty-four men had been killed in action, fifteen more severely wounded and thirty-seven lost as prisoners of war. Fifteen S-boats had been sunk. Coupled with this was a perceptible increase in British home-water seapower. During May 1943 U-boats had reached their peak strength with 118 U-boats at sea, yet they also suffered their most grievous losses with forty-one destroyed in action. Dönitz conceded defeat and the U-boats withdrew from the Atlantic to revive their numbers, never to return in strength again. The Battle of the Atlantic had been lost and although U-boats continued to sail and sink ships, Allied naval and air power had prevailed to such an extent that many destroyers were no longer required for convoy protection, able instead to concentrate their efforts in coastal waters.

Petersen's Channel force received recognition and reinforcement as the newly established 9th S-flotilla, under the command of Kptlt Götz Frhr von Mirbach, arrived in the Netherlands with new boats *S130*, *S144*, *S145* and *S146*, while on 1 January 1944, flotilla commanders KK Bernd Klug and KK Klaus Feldt were awarded the Oak Leaves to their Knight's Crosses.

Invasion fever still prematurely gripped OKW. Petersen countered proposals that S-boat control be devolved from FdS to local commands in the event of Allied landings, reasoning that optimal S-boat conditions for success were only possible under centralised command: Führer der Schnellboote. Through this office he would receive orders from MGK West and co-ordinate his boats accordingly. He also continued to resist the conversion of S-boats into heavier gun platforms, Dönitz himself questioning his tactics by declaring 37mm guns inadequate, instead proposing 50mm or 55mm fixed weapons, even the possibility of incendiary 'Greek fire' weapons. This would eliminate S-boat speed and manoeuvrability and while Petersen continued to resist such moves, he continued the war with what means he possessed.

By 1 January Petersen had forty-six operational boats spread between six flotillas in the west and five more refitting in German harbours. The Luftwaffe had promised a slight increase in available reconnaissance through the use of radar-equipped Junkers Ju88 aircraft. Petersen's decision to abandon large scale minelaying met with belated approval from MGK West, though SKL was keen to point out that 'a mine is a permanent source of danger; a torpedo, once fired, loses its effect'.[108]

Rough seas prevented operations until 5 January when seven 5th S-flotilla boats attacked an eastbound convoy. Divided into three *Rotten* they had narrowly escaped damage after mines exploded near *Führerboot S100* while departing Cherbourg. The S-boats found convoy WP457 between

Land's End and The Lizard during early morning darkness. Ober-steuermann Richard Grüger's *S143* fired a single first torpedo as Plymouth radar reported the unidentified contacts closing fast. Grüger hit 1,408-ton SS *Solstad* headed to London with coal, the ship sinking in less than three minutes with five dead. ObltzS Hinrich Ahrens aboard *S142* reported a '2,000-ton' freighter also hit and sinking, while ObltzS Hans-Jurgen Stohwasser's *S138* torpedoed and sank the 545-ton escorting trawler HMT *Wallasea*. The *Rotte* comprising *S84* and *S141* both torpedoed 403-ton MV *Polperro*, the small collier carrying coal from Manchester and sinking with all eight merchant crew and three gunners. The final confirmed sinking was 1,990-ton MV *Underwood* carrying a cargo of nine fully fuelled invasion craft which burst into flame as the ship sank, fourteen of the twenty-three people aboard killed. Klug's flotilla sailed for Brest as the scattered ships of WP457 retreated into Mounts Bay. The attack against WP457 had been the first use of the new TZ3 magnetic torpedo pistol and, though successful, Petersen was critical of the number of single torpedoes fired at excessive range.

During 16 January Klug's flotilla attempted to repeat their success and attacked westbound convoy PW461 near Lizard Head. Although torpedoes were fired, HM Ships *Talybont* and *Brissenden* fended the S-boats off in bad visibility and the convoy was unharmed. Once again the 5th S-flotilla sailed to Brest before returning to their home port of Cherbourg.

Hinrich Ahrens' *S142* was at the forefront of the attack on CW243 southeast of Beachy Head by Klug's 5th S-flotilla on the night of 30 January. Once again divided into three *Rotten*, one attacking from inshore of the convoy, Ahrens hit and blew the bow off escort HMT *Pine* which continued to fight back, later sinking under tow to shore. Ahrens also hit and sank 806-ton collier SS *Emerald* with the third torpedo he fired, his fourth a failure. The other half of his *Rotte*, ObltzS Hans-Jurgen Stohwasser's *S138*, torpedoed 1,813-ton SS *Caleb Sprague*, twenty of twenty-seven crew and three out of four gunners lost.

During early February Kptlt von Mirbach's 9th S-flotilla moved from Vlissingen to Dunkirk, from where it was planned to operate alongside Cherbourg's 5th S-flotilla against the south coast. Reinforcing this area, Petersen was forced to lose strength from the Netherlands. Following the successful Soviet winter offensive near Leningrad, OKM feared a resurgence of the Soviet Baltic fleet and ordered 6th S-flotilla removed from the west and transferred to the Finnish Bight. Eight boats departed on 7 February, *S128* and *S135* following later, once fitting of 40mm flak weapons was completed in Rotterdam. Petersen then faced yet further potential reduction as OKM vacillated over decisions to move at least two of his flotillas to the harbours of Bordeaux, Arcachon, Bayonne and Saint-Jean-de-Luz, amid fears of an Allied landing on the Iberian Peninsula. However, the idea was eventually dismissed.

On the night of 12 February the 8th S-flotilla mined the waters southeast of the Humber with thirty-six LMB mines, *S99* and *S65* sighting minesweeping trawler HMT *Cap d'Antifer* and sinking her with torpedoes leaving no survivors from the twenty-four crew. Two nights later both the 2nd and 8th S-flotillas sailed from Ijmuiden, the former to lay mines, though they were intercepted and forced away by HM Ships *Shearwater* and *Mallard* off Southwold. Returning to harbour they joined a battle between three German minesweepers and British MTBs near the harbour. *S89*, *S98*, *S92*, *S80* and *S67* raced into the attack, hitting and damaging several British vessels, the commander and three ratings killed aboard *MTB444*. During the confused melee, minesweeper *M3411* was sunk by torpedoes from *MTB455*, and *S89* so severely damaged by cannon fire that she was later towed into harbour, badly holed and low in the water, both torpedoes fired to lighten the hull as the crew doused fires in the stern.

Meanwhile, KK Felix Zymalkowski's 8th S-flotilla were tasked with finding enemy MGBs in the vain hope of capturing one to obtain

Albert Speer disembarking from an 8th S-flotilla boat in 1944; the flotilla emblem of a shield surmounted by an iron cross is visible on the side of the bridge.

intelligence regarding British convoy routes, Petersen's Luftwaffe intelligence having dried up. The same MTB groups that had tangled with Feldt's flotilla now crossed paths with *S93*, *S64*, *S117*, *S127*, *S129*, *S85*, *S133*, *S99* and *S65* as they retreated to Lowestoft. The S-boats were in isolated *Rotten* and swift and accurate gunfire from the MTBs forced a path through the German vessels, damaging *S99* and *S133* and killing one man.

It had been an entirely unsuccessful mission as was the next one for 8th S-flotilla on 22 February when HMS *Garth* engaged the eight boats with cannon fire. Six torpedoes arced toward their attacker, all of them missing, and in the confusion that followed ObltzS Karl Rindfuß' *S128* collided with LzS Karl Boseniuk's *S94*, killing one man. Both boats were so severely damaged that they were scuttled. The two young commanders' inexperience lay at the heart of the disaster. Two nights later, after successfully laying mines, the flotilla torpedoed and sank 2,085-ton SS *Philipp M* from convoy FS71 (Phase 12). Laden with coal, the torpedo hit her starboard side, a vivid blue flash seen by ships three miles away. Her back was broken, and she sank within three minutes as the crew abandoned ship on rafts, their attacker being seen to approach at high speed from astern and then shut off engines and drift near a sandbank until lost in the darkness.

March and much of April saw disappointing mission results and increasingly frequent collisions. Bad visibility, strong enemy action and inexperienced S-boat reinforcements all contributed to the consistent failures. Meanwhile, Allied air power was directed against the S-boat harbours, Ijmuiden being raided by the USAAF 9th Air Force on 25 March. While the bunkers were not penetrated, they took heavy damage, other buildings used by 6th S-flotilla were completely burned out, and *S93* and *S129*, moored outside of the protective shelter, were obliterated. To compound problems, a lighter was sunk immediately outside the bunker entrance, reducing access to during high water until the wreck could be removed.

On the night of 18 April *S64* took a direct hit in the starboard torpedo tube and the midships-mounted twin machine guns while the 8th S-flotilla laid mines near Great Yarmouth. *S133* was also hit, the shell exploding in the captain's empty cabin, the boat already having suffered engine failure following another crankcase explosion. To the west that same night, the 5th S flotilla was fired on by HMS *Middleton* and MTBs while also minelaying in the Channel. One man was killed in *S141*'s engine room before the flotilla escaped back to Cherbourg, avoiding MTBs attempting to head them off.

The pattern continued with S-boats taking casualties and damage with little recompense. On 24 April the Dutch tug *Roode Zee* was sunk defending

CW264 near Dungeness, the only success thus far that month. Ordered to reconnoitre the Channel following yet another invasion scare on 26 April, *S147* of the 9th S-flotilla was sunk by a direct hit from French destroyer *La Combattante* southeast of the Isle of Wight. The French ship closed the burning S-boat in order to rescue survivors, but only had time to pull one man aboard before hydrophone operators reported the approach of other S-boats, the destroyer moving away. *S147*'s skipper, LzS Bernhard Theenhausen, and ten men were later picked up, thirteen others killed.

However, S-boats were still dangerous. On 27 April six boats of the 5th S-flotilla and three of the 9th were ordered to sail against an enemy convoy reported by one of the infrequent Luftwaffe spotting missions. En route to their target area, *S136* and *S138* reported torpedo hits on an enemy destroyer, *S100* and *S143* claiming a 1,500-ton freighter hit and on fire. However, it was the 9th S-flotilla *Rotte S130*, *S145* and *S150* that wreaked the most havoc. They stumbled upon eight large tank-landing ships travelling in convoy as part of Exercise Tiger. An American simulation of the planned assault on Utah Beach, the eight LSTs were part of the mock 'build-up' phase, carrying vehicles and troops of the 1st Engineer Special Brigade. The exercise had already been marred by 'friendly fire' casualties from live ammunition fired by HMS *Hawkins*. Used to accustom men to the sights, sounds and smell of combat, a timing misunderstanding had sent several landing craft into the inferno before the British ship ceased fire.

The LSTs of convoy T4 were escorted solely by corvette HMS *Azalea*, a second escort HMS *Scimitar* having been damaged in a collision with an infantry landing craft the previous night and not replaced. Tragically, the incoming S-boats were sighted by both British radar and coastal gunners, the latter under orders not to fire lest they betray the area's level of coastal defence, the former relaying the news to *Azalea*, who then failed to pass the information onward, assuming incorrectly that the American vessels had received the same message, evidently unaware that they operated on a different radio frequency. In fact, radar echoes of the incoming S-boats *were* detected aboard one of the slow moving LSTs, but the operator assumed they belonged to the convoy. Luck was with the Germans.

Oberleutnant zur See Gunther Rabe's *S130* and ObltzS Franz Behr's *S150* both fired torpedoes at *LST507*, some failing to explode, before one from *S130* blew a hole in the ship's side, setting her on fire. Shortly afterward *LST531* was also hit, this time by Behr, and *LST511* torpedoed as well but by duds. Oberleutnant zur See Hans Schirren's *S145* hit *LST289*, destroying the crew's quarters, rudder and stern guns, although flooding was soon under control and the ship made it to Dartmouth under its own power. The remaining LSTs scattered as the three S-boats withdrew. Behind them they left a scene of devastation with at least 638 American army and naval personnel believed to have been killed, hundreds drowned under the weight of their equipment as they abandoned the burning ships. Even official figures vary as to the final death toll, possibly rising to 946, although news of the disaster was immediately withheld lest it betray the impending invasion of France. More American troops were killed that night than during the landings on Utah Beach in June 1944. All of the S-boats returned without damage.

These were, however, the last torpedo sinkings of the first half of 1944, the S-boats suffering casualties elsewhere. On the night of 13 May ObltzS Walter Sobottka's *S141* was sunk by *La Combattante*, the skipper and five survivors rescued. Amongst the eighteen men killed was LzS Klaus Dönitz, eldest son of Grossadmiral Karl Dönitz. A week later, ObltzS Günter Rathenow's *S87* was severely damaged by two Swordfish aircraft following completion of a successful minelaying mission. The boat sank, with Rathenow and most of his crew later rescued, two others killed and one listed as missing in action. Their mines accounted for HMT *Wyoming* and Dutch minesweeper *Marken* during the same night. American minesweeper USS *Osprey* was also lost to an S-boat mine on 4 June near St Catherine's Point. The explosion blew a hole in the forward engine room, with six men killed. This was, in fact, the first casualty of Operation Overlord, the minesweeper engaged upon sweeping channels for impending invasion traffic.

On 30 May 1944 Kptlt Bernd Klug left the role of 5th S-flotilla commander, and was replaced by Kptlt Kurt Johannsen. Klug moved over to Petersen's FdS staff as chief of staff, his predecessor KK Heinrich Erdmann departing to command destroyer *Z30*.

Air power continued to take its toll on Petersen's S-boats; *S100* was bombed and one man severely wounded in the early morning of 24 May, and *S172* and *S74* were both trapped inside the S-boat bunker in Boulogne Harbour following American bombing throughout the Pas de Calais. Although the S-boats were protected from damage, a shelter door was blown off, blocking the entrance to one of the double-berth pens. Though he could not know it, the intensified Allied air offensive heralded the long-feared invasion: Operation Overlord was about to begin.

17
The Channel

June 1944 – December 1944

The invasion has begun ... Thus all considerations and abstract speculations have been silenced. The strain that prevailed in all quarters was solved. The war entered into its decisive stage as far as Germany is concerned. Once again there is an opportunity to bring about a quick decision of the war by a short but energetic fight.[109]

On the eve of the Allied invasion of France, Petersen possessed thirty-one operational S-boats spread between five flotillas:

2nd S-flotilla (Kptlt Opdenhoff) in Ostend: *S177*, *S178*, *S179*, *S181* and *S189* (*S176*, *S180*, *S182* and *S190* non-operational).
4th S-flotilla (Kptlt Fimmen) in Boulogne: *S169*, *S171*, *S172*, *S173*, *S174*, *S175*, *S187* and *S188*.
5th S-flotilla (Kptlt Johannsen) in Cherbourg: *S84*, *S100*, *S136*, *S138*, *S139*, *S140* and *S142*.
8th S-flotilla (KK Zymalkowski) in Ijmuiden: *S83*, *S117*, *S127* and *S133*
9th S-flotilla (Kptlt von Mirbach) in Cherbourg: *S130*, *S144*, *S145*, *S146*, *S150*, *S167* and *S168*.

Korvettenkapitän Zymalkowski had just completed the transfer of three older boats, *S64*, *S65* and *S85*, to the Schnellbootslehrdivision in Swinemünde. In Sengwarden near Paris, Admiral Krancke exercised overall control as head of MGK West. Alongside Petersen's S-boats and apart from five isolated torpedo boats stationed in Le Havre, Krancke's command included only minesweepers, artillery barges and patrol vessels along the Channel coast. In western France an additional five destroyers were stationed alongside small coastal units. U-boats remained under the control of BdU, by this stage of the war rendered virtually obsolete and impotent by Allied air and sea power. Thus it was that the S-boats comprised the cutting edge of the Kriegsmarine's blunted sword in the west on 6 June 1944.

Facing the Germans was a combined Allied naval strength that numbered 1,213 different warships including seven battleships, two monitors, twenty-three cruisers, eighty fleet destroyers, twenty-five escort destroyers, three cannon boats and fourteen sloops. Additionally, over four thousand landing craft were available. In the air, on the invasion day alone, Allied air forces would fly 14,674 missions – including sweeps by over two thousand fighter aircraft – while the Luftwaffe would mount only 319 sorties in return.

At 0330hrs on 6 June landing craft were reported in the Seine Bay, while heavy air attacks battered the French coast. While further sighting reports tumbled in to MGK West, the eight S-boats of Fimmen's 4th S-flotilla headed south from Boulogne, completing a reconnaissance sweep that, almost miraculously, saw just a single destroyer. Likewise, the 5th and 9th S-flotillas had put to sea northwest and northeast of Cherbourg, sighting nothing of the expected armada. As the Allies gained their foothold on mainland Europe, German defences on land, sea and air were almost paralysed by confusion and inactivity, dependent on orders from Berlin that were tardy at best. OKW believed the Normandy landings a feint, resulting in too much held in reserve for too long. That night the 2nd S-flotilla made an unsuccessful reconnaissance sweep from Ostend, as did 8th S-flotilla from Ijmuiden, their search for the impending 'main landing' expected near Pas de Calais showing nothing.

Sailing from Boulogne, the 4th S-flotilla was harassed by enemy aircraft and one man lightly wounded. A single destroyer was sighted, missed by *S172* at long range before the S-boats returned to harbour. It was left to Kptlt Johannsen's 5th S-flotilla to open the battle proper against the invasion. All seven boats sailed into action, although *S84* had not been at sea long before engine damage forced a return to harbour. Two enemy destroyers were sighted and attacked unsuccessfully with torpedoes before *S139* blundered into a minefield of 202 moored mines laid during May by 'Dog Boats' of the 64th MTB Flotilla. Kptlt Hans-Jürgen Dietrich's *S139* sank quickly with twenty-two dead, and four men, including Dietrich, taken prisoner by British forces. Johannsen's flotilla claimed the sinking of American *LCT875* off St Vaast and the damaging of destroyer USS *Meredith*, killing seven men. The destroyer was towed to an anchorage in the Seine Bay and sunk by Luftwaffe bombers on 9 June. Meanwhile, Johannsen's boats retreated to Cherbourg, searching in vain for *S139* survivors on the way. On 14 June flotilla commander Kurt Johannsen was awarded the Knight's Cross.

Von Mirbach's 9th S-flotilla from Cherbourg operated alongside Johannsen's boats, also sighting gunboats, destroyers and landing vessels and claiming the destruction of American *LCI105* after firing six torpedoes into packed landing craft. However, ObltzS Martin Bongertz's *S140* struck a mine in the same field that had claimed *S139*, sinking with fifteen dead including the skipper and eight survivors picked up by other S-boats.

The FdS situation room with Rudolf Petersen (*centre*) and Klaus Feldt (*right*).

Petersen moved the 2nd S-flotilla from Ostend to Boulogne during the night of 7 June, all flotillas assigned mission areas in search of targets within Seine Bay. Freedom of movement was granted to 4th S-flotilla at the conclusion of their mission, either to return to Le Havre or Cherbourg, Fimmen choosing the former. On the night of 8 June Fimmen's 4th S-flotilla encountered convoy ECM1 in the Channel, sinking American *LST314* and damaging *LST376* so badly she was later scuttled; 250 survivors of both ships were rescued by HMS *Beagle*. Two other landing ships were claimed hit and sunk but they remain unconfirmed.

The Cherbourg S-boats also reported sporadic success, 9th S-flotilla claiming three landing vessels sunk, but also taking damage to most S-boats in combat with MGBs; aboard *S130* two men were killed, four were wounded on the other boats and engine damage was suffered on *S168*. Klug's 5th S-flotilla took engine damage by gunfire aboard *S142* and *S145*, while three men were severely wounded aboard *S84*.

The 4th, 5th and 9th S-flotillas were next tasked with minelaying, attempting to hinder the movement of Allied surface forces, particularly battleships bombarding German forces ashore. Under strong defensive fire, the minefields were laid, two LSTs claimed sunk in return. The futility of the operation, betrayed by ULTRA decryption, was unknown to Petersen. Amidst this confusion, *S180* and *S190* were placed back into operations, attached to 8th S-flotilla as reinforcement and proceeding from Vlissingen toward Boulogne. Zymalkowski's flotilla remained in Ostend to counter a feared landing on the Dutch coast, *S190* hitting a mine during the passage and though suffering no casualties, requiring a return to Rotterdam's dockyard.

The S-boats maintained whatever pressure they could on Allied forces, Cherbourg boats unable to break through strong escort forces north of Barfleur, while others claimed five ships aggregating 11,400 tons sunk. With two S-flotillas operating periodically from the ideally situated Le Havre, alongside torpedo boats of 5th T-flotilla, an acute shortage of torpedoes

Grossadmiral Karl Dönitz and FdS KK Rudolf Petersen visit men of the 4th S-flotilla in June 1943. The relationship between these two men remained tense throughout the last two years of the war, Dönitz accusing Petersen of lacking aggressive spirit and an unwillingness to make a 'total commitment' in combat.

developed in the harbour, necessitating replenishment in Boulogne instead, frustratingly further from the Allied beachhead. However, Le Havre lacked not only torpedo storage but also the requisite workshops and balancing equipment and Cherbourg was so badly threatened by Allied invaders that Petersen requested as much equipment as possible transferred to Le Havre.

The 2nd S-flotilla moved its attention further into the English Channel in search of troop convoys feeding the Allied beachheads. Near the Isle of Wight they found the twenty-ship convoy ETC4W headed to Juno Beach, OblzS Kurt Neugebauer's *S179* torpedoing the 534-ton tanker MV *Ashanti*, laden with a cargo of cased octane fuel which caught fire and spread rapidly through the floundering ship, exploding and killing all seventeen men aboard, including the Merchant Navy's youngest captain, 24-year-old John Robert Smith. Drifting fuel continued to burn for hours on rolling seas when 657-ton SS *Brackenfield* was sunk by ObStrm Alois Sczesny's *S189*. Carrying 660 tons of ammunition, the freighter broke in two, the stern blown completely away, and the bow rising high before rolling to port and sinking with only two survivors rescued. A third vessel, 621-ton ammunition ship SS *Dungrange*, was also hit by both LzS Karl Boseniuk's *S177* and ObltzS Georg Braune's *S178* after assisting *Brackenfield* survivors, the freighter exploding and killing all but two of the twenty. As the remaining ships disappeared behind smoke, cannon fire bounced off the armoured bridge of more than one S-boat, fully vindicating the installation of the *Kalotten*.

To the southeast, on 10 June the 5th and 9th S-flotillas struggled to break through warship perimeters and attack the transports beyond. Johannsen's 5th S-flotilla became locked in a fast moving battle against MTBs, remembered by Lieutenant Commander R J W Timms aboard *MTB448*:

We were engaged by a unit of six E-boats, they came up on our port beam at very high speed. We all opened fire at the same time, the engagement was very close and intense. The noise was terrific, the charthouse filled with cordite smoke as we sustained hits from heavy gunfire of many calibres. Suddenly a body fell through the doorway from the bridge onto the charthouse floor and I was ready to climb up to the bridge to take command. I turned him over but it was not [skipper] Rodney [Sykes] but Thorpe the reporter sailing with us. I could see no blood or head wounds so I tried to find a heartbeat but the gunfire was deafening, I couldn't hear or feel a pulse so I presumed he was dead. (He was). The group of E-boats we came across contained *S112* with damaged steering, *448* attacked *S136* ... and dealt and received lethal blows – both sank. *MTB448* passed between Nos 4 & 5 of the E-boats in line ahead, we dropped a depth charge with a specially designed shallow depth setting. The depth charge was attached to an empty 40 gallon oil drum by a short length of wire. This was designed to explode at shallow depth immediately under the target. All of the enemy gunfire had been directed at *448*'s hull forward just below the waterline so that *448* could not lift her bows.[110]

Both ObltzS Hans-Günter Jürgensmeyer's *S136* and *MTB448* went down, the S-boat with nineteen dead, including the commander. HMS *Duff* steamed through German survivors struggling in the water, unable to stop or deviate from her path as the battle continued elsewhere, though three men were later rescued to become prisoners of war. Destroyer HMS *Halsted* was also hit by a torpedo forward of the bridge which blew away the bow; thirty-three men were killed and the ship was towed back to Portsmouth and declared a constructive loss.

During the early hours of the following morning, von Mirbach's 9th S-flotilla succeeded in sinking a Phoenix Caisson under tow and destined for use in constructing the western Mulberry Harbour, as well as 730-ton tugboat USS *Partridge*, 700-ton British tug HMT *Sesame* and *LST538*. In turn, *S130* was damaged by aircraft while outside Cherbourg, bomb fragments putting the boat out of commission, with her skipper, ObltzS Günter Rabe, and four men wounded. Two others, *S144* and *S146*, headed to Le Havre instead of returning to embattled Cherbourg.

That night six boats of the Cherbourg flotillas, supported by artillery barges of 4th Artillerieträger Flotilla, sailed once more, *S84*, *S100*, *S150*, *S167*, *S138* and *S142* putting to sea to attack the western edge of Allied invasion traffic. Battling against three American destroyers, ObltzS Stohwasser scored a torpedo hit on USS *Nelson*; with twenty-four sailors killed and nine wounded, the destroyer towed to Portsmouth for repair. One man was killed aboard *S100* as cannon fire struck the bridge, causing compass failure, while the S-boats disengaged. The two detached S-boats from 9th S-flotilla in Le Havre – *S144* and *S146* – operated without success that same night, as did the 8th S-flotilla engaged on reconnaissance from Ostend. Off Le Havre the 2nd S-flotilla came under fire by Canadian MTBs and the escort destroyer HMS *Talybont*. One man was killed aboard *S181* when the bridge was hit by cannon fire. During the return to Le Havre, both *S179* and *S181* blundered into their own minefield, and both boats were damaged. Elsewhere, Kptlt Wiencke's *S171* and five other 4th S-flotilla boats engaged British destroyers and MTBS near Boulogne, Wiencke sinking *MGB17* with artillery fire, with three of the British crew killed.

Inevitably, the odds mounted against the beleaguered S-boats. During the night of 12 June all flotillas planned to attack supply traffic from both west and east, but encountered only strong enemy escort groups. Von Mirbach's four Cherbourg boats battled against destroyers, *S138* was hit with one man wounded and the boat in flames before the attack was abandoned, the damaged S-boat shepherded by the remaining three in to Le Havre rather than trying to fight their way back to Cherbourg, from where operations were becoming progressively more difficult. It proved a fateful decision. The 2nd and 4th S-flotilla were unable to find targets, returning to Boulogne and Le Havre respectively, *S169* hitting a mine, causing severe damage to the starboard foreship, but still managing to limp home. The radioed message for S-boats to break off their patrols and return was heard by the Allies who despatched Bristol Beaufighter aircraft to intercept: *S178* received a direct bomb hit, killing skipper OblzS Georg Braune and sixteen men, and *S179* was hit and suffered complete engine failure as she burst into flames. *S189* was also set on fire and sunk during a second wave of attacks, during which ObStrm Alois Sczesny and ten men were killed. *S181* attempted to tow ObltzS Kurt Neugebauer's battered *S179* in to harbour, but further Beaufighter attacks sank the shattered boat, killing thirteen of the crew, as well as Räumboot *R97*, hit by a rocket in its fuel bunker as she attempted to rescue *S179* survivors.

Amidst the chaos of the D-Day battle, KzS Rudolf Petersen was awarded the Oak Leaves to his Knight's Cross on 13 June, Kptlt Götz Frhr von Mirbach receiving the same the following day. While von Mirbach received his award, Allied ULTRA intelligence was used with devastating effectiveness.

With an unusual concentration of S-boats within Le Havre, MGK West planned torpedo patrols for 13 June, bad weather forcing postponement. This message, intercepted, decoded and passed on to Admiral Ramsey, C-in-C Allied Naval Forces, provided an opportunity to deal en masse with the elusive S-boats. After quick co-ordination with the RAF, a mass daylight raid on Le Havre by 221 Lancasters with Mosquito pathfinders and Spitfire escort was arranged. Amongst the Lancaster bombers were aircraft of 617 Squadron, equipped with 12,000lb Tallboy bombs, designed to penetrate the thickest of bunkers.

The attack was shattering. In total, thirteen S-boats were destroyed or damaged beyond use: *S84*, *S100*, *S138*, *S142*, *S143*, *S146*, *S150*, *S169*,

S171, *S172*, *S173*, *S187* and *S188*. As well as myriad patrol vessels and minesweepers, three of the four torpedo boats in harbour were also sunk or severely damaged, and only *T28* left afloat, grazed by bomb splinters. In Le Havre a single boat remained fully operational – *S167* – while *S144* was at first considered repairable, but later scrapped and abandoned. Casualties had been surprisingly light given the devastation: eighteen men killed including the commander of 5th S-flotilla, Kurt Johannsen. Twenty-five other men were wounded, including 9th S-flotilla commander von Mirbach who was lightly injured and the skippers of *S187*, *S167*, *S138* and *S84*. Some two hundred French civilians lost their lives in the bombing.

The Allies attempted to repeat their masterstroke the following day with a mixed force of Lancaster and Halifax bombers against Boulogne's harbour but, although they inflicted shocking loss on small Kriegsmarine vessels and damage to the S-boat bunker, the 2nd S-flotilla's four boats were out of harbour during the bombardment.

On 15 June Petersen possessed thirteen operational S-boats:

8th S-flotilla in Ostend: *S83*, *S127* and *S133*;
2nd S-flotilla in Boulogne: *S176*, *S180*, *S181* and *S182*;
4th S-flotilla in Boulogne: *S174* and *S175*;
9th S-flotilla in Le Havre: *S167*; in Cherbourg: *S130*, *S145* and *S168*;
5th S-flotilla in Cherbourg: *S112* (ready for sailing but not quite combat-ready).

At a stroke the Allies had all but neutralised the S-boat threat, matching their defeat of German destroyers and U-boats from the west and the Channel torpedo boats. German minesweeping and patrol abilities were also severely reduced. The remaining boats from 2nd and 4th S-flotillas were combined under the command of Kptlt Opdenhoff, and personnel from the defunct 5th S-flotilla returned to Germany where they would form the cadre for a rebuilt unit commanded by Kptlt Hermann Holzapfel. Their defective *S112* was passed over to the 9th S-flotilla. In order to disperse his forces, Petersen also began using Dieppe and St Malo as interim bases for Channel operations. On 11 June the return of the 6th S-flotilla from the Baltic had been requested and agreed, although the flotilla was yet to begin its journey and so Petersen awaited reinforcements, his few boats continuing to sail into the inferno.

There was little that they could achieve. Attempting to complete a minelaying mission on 17 June, *S83* was damaged by bombing and suffered engine failure, breaking off and returning to Ostend. The 9th S-flotilla

Inside the Cherbourg S-boat pens. Initially deemed essential for the protection of combat boats, from June 1944 they became a trap as Allied bombers were able to penetrate the shelters with Tallboy and Disney weapons. The leaping tiger insignia marks the boat on the right as part of the 6th S-flotilla.

meanwhile received orders to covertly supply the encircled garrison of Cherbourg with ammunition from St Malo, transporting twenty-four Wehrmacht officers and 19 tons of munitions into the 'fortress' during the night of 22 June. Von Mirbach's flotilla base had moved to Jersey during the previous day, with Cherbourg on the brink of capitulation, all dockside installations except the facilities for unloading S-boats or U-boats already demolished by the garrison.

That night the 8th S-flotilla transferred from Ostend to Boulogne under sustained air attack which wounded two men aboard *S83* and damaged the boats, while 2nd S-flotilla was forced away from a minelaying mission by two destroyers, Kptlt Hugo Wendler's *S190* receiving several direct hits from large-calibre shells, wounding three men before the boat was scuttled with one man missing. The same mission two nights later clashed again with destroyers, *S175* hit by shellfire in the chart room at the back of the bridge, which killed two men and wounded another. As the S-boats raced away under a smokescreen, *S175* leaking fuel from a ruptured forward tank, *S181* was also hit by 40mm cannon fire from pursuing MTBs.

In Cherbourg the city battled vainly against American forces. The 9th S-flotilla, with *S130*, *S145*, *S168* and the defective *S112*, transferred first to

St Malo and then onwards to Alderney. *S112* and *S145* were left behind and later sailed west to Brest during July, finding a single survivor from the destroyed Vorpostenboot *V715* along the way.[111] From Alderney the remaining three boats attempted to break through the enemy destroyer screen for Dieppe, ObStrm Seifert's *S145* badly hit in compartments V and VI and returning to Alderney on only one engine, ditching all secret material from the boat as a precaution. Meanwhile, *S130* and *S168* successfully reached Dieppe. On 29 June German troops in Cherbourg city centre and the naval arsenal surrendered.

The arrival of Kptlt Jens Matzen's 6th S-flotilla – comprising *S39*, *S76*, *S90*, *S91*, *S114*, *S132*, and *S135* in Ijmuiden at the end of June – did little to alleviate the situation. Minelaying along the fringes of Allied traffic and unsuccessful torpedo missions continued, while the transfer of Matzen's unit into Le Havre on 5 July, during which *S90* and *S135* were damaged by enemy aircraft, nearly ended in disaster when the new torpedo maintenance room exploded, forty-one torpedoes blowing the bunker to pieces and killing seven flotilla personnel. Damage to the main bunker left it only capable of accommodating six boats at any one time thereafter.

During the night of 7 July six boats from 2nd and 9th S-flotilla sailed from Le Havre into Seine Bay once more. Despite a critical rudder defect aboard *S182* and 40mm cannon failure on both *S132* and *S177*, six torpedoes were fired at what was believed to be a pair of destroyers detected by onboard FuMB gear. An explosion and huge column of escaping steam was plainly visible: frigate HMS *Trollope* torpedoed with the loss of fifty-four men and another thirty-four injured. The ship was later towed ashore and declared a total constructive loss. Three S-boats were then shadowed by two MTBs, shaking them loose with a sharp turn to the south under a thick smokescreen. Two more MTBs and a pair of destroyers blocked their path, the trio of S-boats speeding between them, an attempt to torpedo the destroyers failing and betraying the S-boats' position. Under fire, *S180*'s engines broke down and *MTB447* closed to within two hundred yards, but was hit by German fire from their quadruple Vierling 20mm flak gun and severely damaged. A second MTB then rammed the damaged British boat at high speed, the pair no longer taking part in the action as the S-boats managed to slip away, all with significant battle damage.

Bad weather prevented S-boat sailings until mid July, whereupon the same suffocating Allied surface forces prevented success. In an environment of near-hysterical cries for 'total commitment' that originated in the Reich Chancellery, Rudolf Petersen's S-boat service came under sharp criticism for what was characterised as undue caution. However, the redoubtable Petersen never wavered in his calm handling of the S-boat service and willingness to risk men in missions that offered possible success, but he remained unwilling to lose men purely on the altar of any national cause. A devoutly religious man, it was perhaps this that prevented him from buckling under pressure to almost 'politicise' the sacrifice of his men and machines. After the 20 July attempt on Hitler's life by Wehrmacht officers, Petersen's brand of resistance to wasteful military decisions marked him as a resolute, and undoubtedly brave, man. Nevertheless, combat damage and a stream of casualties flowed through all of the S-boat operations that month. The introduction of the T5 *Zaunkönig* torpedo into the S-boats' arsenal was championed by OKM, but received a lukewarm response from Petersen.

Hailed as 'destroyer killers', the acoustic warhead homed on high-pitched military propeller sounds, having been used already by U-boats, although frequently without observed results as the firing U-boats dived immediately so as to avoid potential 'circling' accidents. Petersen was aware, however, that the torpedo's top speed of 24 knots was insufficient to catch an alert destroyer moving at maximum revolutions, plus decoy MTBs and MGBs

Close up of an *S30*-class boat in France.

could 'lure' the torpedo away, remaining of too shallow draught to be hit by a contact warhead and too wooden for magnetic pistols. The Kriegsmarine had also begun to fling human torpedoes and explosive motorboats of the Kleinkampfverbände into the fray in true desperation, but with little actual effect.

Facing meagre prospects against the invasion fleet, Petersen returned the S-boats to the coasts of England. During the night of 26 July Matzen's 6th S-flotilla attacked convoy ETM46 proceeding from Southend to the Normandy beaches. Both ObltzS Hemmer's *S114* and ObStrm Waldhausen's *S97* fired FAT torpedoes towards the convoy, damaging 7,046-ton SS *Empire Beatrice* and 7,171-ton SS *Fort Perrot*, the former beached at Dungeness, the latter towed on fire into harbour. *S90* and *S91* fired several shots at escorting destroyers HM Ships *Obedient*, *Savage* and *Opportune* but missed, counter-fire from MGBs hitting *S90* in the fuel tank and badly wounding one crewman.

The same night, as if proof of the folly of their endeavour, five boats from 2nd S-flotilla sailed into the Seine Bay to attack invasion shipping in poor visibility, running squarely into escort forces, whereupon *S182* rammed *MTB430*, gunfire crackling overhead as the close-quarter action raged. The speeding *MTB412* also ran into the wrecked *430*, all three boats scuttled or sinking of their own accord. Eight of the German crew, including skipper Kptlt Kurt Pinger, were killed, and another seventeen men captured as the remaining S-boats were forced away.

On the night of 30 July Petersen directed three boats of Matzen's 6th S-flotilla once again against convoy traffic, targeting the eastbound FTM53 transiting from Normandy to Southend. Operating in the *Stichansatz* pattern, six FAT torpedoes were fired, hitting four freighters, sinking 7,219-ton SS *Samwake* and damaging 7,160-ton SS *Fort Dearborn*, 7,187-ton SS *Fort Kaskaskia* and 7,178-ton SS *Ocean Courier*. Escorting frigate HMS *Thornborough* attacked the distant S-boats, which returned fire before vanishing into darkness and returning home.

The following night Matzen's boats joined those of the 2nd S-flotilla in a *Zaunkönig* attack on British warships, every single torpedo detonating prematurely and drawing heavy fire, *S132* hit in the starboard engine with three men wounded before they escaped over a deep German minefield that the destroyer could not cross and into Dieppe and Le Havre. To compound their injury, 153 Lancaster bombers guided by five Mosquitoes returned to bomb Le Havre: three S-boats moored in the harbour were slightly damaged, *S132* was hit by bomb splinters and a radio man killed. ULTRA intercepts reported this lack of effect and a follow-up raid was mounted on 2 August by 154 more Lancasters dropping 384 tons of bombs on the harbour. Both *S39* and *S114* were sunk in the harbour alongside four other vessels and a floating crane, *S79* lightly and *S91* seriously damaged. The crews' air-raid bunker received a direct hit, but survived the impact.

The following night 2nd S-flotilla acted as diversion for human torpedoes and Linsen explosive motorboats of the Kleinkampfverbände, clashing with British destroyers, MTBs and MGBs. *S180* was badly hit by gunfire in the outer engines and limped away as *S174* and *S176* collided while making evasive manoeuvres, the latter's forecastle crushed above the waterline by the impact. *S181* was hit in the *Kalottenbrücke* by a shell that penetrated the armour, all boats breaking away for home with significant scars. Amongst the wounded men, four had been badly hurt including *S180*'s skipper ObltzS Nikolai von Stempel.

A trickle of reinforcements arrived in Ijmuiden: *S195*, *S196* and *S197* for 8th S-flotilla, and five boats of the newly worked up 10th S-flotilla, commanded by veteran Kptlt Karl 'Charlie' Müller, travelled from Cuxhaven to Ijmuiden and on to Ostend by 12 August. Müller's *S184*, *S185*, *S186*, *S191* and *S192* bolstered Petersen's forces, which were engaged on another tactical experiment about which he harboured grave reservations. Le Havre had taken shipment of the newly developed Dackel torpedo. The Dackel (TIIId) torpedo had been developed as a coastal defence weapon, improvised from the standard G7e electric torpedo. It was designed to be used at exceptionally long range against targets of concentrated shipping where weapon speed was not important. Equipped with the *Lage unabhängiger Torpedo* (LUT) pattern-running, the Dackel was able to cover 57km (35 miles) at 9 knots, while slightly modified LUT gear allowed a straight run of 34,600m (37,800yds) before embarking on the first of what could be a maximum of 2,650 long pattern legs. The torpedo was lengthened – hence the name, which translates to 'Dachshund' – by the addition of an empty battery chamber immediately behind the warhead, into which was fitted compressed air bottles providing enough air for the operation of depth gear and steerage for up to three hours of travel.

It was estimated that if Dackel were fired from Le Havre they could reach Allied disembarkation areas off the Orne River and their bombardment station off Courseulles. Allowed to run their patterns under cover of darkness, MGK West expected great results, despite protestations from Petersen that the S-boats' low profile dictated that any possible targets at such distances would be beyond the visible horizon. He also correctly pointed out that original plans to launch at twilight, giving the entire night in which to run, were untenable due to Allied fighter bombers. Petersen feared that inaccurate firing data, faulty running and the effect of strong tidal movement on slow-running torpedoes might wash one ashore, revealing the secrets of the LUT gear to the Allies. Despite his protests, he was overruled.

Six S-boats launched the first twenty-four Dackel torpedoes between 0137hrs and 0234hrs on 5 August, nine explosions later observed in the general target area. Between that night and 18 August they exhausted available supply of ninety-one Dackel torpedoes. In return they damaged only four ships: elderly cruiser HMS *Frobisher*, repair ship HMS *Albatross*, minesweeper HMS *Vestal* and 5,208-ton transport ship SS *Iddesleigh*. Petersen's scepticism regarding the weapon remained undiminished.

The attritional war continued to grind down the combat abilities of the western S-boats. Between brief bouts of unsettled weather, they sailed on mixed minelaying and torpedo missions with very few successes during August. In addition to the Dackel hits, 7,176-ton American Liberty ship SS *William L Macy* was badly damaged on 7 August, the ship later scuttled with surplus ammunition aboard in the North Sea, and 7,127-ton SS *Fort Gloucester* also damaged on 18 August. Having sailed from Juno Beach in convoy FTM70, *Fort Gloucester* was torpedoed midships: number one boat

An *S26*-class boat at sea.

was blown away, the hatches blown off and number three hold flooded immediately. Abandoned, she was later reboarded and salved. In turn, the S-boats suffered a continuous stream of killed and injured men and battle damage to the boats themselves. Much hope had been placed by the Kriegsmarine in the newly developed 'oyster mine', activated by pressure waves generated by passing ships, but an intact model delivered to the Allies at low tide by the Luftwaffe provided the antidote: a reduction in shipping speed in shallow waters.

Five Tallboy bombs were dropped on the S-boat bunker in a raid on Ijmuiden during the afternoon of 24 August. Two pierced the thick concrete ceiling and exploded in the bunker, destroying all torpedo equipment, the regulating station and general supplies for the S-boats. The bunker foundations were wrecked beyond reconstruction.

On 25 August the 6th S-flotilla lost *S91*, Kptlt Heinz Nolte's boat, hit by multiple cannon shells and set on fire by HM Ships *Retalick* and *Talybont*. The starboard and middle engines failed, and the rudder was disabled as flames took hold. Two men were killed, and Nolte and one other badly wounded as they abandoned ship in the lifeboat after setting scuttling charges. That same night 8th S-flotilla tangled with a convoy escort off Beachy Head, *S701* being hit by shells from HMS *Bleasdale*, set on fire and then rammed by *S196*. Despite heavy damage both boats returned to Dieppe.[112]

However, the S-boats' war against the invasion bridgehead was over; Allied forces had spread through Normandy and now threatened Channel ports from land as well as sea and air. Le Havre began evacuation on the night of 23 August, S-boats escorting smaller craft as they headed east, this convoy traffic suffering greatly from at least forty-three separate aircraft and MTB attacks. Meanwhile, shore-based personnel departed in truck convoys for Belgium and the Netherlands. The 2nd S-flotilla was the last unit to leave Le Havre, fouling the harbour with mines before retreating to Boulogne. Their final withdrawal was hindered by enemy destroyers, MGBs and aircraft, although KK Zymalkowski's *S196* hit the bridge of escort destroyer HMS *Cattistock* with artillery rounds, killing the ship's commander, Lieutenant Richard Keddie, and three other men, and damaging their radar and gunnery control centre.

Within days Dieppe followed by Boulogne were evacuated by the Kriegsmarine, the 10th S-flotilla the final unit to leave as they also mined the harbour entrance. Harried by aircraft and surface forces, the S-boats retreated east to the Netherlands, LzS Bruno Klockow's *S184* receiving a direct hit from Dover's coastal artillery and being holed beneath the waterline. One man was killed, and the crew rescued by *S183* as the boat went under. In four years of transiting the Channel narrows, it was the first time coastal artillery had hit an S-boat. Dieppe was taken without opposition on 1 September, Ostend captured by Canadian troops on 8 September and besieged Le Havre fell after a three-day assault, surrendering on 12 September with the port and much of the city in ruins. German requests for the evacuation of French civilians had been denied and the death toll was high. Boulogne and Wimereux were occupied by the Allies by 22 September, Petersen and his FdS staff having departed for Scheveningen well before the town was attacked.

Once Allied troops had broken out of their Normandy beachhead they raced through France to west and east. The Atlantic ports were placed under siege, a costly battle for Brest dissuading attempts to subjugate the remainder and they, as well as Dunkirk, were held under siege until the war's end. With operational U-boats evacuated to Norway and whatever surface vessels remained penned inside besieged harbours, the Kriegsmarine in France had essentially ceased to exist and Admiral Krancke's MGK West was officially dissolved on 20 October 1944. The Naval Group Commands were no longer appropriate in the west, south or east: local theatre commands used as the boundary of Germany's Reich territory contracted inexorably. Subsequently, the office of Führer der Schnellboote was subordinated to *Marineoberkommando Nordsee* (Naval High Command North Sea).

From Petersen's western flotillas, the 2nd and 6th transferred to Germany, Opdenhoff's remaining two boats of the 2nd sailing to Wilhelmshaven for overdue maintenance on worn engines, while Matzen's 6th headed to the Baltic where they handed over the flotilla's older boats to the Schnellbootslehrdivision. By 6 September Petersen's operational western force numbered eight boats of 8th S-flotilla in Ijmuiden, three boats of 9th S-flotilla in Rotterdam and five boats of 10th Flotilla in Amsterdam. Bad weather hampered minelaying missions and torpedo, and the few patrols that approached Britain's coastline were driven quickly away by destroyers. A trickle of reinforcement with new boats or those emerging from refit continued to arrive in the Netherlands.

During the night of 18 September four boats of the 10th S-flotilla – *S186*, *S185* and *S199* led by Kptlt Walter Knapp's *Führerboot S198* – successfully ran a supply mission, carrying 8 tons of munitions into the besieged port of Dunkirk, while the 10th S-flotilla mounted a diversionary torpedo patrol to the northeast. Despite very poor visibility and a strong destroyer and

MGB group presence offshore, supplies were unloaded by 0245hrs, twelve machine guns and accompanying ammunition dismounted from the S-boats and handed over to infantrymen, while four severely wounded men and Generalleutnant Wolfgang von Kluge and his staff of the 226th Infantry Division were taken aboard for the return trip.[113] Despite being sighted and chased by destroyers, the S-boats evaded the enemy.

However, the three-boat distraction force was less fortunate. Flotilla commander Kptlt Karl Müller led *S183*, *S100* and *S702* into action aboard *S200*, running into destroyer HMS *Stayner* and MTBs *724* and *728* of 64th MTB Flotilla. The night was starless and almost impenetrably dark, *Stayner* making radar contact and vectoring the two 'Dog Boats' onto them. By the time the S-boats were seen, they were so close that they were unable to turn away before the formidably armed MTBs poured full broadsides into the Germans. ObltzS Klaus-Ulrich Hardtke's *S183* was immediately holed and began sinking in flames, the remaining two colliding while turning to avoid gunfire. Many casualties were suffered aboard *Führerboot S200* as it was raked with fire, the boat slewing to a halt and beginning to sink as ObltzS Hilmar Blum's *S702* immediately raced away at high speed. Collision damage had slowed the boat, which was caught and savaged by the MTBs, bursting into flames while the crew abandoned ship. HMS *Stayner* arrived to finish off *S183* and eventually the British collected a total of sixty-seven prisoners, including the flotilla medical officer MStArzt Walter Innerebner and the flotilla chief Müller who spent nearly eleven hours in the water.

After *S200* was sunk, two MTBs stopped at the spot where she had gone down, making no attempt to pick us up. About ninety minutes later another British vessel appeared, which looked to me like a steam gunboat, but this boat also made no attempt to rescue survivors. I find this attitude by the British incomprehensible. During the battle the inflatable boats were so badly shot up as to be unserviceable. Our only remaining life-saving equipment was a large French kapok float on which I first put our wounded. The conduct of the crew in the early stages after the boat sank was very confident and correct ... After about six hours in the water many of the men began to display a ruthless, impulsive urge for self-preservation and only by the admonitions hinting at the direst punishment were excesses prevented ... I watched the wounded commander of the *Führerboot* [LzS Alfred Kellinghausen] and three other men die of exposure after seven or eight hours in the water. Shortly after 0800hrs, some British MTBs appeared sailing in a broad line abreast and began searching for survivors.[114]

The trio of S-boats had thirteen fatalities, including a *Propaganda Kompanie* reporter aboard *S702*, while the MTBs suffered three killed by return gunfire and one man wounded. Kapitänleutnant Dietrich Bludau, former commanding officer of 4th S-flotilla, took charge of the 10th S-flotilla.

Allied airborne landings of Operation Market Garden near Arnhem, Nijmegen and Eindhoven on 17 September sent waves of panic through OKW in Berlin, predicting a full-scale Allied invasion of the Netherlands. The demolition of all dock facilities, including S-boat shelters, in Amsterdam and Rotterdam was authorised by SKL, as FdS transferred from Scheveningen to Den Helder as a precautionary measure. Petersen and other Kriegsmarine officers made urgent appeals to rescind demolition orders, baldly stating that should the demolition of these harbours be carried out, all offensive S-boat operations in the region would cease. Fortunately, cooler heads prevailed and the order was retracted, but not before limited destruction of quayside equipment had already been completed.

September gales halted all S-boat missions as the confusion caused by a failed Market Garden ebbed away. Firm defensive lines had been knitted together from the chaos of troops retreating from France and Belgium. By early October only nine S-boats were ready for action, spread between Ijmuiden and Rotterdam. The 4th and 10th S-flotillas mustered three and two respectively in Ijmuiden, the 8th and 10th another pair each in Rotterdam. By mid-month Kptlt von Mirbach's rebuilt and refitted 9th S-flotilla comprising *S130*, *S167*, *S168*, *S175*, *S206* and *S207* arrived back in Rotterdam. Petersen had by now shifted his operational focus toward mining the Western Scheldt Estuary and its approaches, as Allied forces attempted to clear German forces from the south and north banks of the Scheldt, opening the deep-water port of Antwerp as a primary supply head for the advance into Germany. Von Mirbach's first attempted mission on the night of 7 October was curtailed by poor visibility, *S175* and *S207* hit by 20mm shells from jumpy Vorpostenboote gunners as they returned to harbour. Three nights later, thirteen boats from all three flotillas successfully began minelaying off Walcheren Island, although bad weather prevented any further missions until the last night of the month.

By this stage Petersen had once again lost a considerable number of combat vessels with Kptlt Fimmen's 4th S-flotilla, reconstituted to eight vessels, ordered home via inland waterways for refit and transfer to Norway with the tender *Hermann von Wissman*. The removal of so many combat boats from the Dutch harbours coincided with the launch of Operation Infatuate by Anglo-Canadian forces: landings on Walcheren Island in the

Scheldt Estuary to clear the approaches to Antwerp once and for all. Despite Allied strength, a long, grinding battle against firmly embedded Wehrmacht troops dragged on until 8 November before 40,000 German defenders surrendered. Petersen's flotillas had been ordered to undertake aggressive

A crewman at the controls of his boat's smoke-making apparatus. The ability to lay smoke was key to S-boat tactics, being used as cover to retreat following an attack.

torpedo patrols against all targets in support of the Walcheren defence and on 1 November 8th S-flotilla sailed with *S194*, *S195*, *S197*, *S198* and *S199*; the 9th sailed with *S175*, *S167*, *S168* and *S207*; and the 10th put to sea with *S185*, *S186* and *S192*. One of Kptlt Bludau's 10th S-flotilla boats dropped out with engine damage, as did *S168* with water in the fuel causing a failure of the centre engine. Zymalkowski's 8th Flotilla lost *S198* to rudder failure, the boat escorted home by *S197*. From the various S-boat groups easing through the November darkness, only two of von Mirbach's boats achieved anything. Torpedoes fired at bombarding battleship HMS *Warspite* missed, though a second run allowed ObltzS Franz Behr's *S175* to torpedo 1,141-ton tanker MV *Rio Bravo* lying at anchor two miles north of Ostend, fourteen men were killed with the sinking ship and the survivors rescued by HMS *Kernot*. ObltzS Hans Schirren's *S207* also probably hit and sank 554-ton British trawler HMT *Colsay*, killing thirty-six men aboard. Biber one-man midget submarines were also active in the area, so it is not completely clear who hit the trawler. Stabsobersteuermann Seifert claimed a third ship hit by torpedoes from *S167*, but this was never confirmed. These were to be the final S-boat torpedo successes of 1944. The following night all three flotillas were again engaged on the same operation, but clashed with MGBs, *S185* forced to retire prematurely with a burst barrel on her 40mm flak weapon and the other boats failing to make any headway against their enemy.

The weather once again closed in and by the time S-boats could next sail, Walcheren had fallen. During mid November, the 8th S-flotilla mined the Humber Channel, two boats suffering engine damage and a third rudder failure in heavy seas. Minelaying by the 9th Flotilla was hindered by MGBs and British frigates, HM Ships *Retalick* and *Thornbrough*, *S168* hit in the forecastle and retiring to the Hook of Holland on fire. In effect, mines continued to take a small destructive toll on the Allies: *LCT457*, *LST420*, MV *Saporoea* and SS *Empire Path* sunk during 1944.

In one of November's few operations, an eastbound convoy was attacked by five boats of the 8th S-flotilla on the night of 29 November, three T5 *Zaunkönig* and seven FAT torpedoes all missing and every German boat receiving splinter damage from retaliating escorts. However, the North Sea and its environs remained the only region in which Petersen could take his battle to the enemy. On 12 December his request for more combat units was finally approved, and the 2nd and 6th S-flotillas were ordered from Wilhelmshaven to the Netherlands, arriving in Den Helder and Rotterdam respectively one week later.

During the afternoon of 15 December, Ijmuiden was the target of seventeen Lancaster bombers of the specialist 617 Squadron. Two Tallboys penetrated the bunker roof, destroying *S198* and trapping *S193* behind a mountain of rubble. Six other boats were so badly damaged that they would require extensive shipyard time before they were fit for action once more. Thirteen men had been killed and the entire S-boat maintenance facility was disorganised to the point of being useless. Petersen was forced to abandon future use of the shelters, clearly vulnerable to direct attack. Instead, he scattered the S-boats between harbours, no longer providing a concentrated bombing target. As if to prove his decision correct, sixteen Lancasters of 617 Squadron bombed the Rotterdam S-boat pens on 29 December, slightly damaging *S207* and *S167* and wounding three men.

On 16 December the German Ardennes Offensive began, the Kriegsmarine offered in staunch support by Dönitz to Hitler's last great gamble, doomed to failure from the outset. S-boats put to sea to hunt mythical reinforcement convoys with torpedoes, but the complete absence of Luftwaffe reconnaissance rendered their efforts pointless; nothing was sighted or attacked. Despite Dönitz's displeasure, Petersen reverted to minelaying.

On 22 December harsh winter weather moderated enough for mining of the convoy route trailing from Antwerp to the Thames. Eighteen S-boats were allocated the task, while six boats from 2nd Flotilla mounted a torpedo attack against a westbound convoy. However, two *Rotten* belonging to the 6th S-flotilla were surprised by British MGBs lurking in strength off the Hook of Holland, a mine aboard *S211* blown to pieces by gunfire and two men badly wounded. Another UMB mine aboard *S222* toppled off its carriage, blocking the rails for the remainder of the deadly cargo. Despite this handicap, the S-boats shook loose their pursuers as they raced away at full speed, mines eventually laid on target as ordered.

One *Rotte* from 10th S-flotilla was surprised by a British patrol group of destroyer HMS *Walpole*, frigates HM Ships *Torrington* and *Curzon* and the sloop HMS *Kittiwake*. Vastly outgunned, *S185* and *S192* were bracketed by accurate gunfire and sunk. There were no survivors from LzS Heinrich Holz's *S192*, while ObltzS Klaus-Degenhard Schmidt's *S185* suffered six men killed, including the skipper. Twenty-two survivors were rescued by the British, an officer from *S185* climbing aboard HMS *Walpole* with his boat's ensign wrapped around his waist, surrendering it to the ship's captain. The 6,140-ton SS *Empire Path* was the sole casualty from the two minefields, blown in two with five men dead on Christmas Eve 1944.[115]

18
The End

January 1945 – May 1945

The North

The wastefulness of deploying S-boats to the Norwegian theatre had not ended in 1943. Norwegian Kriegsmarine command had continued to request S-boats in Norway, predominantly to protect the leviathan *Tirpitz* moored in Alta Fjord and subsequently destroyed by bombing, but also as coastal defence. The previous fruitless tenure of S-boats in the Arctic failed to dent their enthusiasm for the idea, although SKL managed to deny all requests, concurring with FdS conviction that the battle lay in British waters. Unfortunately, an executive decision that could not be ignored, made at Führer headquarters on 17 October 1944, sent valuable S-boats once again to Norway.

> The Führer is afraid that an agreement between the Russians and Anglo-Americans has been reached to the effect that German troops in the North could be taken within a pincer action by an Anglo-American landing on the northern coast of Norway and a simultaneous attack by the Russians from the East. Furthermore, the Führer is afraid that transfers [of troops from Norway to the western front] by sea will be strongly harassed. Following a proposal by the Naval Staff, the Commander in Chief, Navy ordered the transfer of one S-flotilla consisting of at least eight boats with an escort ship to the area of the *Admiral Polarküste*.[116]

Correspondingly, the following day Kptlt Fimmen's 4th S-flotilla (*S201*, *S202*, *S203*, *S204*, *S205*, *S219*, *S220* and *S703*) departed the Netherlands for refit in Kiel and installation of heavier deck weapons, before transferring with the tender *Hermann von Wissman* to northern Norway. Severe weather resulted in *S203* colliding with an R-boat near Lindesnes, the boat abandoned and scuttled, but not before *S201*, *S203*, *S205* and *S703* were all damaged while saving the crew.

In the meantime, MOK Norway (*Marineoberkommando Norwegen*), perhaps emboldened by acquiescence to an S-flotilla request, asked for a second to be sent north for ASW work. Once again their application was successful, although this time, rather than deplete the ranks of combat boats, the training unit, 1st S-training Flotilla (*Schnellbootsschulflottille*) commanded by Kptlt Friedrich Wilhelm Wilcke, was earmarked for transfer. Instead of 4th S-flotilla continuing its journey north, Fimmen's boats transferred to the jurisdiction of Admiral Westküste to satisfy the ASW requirements, Wilcke's training boats instead assigned to the polar seas.

The launching of Germany's Ardennes Offensive and demand for total S-boat combat commitment in the west saw Fimmen's boats returned to the Netherlands, without *S201* and *S220* which were both damaged during transit. Meanwhile, 1st S-training Flotilla arrived in southern Norway, remaining there as convoy escorts until the war's end. It was an exercise in wasteful futility that resulted in the destruction of only a single ship.

On 29 March 1945 *S13* accidentally fired a torpedo that hit and sank 543-ton Norwegian passenger ship *Kommandøren* in Bergen harbour. *S13* was moored in the Homen bunker with bow facing to sea when an inexperienced torpedo man misunderstood instructions from the bridge and fired a single torpedo, hitting the steamer 300m (330yds) distant and sinking her, killing seaman Alf Larsen in the blast.

The West

On New Year's Day 1945, the S-flotillas on the western front numbered thirty-three operational boats.

2nd S-flotilla (KK Opdenhoff): *S74*, *S177*, *S180*, *S181*, *S209*, *S210* and *S221*; *S176* in a Wilhelmshaven shipyard.

4th S-flotilla (Kptlt Fimmen): *S202*, *S204*, *S205* and *S703*; *S219* out of service in Rotterdam, *S201* out of service in Norway and *S220* under repair in Wilhelmshaven.

6th S-flotilla (Kptlt Matzen): *S211*, *S212*, *S222*, *S223*, *S704* and *S705*; *S706* out of service in Wilhelmshaven.

8th S-flotilla (Kptlt Zymalkowski): *S194*, *S196*, *S197* and *S701*; *S198* trapped in the damaged Ijmuiden bunker, *S195* in an Emden shipyard.

9th S-flotilla (Kptlt von Mirbach): *S130*, *S168*, *S175* and *S206*; *S167* and *S207* under repair in Rotterdam; *S112* out of service at St Peter Port.

5th S-flotilla (Kptlt Holzapfel): *S48*, *S67*, *S85*, *S92*, *S98*, *S110* and *S127*; *S132* out of service in Cuxhaven.

10th S-flotilla (Kptlt Bludau): *S191* in Amsterdam; *S186* out of service in Wilhelmshaven; *S215* and *S224* undergoing trials by the Erprobungs-kommando für Kriegsschiffneubauten (EKK) in the Baltic.

The Kriegsmarine's plan was to raise the level of combat-ready boats in the west back to fifty, requiring a stockpile of mines, fuel and torpedoes that would be difficult to meet with production hampered in Germany by round-the-clock bombing. The western front now stretched from the Netherlands, roughly following the German border to Switzerland, although the first Allied troops had already entered Germany in September 1944 at the beginning of the costly battle for Aachen.

For S-boats, the beginning of 1945 was marked with bad weather, keeping them penned in harbour until conditions moderated. During December Dönitz had reprimanded Petersen for his minelaying activities within the Scheldt, fearing that it would endanger operations by newly committed two-man *Seehund* midget submarines. With Dönitz's mind still centred on U-boat warfare, he placed what hindsight shows as undue faith in the ability of the midgets to inflict severe damage on Allied convoy traffic between the Thames and Scheldt. He therefore forbade further S-boat mining of the Scheldt, robbing Petersen of his more effective weapon. The sheer power of free-roaming Allied surface forces had virtually nullified all but the slightest chances of successful torpedo missions and so a frustrated Petersen turned his attention back to the English east coast.

On the night of 14 January six 5th S-flotilla boats laid four UMB and fifteen LMB mines along the convoy route off Cromer, seven boats of 2nd S-flotilla also dropping six LMB and eight UMB mines in a complementary field. That night 5,835-ton SS *Dalemoor* travelling in ballast from Antwerp was sunk by one of the mines; 3,936-ton Norwegian SS *Carrier* also sank four days later. However, during the return to harbour, ObltzS Albrecht Pillet's *S180* hit a German mine off Texel, which detonated the boat's torpedoes, immediately destroying the boat. Accompanying boats only managed to rescue twelve crewmen and retrieve three dead from the shattered remains, the bodies of Pillet and seven other men washing ashore a week later.

A torpedo mission launched by eight boats of 2nd and 5th S-flotillas on 15 January was detected and forced away with light damage, unable to find merchant targets. Within twenty-four hours, five 8th S-flotilla boats repeated the attempt and although attacked by aircraft while outbound, eight FAT and LUT torpedoes were fired at a convoy of landing craft, *LST415* hit and so severely damaged that she was beached near the Tongue lightship. Artillery fire from the 3.7in guns of Tongue Sands Fort also began landing around the S-boats, which broke away and returned undamaged.

During this period there were again bitter recriminations directed toward Petersen and his 'conservative' methods from Grossadmiral Dönitz. Once again clutching his 'total commitment' rationale, he told Petersen in a private letter that:

> too much emphasis was placed upon sparing our forces and avoiding big risks when weighing up demands, exigencies and pressures needed to inflict extensive harm on the enemy ... Things were, and are, different in the U-boat arm ... sparing our forces and avoiding too high a risk does not play anything like the role it does in the S-boat arm.[117]

Tantamount to an accusation of cowardice, Petersen replied with a written list detailing his principles of action and appealed for a free hand in operational planning, including the forbidden laying of mines within the Scheldt. Petersen had previously proven that he was unafraid of demanding full and dangerous commitment from his men, but only when it offered some prospect of success. The suicidal application of 'total commitment' in the face of almost certain failure was beyond his responsibility for the welfare of men under his command, let alone the ability to keep S-boats serviceable and ready for action when needed.

Harsh weather again halted operations until the night of 21 January when a combined torpedo mission by sixteen boats of 4th, 6th, 8th and 9th S-flotillas attacked various points along the Thames–Scheldt convoy route. Facing them were forty-four MGBs, as well as the sloop HMS *Guillemot* and frigate HMS *Torrington*. Lacking any kind of Luftwaffe reconnaissance, the S-boats trusted to good fortune, only a *Rotte* of the 9th S-flotilla actually finding any merchant shipping: straggling 2,365-ton steamer SS *Halo* of convoy TAC114 hit by one of four torpedoes fired by *S168* and *S175*. The ship, carrying wooden sleepers and military supplies, was badly holed and sank the following day under tow. Detected by the escort, ObltzS Dau's *S168* was hit in the bridge by an artillery round from HMS *Stayner*, the blast destroying the port torpedo tube and killing one man, wounding six others. ObltzS Franz Behr's *S175* was also slightly damaged by gunfire.

Originally published in Die *Kriegsmarine* magazine: crewing a stern 40mm Bofors at night aboard an *S38*-class boat.

In return for the destruction of one steamer, the Germans paid dearly. Outbound, the 8th S-flotilla's five boats had come under bombing attack by an RAF Wellington, although they successfully escaped serious damage. HMS *Guillemot* had been made aware of the S-boats' presence, finding them and opening fire at 800m (875yds) range, wounding one man aboard *S194*, the stored life raft also being hit and catching fire until jettisoned overboard. A T5 torpedo was launched toward the attacker, but to no avail, as British reinforcements arrived in the shape of frigate HMS *Seymour* and seven MTBs. Frantically, the S-boats attacked, retired, then probed forward again in an effort to break the British line. *S701* and *S199* collided, the latter damaged so badly that ObltzS Joachim Quistorp and his crew scuttled the boat. The chaos was not confined to the Germans as *MTB495* was also badly damaged, one man killed and three wounded. Into the maelstrom, artillery fire from Tongue Sand Forts began landing, often attributed to sinking the already doomed *S199*.

Quistrop and his men went into the water and drifted in life rafts for six and a half hours, eventually rescued by minesweeper HMS *Neave*, though the propeller of the ship accidentally killed one German and injured three others before they could be pulled aboard, Quistorp and seventeen of his crew being rescued. Meanwhile, the remaining exhausted flotilla boats reached Ijmuiden, *S194* briefly running aground before refloating and reaching harbour. The damaged *S701*, late into harbour, was mistakenly fired on by a Vorpostenboot, killing one man and wounding two others, the boat so badly damaged that it was taken into the shipyard never to sail again.

Between bouts of bad weather, torpedo and minelaying missions continued, though with no confirmed successes. Frequently attacked by sea and air, the flotillas suffered a grinding succession of damaged boats and injured men. Drifting ice from the Maas River had forced six serviceable boats to transfer from Rotterdam to Ijmuiden towards the end of January, the latter harbour bombed once again by RAF Lancasters on 3 February, 617 Squadron returning five days later. Almost miraculously, there appears to have been no significant damage inflicted on scattered S-boats, though port facilities for lifting Biber one-man midget submarines in and out of the water were destroyed. The USAAF mounted its first ever 'Disney' mission against the Ijmuiden shelter on 10 February, nine B17s using 4,500lb (2,000kg) rocket-boosted concrete-piercing bombs, penetrating the pens, though they were empty as per Petersen's instructions.

The next break in the weather, on 16 February, allowed S-boats to sail from Den Helder and mine the Humber Estuary, which claimed French destroyer *La Combattante* and 187-ton British trawler *Aquarius*, as well as damage to two large freighters. A failed torpedo mission on 20 February by 2nd S-flotilla was followed by twenty-two boats from six flotillas sailing into the old hunting ground of 'E-boat Alley', although shadowing Allied aircraft vectored surface forces on to the boats from 4th, 6th and 9th S-flotillas, forcing them home without encountering targets. Meanwhile, in extremely poor visibility, the 2nd S-flotilla *Rotte S174* and *S209* suddenly found themselves in the midst of FS34 (Phase 17) convoy as drifting banks of fog cleared momentarily. *S174* hurriedly launched two LUT torpedoes and ObltzS Kurt Neugebauer's *S209* fired two standard G7a torpedoes as they gunned engines and broke away, *S209* hitting 1,345-ton Danish SS *Skjold* with artillery fire and setting her aflame during the retreat, in which escort ships also hit Neugebauer's boat several times in a fuel tank and the starboard, fires aboard quickly extinguished by the German crew, two of whom were wounded. The S-boats reloaded and *S209* fired its last two torpedoes, hearing the sound of five detonations later, although nothing was confirmed by Allied records. Although the two boats reached home without further trouble, all of the 2nd S-flotilla had suffered engine problems, the cause found to be salt added to the diesel fuel. The entire flotilla was non-operational for two days while fuel bunkers were emptied and cleaned.

The 5th S-flotilla attacked the same convoy north of Great Yarmouth, torpedoing and sinking 2,780-ton SS *Goodwood* and 1,109-ton SS *Blacktoft*, with HMS *Valorous* damaged by gunfire from one of the convoy's merchant ships while attempting to rescue men from *Goodwood*. To the south, boats of the 8th S-flotilla found a small convoy of landing craft and torpedoed and sank *LCP707*. During ensuing combat against escorts, ObltzS Horst Schuur's *S193* was lost; StObStrm Seifert's *S167* also sank during the return to port following collision damage. The entire twenty-three-man crew were captured by the British.

During the night of 22 February, the 4th, 6th, 8th and 9th S-flotillas laid mines along the convoy lanes leading to the Scheldt, also managing to successfully shoot down a shadowing fighter bomber. Ultimately, the minefield would sink five ships totalling 25,226 tons, vindicating Petersen's request to reopen mining within the Scheldt itself, despite *Seehund* operations, the success in accrued tonnage of shipping destroyed by S-boat mines outstripping that sunk by midget submarines, despite the best efforts of the Kleinkampfverbände.

During the night of 24 February, five 4th S-flotilla boats once again mined the convoy route, but this time were found and attacked by free-ranging British surface units after dropping all twenty-four mines. One man was killed aboard *S205* by MTB gunfire, while Kptlt Helmut Dross's *S220* took a shell hit in the starboard engine room from HMS *Cotswold*, the boat burning as firefighting equipment failed. With little choice, Dross ordered *S220* abandoned and scuttled, further shells hammering into the listless wreck. Three men were killed, the remainder rescued as prisoners of war.

The month of March continued this pattern. Fog curtailed several attempted operations, those that were able to continue frequently encountering strong enemy forces and being forced home with damage. Not until 18 March was there any success to report after seven boats of the 6th S-flotilla laid forty-two mines off the east coast and continued on to attack FS59 (Phase 18) off Lowestoft. Reporting seven ships sunk and a destroyer damaged with torpedoes, the flotilla had actually destroyed two freighters: the 1,097-ton SS *Crichtown* and 2,871-ton SS *Rogate*, while the mines claimed two freighters – 7,062-ton SS *Empire Blessing* and 7,253-ton SS *Samselbu*. Trawler *Nelly* and *LST80*, a Liberty ship, were also damaged.

Although they could not yet know it, the S-boat service had made its final torpedo sinkings in the west and the war of attrition had reached its inevitable conclusion. Nine B17 bombers returned on 14 March with Disney rocket-powered bombs to attack the Ijmuiden bunker and, although not sinking any S-boats, the 8th S-flotilla was declared non-operational with damage to all boats. Three other S-boats of the western flotillas were lost due to USAAF bombing during the month, B24s attacking Wilhelmshaven on 30 March and destroying *S194*, *S186* and *S224*, all in the port for repairs and overhaul.

Seven nights after the Ijmuiden raid, the four remaining boats of the 2nd S-flotilla mounted a torpedo mission, engine failure aboard *S201* reducing the number to three until flotilla commander KK Opdenhoff, aboard *Führerboot S181*, curtailed the mission. During their return, 236 Squadron Beaufighters attacked with machine guns and rockets, hitting *S181* in a fuel tank, compartment VII and also the bridge. As the S-boat burst into flames, *S209* moved in to evacuate the crew: Opdenhoff, the first man of the S-boat service to have received the Knight's Cross in 1940, skipper ObltzS Martin Schlenk and twelve men lying dead aboard the burning boat, which sank shortly afterwards. *S210* was also hit, severing air lines leading to the engine ignition and forcing the boat to limp home. Kapitänleutnant Hugo Wendler, erstwhile skipper of *S174*, took control of 2nd S-flotilla.

Bravely, S-boats continued to sail whenever possible into an almost certain inferno of enemy fire. Mines continued to be sown, destroying *ML466*, Belgian trawler *St Jan* and *LCP840* during March. On land, the Allies had resumed their drive into Germany, and German forces in the Netherlands were cut off by the beginning of April. Rudolf Petersen had moved FdS headquarters from Den Helder to Sonderburg and continued

Minelaying continued until the last days of the war, often a more effective weapon than torpedoes. Here, EMC mines are loaded aboard an S-boat.

to direct his forces, although their movements were increasingly hindered by fuel shortages. Although relatively substantial fuel stocks had been allocated by the Kriegsmarine to S-boats at the beginning of the month – with no chance of resupply – they were shortly thereafter ordered passed to the army, whose forces were immobilised in their struggle against advancing Canadian troops.

On 2 April the boats of the 5th S-flotilla were transferred to the Baltic to face the inexorable onslaught of Soviet power, while the first operation of April was mounted by Kptlt Wendler's 2nd S-flotilla four nights later. Six boats left harbour and, shadowed by aircraft, soon clashed with HMS *Cubitt* and *Haydon* and *MTB781* and *5001* of 68th flotilla. Twenty-six LMB mines were laid under fire and *MTB5001* was hit by S-boat cannon shells, exploding with three men killed. The S-boats sped for home under smokescreens, but were intercepted by another unit of MTBs. Oberleutnant zur See Friedrich Wilhelm Stockfleth's *S176* rammed *MTB494*, which turned over and sank with fourteen men, while ObltzS Karl Boseniuk's *S177* also collided with *MTB493*, which in turn hit the submerging wreck of *494*, and later limped to England stern-first, badly holed. Boseniuk's boat was struck several times by cannon fire below the waterline and the entire crew were evacuated by *S174* as the boat sank. Meanwhile, *S176* had burst into flames after also taking shell hits, five men killed and the remainder, including Stockfleth, rescued by MTBs. The remaining four S-boats reached Den Helder by 0645hrs, the skipper of *S209*, ObltzS Kurt Neugebauer severely wounded by machine-gun fire and dying in hospital the following day. Three men had also been killed by shell hits on *S221*, during what was the last mission mounted by the 2nd S-flotilla. That evening, fifteen Lancaster bombers of 617 Squadron and two Mosquito pathfinders bombed the Den Helder S-boat bunker.

The western S-boats' final losses occurred on the night of 7 April, when six boats of the 4th S-flotilla and seven of the 6th S-flotilla were conducting minelaying in the Scheldt approaches. Shadowed by aircraft, they were attacked by MTBs, Kptlt Wiencke's *S202* and ObltzS Steinhauer's *S703* colliding at high speed in the action that followed, both boats sinking with thirteen men killed, including Wiencke, the remainder rescued by the British. During their return, ObltzS Brandi's *S223* struck a mine and sank off Ostend, and only the skipper and eight men were rescued.

Five nights later, twelve boats from 4th, 6th and 9th S-flotillas sailed their final minelaying mission again in the Scheldt approaches. Reported by aircraft, they were attacked by HMS *Ekins* and two MTBs; the close-range,

First holder of the Knight's Cross within the S-boat service, Korvettenkapitän Hermann Opdenhoff, with comrades. Opdenhoff was killed in action on 21 March 1945.

fast-moving action saw *S205* severely damaged, but escaping to the Hook of Holland. In April the 8,208-ton tanker MV *Gold Shell* was possibly sunk by S-boat mine, and three other freighters damaged. The western S-boats were now immobilised by lack of fuel, awaiting the end within their Dutch bases. On 10 April 1945 in a brief ceremony, the commander of the 8th S–flotilla, KK Feliz Zymalkowski, received his Knight's Cross. Less than a month later, on 2 May Kaptlt Jens Matzen, commander of the 6th S-flotilla, also received the coveted decoration. In one final act, *S174* and *S209* departed for Germany on the day of capitulation, carrying SS Obergruppenführer Artur Seiß-Inquart back to Germany, the oppressive Reichskommissar in the Netherlands having been appointed Foreign Minister to Dönitz's new government following Adolf Hitler's suicide.

The East

The year 1944 had seen little combat S-boat activity within the Baltic. Following the fall of Novgorod to the Red Army on 20 January, the abandonment of the German siege of Leningrad and subsequent retreat to the Narva River, Wehrmacht command feared a Soviet landing behind German lines in Estonia. Dönitz and his staff were also wary of a reactivation of the dormant Soviet Baltic fleet and requested an S-flotilla despatched to the area, Petersen reluctantly sending Kptlt Obermaier's 6th S-flotilla from Ijmuiden to the eastern Baltic on 6 February. Obermaier's eight boats – *S39*, *S76*, *S79*, *S90*, *S91*, *S97*, *S114* and *S132* – rendezvoused with the depot ship *Carl Peters* in Reval, with two others due to follow once work in Rotterdam was completed. There, with freezing temperatures icing the Gulf of Finland, the flotilla operated against small Soviet gunboats, frequent gun battles amongst the Finnish skerries achieving only the sinking of *MO122* on 14 May, the final torpedo sinking of an enemy vessel by S-boat within the Baltic Sea. With Allied landings in Normandy on 6 June, Obermaier's flotilla was soon headed back to the western front.

However, on 9 June the Soviet juggernaut launched its offensive against Finland; four Finnish crews arrived at Saßnitz six days later to take over the boats *S64*, *S83*, *S99* and *S117*. Finland was correctly judged by OKW to be wavering in the face of the onslaught and Dönitz demanded an immediate S-boat presence in the eastern Baltic. Petersen selected Kptlt Holzapfel's 5th S-flotilla, all of the unit's boats having been destroyed or neutralised in the west, but still comprising a cadre of experienced combat crews. Holzapfel's men took charge of *S65*, *S67* and *S80* from the 10th S-flotilla training in German waters, and *S120* and *S68* from the 2nd S-training Flotilla, as well as *S85* from the 3rd S-training Flotilla. Later the boats *S110* and *S116*, undergoing refit and the fitting of 40mm Bofors cannons, were added. Coupled with the tender *Hermann von Wissman*, the 5th S-flotilla began transferring to Finland during July. Over the months that followed, the flotilla was employed on patrol duties and occasional minelaying, ObStrm Borkenhagen's *S80* being lost to a mine on 1 September near Vibord with five men killed. The following day Finland declared its intention to withdraw from the war after agreeing an armistice with Soviet Russia. German forces were given notice to leave and Holzapfel's flotilla sailed to Paldiski in Estonia until the fall of Reval to the Red Army on 22 September, moving southwest to Windau in Latvia.

The 5th S-flotilla took part supporting minelaying for the abortive Operation *Tanne Ost* centred on German occupation of Suursaari Island in the heart of the Gulf of Finland. S-boats mined the waters off Kotka to the north, in an attempt to frustrate potential Finnish naval interference in the planned landings, but the minelaying was observed and the mines' effect nullified. The S-boats passed several Finnish patrol ships with no shots exchanged, the former allies merely keeping a wary eye on one another. Indeed, a Finnish patrol ship was preparing to leave the island with a stranded German observation unit when the Wehrmacht occupation force arrived. Demands for the Finnish garrison's surrender were refused and the German troops – a hastily gathered mixture of personnel from the Heer, Luftwaffe and Kriegsmarine – began landing, defenders opening fire and marking the beginning of German-Finnish hostilities. Ultimately, the attempt ended in complete failure within twenty-four hours, 153 Germans killed and 1,231 surrendering to the Finns, who lost thirty-six confirmed dead. The 5th S-flotilla took no active part in the operation, not even receiving full orders regarding the planned attack. On 17 September S-boats lifted some Kriegsmarine personnel stranded on the small island of Pein Tytarsaari, including the commander of 7th Artillerieträgerflottille KK Dr Theodor Sonnemann who had been stranded there since *Tanne Ost*.

To bolster the S-boat presence within the Baltic, elements of Kptlt Hans Helmut Klose's 2nd S-training Flotilla were activated as combat boats, *S64*, *S76*, *S81* and *S135* arriving in Windau with the depot ship *Tsingtau*, the *Hermann von Wissman* returned to Germany. Together the boats of the training group and 5th S-flotilla reconnoitred the Baltic front facing both the Soviets and Finns, *S110* being attacked and damaged by Soviet aircraft on 26 October. Multiple minefields were laid, which accounted for several Soviet warships during September and October, including submarine *M96*, seven minesweepers, three patrol boats, five MTBs, two tugs and the gunboat *Amgun*.

As minelaying continued, German forces were pushed back by a seemingly unstoppable Red Army. The island of Hiiuma was taken on 2 October, Saaremaa attacked three days later. Hitler had ordered that the Sworbe Peninsula be held 'to the last round', and S-boats laid mines to support the land battle, probing the waters around the peninsula in order to intercept Soviet landing forces. Holzapfel led *S69*, *S65*, *S68* and *S116* in search of the enemy on 18 November, encountering three MGBs and fourteen smaller craft. *S69* fired two torpedoes, followed by *S65*, all shots going wide as cannon fire erupted in the early morning darkness. In the confused fight that followed, *S68* and *S116* suffered hits from intervening Russian aircraft, one man killed aboard *S116* and the starboard engine disabled. Four boats in total collided during the night and the S-boats retreated, repairs required before the majority would sail again. On 23 November, the last German troops were evacuated from Sworbe.

Minelaying continued into December, before the 5th S-flotilla was withdrawn to the western front in support of the Ardennes Offensive, leaving Windau on 21 December, and exchanging some boats with 1st S-training Flotilla in order to take the strongest into action in the west.

Meanwhile, Klose's training unit, based in Windau, continued to lay mines and conduct small harassing raids against the enemy, sometimes landing small sabotage troops behind Russian lines.

During February Soviet MTBs began attacking convoy traffic streaming to and from Kurland, and MOK Nord pleaded for the return of the 5th S-flotilla to the Baltic, heavier warships being used as floating artillery platforms and S-boats the most effective naval strike force remaining. However, Petersen instead recommended using the cadre of experienced men from the 1st S-flotilla recently returned from the Black Sea, where they had experienced combat against Russians. The newly reconstituted 1st S-flotilla commanded by KK Büchting had begun working up new boats *S216*, *S217*, *S218*, *S225*, *S226*, *S707* and *S708* within the Baltic. By mid March they had completed their training and transferred from Kiel to Saßnitz on the island of Rügen and home to the 11th S-flotilla. The latter never passed the initial stages of formation, following subordination to the needs of the 5th S-flotilla.

Unfortunately, their timing was atrocious, as the RAF targeted Saßnitz for attack on 6 March. Crowded with refugees from East Prussia, the small harbour was bombed by 150 Lancaster bombers guided by Mosquito pathfinders. A further forty-one Lancasters dropped magnetic mines into the harbour and its approaches. Destroyer *Z38* and hospital ship *Robert Möhring* were sunk, as well as the 21,600-ton liner *Hamburg*, sunk the next day by mines. The headquarters and facilities of the 11th S-flotilla were destroyed and the flotilla engineer Oblt (Ing) Rudolf Röhl and an administrative officer killed.

By this stage of the war, the exodus of refugees fleeing East Prussia had become an avalanche, the Kriegsmarine actively participating in the evacuation of a terrified civilian population, alongside whatever fighting units could be salvaged from battles they could not win, but from which they were seldom allowed to retreat. The Soviet Air Force continued to ask for Anglo-American assistance in the bombardment of Baltic ports, the majority crowded with more civilians than troops. Swinemünde was hit by the USAAF on 12 March, and an estimated 23,000 people killed, the majority refugees.

The 2nd S-training Flotilla patrolled off Libau as Russian gunboats pushed further west, harassing evacuation traffic. On 18 March *S64* and *S81* clashed with nine such gunboats, the small 66-ton *TK66* sunk by artillery fire and *TK195* badly damaged. Nine days later the same S-boats, with an additional *S69*, rescued survivors from 694-ton tanker *Saßnitz*, which had been attacked and sunk by Soviet aircraft along with three minesweeper escorts. The Luftwaffe intervened, destroying eleven of the attackers, and driving the rest away as the three S-boats arrived to haul shocked survivors aboard. After landing them in Libau, they returned to the scene of the still-burning tanker, expecting correctly that Russian MTBs would attempt to find survivors for interrogation, as well as papers, signal books or any material that could provide intelligence. Surprising a group of Soviet MTBs – described by ObltzS Bernhard Wülfring as 'a disorderly bunch of craft with stern lights burning and which kept getting in one another's way' – a fierce and fast-moving gun battle ensued, in which LzS Runge's *S69* destroyed *TK166* and Wülfing's *S81* hit and sunk *TK181* with artillery fire. Obersteuermann Deckert's *S64* disabled *TK199* with gunfire, boarding the boat and capturing eleven men, including the wounded commander of the TKA (MTB) Division, Captain (Third Rank) Čubujkin, five other officers and five seamen. Although the battle had at times been fought at a range of only 300m, one German sailor was wounded, and at least four other Soviet MTBs damaged as they retreated in disarray.

On 22 March *S216* and *S218* transported Generaladmiral Oskar Kummetz, chief of MOK Ost, and elements of his staff to Hela Peninsula near Danzig, a jumping-off point for troops and civilians trapped in Pomerania. They were joined for the voyage by *S217*, *S226* and *S225*, two of the S-boats suffering engine breakdowns that required shipyard replacement. Somewhat ironically, at the end of the month KK Büchting was forced to order two of his 1st S-flotilla boats – *S217* and *S707* – to torpedo the hulk of the battleship *Gneisenau*, sunk on the shallow floor of Gotenhafen harbour, its tall central mast used as a spotting platform by Russian artillery observers. The S-boats each fired two torpedoes into the ship's hull in an attempt to bring down the mast, but failed. Büchting later described it as the 'saddest order that the flotilla had been ordered to carry out during his time'.

There only remained the final act of the war to play out in the east. By the beginning of April Hela was under Soviet artillery fire, enemy aircraft dominated the skies and the S-boats were more frequently engaged on shepherding crowded transports and rescuing shipwrecked survivors than taking the futile fight to the enemy. On 2 April Kptlt Holzapfel's 5th S-flotilla was ordered to transfer from Den Helder via Kiel to Swinemünde, arriving at Bornholm with seven boats thirteen days after their voyage began.

During the night of 9 April, *S225* and *S708* were operating off Gotenhafen against Russian MTBs that prowled Danzig Bay following the

An S-boat transporting troops evacuated from Libau, May 1945. One of the few units still capable of striking back against Soviet naval power during the frantic Baltic flight of troops and civilians from the advancing Red Army, S-boats continued to sail both as a defensive measure for transport vessels and to take as many people aboard as possible and ferry them west.

fall of that city. Hela still functioned as a tiny bridgehead, enabling the final evacuation of refugees, and both S-boats sailed to aggressively defend the escape route west. One of the last refugee transports had departed Pillau that night, sailing to Hela, where those aboard could be transferred to larger vessels. Crowded with people, the 807-ton steamer *Neuwerk* became separated from her escort and was challenged by *S708*. With no return signal given, LzS Carl Silies fired a single torpedo which hit the ship amidships. Carrying a thirteen-man crew, 854 wounded troops, sixty railwaymen, seven medical orderlies and approximately a hundred refugees, the ship went down in minutes. S-boats rescued only seventy-eight people from the water. The last torpedo sinking of the war had been a costly and tragic mistake.

S-boats continued shuttling back and forth evacuating whoever they could find. On 5 May 1945 German capitulation in the west became known to the flotilla commanders, Kptlt Holzapfel deciding to take his 5th S-flotilla west in company with torpedo boat *T28*. However, before they could begin their voyage, *T28* was ordered to assist in the evacuation of Hela, Holzapfel following with his flotilla back into the fray. All crewmen were given an option to leave and head west independently before they were recommitted to the action, but not a single man opted to do so. Holzapfel led his boats to Pillau where both the 1st S-flotilla and 2nd S-training Flotilla were stationed. Elsewhere, S-boat men had been drafted into the infantry, Marine-Schützen-Bataillon 1011 formed in Swinemünde from 1st Abteilung der Schnellboot-Lehrdivision.

On the morning of 8 May all available S-boats loaded 165 exhausted troops aboard and, alongside similarly encumbered *Tsingtau*, various minesweepers, patrol boats, tugs, coasters and lighters headed west; in total some 14,400 troops were carried out of the grasp of the Red Army in this final evacuation. All nineteen S-boats entered the Geltlinger Bight the following evening.

Kapitänleutnant Ernst-August Seevers' *S216* had remained in Hela to carry ninety-nine more troops to safety. Sailing in company with two minesweepers and the steamer *Ruggard*, the tiny convoy was attacked by thirty-five Il2 Sturmovik aircraft on the afternoon of 9 May, one bomb hitting *S216* and penetrating the forecastle without exploding, passing centimetres from the starboard torpedo warhead. Two soldiers were killed, thirteen severely injured and seven lightly wounded in the attack. On 10 May *S216* moored in Kappeln to unload able-bodied troops and the two corpses, before continuing onward to Schleswig, still carrying wounded men. There they dropped anchor and transported the casualties to hospital.

On 1 May 1945 at 1100hrs, Kapitän zur See Rudolf Petersen addressed assembled S-boat crews from 1st S-flotilla, 5th S-flotilla and 2nd S-training Flotillas in a final parade within the Geltlinger Bight. As the ceremony ended the Kriegsmarine battle ensign was lowered for the last time. The S-boats' war was over.

In total, 112 S-boat men received the *Deutsches Kreuz* in gold during the Second World War, visible at lower left. This *Bootsmannmaat* sports the DKG, and the Iron Cross, first and second class, as well as the Eastern Front medal and S-boat badge.

Appendix 1

S-boat dispositions at the end of hostilities

Germany

Geltlinger Bight

1st S-flotilla: *S208, S216, S217, S218, S225, S707, S708, S306*
5th S-flotilla: *S48, S65, S67, S85, S92, S98, S127, S132*
8th S-flotilla: *S196*
9th S-flotilla: *S227*
10th S-flotilla: *S110, S215, S228, S305*
2nd S-training Flotilla: *S64, S69, S76, S81, S83, S99, S117, S135*
3rd S-training Flotilla: *S19, S20, S21, S24, S25, S50, S68, S82, S95, S97, S101, S105, S107, S108, S113, S115, S118, S120, S122, S123*
Tenders: *Hermann von Wissman, Tanga, Tsingtau, Carl Peters,* and *Buea*
Brunsbuttel
2nd S-flotilla: *S174*
List
2nd S-flotilla: *S209*

On 13 May 1945, *S204* and *S205* arrived in Felixstowe harbour. Both boats had surrendered in Rotterdam to British forces, but had subsequently transported Konteradmiral Erich Alfred Breuning and other officers to England. Breuning, brought ashore aboard Kaptlt Hans-Jurgen Seeger's *S205*, was the chief of staff of the *Nationalsozialistischen Führungsstabes*, responsible for the 'National Socialist political education' of the Wehrmacht. *S204* carried KK Kurt Fimmen (4th S-Flotilla commander) and Kaptlt Bernd Rebensburg (operations officer of the FdS staff) into captivity.

Norway

Bergen
1st S-training Flotilla: *S10, S11, S13, S15, S16*
Tender: *Adolf Lüderitz*
Egersund
8th S-flotilla: *S195, S199*

The Netherlands

Den Helder
2nd S-flotilla: *S201, S221*
8th S-flotilla: *S197, S701*
Rotterdam
4th S-flotilla: *S204, S205, S219, S304*
6th S-flotilla: *S211, S212, S213, S222, S704, S705, S706*
9th S-flotilla: *S130, S168, S175, S206, S207, S214*

Appendix 2
The S-Boat Service
1935–1945

Führer der Torpedoboote

KA Günther Lütjens (October 1937 – October 1939)

KzS Friedrich Bonte (October 1939 – November 1939)

KzS/KA Hans Bütow (28 November 1939 – 20 April 1942)

Führer der Schnellboote

FK/KzS/Kommodore Rudolf Petersen(April 1945 – May 1945)

1st S-division

FK Herbert-Max Schultz (July 1943 – March 1945)

Kptlt Siegfried Wuppermann (March 1945 – May 1945)

Combat units

1935–1938

1st Schnellbootshalbflottille

Commander: Kptlt Erich Bey (until 12 September 1934)

                            Kptlt Günther Schubert

1st Schnellbootsflottille

Commander: Kptlt Günther Schubert (September 1934 – September 1936)

                            KK Heinz Dietrich von Conrady (October 1936 – June 1938)

                            Kptlt Kurt Sturm (2 June 1938 – November 1939)

                            Kptlt Heinz Birnbacher (26 November 1939 – 1 September 1942)

                            KK Georg-Stuhr Christiansen (2 September 1942 – September 1943)

                            KK Hermann Büchting (September 1943 – May 1945)

2nd Schnellbootsflottille

Commander: Kptlt Rudolf Petersen (1 August 1938 – 20 October 1941)

Kptlt Klaus Feldt (20 October 1941 – February 1944)

KK Hermann Opdenhoff (February 1944 – 22 February 1945)

Kptlt Hugo Wendler (23 February 1945 – May 1945)

3rd Schnellbootsflottille

Commander: ObltzS Werner Töniges (15 May 1940 – 23 May 1940)

Kptlt Friedrich Kemnade (23 May 1940 – 9 July 1943)

Kptlt Albert Müller (9 July 1943 – 16 July 1943)

FK Herbert-Max Schultz (16 July 1943 – 1 September 1944)

Kptlt Albert Müller (1 September 1944 – 12 October 1944)

Kptlt Günther Schulz (13 October 1944 – 3 May 1945)

4th Schnellbootsflottille

Commander: Kptlt Niels Bätge (1 October 1940 – March 1943)

KK Werner Lützow (March 1943 – 25 October 1943)

Kpt Albert Causemann (26 October 1943 – November 1943)

KK Kurt Fimmen (November 1943 – May 1945)

5th Schnellbootsflottille

Commander: KK Bernd Klug (15 July 1941 – 31 May 1944)

Kptlt Kurt Johannsen (1 June 1944 – 14 June 1944)

Kptlt Hermann Holzapfel (July 1944 – May 1945)

6th Schnellbootsflottille

Commander: KK Albrecht Obermaier (1 March 1941 – July 1944)

Kptlt Jens Matzen (July 1944 – May 1945)

7th Schnellbootsflottille

Commander: KK Bernd Klug (1 October 1941 – May 1942)

KK Hans Trummer (June 1942 – July 1944)

Kptlt Günther Schulz (July 1944 – 3 May 1945)

8th Schnellbootsflottille

Commander: KK Georg-Stuhr Christiansen (1 November 1941 – 20 July 1942)

KK Felix Zymalkowski (1 December 1942 – May 1945)

9th Schnellbootsflottille

Commanders: KK Götz Frhr von Mirbach (1 April 1943 – May 1945)

10th Schnellbootsflottille

Commander: Kptlt Karl Müller (15 March 1944 – 19 September 1944)

Kptlt Dietrich Bludau (20 September 1944 – May 1945)

11th Schnellbootsflottille (MAS boats in Black Sea)

Commanders: Kptlt Hans-Jürgen Meyer (1 June 1943 – 28 September 1943)

11th Schnellbootsflottille

Commander: Kptlt Hermann Holzapfel (May 1944 – June 1944)

Kptlt Nikolai Baron von Stempel (10 December 1944 – April 1945)

21st Schnellbootsflottille

Commander: Kptlt Siegfried Wuppermann (September 1943 – February 1944)

Kptlt Ludwig Graser (March 1944 – 18 October 1944)

22nd Schnellbootsflottille

Commander: Kptlt Siegfried Wuppermann (1 December 1943 – 15 December 1943)

Kptlt Friedrich Hüsig (15 December 1943 – 15 September 1944)

24th Schnellbootsflottille

Commander: Kptlt Hans-Jürgen Meyer (1 November 1943 – 25 October 1944)

Training Units

Schnellbootslehrdivision

Commander: Kptlt Hermann Opdenhoff (1 November 1943 – February 1944)

KK Klaus Feldt (February 1944 – May 1945)

1st Schnellbootsschulflottille

Commander: Kptlt Friedrich Wilhelm Wilcke (1 November 1943 – May 1945)

2nd Schnellbootsschulflottille

Commander: Kptlt Hand-Helmut Klose (15 December 1943 – 8 May 1945)

3rd Schnellbootsschulflottille

Commander: Kptlt Klaus-Dietrich Siems (15 June 1944 – January 1945)

Kptlt Hans Detlefsen (January 1945 – May 1945)

Select Bibliography

Primary Source material

KTB SKL 1939–1945
KTB FdT 30 November 1939 – 20 April 1942
KTB FdS 20 April 1942 – 31 January 1945
KTB 1 S-flotilla
KTB 2 S-flotilla
KTB 3 S-flotilla
KTB 5 S-flotilla
KTB 6 S-flotilla
KTB 7 S-flotilla
KTB 8 S-flotilla
KTB 1 S-division

Books and Publications

Aguilera y Elias, *Buques de Guerra Españoles 1885–1972*, Editorial San Martín, Spain.

Barnett, Correlli, *Engage the Enemy More Closely*, Hodder & Stoughton, London, 1992.

Bräckow, Werner, *Die Geschichte des deutschen Marine-Ingenieur-offizierkorps*, Stalling Verlag, Hamburg, 1974.

Camil Busquets i Vilanova, 'Lanchas Torpederas en la Marina de Guerra Española', *Modelismo e Historia*, Spain.

Collier, Richard, *The Sands of Dunkirk*, Dutton, 1961.

Connelly, T Gath and Krakow, David L, *Schnellboote in Action*, Squadron/Signal Publications, Carollton, 2003.

Cooper, Brian, *The E-Boat Threat*, MacDonald and Janes, London, 1976.

Dallies-Labourdette, Jean-Phillippe, *S-Boote*, Histoire & Collections, Paris 2003.

Escuadra, Alfonso, *Bajo las banderas de la Kriegsmarine. Marinos de españoles en la Armada Alemana (1942–43)*, Editorial Fundación Don Rodrigo, Spain.

Fock, Harald, *Die deutschen Schnellboote*, Koehler Verlag, Hamburg, 2001.

Frank, Hans, *S-Boats in Action in the Second World War*, Seaforth Publishing, Barnsley, 2007.

Guard, J S, *Improvise and Dare*, The Book Guild, Lewes, 1997.

Haarr, Geirr, *The Battle for Norway: April–June 1940*, Seaforth Publishing, 2010.

Hümmelchen, Gerhard, *Die Deutschen Schnellboote*, E S Mittler & Sohn Verlag, Hamburg, 1996.

Isby, David, *The Luftwaffe and the War at Sea 1939–1945*, Chatham Publishing, London, 2005.

Johnson, Brian, *The Secret War*, British Broadcasting Corporation, London, 1978.

Kemnade, Friedrich, *Die Afrika Flottille*, Motorbuch Verlag, Stuttgart, 1978.

Kent, Captain Barrie, *Signal: A History of Signalling in the Royal Navy*, Permanent Publications, 2004.

Kurowski, Franz, *Korvettenkapitan Werner Töniges*, Flechsig Verlag, Würzburg, 2007.

Lohmann W and Hildebrand H H, *Die Deutsche Kriegsmarine 1939–1945* (3 vols), Podzun Verlag, Bad Nauheim, 1956.

Mallmann Showell, Jak P, *Fuehrer Conferences on Naval Affairs*, Chatham Publishing, London, 2005.

Mann, Christopher and Jörgensen, Christer, *Hitler's Arctic War*, Brown Partworks, London, 2002.

Müller, Wolfgang and Kramer, Reinhard, *Gesunken und Verschollen*, Koehlers Verlag, Herford, 1994.

Rohwer, J, and Hümmelchen, G, *Chronik des Seekrieges 1939–1945*, Gerhar Stalling Verlag, 1968.

Ruge, Friedrich, *The Soviets as Naval Opponents*, USNI, Maryland, 1979.

Schramm, Percy E, *Kriegstagebuch des OKW*, 8 vols, Bernard & Graefe Verlag, 2002.

Tarrant, V E, *The Last Year of the Kriegsmarine*, Arms and Armour Press, London 1994.

Weichold, Eberhard, *Axis Naval Policy and Operations in the Mediterranean, 1939 to May 1943*, Washington Navy Dept, 1951.

Whealey, Robert H, *Hitler and Spain: The Nazi Role in the Spanish Civil War, 1936–1939*, University Press of Kentucky, 2004.

Wilson, Kevin, *Men of Air*, Phoenix Publishing, London, 2008.

Winton, John (ed), *The War at Sea*, Book Club Associates, London, 1974.

Notes

1 This written order was used by American prosecutors against Raeder during the Nuremberg Trials, listed in evidence as 'C-141 Order for concealed armament of E-boats, 10 February 1932, signed by Raeder (USA 47) VI 955'.

2 Bey had already headed the UZ Flotilla and was considered the 'Father of S-boat operations'. In 1937 he was transferred to destroyers, commanding the 4th Destroyer Flotilla in 1939. Later still he ascended to Führer der Zerstörer and was killed aboard the *Scharnhorst* while operating in that capacity as commander of the Northern Battle Group aboard the ship.

3 The post of Führer der Zerstörer was established independently in November 1939, removing destroyers from FdT command.

4 The Italian Regia Marina, for their part, sent a total of fifty-eight submarines to covertly operate as part of the Nationalist Navy – though their presence was widely known.

5 A further development – the 3000HP MB518 – was tested in 1942, though not field tested until February 1944. Designed to increase top speed after the standardised fitting of an armoured bridge and heavier flak weaponry, it was capable of pushing the fully armed boat to a maximum of 45 knots, far in excess of any other MTB. However, some minor teething problems combined with production delays caused by Allied bombing led to the design's cancellation in favour of continued production of the proven MB511.

6 SKL KTB 3 November 1939.

7 Initially, MGK West had lobbied for only eight of the available S-boats to be used in total for *Weserübung*, reasoning that more would be needed in immediate defensive reserve should hostilities break out of the static western front. SKL overruled the request, stating that all available boats must be used.

8 Wuppermann was soon promoted to Oberleutnant zur See and placed in command of *S25*, LzS Götz Frhr von Mirbach taking over *S21*.

9 The freighter was later refloated, towed to Gothenburg and repaired.

10 *Karlsruhe* immediately began the return journey to Germany under torpedo-boat escort but was hit by two torpedoes from submarine HMS *Truant*, abandoned and sunk by another pair of torpedoes from *Greif*.

11 HMS *Birmingham* was escorted by four destroyers (HM Ships *Janus*, *Hyperion*, *Hereward* and *Havock*) and joined by four extra ships of the 5th Destroyer Division: HM Ships *Kelly*, *Kandahar*, *Kimberley* and *Hostile* for the interception mission. Five other destroyers led by HMS *Fury* were also sailing from Scapa Flow to join the group: HM Ships *Mohawk*, *Foresight*, *Bulldog* and *Gallant*. The target for this impressive group was a minelaying mission comprised of minelayers *Roland*, *Cobra*, *Preussen* and *Kaiser* with destroyers *Richard Beitzen*, *Hermann Schoemann* and *Bruno Heinemann*.

12 HMS *Kelly* lost twenty-seven men during the action, and was mistakenly believed sunk by the Germans. She would eventually be sent to the bottom after air attack in action off Crete on 23 May 1941.

13 Opdenhoff had already received the Iron Cross, second class, on 27 April 1940 and first class on 11 May 1940.

14 SKL KTB 14 May 1940.

15 Interrogation Report S38.

16 The identity of the ship remains unconfirmed, though several sources cite it as the 3,060-ton auxiliary mine destructor ship HMS *Corburn*. However, I do not believe this to be correct. *Corburn* was equipped with a powerful magnet in the forward hold that was used to detonate magnetic mines at a safe distance. While operating off Le Havre (too far west for *S32*'s attack) the circuit breakers that carried current from the alternators to the magnet were disabled by a mine explosion. The magnetic mines of that field had been laid so densely that in spite of the *Corburn*'s engines having been put full astern, she drifted over the next mine which detonated immediately under her, cutting her in half and sending her to the bottom.

17 SKL KTB 21 May.

18 Further members of the crew were killed aboard the minesweeper *Emile Deschamps* when she struck a mine at the mouth of the River Thames while evacuating French troops as part of Operation Dynamo.

19 No Allied submarine is confirmed as having been sunk on this date. The only such vessel operating in this area at that time was the French submarine *Antiope*, though they recorded no depth-charge attack.

20 SKL KTB 28 May 1940.

21 Both Sub Lieutenant Wills-Rust and Captain Morris-Woolfenden were the first to receive the newly established Lloyd's War Medal for Bravery at Sea. Years later, while serving in the Bundesmarine as part of NATO, Obermaier asked for an independent investigation into the event which concluded it had indeed been British gunners responsible for the accident.

22 *The Sands of Dunkirk*, Richard Collier, Dutton, 1961, p97.

23 In order to assist survivors from *Sirocco*, *Blyskawica* handed over escort duties for *Cyclone* to the French torpedo boat *Bouclier* and minesweeper *Arras* who saw the damaged vessel safely to Dover. After emergency repairs, *Cyclone* proceeded to Brest minus its bow and was found there in dry dock by German troops on 18 June. French naval personnel had sabotaged what was left of the destroyer.

24 SKL KTB 31 May 1940.

25 Both the FN (northbound) and FS (southbound) convoys used an unusual numbering system. The numbering ranged from 1 to 100 rotating in 'phases'. For example, once the 101st FN convoy had been reached it was then known as 'FN1 (Phase 2)'. I have chosen to keep this original numbering technique rather than convert it to a consecutive numbering. Therefore, in other publications, FS71 (Phase 3) can be referred to as 'FS271'.

26 SKL KTB 10 June 1940.

27 Depot ships were not deployed into Channel areas, deemed too vulnerable to air attack.

28 The Romney Marsh Research Association paper, 'Shipwrecks' (2009) (no longer available in pdf form: quoted on ww2talk.com, RNLI in WW2).

29 Salvaged pit-props from the beached ship were used to rig a temporary boom defence off Dungeness against S-boats or any other invasion craft.

30 One of the gunners aboard HMS *Foylebank*, Leading Seaman John F Mantle, continued to fire at the attacking Stukas as the ship sank, despite being fatally wounded, and was probably responsible for the sole Stuka lost. He was awarded a posthumous Victoria Cross.

31 Churchill, Winston, *The Second World War*, vol 2, p505.

32 FdT KTB 3 July 1940.

33 The five steamers aggregated 5,117 tons for the Luftwaffe pilots, who actually claimed to have sunk eleven ships, totalling 43,000 tons.

34 At least one body from the *Fife Coast* later washed ashore in France and was buried there.

35 NA ADM 199/2133 Survivors' Reports: Merchant Vessels 1 June 1940 to 31 August 1940, p213.

36 Klug mistook the small ship for a 4,000-ton tanker.

37 SS *Polly* was so badly damaged that the crew abandoned her believing that she would soon sink. They reboarded her the following day and limped to Newhaven.

38 SKL KTB 8 August 1940.

39 SKL KTB 10 August 1940.

40 SKL KTB 15 August 1940.

41 *TM52* and *TM53* were both commissioned in August 1940. They were sent to Germany for trials, but deemed unsatisfactory due to sabotage by a dockyard engineer at Gusto. *TM54*–*TM61* were commissioned in the period between December 1941 and September 1942 with modified designs by Lurssen Werft in Vegesack, Germany.

42 The 8,663-ton steamer *Baronesa* would be the final victim from FS71 (Phase 3), bombed and sunk by the Luftwaffe in London on 9 September.

43 SS *Gasfire* was later sunk by a mine on 21 June 1941; all her crew survived.

44 CB4051 (17): German E-Boat 'S 38' Interrogation of Survivors, February, 1941, Naval Intelligence Division, Admiralty.

45 IWM Docs 75/105/1 Phipps, W J, p80, quoted in Nick Hewitt, *Coastal Convoys 1939–1945: The Indestructible Highway* (Kindle Location 3590), Casemate Publishers, Kindle Edition.

46 Fred Bailey quoted as part of the BBC's 'People's War' series, www.bbc.co.uk/history/ww2peopleswar/stories/87/a3799687.shtml.

47 Lind's account was included in Imperial War Museum Docs 99/43/1 Lind, William, quoted in *Coastal Convoys 1939–1945: The Indestructible Highway*, Nick Hewitt. Lind was transferred by a German guard to hospital and thence onward to Milag Nord. Milag (*Marineinterniertenlager*, or 'marine internment camp') Nord was built specifically to house civilians of the merchant naval service taken prisoner. It was partnered with Marlag Nord (*Marinelager*, or 'navy camp') for men of the Royal Navy, both located near the village of Westertimke, northeast of Bremen.

48 Führer Directive No 21: Operation Barbarossa (OTL document). On 18 December 1940, Hitler issued this direct order to the Wehrmacht leadership outlining their specific roles in his planned invasion of the Soviet Russia.

49 The depot ship *Adolf Lüderitz* remained in Swinemünde.

50 Accompanying boat *S35* carried *Propaganda Kompanie* reporter Paul Reymann, who photographed the incident and would later include such photos in his 1942 book *Schatten Voraus! 'Sophie Toni!'* sanctioned by the Kriegsmarine.

51 The 2nd S-flotilla's War Diary (*Kriegstagebuch der 2 Schnellbootsflottille*) records the lightship as Soviet patrol ship *MO-238*, but this is incorrect. In actuality this ship did not exist; she was *PK-238* (*MO-4* class), later renamed *MO-306* on 25 July 1941 and sunk the following day by Finnish gunboat *Uuismaa*. The bell of the *Hiiumadal* has been raised by divers, firmly identifying the ship that was sunk that night.

52 The S-class submarines – most successful of Russian types – were actually a result of Russo-German engineering co-operation in the interwar period when Versailles treaty terms forbade U-boat construction.

53 The Russian minelaying mission continued once the S-boats had departed. The heavily damaged *Storoževoj* remained afloat and was towed to harbour and subsequently dry-docked at Kronstadt. There she was damaged further during the Siege of Leningrad. Eventually, the destroyer was repaired using the bow section of the incomplete *Ognevoi*-class ship *Organizovannyi*, and refitted with a twin turret forward instead of two singles, and reclassified as a training destroyer.

54 Russian forces claimed to have hit and sunk a German destroyer, undoubtedly the misidentified *MRS11*. Russian destroyer *Silnyi* was hit by a shell from the minesweeper *M31*, which killed four and wounded seven as well as set a stored mine ablaze, though it was successfully jettisoned overboard before it exploded.

55 *Führer Conferences on Naval Affairs*, 25 July 1941, p224.

56 *Führer Conferences on Naval Affairs*, 18 March 1941, p185.

57 This was the same *Gasfire* that had been hit and damaged the previous October. During the return from the minelaying that destroyed *Hull Trader* the S-boats chanced upon two Dutch flying officers attempting to escape occupation and sail to England. They were taken aboard and interned within a POW camp.

58 Survivor Report dated 22 September 1941 and quoted on www.warsailors.com.

59 *The War At Sea: We Fought Them in Gunboats*, pp255–6.

60 *The War At Sea: We Fought Them in Gunboats*, p257–8. Hitchens was the first officer of the Royal Navy Volunteer Reserve to command an MGB and then an MGB flotilla. He was also the most highly decorated officer of the RNVR, awarded two Distinguished Service Orders, three Distinguished Service Crosses and three Mentions in Despatches. He was recommended for a Victoria Cross for an action in February 1943, though refused the recommendation as he felt he had endangered the lives of all aboard two boats when he had brought *MGB77* alongside a crippled *MGB79* under heavy fire to rescue the crew. He was killed in action in April 1943.

61 SKL KTB 3 December 1941.

62 SKL KTB 16 December 1941.

63 1st S-flotilla was undergoing overhaul in Kiel. 2nd S-flotilla had four operational craft, plus one from the 1st on attachment in Rotterdam. 4th S-flotilla fielded six vessels in Rotterdam. 6th S-flotilla had one vessel in Rotterdam (*S24?*).

64 Glycerine, a key ingredient in the manufacturing of high explosives, was a fish oil extract.

65 *Führer Conferences on Naval Affairs*, p260.

66 SKL KTB, 22 January 1942.

67 SKL KTB 27 December 1941.

68 The ten ships, known as the 'Kvarstad ships' in Norway, began their attempt to break the German blockade on the evening of 31 March, code-named by the British Operation Performance. Two ships were intercepted and sunk, four scuttled themselves under fire by Kriegsmarine ships, two returned to Gothenburg and two reached Britain.

69 The elimination of the post of Führer der Torpedoboote had been decided by OKM, leading to creation of the new office of Führer der Schnellboote on 20 April 1942.

70 SKL KTB 18 May 1942.

71 SKL KTB 6 Feb 1942.

72 IWM Document 96/456/1 Ditcham, Lieutenant A G F, p59.

73 SKL KTB 23 February 1942.

74 *Stier* sank four merchant ships before herself being damaged by artillery fire from her final victim, Liberty ship SS *Stephen Hopkins,* and scuttled on 27 September 1942.

75 Hewitt, Nick (2012), *Coastal Convoys 1939–1945: The Indestructible Highway* (Kindle Locations 4608-4610), Casemate Publishers Kindle Edition.

76 Hans Meier-Welcker, *Zur deutsch-italienischen Militärpolitik und der Beurteilung der italienischen Wehrmacht vor dem Zweiten Weltkrieg*, p71.

77 SKL KTB 8 February 1942.

78 SKL KTB 8 February 1942.

79 HMS *Welshman* was a valuable target, bringing 105 RAF maintenance personnel from Gibraltar and 540 tons of stores, including 15 tons of smoke-making compound, ninety-six Rolls-Royce Merlin aircraft engines, over 80,000 rounds of Bofors shells, plus medicines, tinned meat, powdered milk and dehydrated foodstuffs. The Kriegsmarine at first feared that, to add insult to injury, *S31* had been sunk by a German mine. However, an investigation concluded on 4 June that the 'Underwater Obstacles Branch, Naval Ordnance Division, does not feel that the sinking of S-boat "*31*" off Valletta ... was due to the surfacing of one of our own torpedo mines, Type A.' It was concluded that it had been a stray mine come adrift from its anchor and of indeterminate origin.

80 The breakdown of exactly what had been laid is as follows: 133 TMA, 8 LMF, 4 UMA, 216 UMA and 196 FMC mines. 308 explosive buoys and 108 cutter buoys.

81 The final boat of this class to enter service, *S158*, was commissioned on 9 September 1942.

82 Due to the basic facilities in the harbour, which was also being used a supply head for the Afrika Korps, there was some competition for space. SKL recorded on 15 June: 'The cargo unloaded in Derna on 15 June amounted to 774 tons. This is a very good record, although unloading was hampered by the fact that the 3rd S-flotilla was fuelling and taking on torpedoes at the same time.'

83 SKL KTB 20 June 1942.

84 British *MTB314* was captured by boats of the 6th R-flotilla after running aground near Tobruk on 14 September. It was later repaired and saw service under the Kriegsmarine ensign.

85 SKL KTB 21 June 1942.

86 *S59* would follow on, but was delayed in leaving Sicily after having to wait for a group of naval war correspondents bound for North Africa, reaching Tunisia two days later with *S54* and *S55*.

87 On 3 January 1943 five Royal Navy two-man 'Chariots' managed to sink the new Italian cruiser *Ulpio Traiano* in Palermo, which severely hampered use of the dockyard for S- and R-boat repairs.

88 'The Story of HMS *Lightning*', tribute website created by Eric Gilroy, son of George 'Geordie' Gilroy AB LR3 aboard HMS *Lightning* May1941 – March 1943, http://freespace.virgin.net/e.gilroy/index.htm.

89 SKL KTB 27 Oct 1943.

90 Bereft of a boat to skipper, ObltzS Horst Weber was transferred ashore to the staff of 1st S-division.

91 The Kriegsmarine artillery officer Bünsche excelled in his new assignment and later commanded the Kriegsmarine's 605th Security Battalion between October 1944 and January 1945.

92 SKL KTB 18 August 1944.

93 For a fuller examination of the Kleinkampfverbände see *Weapons of Desperation*, Chatham Publishing.

94 The siege of Sevastopol even affected Army Group North, in that the huge pieces of siege artillery originally planned to force Leningrad's surrender were instead used in the Crimea. Subsequently, Leningrad never fell.

95 Although treated well by his Kriegsmarine captors, Novikov was later taken to Flossenbürg concentration camp where he was executed by the SS in 1944.

96 SKL KTB 2 July 1942.

97 Admiral Black Sea KTB 7 January 1943.

98 With one engine shaft out of action, *S49* suffered a second engine failure while attempting to return to Constanta on 1 February, forced to limp from Ivan Baba to Yalta, Sevastopol and onwards later that month.

99 *Admiral Black Sea KTB* 28 February 1943.

100 Kieseritzky had held the post since February 1943 and was killed on 19 November 1943, succeeded by Van Helmuth Brinkmann, previously his chief of staff.

101 The 11th S-flotilla was planned to be rebuilt in Saßnitz on the island of Rügen. A flotilla headquarters was established there under the command of Kptlt Baron von Stempel, but was subordinated to the 5th S-flotilla after the latter was destroyed in the west and began reforming within the Baltic.

102 During February *S40* and *S52* were equipped with the new armoured bridge: the *Kalottenbrücken*.

103 The six boats sold to Spain were *S73*, *S78*, *S124*, *S125*, *S126*, and *S134*.

104 Bätge was killed after his ship ran on to a German mine in the Gulf of Finland on 12 December 1944. Though he and twenty-four crewmen survived the sinking and managed to abandon ship on a life raft, they froze to death and later washed ashore on the Åland Islands.

105 Petersen requested a new bunker constructed in Aberwrac'h, an ideal base from which to attack Britain's westernmost coastal shipping. However, by 1943 there was no chance of the new construction passing ground planning stage. Likewise at Lézardrieux, another of Petersen's planned future bases.

106 *Trawlers Go To War*, Paul Lund, Harry Ludlam, New English Library.

107 The so-called 'Z-line' was a British picket line developed in 1942 seaward of the east-coast convoy routes in an attempt to detect and intercept S-boats. British coastal forces would lie in wait, much as the S-boats had done in their offensive tactics, until either making contact or summoned by other units to the scene of any action.

108 *SKL KTB* 2 January 1944.

109 *SKL KTB* 6 June 1944.

110 http://www.rodericktimms.royalnavy. co.uk/flag_battleship.html.

111 Both S-boats were non-operational and stored within the cavernous U-boat bunker. On 5 August RAF 617 Squadron hit the bunker with Tallboy bombs, damaging *S145* in dry dock; her starboard torpedo tube was destroyed. They attempted to leave the embattled harbour for the Channel Islands but were forced to return with engine problems. *S112* eventually transited to Lorient, planning to evacuate the commander of the Brest garrison, General Ramcke, though that mission was abandoned. While in Lorient the skipper, LzS Nikelowski, was killed in a road accident during April 1945. Both unserviceable boats were later captured when the port cities fell.

112 The planned series of boats from *S701* to *S800* – of which only nine were commissioned at the Danziger Waggonfabrik Yard – incorporated two extra stern torpedo tubes in an experiment to allow defensive firing of T5 torpedoes at pursuing destroyers. The merits of the idea were never properly evaluated before the war's end.

113 Von Kluge had been the fortress commandant, but was relieved of his command, handing the duty over to VA Friedrich Frisius after being ordered back to Germany. His crime was to be the brother of Günther von Kluge who had been implicated in the 20 July bomb plot. Von Kluge was discharged from the Wehrmacht shortly thereafter for 'political reasons'.

114 Report from Karl Müller dated 1 December 1944 and handed in to OKM. Müller had been repatriated to Germany in exchange for Captain Michael Foot, later the Labour Party leader in Great Britain.

115 The wreck lay close to the surface in shallow water for several months, sinking 613-ton Belgian SS *Emeraude* on 2 July 1945 after collision with it, three men being killed as the ship sank. Both wrecks were finally dispersed in 1960.

116 *SKL KTB* 18 October 1944.

117 Letter quoted in *German S-boats in Action*, p125.

Index